Essential Study Skills

FOURTH EDITION

Essential Study Skills

FOURTH EDITION

LINDA WONG

HOUGHTON MIFFLIN COMPANY Boston New York

Editor-in-Chief: *Patricia A. Coryell*
Senior Sponsoring Editor: *Mary Finch*
Associate Editor: *Shani B. Fisher*
Editorial Assistant: *Andrew Sylvester*
Project Editor: *Cecilia Molinari*
Editorial Assistant: *Kristin Penta*
Senior Production/Design Coordinator: *Sarah Ambrose*
Senior Manufacturing Coordinator: *Marie Barnes*
Marketing Manager: *Barbara LeBuhn*

Cover image: © Celia Johnson c/o The iSpot Showcase.

Text credits can be found at the back of the book, on page A10.

Photo Credits:
Page 8: David Joel/Getty Images; **Page 19:** Bonnie Kamin/Photoedit; **Page 32:** Michelle D. Bridwell/Photoedit; **Page 43:** © Getty Images; **Page 62:** David Young-Wolff/Photoedit; **Page 69:** Michelle D. Bridwell/Photoedit; **Page 87:** Spencer Grant/Photoedit; **Page 99:** Gary Connor/Photoedit; **Page 114:** Stewart Cohen/Getty Images; **Page 118:** David Young-Wolff/Photoedit; **Page 147:** Mary Kate Den/Photoedit; **Page 151:** © Index Stock Imagery; **Page 174:** © Photodisc; **Page 179:** Spencer Grant/Photoedit; **Page 183:** David Young-Wolff/Photoedit; **Page 186:** © David Riecks; **Page 202:** Bob Daemmrich/Stock Boston; **Page 217:** Michael Newman/Photoedit; **Page 240:** Amy Etra/Photoedit; **Page 241:** Elizabeth Crews/Stock Boston; **Page 261:** Bob Daemmrich/Stock Boston; **Page 272:** Greg Ceo/Getty Images; **Page 287:** Richard Pasley/Stock Boston; **Page 288:** Grant LeDuc/Stock Boston; **Page 318:** Gary Connor/Photoedit; **Page 339:** Bob Daemmrich/Stock Boston; **Page 37:** Bonnie Kamin/Photoedit; **Page 373:** Michael Newman/Photoedit.

Printed in the U.S.A.
Library of Congress Control Number: 2001098587

ISBN Number: 0-618-24207-4
56789–HS–06 05 04 03

Table of Contents

UNIT IV: Using Effective Notetaking Techniques

UNIT V: Strengthening Your Test-Taking Skills

Preface

The fourth edition of *Essential Study Skills*— a text appropriate for all postsecondary students interested in learning effective study strategies and especially helpful for returning adults and underprepared students—presents innovative new features, a regrouping of chapter content, and new instructional content and strategies. This new organization lays the foundation for and allows the development of metacognition, the process of using knowledge about one's own memory system and learning strategies to tackle intellectual tasks. The metacognitive approach used throughout the fourth edition enables students to assume responsibility for their own learning and to realize that academic success is a product of skills and behaviors they can acquire, customize, and effectively implement. In addition to the step-by-step approach, encouraging tone, clear rationales, and versatile exercises of previous editions, the new features and the revisions of the fourth edition provide a greater array of practical strategies and exercises. This worktext approach will bring students not only higher grades and a more thorough learning of information, but, ultimately, it will bring increased confidence, self-esteem, and empowerment.

Student-Oriented Features Continued in the Fourth Edition

- The ***Quick Start Checklist*** at the beginning of the textbook presents essential study skills that students can implement at the beginning of the term to familiarize themselves with registration, campus resources, computer access, textbook organization, syllabi, and other successful study strategies.
- **Chapter visual mappings** use a graphic form to show the main headings in each chapter.
- **Chapter profiles** provide students with a self-correcting tool to assess their current attitudes and behaviors. To show progress and changes made through the course of the term, students complete the profiles again at the end of the term. Students record their scores on the Master Profile Chart located in Appendix A.
- **Boxed information** provides students with highlights of key points to use while previewing, reading, and reviewing the chapter for tests.
- **Ample exercises** provide guided practice in applying the skills of the chapter whether in class, in small groups, with partners, or as individual homework assignments.
- **LINKS exercises** connect content in the chapter to skills, concepts, and excerpts presented in previous chapters.
- **Chapter summaries** review the main points in succinct lists that students can use when previewing and reviewing a chapter.
- **Review questions** at the end of the chapter assess students' understanding and application of the chapter content.

New Student-Oriented Features Enriching the Fourth Edition

- **Terms to Know** listed on the opening page of each chapter help students easily identify the key terms that they will need to learn in the chapter.
- Three **Reflection Writing Assignments** provide students with the opportunity to personalize the chapter content and integrate the chapter's skills with other study skills. The first Reflection Writing provides instructors with

information about the students' profile scores and current skill levels related to the chapter content. The second Reflection Writing shows students' understanding and application of the chapter content to their personal experiences and approach to studying. The third Reflection Writing, which promotes critical thinking and integration of strategies and concepts presented in the chapter, serves as a culminating assignment. The Instructor's Resource Manual provides suggestions for assigning one, two, or three writing assignments, as well as for using the assignments in portfolio projects.

- **Photographs** in each chapter are accompanied by discussion questions that integrate the content of the chapter with real-life situations and applications.
- **Group Processing—A Collaborative Learning Activity** in each chapter provides a small-group activity that enhances student interest; creates a forum for student interaction through brainstorming, discussion, and cooperative work; and promotes critical thinking skills.
- **Learning Options** at the end of each chapter offer students the opportunity to demonstrate their understanding of the content and skills in the chapter by selecting an assessment activity that capitalizes on their learning preferences, motivates or interests them, and allows them to express their ideas creatively. The Instructor's Resource Manual includes options for using these Learning Options in one or more chapters.
- The **web site activities** for the fourth edition provide interactive practice tests and exercises that can be scored online or emailed to the instructor. Instructors can use the exercises and links for course assignments or as part of an online course. Students may also access the web site on their own to complete the exercises for enrichment and review for tests.
- The **Personal Insights** form located in Appendix B reflects the metacognitive approach used throughout this textbook. *Personal Insights* provides students with a form to summarize and integrate the various learning styles, patterns, and preferences they have identified as part of their individualized approach to learning.

New Chapter Content

Chapter revisions of content and exercises, the repositioning and combining of topics from the third edition, and the addition of new content for learning styles, time management, goal setting, listening and notetaking, reading comprehension and critical thinking, and test taking provide students with additional strategies to incorporate into their strategies for success. New topics in the fourth edition include strategies for decreasing stress and procrastination, reading and notetaking skills for math, surveying textbooks and articles, and Bloom's Taxonomy for levels of questioning.

Unit I Understanding How You Process and Learn

Unit I provides students with a fundamental understanding of their learning styles or preferences and knowledge about learning and memory systems. Chapters 1 and 2, which lay a strong foundation on which students can build solid study skills, provide the rationale for the learning strategies presented throughout this textbook. The metacognitive approach and pedagogy woven into the fourth edition of *Essential Study Skills* support contemporary theories of learning and views on student success.

Chapter 1 Discovering Your Learning Style
Three Cognitive Learning Styles, Learning Styles Inventory, Learning Strategies, Howard Gardner's Multiple Intelligences

New for this chapter: Global/Linear Learners with an inventory, Structured, Interactive, and Independent Learners

Chapter 2 Processing Information into Your Memory System
The Information Processing Model, Twelve Principles of Memory

New for this chapter: Introduction on the use of visual mappings

Unit II
Preparing Yourself for Optimal Learning

Unit II now includes *four* chapters that provide students with the skills necessary to become effective, self-motivated, independent, and successful students. Instructors who prefer to begin the term by addressing self-management, organizational, affective domain, and personal improvement skills may want to reverse the order of presentation by working with Unit II before Unit I.

Chapter 3 Managing Your Time
Balancing Your Life, Pie of Life, Creating a Weekly Schedule, Applying Time-Management Skills

New for this chapter: Discussion of four kinds of schedules: term, weekly, daily, and task schedules

Chapter 4 Setting Goals
Kinds of Goals, Four-Step Approach for Writing Goals, Goal-Setting Techniques, Combining Goal Setting and Time Management

New for this chapter: Reasons Some People Do Not Set Goals; Five-Year and Two-Year Goals; Using a Goal Organizer; Types of Summary Notes to Use in a Five-Day Study Plan

Chapter 5 Increasing Concentration; Decreasing Stress and Procrastination
Physical Stage for Concentration, Mental Stage for Concentration, Concentration Strategies

New for this chapter: Techniques to Decrease Stress; Techniques to Decrease Procrastination; Choosing a Healthy Lifestyle; Introduction on Creating Comparison Charts

Chapter 6 Boosting Your Memory and Preparing for Tests
Five Theories of Forgetting, Five-Day Study Plan, Summary Notes, Test-Preparation Skills, Dealing with Test Anxiety

New for this chapter: Mnemonics to Boost Memory; Writing Practice Questions Using Bloom's Taxonomy

Unit III
Developing Effective Textbook Reading Strategies

Unit III combines reading skills from the third edition and presents these skills in two chapters rather than three. Instructors who used the third edition will notice that no content from the third edition has been deleted; instead, it has been shifted to other chapters. Unit III introduces students to an array of reading skills and strategies that will strengthen their reading comprehension and increase their ability to learn textbook information.

Chapter 7 Using a Reading System
Surveying a Chapter, the SQ4R Reading System

New for this chapter: Surveying a Textbook; Surveying an Article; Reading Math Textbooks; Recording (Notetaking) on Index Cards; Recording (Notetaking) in the Margins

Chapter 8 Strengthening Comprehension and Critical Thinking Skills
Third edition comprehension strategies moved to this chapter include understanding what you read (comprehension strategies): using definition, word

structure, and context clues; substituting words; identifying main ideas; identifying organizational patterns; highlighting and marking (annotating) the textbook; making marginal notes; and writing summaries.

New for this chapter: Active Reading and Thinking; Verbalizing and Visualizing, Converting Words to Pictures

Unit IV
Using Effective Notetaking Techniques

Unit IV prepares students for a variety of notetaking situations and notetaking options. The content from the third edition appears in a similar format in the fourth edition; the fourth edition includes new excerpts and assessment forms.

Chapter 9 Creating Cornell Notes for Textbooks
Preparing for Notetaking, Using the Five *R*'s of Cornell, Combining Cornell and SQ4R

New for this chapter: New Notetaking Assessment Form; Exercise on Taking Cornell Notes for Math

Chapter 10 Listening and Taking Lecture Notes
Understanding Listening Skills, Strengthening Listening Skills, Using the Cornell System for Lecture Notes, Techniques for Recording and Organizing Information, Finding Solutions to Notetaking Problems

New for this chapter: Steps in the Listening Process; Listening Inventory; Taking Lecture Notes in Math Classes; New Notetaking Assessment Form

Chapter 11 Using a Variety of Notetaking Systems
Using Visual Notetaking (Visual Mappings, Hierarchies), Creating Comparison Charts

New for this chapter: Tailoring Your Approach to Learning, Creating Formal Outlines, Creating Three-Column Notes

Unit V
Strengthening Your Test-Taking Skills

Unit V now consists of two chapters for test-taking skills that focus on *performing well* on test day by using effective strategies for objective, short-answer, math, and essay tests. The test-preparation and test anxiety topics in the third edition now appear in Chapter 6 of the fourth edition.

Chapter 12 Developing Strategies for Objective Tests
Performing Well on Tests, Using Four Levels of Response, Taking Objective Tests (True-False, Multiple Choice, Matching), Using Educated Guessing, Taking Computerized Tests

Chapter 13 Developing Strategies for Recall, Math, and Essay Tests
Answering Recall Questions (Fill-in-the-Blank, Listing, Definition, and Short Answer), Strategies for Different Kinds of Essay Tests, Direction Words, Writing Practice Answers for Essay Questions, Essay Writing Tips

New for this chapter: Taking Math Tests; Six Types of Test-Taking Errors; RSTUV Problem-Solving Method; Identifying Themes for Essay Questions

Appendixes

Appendix A—Chapter Profiles consists of the Master Profile Chart to use at the beginning and the end of the term and the Profile Answer Key.

Appendix B—Useful Forms consists of a Learning Option Assessment Form, a Class Schedule Form, a Weekly Time-Management Form, a Goal Organizer, and a Personal Insights Form to use at the end of the term.

Instructor's Resource Manual

Essential Study Skills, Fourth Edition, is accompanied by an Instructor's Resource Manual, which provides teaching tips, answer keys for textbook exercises, answer keys for chapter review questions, enrichment activities, and masters for making overhead transparencies in a chapter-by-chapter format. Additional excerpts from a variety of college textbooks are included to use for textbook reading, notetaking, or test-taking practice.

To facilitate the use of the Instructor's Resource Manual, the following revisions and additions have been incorporated into the fourth edition:

- Suggestions for using Reflection Writing Assignments, the Learning Options at the end of each chapter, and the web site exercises and links for this textbook
- Suggestions for creating portfolio projects
- A reorganization that places the material for each chapter in its own section
- A convenient list with textbook pages for reading assignments, student exercises and activities, Reflection Writing Assignments, and chapter review questions for reference when making lesson plans

Web Site

The fourth edition of *Essential Study Skills* includes a comprehensive web site that can be used for course assignments, in online courses, or by students for enrichment. An icon appears throughout the textbook to indicate companion exercises, online response forms for students to use, or related links. Online applications for each chapter include such features as Chapter Profiles, which will be scored online; text boxes for Reflective Writing Assignments, Case Studies, and other activities, that allow students to email their responses to the instructor; ACE practice tests and exercises that provide students with feedback and their scores; and links to a multitude of other web sites with related topics, exercises, or articles.

Optional unit tests that assess students' retention and integration of material across the chapters for Unit I (Chapters 1 and 2), Unit II (Chapters 3–6), Unit III (Chapters 7 and 8), Unit IV (Chapters 9–11), and Unit V (Chapters 12 and 13) can be found on the Instructor's web site. The Instructor's web site also provides you with a test bank of objective test questions that you may use to construct customized tests, modify existing tests, or create original midterm exams or final exams.

Power Point Slides

Power Point slides are available for each chapter to assist in classroom instruction online through the *Essential Study Skills,* Fourth Edition, instructor's web site. To access the web site, go to **http://college.hmco.com/collegesurvival/instructor**. Select Wong, *Essential Study Skills,* 4e, from the drop-down menu of Student Success/Study Skills texts.

Optional Resources to Accompany This Textbook

The College Survival Student Planner

Our week-at-a-glance College Survival Student Planner includes a "Survival Kit" of helpful success tips.

Myers-Briggs Type Indicator (MBTI®) Instrument

This widely used personality inventory determines preferences of four scales: Extraversion-Introversion, Sensing-Intuitive, Thinking-Feeling, and Judging-Perceiving. Qualified schools may purchase this inventory; MBTI and Myers-Briggs Type Indicator are registered trademarks of Consulting Psychologists Press, Inc.

Retention Management System College Student Inventory

The Noel Levitz College Student Inventory identifies students with tendencies that contribute to dropping out of school. This instrument works with campus advisors as an early-alert intervention program.

For more information on including these products with your order of *Essential Study Skills,* contact your College Survival consultant (1-800-528-8323) or your local Houghton Mifflin Sales Representative, or visit the Instructor Section of this textbook's web site.

Consulting and Support Services

Correspondence with the Author

Linda Wong, the author of *Essential Study Skills,* welcomes the opportunity to discuss the use of *Essential Study Skills* with you. Visit the instructor web site for this textbook to locate her email address.

College Survival Consulting Services

Expert conultants are available to provide your campus with training programs and materials for designing, implementing, and administering student success and first-year courses. Contact us at 1-800-528-8323 or visit us on the web at **http://college.hmco.com/instructors**.

Acknowledgments

The fourth edition of Essential Study Skills is dedicated to all the teachers of study skills courses who devote tremendous amounts of time, energy, and enthusiasm to guide students along the paths of higher learning.

Appreciation is extended to the following reviewers who contributed valuable ideas to further strengthen the effectiveness of this textbook for college students: Alison Parry, Capilano College, British Columbia; Judith Drabkin, Ulster County Community College, NY; Robert Flagler, University of Minnesota, MN; Lorraine Gregory, Duquesne University, PA; Barbara B. Hamilton, Oakland University, MI; Bill Hoanzl, El Camino College, CA; Suzanne F. Iovino, Delaware State University, DE; Rita M. McReynolds, Mississippi State University, MS; Annette Wadiyah E. Nelson-Shimabukuro, Seattle Central Community College, WA; Laura M. Powell, Danville Community College, VA; Gretchen Starks-Martin, St. Cloud State University, MN; Beverly Walker, North Central State College, OH; Runae Edwards Wilson, College of Staten Island, NY.

I applaud the outstanding editorial and production staff that has worked with me through the stages required to develop and produce this book. I extend very special thanks and appreciation to Shani Fisher, Cecilia Molinari, Andrew Fisher, and Manuel Munoz for their organizational skills, attention to minute details, team spirit, and dedication.

Linda Wong

To the Student

Essential Study Skills is designed to provide you with skills that will unlock your learning potential. By consistently using the skills presented in this book, you will learn information more thoroughly and remember it more easily. This section tells you how to get the most out of *Essential Study Skills.*

How to Start the Term

As soon as you purchase your book (and read this), read the Quick Start Checklist section preceding the text chapters. As you complete each task designed to prepare you for an excellent start to the term, check off the item. Continue through the checklist until you complete all the items.

How to Start Each Chapter

1. Read the paragraph on the first page for a glimpse of the skills you will learn in the chapter.
2. Study the visual mapping on the first page of the chapter. This mapping is a picture form of the main headings or topics in the chapter.
3. Read through the Terms to Know to familiarize yourself with the chapter vocabulary.
4. Answer the chapter profile questions on the second page of the chapter honestly. This will not be graded; it will be used to show your current attitude, habits, and knowledge of skills that will be presented in the chapter. If you prefer, you can complete the profile online at the web site for this textbook.
5. Score your profile by counting the number of your answers that match the answer key on page A3 in Appendix A. If you complete the profile online, you will receive your score automatically. Then chart your score on the Master Profile Chart on page A2 in Appendix A.
6. Complete the Reflection 1 Writing Assignment—even if your instructor does not assign it.
7. Prepare your mind for the content of each chapter by *surveying* the chapter before you begin the careful reading. Survey, or preview, the chapter by
   - reading the headings and subheadings.
   - reading the highlighted boxed information.
   - noticing the key words in bold green print.
   - reading the chapter summary.
   - reading the chapter review questions.
8. Begin the process of thorough, accurate reading. Read one paragraph at a time and think about what you have read. Your goal should not be to race through the chapter reading quickly; fast reading is not a reading approach that will lead to comprehension or retention of the information.

How to Use the Special Features in the Chapter

Visual Mapping

This overview shows the "big picture" of the chapter, that is, the most important information or ideas that develop the overall topic of the chapter. The chapter title is in the center of the mapping; the chapter headings branch out from the title beginning at the "11:00 position" and move clockwise.

Introductory Paragraph

The introductory paragraph on the opening page of each chapter reflects the main points that appear on the chapter mapping. Reading the paragraph carefully helps you formulate a "big picture" of the topics you will be studying in the chapter.

Terms to Know

The list of terms on the opening page of each chapter introduces you to the vocabulary you will need to learn to define. As you survey and later read the chapter, note that the *Terms to Know* appear in bold green print throughout the chapter.

Reflective Writing Assignments

Three Reflective Writing Assignments appear in each chapter. Your instructor may assign one, two, or all three writing assignments as individual assignments or entries in a journal, or as a portfolio project (larger-scale assignment). If your instructor does not use the Reflective Writing Assignments, you have the option of writing responses for your own records and your own benefit. The Reflective Writing Assignments are designed to promote interest, strengthen critical thinking skills, and assist you in personalizing the content of the chapter.

Exercises

This textbook contains a wide variety of exercises to practice the skills and techniques presented in the chapter and to integrate the new skills with previously learned skills. Your instructor might not assign all of the exercises, so pay close attention to the assignments given in class. Work carefully and thoughtfully to complete each exercise. Remember, your work should reflect the quality of work that you are capable of producing, so allot sufficient time to complete the assignments. For practice and personal enrichment, you can complete on your own any of the exercises not assigned by your instructor.

Boxed Information

As you preview, read, and review, pay special attention to the boxes throughout each chapter. Read each box carefully; then read the text following, which discusses each point in detail. Review the boxes when you prepare for tests.

Companion Web Activities

The web page icon ( ) used throughout each chapter indicates companion activities and exercises that are online for *Essential Study Skills,* Fourth Edition. When accessing the Internet and conducting web searches, realize that "surfing the web" can be very time consuming. Set a limit for yourself so you do not consume an excessive amount of time on the Internet. Bookmark the following web site for quick access; then click on the chapter you are studying. Go to **http://college.hmco.com/collegesurvival/students.** Click on *List of Sites by Author.* Use the arrow to scroll down to Wong, Essential Study Skills, 4e. Click on the title.

Summary

For a brief list of key points in the chapter, turn to the summary. Read it when you preview, and again after you have read the chapter thoroughly. Practice expanding the summary's points by adding additional details you have learned about each point. Use the summaries as review tools to prepare for tests.

Learning Options

Learning Options provide an alternative form of assessment to show how well you understand the concepts and skills in the chapter and how effectively you can apply them in new ways. Learning Options add excitement to the learning process, for you are able to express your understanding in ways other than written or computerized tests. Learning Options may be used by your instructor in a variety of ways: he or she may assign a specific option, allow you to select the option that is most appealing to you, or require you to complete a given number of Learning Options through the course of the term. Follow your instructor's directions for using the Learning Options at the end of each chapter.

Review Questions

The questions at the end of the chapter will help you check how well you have learned and applied the chapter's study skills. You should be able to complete the questions without looking back at the chapter or your notes. Be sure to read the directions carefully before answering the questions. Additional practice tests are available online at this textbook's web site.

General Recommendations

1. Strive to complete your reading and assignments on time. You can gain a sense of being organized, progressing, and being in control of the learning process if you finish your work on time.
2. Have an open mind that is willing to try new strategies for learning. Many of the strategies you used in previous years are perhaps not the most efficient or effective. This is your opportunity to discover the excitement, creativity, and benefits of learning new ways to process academic information.
3. See this course as an opportunity to work hard, apply yourself, and push to work closer to your true potential. Your rewards will be a greater sense of accomplishment, confidence, empowerment, and success. You will learn valuable skills that will become your individualized approach to learning.

Your goal is not to learn *about* study skills; your goal is to learn *to use* powerful study skills consistently to enable you to accomplish other goals and achieve success. Learning, after all, is a lifelong process. Each time you are faced with a new learning situation—whether at school, at home, or at work—you can draw upon the skills you have learned in this book. Apply the skills of goal setting, time management, concentration, processing information, strengthening memory, and acquiring new knowledge to any new task at hand. You will be prepared to experience the rewards of success . . . again and again and again.

Linda Wong

Quick Start Checklist for the First Week of Classes

❒ **Register for your classes before the term begins.**

❒ **Obtain a printout of your classes.**

❒ **Become familiar with the campus and the locations of key departments, services, and facilities.**

If campus tours are not available, use a campus map to explore the campus and its facilities. Take time to locate the following areas:

1. Your classrooms and closest restrooms
2. Most convenient parking areas or bus stops
3. Financial Aid office
4. Career Counseling, Counseling/Advising offices
5. Student Records or Registrar's office
6. Student Health
7. Library
8. Computer labs
9. Bookstore
10. Tutoring centers
11. Student Activities/Student Government
12. Cafeteria

❒ **Inquire how to access computer labs, an email account, and the Internet.**

❒ **Visit the library.**

Learn the procedures for locating and checking out materials, the hours the library is open, and the availability of library orientation workshops.

❒ **Organize your notebooks.**

Use dividers to set up a three-ring notebook with sections for each of your classes. If you need to use more than one notebook, consider a notebook for the MWF classes and another for the T/Th classes. In each section of your notebook, organize the following materials:

1. Your weekly schedule of classes (See the Class Schedule form in Appendix B.)
2. The course *syllabus* (which is an outline of the class and the requirements)
3. A list of names and phone numbers of other students in class whom you may want to call to discuss homework assignments or meet for a study group
4. All of your class notes, handouts, and completed assignments arranged in chronological order

❒ **Create a term-long calendar.**

Locate a month-by-month planner or use a regular calendar to record all scheduled tests, midterms, due dates for projects, study-group meetings, conferences, and final exams. Begin by carefully examining each course syllabus for important test dates, project dates, and final exam dates. Also, refer to your college calendar for the term for additional dates of importance (holidays, last day to change grade options or drop courses, and special college events). Keep the monthly calendar in the front of your notebook. Plan to update it throughout the term.

❒ **Decide on a system to use to record all homework assignments.**

Select an easy-to-use system for recording your homework assignments. While some instructors provide students with daily assignment sheets, most do not. The system you select should provide you with a list of tasks or assignments that need to be done.

One system that works effectively is to title a sheet of notebook paper "Assignments." Place this Assignments page in the front of each section of your notebook. Use this page *every time* an assignment is given. Write the date the assignment is given, the specific assignment, the date it is due, and a place to check that the assignment is done. Your assignment sheet will look like this:

Assignments—Math 60

Date	Assignment	Due	Done
10/3	Read pages 110–125	10/5	x
	Do odd-numbered problems on 112, 115, 118, 125	10/5	x
10/5	Study for quiz on Chapter 3	10/7	

A second system involves using a commercial daily or weekly planner that has enough room for you to write assignments and their due dates. Check off the assignments as you complete them. A week in your weekly planner would show the assignments on the days they were given.

You can create your own weekly planner page using unlined notebook paper. Make six columns (one for each school day of the week and one to list your classes) and enough rows to show all of your classes. Each time an assignment is given, write the assignment on your planner page. Assignments can be checked off after they are completed. Your weekly planner page would look like this:

classes	Mon.	Tues.	Wed.	Thurs.	Fri.
math					
writing					
theater					
psych.					

❒ **Become familiar with your textbooks by surveying each textbook.**

Before you begin attending classes, get a head start by *surveying* your textbooks. Surveying a textbook involves becoming familiar with the features of the book by previewing or looking through specific sections in the textbook before you begin reading. Surveying, which often takes fifteen minutes to half an hour per book, will enable you to use the book more effectively and more efficiently throughout the entire term. Take time to complete the following six steps to survey your textbooks.

Step 1: Look at the title page, copyright page, and table of contents in the front of the book.

Step 2: Locate and read the introductory information. This section may also be labeled *Preface, To the Teacher,* or *To the Student*. This introductory material often provides valuable background information on the book and the author and clarifies the book's purpose.

Step 3: Look in the back of the book for an *appendix*. An appendix provides you with supplementary materials that were not included in the chapters. You may find answer keys to exercises; additional exercises; practice tests; additional readings; frequently used charts, formulas, or theorems; maps; or lengthier documents (such as the Bill of Rights).

Step 4: Look to see if the textbook has a *glossary* (a mini-dictionary that defines key terms used in the textbook).

Step 5: Look to see if your textbook has a section in the back of the book titled *References* or *Bibliography*. This section provides you with the names of authors and the books, magazines, or articles that were used by the author as sources of information. This list of references can also be used if you wish to research a topic further.

Step 6: The last step of surveying is to locate the *index* in the back of the book. The index is an alphabetical listing of subjects used throughout the textbook. An index can be used to quickly locate page numbers when you want to

1. review a specific topic that was discussed in class.
2. locate a topic for a class assignment or discussion.
3. review specific information for a topic for an essay.
4. clarify information written in your notes.

❒ **Show up the first day of class ready to learn.**

Many students know that the term begins more smoothly when they are in class the first day and are ready to work. This is the day that the syllabus is usually discussed, introductions are made, and class expectations are explained. The following suggestions can help you get off to a good start:

1. Be on time.
2. Sit toward the front of the classroom rather than "hiding" in the back row. You will be able to see better, will concentrate more easily, and will show you are interested in the course.
3. Come prepared with your notebook, paper, pencils, pens, the textbook, and any other materials that you might need.
4. Be friendly! Show others that you are approachable and willing to be a part of the group. Your friendliness can help set a positive tone in the classroom.
5. Plan to listen carefully and be attentive.
6. Use a highlighter to highlight important information discussed on the syllabus.
7. Plan to take notes. Later in the term, you will learn an effective notetaking system. For now, the format you use for notes is not as important as the habit of writing down information as it is presented. Your notes should also include a record of your homework assignments.

❒ **Make a commitment to dedicate sufficient time each week to studying.**

One of the most common mistakes students make involves allocation of time. *Time on task,* or time devoted to studying, is highly correlated to academic success. Students who spend too little time reading, studying, memorizing, and applying information in a variety of ways often struggle with the process of learning. In addition to completing reading assignments, written work, papers, and problems, you should dedicate some time each week to reviewing information that has been covered. Time management will be covered later in the term, but for now, you can use a time-management technique called the *2:1 ratio.* For most or all of your classes that involve textbook reading assignments and written work, plan to study two hours for every one hour in class. Therefore, if one of your classes meets for three hours a week, plan to study six hours a week for that class. The six hours of study time can be spread throughout the week. You can use your weekly planner or schedule to identify the total hours you plan to study during the week for each of your classes. Your classes and study blocks for each class can be planned on the chart in Appendix B, page A7.

❒ **Plan to ask questions about the class, the expectations, and the assignments.**

Becoming an *active learner* is important. Be willing to show your interest by asking questions in class. Most instructors are very willing to expand directions or give further explanations about classroom or textbook topics. Student questions also help promote interesting classroom discussions.

❒ **Monitor your stress levels.**

Some stress is normal. Normal stress is manageable and can even be a motivator. New or unfamiliar situations are commonly linked to feelings of self-doubt, lower confidence levels, and lower self-esteem. These feelings are part of the "learning cycle" and weaken or dwindle as you gain familiarity with and "settle in" to the new routine, expectations, and tasks to be completed. Chapter 5 introduces you to a variety of concentration, relaxation, and stress-reduction techniques that will assist you in keeping your stress at a comfortable, manageable level. In addition, this course itself will reduce stress levels as you gain skills and confidence by learning strategies designed to strengthen your ability to do well academically.

Stressors, or occurrences in the process of life that cause stress, can occur unexpectedly. Most colleges or universities have counselors, support groups, workshops, or courses that can help individuals with stress reduction and with periods of transition. Schedule a time with a counselor to explore the resources and options available on your campus.

CHAPTER 1

Discovering and Using Your Learning Styles

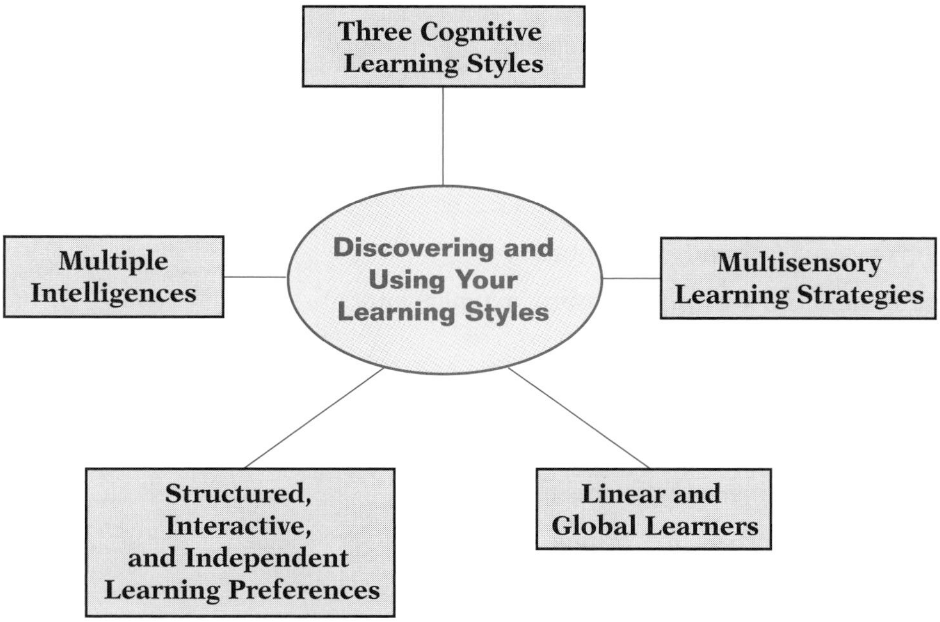

Understanding your individual style of learning can help you become a more effective learner. In this chapter, you will determine whether you prefer using your visual, auditory, or kinesthetic modality to learn information. You will become familiar with a wide range of multisensory strategies to use when studying. After completing two short inventories, you will discover whether you are a linear or global learner, and whether you are a structured, interactive, or independent learner. Finally, you will learn about the eight intelligences. Through this process of learning more about yourself as a learner, you will quickly discover that you already have many skills and abilities that will contribute to your college success.

Terms to Know

cognitive learning styles
learning modalities
learning style preference
visual learner
auditory learner
kinesthetic learner
multisensory learning strategies
brain dominance theory
linear learner
global learner
structured learner
interactive learner
independent learner
Theory of Multiple Intelligences
subintelligences
verbal/linguistic intelligence
musical intelligence
logical-mathematical intelligence
visual-spatial intelligence
bodily-kinesthetic intelligence
intrapersonal intelligence
interpersonal intelligence
naturalist intelligence

CHAPTER 1 Learning Styles Profile

DO the following profile. Answer each question honestly to show your current attitudes and study habits. Your answers should reflect what you do, not what you wish to do. Check YES if you do the statement always or most of the time. Check NO if you do this seldom or never.

SCORE the profile. Compare your answers to the answer key on page A3. Star your answers that are the same as the answer key. Count the stars. This is your score.

RECORD your score on the Master Profile Chart on page A2 in the column that shows the chapter number.

ONLINE: You can complete the profile and get your score online at this textbook's web site.

	YES	NO
1. I am aware of my learning style preference as a visual, auditory, or kinesthetic learner.	______	______
2. I can describe four or more learning strategies that can be effective for each learning preference: visual, auditory, and kinesthetic.	______	______
3. I know how to use multisensory learning strategies when I study.	______	______
4. I use a consistent method of studying for all of my courses.	______	______
5. I usually study new information in a straightforward manner without spending time making creative study or review tools.	______	______
6. I know whether my thinking and listening patterns reflect global learning or linear learning.	______	______
7. I use one of these learning preferences consistently for all of my classes: structured learning, interactive learning, or independent learning.	______	______
8. I know how to use a multisensory approach to learning.	______	______
9. I recognize which of Howard Gardner's eight intelligences are strongest in me.	______	______
10. I use study strategies that capitalize on my different learning styles and preferences.	______	______

Reflection Writing 1 — CHAPTER 1

On a separate piece of paper or in a journal, do the following:

1. Discuss your profile score for this chapter. What was your score? What does it mean to you?
2. Describe in general terms how you tend to proceed when learning something new. How do you begin to tackle the new task? What approaches do you use to work your way through the new learning process? What learning techniques generally work best for you? Your responses should reflect what you already know about yourself as a learner.

Three Cognitive Learning Styles

Learning is an individualized process; different educational and background experiences, personality traits, levels of motivation, and numerous other variables affect the way you learn. The term *cognitive* refers to thinking and reasoning processes, so **cognitive learning styles** refers to the general way people *prefer* to problem solve and to process, learn, and remember new information. Three commonly recognized learning styles (also called **learning modalities**) are *visual, auditory,* and *kinesthetic.* You can lay a strong foundation for learning thoroughly and effectively when you understand your preferred learning style and select study strategies that capitalize on your learning preferences and personal strengths.

Learning Styles Inventory

Before you acquire too much information about learning styles that may affect the way you answer the Learning Styles Inventory, complete the following inventory by reading each statement carefully. Check YES if the statement relates to you *all* or *most* of the time. Check NO if the statement *seldom* or *never* relates to you. There is no in-between, so you must check YES or NO. Your first, quick response to the question is usually the best response to use.

	YES	NO
1. I like to listen and discuss work with a partner.	______	______
2. I could likely learn or review information effectively by hearing my own voice on tape.	______	______
3. I prefer to learn something new by reading about it.	______	______
4. I often write down directions someone gives so I do not forget them.	______	______
5. I enjoy physical sports and exercise.	______	______
6. I learn best when I can see new information in picture or diagram form.	______	______
7. I am easily able to visualize or picture things in my mind.	______	______
8. I learn best when someone talks or explains something to me.	______	______
9. I usually write things down so that I can look back at them later.	______	______
10. I am aware of the rhythm or the individual syllables of multisyllablic words when I hear them in conversations or music.	______	______
11. I have a good memory for the words and melodies of old songs.	______	______
12. I like to participate in small-group discussions.	______	______
13. I often remember the sizes, shapes, and colors of objects when they are no longer in sight.	______	______
14. I often repeat out loud verbal directions that someone gives me.	______	______
15. I enjoy working with my hands.	______	______
16. I can remember the faces of actors, settings, and other visual details of movies I have seen.	______	______
17. I often use my hands and body movements when explaining something to someone else.	______	______
18. I prefer standing up and working on a chalkboard or flip chart to sitting down and working on paper.	______	______
19. I often seem to learn better if I can get up and move around while I study.	______	______

	YES	NO
20. I would need pictures or diagrams to help me with each step of the process to assemble something, such as a bike.	______	______
21. I remember objects better when I have touched them or worked with them.	______	______
22. I learn best by watching someone else first.	______	______
23. I tap my fingers or my hands a lot while I am seated.	______	______
24. I speak a foreign language.	______	______
25. I enjoy building things.	______	______
26. I can follow the plot of a story on the radio.	______	______
27. I enjoy repairing things at home.	______	______
28. I can understand information when I hear it on tape.	______	______
29. I am good at using machines or tools.	______	______
30. I find sitting still for very long difficult.	______	______
31. I enjoy acting or doing pantomimes.	______	______
32. I can easily see patterns in designs.	______	______
33. I need frequent breaks to move around.	______	______
34. I like to recite or write poetry.	______	______
35. I can usually understand people with different accents.	______	______
36. I can hear many different pitches or melodies in music.	______	______
37. I like to dance and create new movements or steps.	______	______
38. I enjoy activities that require physical coordination.	______	______
39. I follow written directions better than oral ones.	______	______
40. I can easily recognize differences between similar sounds.	______	______
41. I like to create or use jingles/rhymes to learn things.	______	______
42. I wish more classes had hands-on experiences.	______	______
43. I can quickly tell if two geometric shapes are identical.	______	______
44. The things I remember best are the things I have seen in print or pictures.	______	______
45. I follow oral directions better than written ones.	______	______
46. I could learn the names of fifteen medical instruments more easily if I could touch and examine them.	______	______
47. I often need to say things aloud to myself to remember them later.	______	______
48. I can look at a shape and copy it correctly on paper.	______	______
49. I can usually read a map without difficulty.	______	______
50. I can "hear" a person's exact words and tone of voice days after he or she has spoken to me.	______	______
51. I remember directions best when someone gives me landmarks, such as specific buildings and trees.	______	______
52. I have a good eye for colors and color combinations.	______	______

	YES	NO
53. I like to paint, draw, or make sculptures.	______	______
54. I can vividly picture the details of a meaningful past experience.	______	______

Scoring Your Profile

1. Ignore the NO answers. Work only with the questions that have a YES answer.
2. For every YES answer, look at the number of the question. Find the number in the following chart and circle that number.
3. When you finish, not all the numbers in the following boxes will be circled. Your answers will very likely not match anyone else's.
4. Count the number of circles for the Visual box and write the total on the line. Do the same for the Auditory box and Kinesthetic box.

Visual					Auditory					Kinesthetic				
3,	4,	6,	7,	9,	1,	2,	8,	10,	11,	5,	15,	17,	18,	19,
13,	16,	20,	22,	32,	12,	14,	24,	26,	28,	21,	23,	25,	27,	29,
39,	43,	44,	48,	49,	34,	35,	36,	40,	41,	30,	31,	33,	37,	38,
51,	52,	54			45,	47,	50			42,	46,	53		
Total: ______					Total: ______					Total: ______				

Analyzing Your Scores

1. The highest score indicates your *preference*. The lowest score indicates your weakest modality.
2. If your two highest scores are the same or very close, both of these modalities may be your preference.
3. If all three of your scores are identical, you have truly integrated all three modalities and can work equally well in any of the modalities.
4. Scores that are *10 or higher* indicate the modalities you use frequently.
5. Scores that are *lower than 10* indicate the modalities that you use infrequently or not at all. For modalities with scores lower than 10, examine possible reasons for these scores.
   - Do you have a physical or neurological impairment (such as a learning disability) that makes using this modality difficult or impossible? For students who have physical or neurological impairments, strategies that capitalize on other strengths and academic accommodations provided by their colleges provide effective learning options.
   - Do you have limited experience with or training in ways to use different modalities when you work or study? For the majority of students who have learning modality scores below 10, the low scores are due to limited experience or training using different modalities.
   - Learning and using multisensory strategies can strengthen your ability to use the three cognitive modalities more comfortably and effectively.

Learning Style Preferences

The Learning Style Inventory indicates your **learning style preference**. This basically means that you would tend to use the cognitive learning style or modality with the highest score when you have a choice of how to learn or process new information. For example, if you are in a work situation and your employer asks you to learn a new process on a computer or the operation of a new piece of equipment, you would learn most comfortably if you used your strongest modality. A **visual learner** may prefer to read the manual or learn from pictures, charts, or graphs. An **auditory learner** may prefer to be told how the new process or equipment works. A **kinesthetic learner** may prefer to be shown how the process or piece of equipment works and then be given an opportunity to try each step during the training session.

Cognitive Learning Style Preferences

1. **Visual learners** learn and remember best by *seeing* and *visualizing* information.
2. **Auditory learners** learn and remember best by *hearing* information.
3. **Kinesthetic learners** learn and remember best by using large and small body *movements* and *hands-on experiences*.

As an adult, you have most likely developed a *preference* for one modality over the others, but can probably use all three modalities if needed. This has not always been the case. Children often begin by experimenting with all three modalities but favor one specific modality. Children who are strongly drawn to books, pictures, colors, shapes, and animation show a visual modality preference. Young children who are nonstop talkers, who continuously ask questions, and who frequently sing or recite nursery rhymes show an auditory preference. Children who actively explore their surroundings, have difficulty sitting still (often run, jump, hop, and roll around), and enjoy taking things apart and working with their hands show a kinesthetic modality preference. As children mature, expectations of them change; as they enter the educational system, they begin working with all three cognitive modalities on a more regular basis. Integration of all three modalities occurs over the years, thus enabling teenagers and adults to function in a variety of situations using a combination of the cognitive learning modalities.

Because the process of learning is a highly individualized process, it is not surprising to find differences among adults in terms of how they process and learn new information. For a variety of reasons, some adults have difficulty learning or functioning effectively in one or two of the modalities. The following examples demonstrate differences in adult learners:

1. Patrice had a low score in the visual category of the Learning Styles Inventory. She has more than average difficulty reading a map or following a set of directions drawn in the form of diagrams or pictures. She has difficulty interpreting charts and diagrams in her textbooks. She lacks the spatial skills necessary to understand information in pictorial forms.
2. Mandy had a low score in the auditory category of the Learning Styles Inventory. She has problems following and comprehending lectures. The information gets scrambled, and she finds following the sequence of ideas difficult. Mandy does not have a hearing loss, but she does have an auditory processing disability. The auditory signals do not travel clearly to her brain, where the information needs to be interpreted and processed.
3. Ralph had a low score in the kinesthetic category. He readily admits that he has always had poor coordination skills. He finds detailed work that requires the use of his hands difficult to complete to his satisfaction. He has poor—sometimes almost illegible—handwriting. In his science lab, he feels as though he is "all thumbs" and that his finished products look immature and incomplete.

Each of the preceding examples shows outcomes of specific situations in which students try to complete tasks that use their weakest modality. Each of these students should strive to learn new strategies to strengthen his or her weakest modality; when given a choice, however, students can choose to process information using their modality strengths. Patrice could participate in discussion groups or work with a tutor to verbalize the meaning of graphic material. Mandy could request accommodations for her lecture class; perhaps the lectures could be taped on a recorder with variable speeds so she could slow them down and listen to them later, or perhaps a classmate could provide her with copies of lecture notes. She could also request copies of overheads used by the instructor. Ralph could use a computer for his written assignments and elicit the help of another classmate or tutor to help him break down the steps and work more slowly and carefully on any hands-on projects.

Fortunately, the ability to strengthen and integrate the visual, auditory, and kinesthetic modalities increases with age and experience. In this book you will learn to use a wide variety of strategies to help you with the process of learning. Strive to use strategies that capitalize on your learning preferences, but be willing to experiment with strategies that involve your weaker learning modalities. Strive to become more comfortable and confident working outside your learning preference. Experiment with ways to process information and complete tasks by using a **multisensory approach** involving a combination of two or three modalities. A strategy that would use all three modalities would involve *seeing, saying,* and *moving,* either through full body movement or hands-on experience. The goal is to strengthen and utilize all three modalities effectively so that you can function comfortably and successfully in any situation and with any kind of task.

Group Processing: A Collaborative Learning Activity

Form groups of three or four students. Complete the following directions.

1. On the top of a large piece of paper, ask each student in the group to write his or her visual, auditory, and kinesthetic scores from the Learning Styles Inventory. Do not attach names next to the scores.
2. Discuss the following questions:
   a. Are any of the scores identical? Very seldom will you find another person in your group or in your entire class who has a score identical to yours.
   b. Why do you think it is unusual to find identical scores in an entire class of students?
3. Create a chart with three columns. Label the columns *visual, auditory,* and *kinesthetic.* As a group, brainstorm different learning strategies or "things you can do when you study" that capitalize on each of the learning modalities. Use your own experiences and ideas for study strategies on the chart; do not refer to your textbook. You may use the following examples to begin your chart.

Group scores:		
Visual	*Auditory*	*Kinesthetic*
Use colored pens to highlight	Talk out loud to study	Make wall charts to review

Common Characteristics of Visual, Auditory, and Kinesthetic Learners

The following chart shows common characteristics of each of the three types of learners or learning styles. A person does not necessarily possess abilities or strengths in all of the characteristics but may instead "specialize" in some of the characteristics. Some of this may be due to a person's educational or personal background. For example, an auditory learner may be strong in the area of language skills but may not have had the experience to develop skills with a foreign language or music.

Common Characteristics

Visual	• Learn best by seeing information • Can easily recall information in the form of numbers, words, phrases, or sentences • Can easily understand and recall information presented in pictures, charts, or diagrams • Have strong visualization skills and can look up (often up to the left) and "see" information • Can make "movies in their minds" of information they are reading • Have strong visual-spatial skills that involve sizes, shapes, textures, angles, and dimensions • Pay close attention and learn to interpret body language (facial expressions, eyes, stance) • Have a keen awareness of aesthetics, the beauty of the physical environment, and visual media
Auditory	• Learn best by hearing information • Can accurately remember details of information heard in conversations or lectures • Have strong language skills that include well-developed vocabularies and appreciation of words • Have strong oral communication skills that enable them to carry on conversations and be articulate • Have "finely tuned ears" and may find learning a foreign language relatively easy • Hear tones, rhythms, and notes of music and often have exceptional musical talents
Kinesthetic	• Learn best by using their hands ("hands-on" learning) or by full body movement • Learn best by doing • Learn well in activities that involve performing (athletes, actors, dancers) • Work well with their hands in areas such as repair work, sculpting, art, or working with tools • Are well coordinated, with a strong sense of timing and body movements • Often wiggle, tap their feet, or move their legs when they sit • Often have been labelled "hyperactive"

Multisensory Learning Strategies

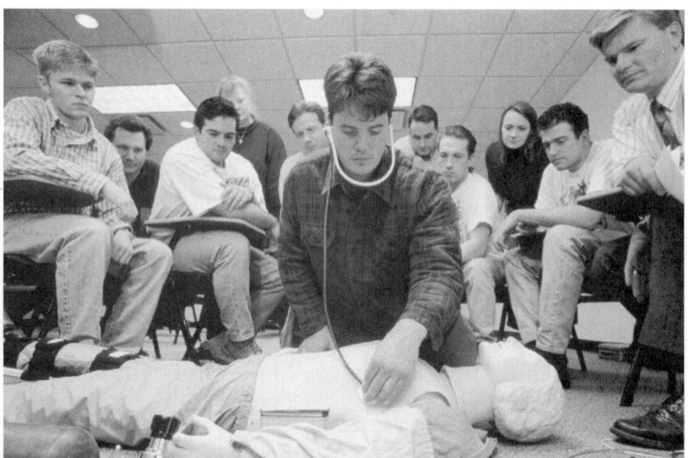

Does this learning strategy work with your strengths? Consider trying it out before you make a decision.

Now that you are aware of your own learning style, you can begin to select learning strategies that work with your strengths. In the following chart you will find a wide array of learning strategies to try; the majority of your strategies will likely come from your area of strength. However, a valuable goal to set for yourself is to strive to integrate all of the modalities into your learning process; therefore, try using several of the strategies for your weaker modalities as well. As you will also notice, some learning strategies will incorporate more than one modality. **Multisensory learning strategies** have the capability of strengthening your memory even more.

Multisensory Learning Strategies That Utilize Modalities

Visual	• Create stronger visual memories of printed materials by highlighting important ideas with different colored highlighters or by highlighting specific letters in spelling words or formulas or equations in math. • Take time to visualize pictures, charts, graphs, or printed information, and take time to practice recalling visual memories when you study. • Create "movies in your mind" of information that you read; use your visual memory as a television screen with the information moving across the screen. • Use visual study tools such as visual mappings, hierarchies, and comparison charts to represent information you are studying. Expand chapter mappings or create your own chapter mappings to review main ideas and important details in chapters. Add colors and/or shapes or pictures. (Visual study tools are discussed in Chapter 11.) • Enhance your notes, flash cards, or any other study tools by adding colors and pictures (sketches, cartoons, stick figures). • Color code study tools. (Different colors imprint into memory more easily for some students.) Colors can be used to accentuate specific parts of textbooks, notes, or any written materials you work with or have created. • Copy information in your own handwriting if seeing information on paper in your own handwriting helps you learn and remember more easily. Practice visualizing what you write. • Use your keen observational skills to observe people and pick up on clues they may give about important information, emotions, or their general state of being. • Always be prepared with a pen and notepaper (or a small notepad) to write down information or directions. (Written information is easier to recall more accurately.)
Auditory	• Talk out loud to explain new information, express your ideas, practice information you are studying, or paraphrase another speaker. • Recite frequently while you study. Reciting involves speaking out loud in complete sentences and in your own words. • Read out loud. (Reading out loud often increases a person's comprehension or clarifies confusing information that has been read silently.) • Work with tutors, with a "study buddy," or in a study group to have ample opportunity to ask questions, articulate answers, and express your understanding of information orally. • For lectures, take your own notes, but back up your notes with a tape-recorded version of the lecture. (Request approval first from the instructor.) Review only the parts of the lecture that are unclear or confusing. • When you practice reciting your notes, flash cards, study tools or information from a textbook, turn on a tape recorder. Tapes made in your own voice often become valuable review tools. • Verbally explain information or processes to someone or to an imaginary person. Explaining verbally provides immediate feedback of your level of understanding. • Make review tapes to review the most important information (rules, definitions, formulas, lists of information, dates, or other factual information) prior to a test. • Create rhymes, jingles, or songs to help you remember specific facts. • Read confusing information using exaggerated expression. The natural rhythm and patterns of your voice often group information in such a way that it becomes easier to understand. • Use computerized technology (electronic spell checkers, calculators with a "voice," speech synthesizers on computers) to help with the learning process. Access multimedia software and CD-ROM programs that provide auditory and visual stimuli for learning.

(continued)

Kinesthetic

- Handle objects, tools, or machinery that you are trying to learn. For example, handle the rocks you study in geology, repeat applications several times on a computer, or hold and use tools or parts of machinery that are discussed in class or in your textbook.
- Create manipulatives (study tools that you can move around with your hands). These may include flash cards or index cards that can be shuffled, spread out, sorted, or stacked as a way to categorize information.
- Cut charts or diagrams apart; reassemble them in their correct order.
- Use exaggerated movements and hand expressions, drama, dance, pantomime, or role playing to assist the development of long-term memory. Muscles also hold memory, so involving movement in the learning process creates muscle memory.
- Type or use a word processor. Using a keyboard involves fine motor skills and muscle memory; it may be easier to remember information that you type or enter into a computer.
- Talk and walk as you recite or practice information. Pacing or walking with study materials in hand helps some people process information more naturally.
- Work at a chalkboard, with a flip chart, or on large poster paper to create study tools. List, draw, practice, or write information while you stand up and work on a larger surface.
- Learn by doing. Use every possible opportunity to move as you study. For example, if you are studying perimeters in math, tape off an area of a room and walk the perimeter.

EXERCISE 1.1 Personalizing the Charts

1. Return to the chart of common characteristics of visual, auditory, and kinesthetic learners (page 8). Highlight the characteristics in each category that you think accurately describe you. Most likely you will highlight several characteristics in each modality. List the characteristics below.

2. Return to the chart showing learning strategies that utilize modalities (pages 9–10). Highlight visual, auditory, and kinesthetic strategies that you feel would be most beneficial for you to learn to use effectively. List the strategies below.

3. The information you highlighted in both charts will be used in later assignments.

Name ______________________ Date ____________

✎ EXERCISE 1.2 Group Discussion

Part 1: *Complete tasks 1 and 2 by yourself. Discuss your answers with the members of your group.*

1. Most people have a daily routine when they get up in the morning. Close your eyes and try to make a movie in your mind that shows you going through your daily routine. Answer the following questions after you have pictured this routine in your mind.

Was the picture clear? ____________________

What colors were visible? ____________________

Name several specific details you saw in your movie. ____________________

____

____

2. Think back to the last conversation you had with a close friend. Answer the following questions.

Can you remember one complete sentence spoken by your friend? ____________________

If yes, write the sentence: ____________________

____

____

Can you "hear" the tone of your friend's voice? ____________________

Oftentimes when a person tries to recall information that was processed through the auditory channels, the person looks to the left (toward the ear) to try to recall the words or sounds. Did you look to the left as you tried to recall your friend's words? ____________________

Part 2: *As a group, solve the following puzzle, using any method that works. As you search for the solution, pay attention to the strategies you use.*

> A parent and a child are standing together on the sidewalk. They both start walking at the same time. Each person begins the first step with the right foot. The child must take three steps for every two steps the parent takes. How many steps must the child take until they both land again on the same foot?

1. How many steps did the child need to take?

2. Did they both land on the right foot or the left foot?

3. Explain how you solved this puzzle.

____

____

____

EXERCISE 1.3 Using Cognitive Modalities

Work by yourself, with a partner, or in a small group to complete parts 1 and 2.

Part 1: *Read each statement below. Circle **V** (visual), **A** (auditory), or **K** (kinesthetic) to indicate the most dominant modality used by the person.*

V A K 1. Without reviewing his textbook, Mark can see details of pictures he studied in a previous chapter.

V A K 2. Jorge may distract others, but jiggling his legs and tapping his pencil on the desk actually help him maintain his concentration.

V A K 3. Lori is studying interior design, for which she seems to be well suited; she has always had an appreciation for aesthetics and a good eye for coordinating colors, fabrics, and accessories.

V A K 4. In our Acting 1 class, James amazed us with his refined movements and facial expressions during his mime performance.

V A K 5. LinLee recounted her conversation with her grandfather; she described the tone of his voice and specific words of advice that he shared with her.

V A K 6. Leroy wants to capitalize on his talent for working with lighting, shading, angles, and composition, so he is majoring in photography.

V A K 7. Raina has notebooks filled with original poetry; she participates in a poetry reading group that meets twice a month.

V A K 8. Bobby, our jazz band's most talented musician, plays drums and keyboard at his church.

V A K 9. Anthony has developed the endurance, speed, and strategies to compete in national marathons.

V A K 10. Maggie won a blue ribbon for her bronze sculpture at the mayor's art show; several of her pieces of pottery also received recognition.

Part 2: *The following learning strategies may involve using one or more modalities. Circle **V, A,** or **K** to indicate the modality or modalities each strategy emphasizes.*

V A K 1. Within the first week of every class, Sharon finds a "study buddy"— someone who wants to meet on a regular basis to discuss class work and topics.

V A K 2. Simon learns shapes for his geometry class by tracing over them several times with his finger and then repeating the process on his desk.

V A K 3. Liz types all her papers on a computer and then asks a tutor or a friend to read each paper out loud so she can listen to the way she expressed her ideas.

V A K 4. Cindy is an excellent note taker. After each class, she uses three different colors to highlight important information: yellow for main ideas, blue for terminology, and pink for important details.

V A K 5. Mark loves history and gets excited thinking about the relationships among different events. He tacked a long piece of paper across his bedroom wall so he can chart all kinds of events on a continuous time line.

V A K 6. Kathryn enjoys reading, but no one likes to be around her when she reads. She reads everything out loud with her own style of expression.

V A K 7. Lily loves to make flash cards for all her classes. She color codes them by chapter and then practices reciting the information out loud. She shuffles all the stacks together and uses a variety of interesting review activities for herself and the members of her study group.

V A K **8.** After Paula reads each literature assignment, she closes her eyes and tells her friends she is studying. At first they did not believe her, but then she told them that she creates an entire movie in her mind about the literature she just read.

V A K **9.** Len has always been dramatic. For an extra-credit project in his psychology class, he convinced two other students to work on a skit that incorporated key concepts from the psychology course.

V A K **10.** Gustav aspires to be a writer. He has created his own web site so he can post his work and, possibly, gain some recognition for his writing.

Reflection Writing 2

CHAPTER 1

On a separate piece of paper or in a journal, write responses to the following questions. Number each of your responses so your instructor can identify them.

1. What were your *visual*, *auditory*, and *kinesthetic* scores on the learning style inventory? Do you agree that the highest score reflects your preferred learning style? Explain.
2. Do you agree that the lowest score is your least preferred learning modality? Explain.
3. Return to the chart of common characteristics on page 8. If you completed Exercise 1.1, you have already highlighted characteristics that reflect how you see yourself (if not, complete Exercise 1.1 before continuing here). Summarize the visual, auditory, and kinesthetic characteristics that you highlighted on the chart. (When you summarize, use some of your own words to shorten, combine, or regroup the ideas or the information.)
4. From what you remember about your childhood, do you think your current learning style preference is the same as your childhood learning preference? Explain.
5. Make a chart with two columns. In the first column, list the strategies from the chart of learning strategies on pages 9–10 that you currently use. In the second column, list the strategies that you will strive to learn to use this term.

Currently use	Goals to learn to use

Linear and Global Learners

The cognitive learning styles model with three basic modalities (visual, auditory, and kinesthetic) is but one of many learning styles models that encourages individuals to identify their preferred ways to process new information. Your instructor, the Internet, your school's counseling department, or your school's career and life planning office may have additional learning styles inventories that you can use to become even more aware of your individual style of learning.

The goal behind every learning styles inventory is for you to increase your awareness about the conditions and the strategies that work most effectively for you to learn information. Sometimes the results of learning styles inventories may also serve as reminders to adjust your strategies when the strategies you currently use are not bringing you the desired results. Remember in all cases that no one learning style is better than another; each style is simply a distinctive way of learning, interacting, or responding.

The **brain dominance theory**, another cognitive model, demonstrates different listening and thinking patterns based on right-hemisphere or left-hemisphere dominance. To gain some insight into this theory, read the following excerpt from Roy Berko's *Communicating*. On pages 15–16 you will have the opportunity to take a short inventory to assess your degree of left- or right-brain dominance. In this model, left-brain learners are called **linear learners**; right-brain learners are called **global learners**.

> **The Role of Global/Linear Thinking/Listening** We are unique in the way we listen and learn. Part of the differences among us is based on the way our brain works. The human brain is divided into two hemispheres, and research shows that some people are prone to use one side of the brain more than the other. This brain dominance accounts for learning and listening in patterned ways.
>
> The left hemisphere of the brain is most responsible for rational, logical, sequential, linear, and abstract thinking. People who tend to be left-brain dominant listen and learn best when materials are presented in structured ways. They tend to prefer specifics and logic-based arguments. Because they tend to take information at face value, abstractions and generalizations don't add much to their learning. Because they are so straight-line in their learning preferences, they are often referred to as **linear learners/listeners**.
>
> The right hemisphere of the brain is responsible for intuitive, spatial, visual, and concrete matters. It is from the right side of the brain that we are able to visualize. Those with this listening/learning dominance prefer examples rather than technical explanations. They prefer knowing the information can be useful and applied. The right-brain dominant person tends to be creative and rely on intuitive thinking, can follow visual/pictographic rather than written instructions, likes to explore information without necessarily coming to a conclusion, and enjoys interaction rather than lecturing. Because of their preference for a generalized rather than specific description, right-brain dominant persons are often labeled as **global listeners/learners**. Many global learners find much of the traditional lecture method of teaching in U.S. schools and universities, a linear methodology, to be dull and frustrating.
>
> Most people are a combination of global and linear learner/listeners. If you fall into this classification, you can be more flexible in how you listen and learn than those with extreme style preferences.
>
> It is important for you to recognize your listening/learning style; it can make a difference in the way you approach the listening/learning environments. If you know that you need examples and the speaker is not giving them, you should ask for them. If the speaker is not drawing specific conclusions and not speaking in a structured format, and these are necessary for your understanding, then you must probe for information that will allow you to organize the ideas. Don't assume that the speaker knows how you need to receive information; he or she doesn't. Many classroom instructors teach based on their own listening/learning style, forgetting that all students don't learn that way. If you are a global listener/learner, this may account for why you had trouble with some math or science classes. On the other hand, if you are a linear listener/learner, literature and poetry classes may have been difficult for you.
>
> Berko, *Communicating*, pp. 58–59, 1998.

Dominance Inventory—Left/Right, Linear/Global Dominance

Answer all of these questions quickly; do not stop to analyze them. When you have no clear preference, choose the one that most closely represents your attitudes or behavior.

1. When I buy a new product, I

A. _____ usually read the directions and carefully follow them.

1 B. _√_ refer to the directions, but really try and figure out how the thing operates or is put together on my own.

2. Which of these words best describes the way I perceive myself in dealing with others?

A. _____ Structured/Rigid

2 B. _√_ Flexible/Open-minded

3. Concerning hunches:

A. _____ I generally would not rely on hunches to help me make decisions.

3 B. _√_ I have hunches and follow many of them.

4. I make decisions mainly based on

A. _____ what experts say will work.

4 B. _√_ a willingness to try things that I think might work.

5. In traveling or going to a destination, I prefer

A. _√_ to read and follow a map.

B. _____ to get directions and map things out "my" way.

6. In school, I preferred

A. _____ geometry.

B. _____ algebra.

7. When I read a play or novel, I

A. _√_ see the play or novel in my head as if it were a movie/TV show.

B. _____ read the words to obtain information.

8. When I want to remember directions, a name, or a news item, I

A. _____ visualize the information, or write notes that help me create a picture, maybe even draw the directions.

B. _√_ write structured and detailed notes.

9. I prefer to be in the class of a teacher who

A. ______ has the class do activities and encourages class participation and discussion.

B. __√__ primarily lectures.

10. In writing, speaking, and problem solving, I am

A. __√__ usually creative, preferring to try new things.

B. ______ seldom creative, preferring traditional solutions.

Scoring and interpretation: Give yourself one point for each question you answered "b" on items 1 to 5 and "a" on 6 to 10. This total is your score. To assess your degree of left- or right-brain preference, locate your final score on this continuum:

Left ____ Right
1 2 3 4 5 6 7 8 9 10

The lower the score, the more left-brain tendency you have. People with a score of 1 or 2 are considered highly linear. Scores of 3 and possibly 4 show a left-brain tendency.

The higher the score, the more right-brain tendency you have. People with scores of 9 or 10 are considered highly global. Scores of 7 and possibly 6 indicate a right-brain tendency.

If you scored between 4 and 7 you have indicated you probably do not tend to favor either brain and are probably flexible in your learning and listening style.

Please bear in mind that neither preference is superior to the other. If you are extremely left- or right-dominant, it is possible to develop some of the traits associated with the other hemisphere, or you may already have them.

Berko, *Communicating,* pp. 75–77, 1998.

EXERCISE 1.4 Creating a Comparison Chart

A comparison chart is a form of visual notetaking that organizes information concisely into a chart. (See Chapter 11 to learn more about comparison charts.) The subjects appear in the left column. The following chart has only two subjects: linear learners and global learners. Categories of information appear at the tops of the columns. Use the information from page 14 to complete this chart by adding key words or characteristics in each of the cells or boxes of the chart. Be selective; use only key words or phrases, not full sentences. If you need more writing space, complete the chart on separate paper.

	Hemisphere used and its responsibilities	**Characteristics of learner**	**Potential classroom problems**
Linear learners			
Global learners			

Structured, Interactive, and Independent Learning Preferences

Other learning styles or preferences relate to emotional, personality, and behavioral patterns that affect how individuals interact, think, and process new information. The following informal learning styles inventory is situational; your preferences may change depending on the course. Examine your preferences for being a *structured,* an *interactive,* or an *independent learner* in different situations. Use the following descriptions:

Structured Learner You want homework assignments to be clearly structured and organized. You want the teacher to provide as much direction as possible, including step-by-step instruction on how to proceed in the course. Teacher feedback motivates you. You want to be able to check off the work you have completed and know you have met the teacher's expectations.

Interactive Learner You want to work with a partner, a tutor, or a small study group to discuss and complete the homework assignments. You want to listen to others and exchange ideas. Group interaction and the feeling of belonging to a group motivate you. You want to use group feedback to give you a sense of your progress.

Independent Learner You want to work by yourself at home or at school. You have your own system for learning information and do not want to get confused by other people's methods or ideas. You want to explore ideas, discover relationships of ideas, study, and review on your own. You have confidence in your methods.

In the following inventory, check the box that shows your preference. Decide whether you have one specific learning style preference for all subjects or if you vary the preference among different courses or content areas.

	Structured Learning	Interactive Learning	Independent Learning
For a reading class, I would prefer:			
For a foreign language class, I would prefer:			
For a writing class, I would prefer:			
For a sociology class, I would prefer:			
For a math class, I would prefer:			
For a computer class, I would prefer:			
For a science class, I would prefer:			
For a health class, I would prefer:			

Discovering Patterns

1. *Structured learning:* Consider the classes for which you checked "structured learning" as your preference for studying. What do those classes have in common? Why do you feel structured learning is best for those classes?

2. *Interactive learning:* Consider the classes for which you checked "interactive learning" as your preference for studying. What do those classes have in common? Why do you feel interactive learning is best for those classes?

3. *Independent learning:* Consider the classes for which you checked "independent learning" as your preference for studying. What do those classes have in common? Why do you feel independent learning is best for those classes?

EXERCISE 1.5 Case Studies

Each of the following case studies describes a student situation. Read each one carefully and highlight key ideas or student issues. Then, answer the question that ends each case study. In your response, address the key points that you highlighted that relate directly to the question. Use complete sentences in your answers and write them on separate paper. These case studies are also available online; you can email your response to your instructor or print a copy of your work online.

1. Elaine is usually an outgoing person. She started college in the middle of the year and does not know anyone on campus. After she received her midterm grades, she became concerned because she knew her work did not reflect her abilities. She knows she has strong auditory skills and is an interactive learner and a global thinker. She studies three or four hours every day alone in the library. She turns in her assignments on time but has difficulty retaining information. She also has trouble motivating herself and getting interested in her classes. What changes can Elaine make to combat the problems she has encountered in the first half of this term?
2. Conor is enrolled in a poetry class to complete one of his program requirements. He has never enjoyed or really understood poetry. He had hoped that this class would provide him with specific methods to analyze, interpret, and respond to poetry. Instead of learning specific steps or guidelines, the class time consists of open-ended discussions that seem to be nothing more than a lot of different opinions. He is frustrated with the instructor and the lack of structure, direction, or specific answers. He is not comfortable talking to other students about this because they seem excited about the class, the instructor, and the content. He is doing well in all of his other classes, which include math and advanced physics, and is afraid that this class is going to lower his GPA. What are Conor's learning styles and how do they contribute to the problems and frustrations he is experiencing in the poetry class?

Multiple Intelligences

Learning styles provide one framework for understanding how people learn. Howard Gardner's **Theory of Multiple Intelligences** provides another framework for understanding cognitive development. In 1983, Gardner, a noted Harvard University psychologist, presented his theory in his book *Frames of Mind: The Theory of Multiple Intelligences*. This Theory of Multiple Intelligences (MI) challenges the traditional intelligence quotient (IQ) tests, which measure intellectual abilities in the areas of verbal, visual-spatial, and logical mathematics. The MI theory defines intelligence as areas of *human potential.* Under this theory, individuals have a wide range of distinct aptitudes, talents, and abilities, each of which can be cultivated and expanded. When Gardner first presented his theory he had identified seven different intelligences. In 1996, Gardner added an eighth intelligence, the naturalist, and contends that very likely additional intelligences will be identified in the future.

What are the different intelligences a director and an actor rely on to work together to produce a play?

The Eight Intelligences in Howard Gardner's MI Theory

Verbal/Linguistic	Musical	Logical/Mathematical	Visual-Spatial
Bodily-Kinesthetic	Interpersonal	Intrapersonal	Naturalist

Gardner notes **subintelligences** under each of these eight intelligences. For example, people can exhibit many different talents and abilities under the category of musical intelligence. A person with a high musical intelligence may not have all of the subintelligences of music well developed. Singing, playing different instruments, composing, conducting, critiquing, and appreciating a variety of music require different skills, abilities, and processes. The level of accomplishment or degree of mastery will vary within an individual among the subintelligences, but the *potential* to acquire more skills and perform on a higher level exists.

Verbal/linguistic intelligence includes verbal and written language abilities. Common characteristics of this intelligence include a love of language—a curiosity and fascination with words, meanings (semantics), and structure (syntax). Sensitivities to how words are used, how they sound (phonology), and how they evoke feelings are other characteristics. People with these developed abilities may exhibit sharp, detailed, vivid memories about written or spoken language; excel in word games such as crossword puzzles or Scrabble; and enjoy creating and reciting puns, jingles, or poetry. They may exhibit the ability to express ideas well in public presentations, storytelling, or debates and may express ideas well in writing, whether in journals, prose, or poetry.

Musical intelligence consists of an acute sensitivity to sounds, melody (pitch), rhythm, tones (timbre), and harmony. People with these developed abilities may exhibit strong auditory memories and may use vocal or instrumental music to express creativity, imagination, and the gamut of human emotions. They may be skilled in reading and writing music. Other characteristics that reflect musical intelligence include an understanding of music theory and symbols; a passion for different types and structures of music; and an enjoyment of singing, chanting, humming, or drumming.

Logical-mathematical intelligence involves the use of logic, sound reasoning, problem solving, analysis, identification of patterns, sequential thinking, and mathematical calculations. People with logical/mathematical intelligence may think concretely and abstractly, understand and apply abstract numerical symbols and operations, and perform complex calculations. They may also use systematic, logic-based, sequential problem-solving techniques and scientific methods to measure, hypothesize, test, research, and confirm results.

Visual-spatial intelligence involves keen, accurate, precise perceptions of the physical world, including sizes, shapes, textures, lines, curves, and angles. People with developed visual-spatial intelligence are able to present their ideas graphically. They often possess strong visual imagery or visualization skills, creativity, and active imaginations. For example, a gifted chess player can play a challenging game of chess blindfolded, or an architect can picture the floor plans of a building before drawing them. People with strong visual-spatial intelligence often enjoy the arts, such as painting, sculpting, drawing, drafting, or photography.

Bodily-kinesthetic intelligence encompasses fine, precise body rhythms, body movements, motor coordination skills, an acute sense of timing, balance, dexterity, flexibility, and possibly strength and speed. People with well-developed gross (large) motor skills are able to judge how their bodies will respond to certain situations and are able to fine tune and train their bodies to perform at higher levels. People with well-developed fine (small) motor skills work well with their hands to create or modify the objects they work with. They can "sense" through their hands. For example, a mechanic unable to see inside an engine may be able to locate and fix a problem using only his or her hands. People with developed bodily-kinesthetic intelligence often enjoy physical exercise, sports, dancing, drama, role playing, inventing, building, and repairing things. They prefer "hands-on" or activity-oriented tasks.

Intrapersonal intelligence focuses on personal growth, self-understanding, personal reflection, intuition, spirituality, and motivation to achieve personal potential. People with this developed ability enjoy exploring their feelings, values, goals, strengths, weaknesses, and personal history. They often use life experiences as lessons and guides to change aspects of their lives and to give their lives meaning. They frequently project a sense of pride, self-esteem, confidence, self-responsibility, control, and empowerment; they tend to be self-motivated and goal-oriented. People with strong intrapersonal intelligence are usually able to adapt to a wide variety of situations and circumstances; consequently, they succeed in many fields of work.

Interpersonal intelligence emphasizes effective interpersonal communication skills, social skills, leadership ability, and cooperative team work. Such individuals participate actively in groups, create bonds with diverse groups of people, and feel a sense of global responsibility toward others. Other common characteristics include the ability to interpret nonverbal clues that appear in the form of facial expressions, gestures, or general body language and the ability to interpret the behavior, motivation, and intentions of others. People with these developed abilities often enjoy socializing, helping others, sharing their skills, tutoring or teaching others, and contributing to the development of positive group dynamics.

Gardner identified the eighth intelligence, **naturalist intelligence**, in 1996, several years after he identified the first seven intelligences. People with a naturalist intelligence are sensitive to the physical world and aware of the balance (or imbalance) of plants, animals, and the environment. They are keen observers of nature's elements—such as daily, seasonal, and cyclical changes—and of the relationships in nature. People with developed naturalist intelligence often demonstrate detailed knowledge and expertise in recognizing and classifying plants and animals. They may exhibit the ability to organize, classify, arrange, or group items and ideas into logical units or categories.

The Theory of Multiple Intelligences serves as a reminder that we are all "evolving beings." We have the ability to expand our abilities and intelligences to reach greater levels of potential, performance, and fulfillment. We can also consciously make choices to capitalize on our abilities and intelligences and strive for ways to cultivate and enhance them. Not surprisingly, many people seek and find success in careers that emphasize their stronger intelligences. The following chart shows a sampling of typical careers that capitalize on the abilities associated with each of the intelligences.

Intelligence	**Careers**
Verbal/linguistic	author, journalist, editor, poet, newscaster, television announcer, motivational speaker, playwright, politician, consultant
Musical	music teacher, composer, conductor, performer, sound engineer, film maker, television crew or director, marketing or advertising personnel
Logical-mathematical	mathematician, math or business teacher, scientist, computer programmer, accountant, tax expert, banker, researcher
Visual-spatial	architect, designer, interior decorator, artist, painter, sculptor, fashion designer, landscaper, carpenter, contractor, graphic artist, advertiser, cartographer, inventor
Bodily-kinesthetic	dancer, athlete, actor, musician/instrumentalist (guitarist, drummer, pianist), dance teacher, choreographer, photographer, mime artist, painter, sculptor, surgeon, inventor
Intrapersonal	psychiatrist, spiritual or personal counselor, self-help or motivational writer or speaker, philosopher, biographer
Interpersonal	parent, tutor, teacher, therapist, counselor, healer, social activist, motivational/personal growth workshop leader, religious leader, sociologist, anthropologist, political organizer
Naturalist	meteorologist, geologist, botanist, herbalogist, biologist, naturopath, holistic healer, medicine man, gardener

Howard Gardner's Theory of Multiple Intelligences has opened a new door to understanding individual differences, skills, abilities, and interests. This theory recognizes that most people have some degree of each of the intelligences, but that some intelligences are more developed than others in the individual. Through effective training, experience, and conducive environments, people have the potential to develop and strengthen each of the intelligences. Many educators and leaders of the educational reform initiatives in the United States use Gardner's research and philosophy to create or modify classroom teaching methods and curricula. Many educators are exploring both practical applications for classroom teaching and assessment of student performance based on the understanding that students' abilities are diverse and that students will excel in the areas of academics and personal growth when their wider range of talents or intelligences are recognized and nurtured.

EXERCISE 1.6 Discussing Multiple Intelligences

Work with a partner or in a small group to complete the following sets of directions.

1. List any fifteen different occupations or careers.

____________	____________	____________
____________	____________	____________
____________	____________	____________
____________	____________	____________
____________	____________	____________

2. Use the letter codes shown after each of Howard Gardner's intelligences below. Discuss which intelligence you feel is most actively used for people who excel in the above professions. Next to each profession listed above, write the code.

   a. verbal/linguistic (VL)
   b. musical (M)
   c. logical/mathematical (LM)
   d. visual-spatial (VS)
   e. bodily-kinesthetic (BK)
   f. intrapersonal (INTRA)
   g. interpersonal (INTER)
   h. naturalist (N)

3. The Theory of Multiple Intelligences has many implications for education and educational reform. Many teachers are exploring new teaching methods, activities, and forms of assessment that are directly linked to the Theory of Multiple Intelligences. After each educational activity below, use the codes from above to indicate which intelligence is most encouraged by the activity.

   a. Form a group to create a student handbook for incoming freshman. ________

   b. Act out a scene from a book in a literature class. ________

   c. Conduct four interviews with people who work in the career field of interest to you. ________

   d. Construct and conduct a survey of students on your campus. Analyze the data and present it in a report format to the president of the college. ________

   e. Collect samples of music from different cultural or ethnic groups. ________

f. Use a computer graphics program to create an eye-catching presentation. ________

g. Write a poem about your heritage or cultural ties. ________

h. Create a collage of international flags to hang in the library. ________

i. Organize a photography exhibit of your best photographs. ________

j. Write a paper contrasting American English and British English terms for common objects. ________

k. Roleplay a conflict resolution strategy. ________

l. Keep a daily journal or log to record your progress in reaching a specific goal. ________

m. Counsel a friend about a personal problem. ________

n. Attend a movie and then write a critique to present to the class. ________

o. Design a tee shirt for an organization on campus. ________

Exercise 1.7 LINKS

The three cognitive learning styles (visual, auditory, and kinesthetic) provide a framework for ways people prefer to process and learn new information. Howard Gardner's Theory of Multiple Intelligences provides a framework for understanding human potential and intelligences that can be cultivated and strengthened. Which cognitive learning styles are actively used in each of the eight intelligences? Write your response below in one or more paragraphs or in the form of a chart.

Reflection Writing 3 — CHAPTER 1

The primary goal of learning style, personality, or other kinds of inventories is to help you become aware of the way you operate, identify approaches to learning that are effective, and acquire the tools to adjust your strategies so you can perform on a higher level and achieve your goals. As part of this process, you are also strengthening your *intrapersonal skills.*

On a separate piece of paper or in your journal, summarize what you learned about yourself in each of the following areas. Then briefly explain how you can use this information in your courses this term.

1. *Cognitive learning styles*
2. *Linear and global learners*
3. *Structured, interactive, independent learning preferences*
4. *Multiple intelligences*

SUMMARY

- Three main cognitive learning styles or learning modalities determine how individuals prefer to learn: visual, auditory, and kinesthetic.
- Most adults have a learning style preference but are able to function using all three modalities.
- The most effective study tools are those that are compatible with your visual, auditory, or kinesthetic strengths.
- Weak learning modalities may be due to lack of experience or training or to physical or neurological conditions.
- Howard Gardner's Theory of Multiple Intelligences proposes that intelligences are human potentials that can be learned and strengthened.
- Gardner identified eight intelligences or abilities that people possess to varying degrees: verbal-linguistic, musical, logical-mathematical, visual-spatial, bodily-kinesthetic, intrapersonal, interpersonal, and naturalist.
- Each of the eight intelligences has subintelligences. A person may not exhibit developed abilities in all of the subintelligences.
- The brain dominance theory groups thinking patterns into right-hemisphere and left-hemisphere thinking. Linear learners are left-brain learners. Global learners are right-brain learners.
- Another learning preference model groups people into structured, interactive, or independent learners. However, these categories are situational; a person may vary his or her preference based on the course and the content.

ACE Practice Tests, which are scored online, supplementary exercises, enrichment activities, and related web site links are available online for *Essential Study Skills*, 4e. Use the following directions to access this web site:

Type: **http://college.hmco.com/collegesurvival/students**

In the Student Success/Study Skills box, use the arrow to scroll down to Wong *Essential Study Skills*, 4e. Click GO.
If you are working on your own computer, bookmark this web site.

LEARNING OPTIONS

The following learning options provide you with opportunities to demonstrate your understanding of the topics in Chapter 1. Your instructor may assign one or more specific options or ask you to select one or more options that interest you the most.

1. Expand the Chapter 1 mapping on page 1. Notice that the name of the chapter appears in the center and each of the chapter headings extends outward from the center of the mapping. Copy this structure on a blank piece of paper, then reread the information under each heading in your textbook. Extend branches on the mapping to show important key words or phrases for each heading. (See Chapter 11 for additional information.) You can add pictures and colors to your mapping to accentuate the points. The first heading is done as an example.

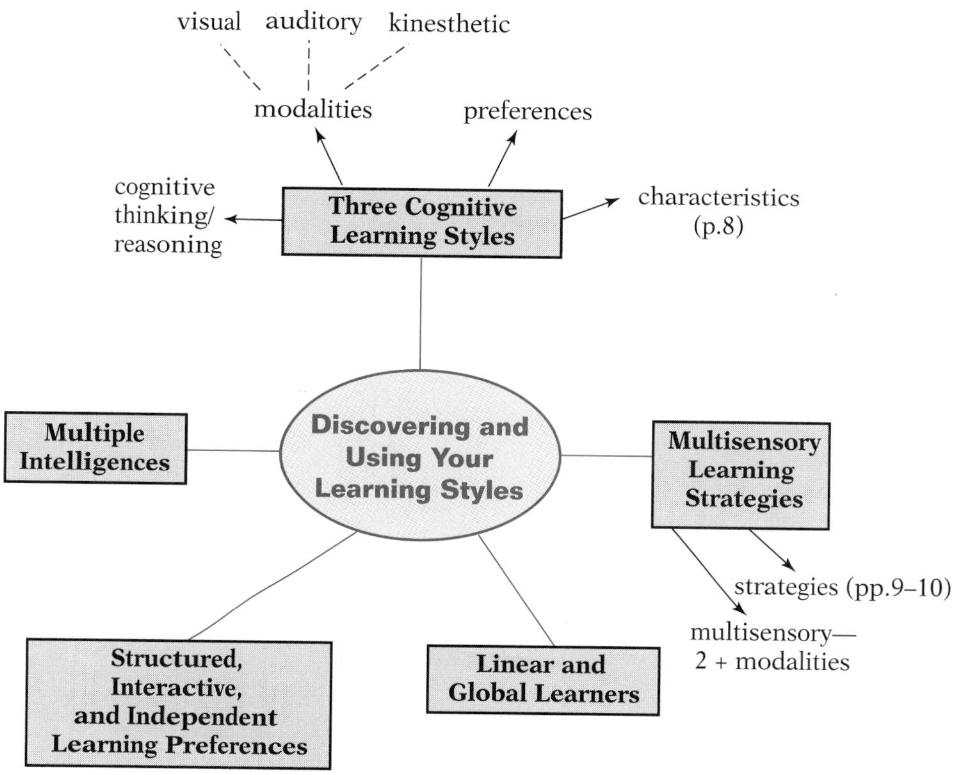

2. Use the directions from Learning Option 1 to make a visual mapping of Howard Gardner's Theory of Multiple Intelligences. Include a picture or symbol on your mapping for each of the intelligences. Extend branches from each intelligence to show key characteristics and common careers related to each intelligence. Add colors to your visual mapping. You may use a computer graphics program for this option.
3. Use the Internet to locate an informative web site for one of the following topics: *learning styles, Howard Gardner's Theory of Multiple Intelligences, the brain dominance theory, or right-hemisphere (brain) and left-hemisphere (brain) thinking.* Print the information. Prepare a short presentation or a written summary of the most significant information. In your presentation or summary, explain how the contents of the web site relate to the content of this chapter.

4. The comparison chart on page 21 shows each of the eight multiple intelligences and typical careers that capitalize on the associated abilities. On your own paper, expand this chart by adding two more columns: *common characteristics* and *famous people.* In one column, write key characteristics for each intelligence. In the other new column, list famous people who best exemplify the traits associated with that intelligence. You may add colors and pictures to your chart.
5. Create a poster or collage that depicts the various kinds of learning styles and preferences discussed in this chapter. You may use magazine pictures, photographs, or your own drawings to represent the following: *visual, auditory, and kinesthetic learners; linear and global learners; structured, interactive, and independent learners;* and *the eight intelligences.* Organize the information in a logical, appealing manner.
6. Form a study group with three or more students and meet outside class to review the content of this chapter. In addition to the review work, spend time discussing the different learning styles and preferences of each member of the group. Write a summary paper that discusses the highlights.
7. Create a study tape for yourself for Chapter 1. On your tape, summarize or explain the most important points of the chapter. This will serve as an excellent review tool later in the term.

Chapter 1 REVIEW QUESTIONS

True-False

Carefully read the following statements. Write T if the statement is true and F if it is false.

_________ **1.** *Cognitive learning styles* refers to the way people interact in a group setting.

_________ **2.** The three cognitive learning styles are *hands-on, visual,* and *kinesthetic.*

_________ **3.** All adults are capable of developing all three cognitive modalities to equally high levels of functioning.

_________ **4.** Learning styles indicate people's preferred ways of learning and processing new information, but students cannot always use their preferred modality in every learning situation.

_________ **5.** A study strategy that uses a multisensory approach incorporates more than one cognitive learning style or modality.

_________ **6.** Visual learners have strong memories for printed material or pictures, diagrams, and charts.

_________ **7.** Auditory learners often have strong language skills and auditory memories.

_________ **8.** People with a kinesthetic learning style should always stand or move around when they study or perform an important task.

_________ **9.** An *interactive learner* would likely benefit from discussing coursework with others and from hearing other students' study techniques and ideas.

_________ **10.** Linear learners are likely to use intuition, visually graphic formats, and methods for organizing specific details.

_________ **11.** Global learners tend to be more creative, interactive, and effective at visualizing information than are linear learners.

_________ **12.** *Interactive learners* have characteristics similar to those of a person with a developed interpersonal intelligence, a global learner, and a learner with an auditory learning preference.

_________ **13.** *Independent learners* are self-directed and prefer to use their own methods of studying and reviewing information.

_________ **14.** Howard Gardner's Theory of Multiple Intelligences consists of eight intelligences and numerous subintelligences that reflect an individual's learning potentials.

_________ **15.** The skills exhibited by a person with a well-developed logical-mathematical intelligence reflect characteristics of a linear thinker.

_________ **16.** Individuals with a well-developed bodily-kinesthetic intelligence always exhibit their abilities through full body movements, such as dance, sports, or acting.

_________ **17.** People who work well with others and show leadership skills exhibit characteristics of intrapersonal intelligence.

_________ **18.** The Theory of Multiple Intelligences states that each person is born with a level of intelligence for each of the eight intelligences and that these levels remain constant throughout the person's lifespan.

Short Answer and Critical Thinking

Use complete sentences to answer each of the following questions.

1. The Theory of Multiple Intelligences is based on the premise that traditional IQ tests are too limiting. What intelligences did Howard Gardner add to expand the concept of traditional intelligence and include a wider range of talents and abilities?

2. Teaching styles frequently reflect a teacher's own learning styles and preferences. Give an example of the difficulties a student with a specific type of learning style might encounter in a classroom with an instructor with a different learning/teaching style. Choose and describe the student's and the teacher's teaching styles; then discuss the kinds of difficulties the student might encounter in that class.

3. What would be an ideal classroom environment and instructional approach for you that would allow you to capitalize on your various learning styles and preferences? Use specific details to describe the classroom and the instructional approach.

Processing Information into Your Memory System

CHAPTER 2

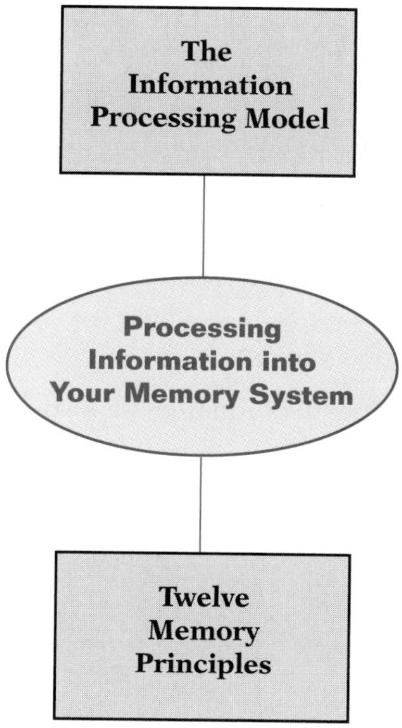

For centuries people have been fascinated by the workings of the human mind. In this chapter, you will learn a basic cognitive model that represents one view of how the mind works to process incoming information. You will also learn twelve principles of memory that can help you strengthen your abilities to process, recognize, and recall important information. By familiarizing yourself with the model and the principles, you will gain a better understanding of your own thinking and memory/learning systems.

Terms to Know

- Information Processing Model
- sensory input
- sensory stimuli
- short-term memory (STM)
- "trap door"
- rehearsal path
- encoding
- rote memory
- elaborative rehearsal
- self-quizzing
- feedback loop
- long-term memory (LTM)
- schemas
- neurotransmitters
- imprinted
- long-term retrieval
- output
- twelve memory principles
- SAVE CRIB FOTO
- selectivity
- association
- memory search
- retrieval cue
- visualization
- effort
- concentration
- recitation
- interest
- big and little pictures
- feedback
- organization
- time on task
- 2:1 ratio
- marathon studying
- massed studying
- distributed practice
- ongoing review

CHAPTER 2 Information Processing Profile

DO, SCORE, and **RECORD** your profile before you read this chapter. If you need to review the process, refer to the complete directions given in the Profile for Chapter 1 on page 2.

ONLINE: You can complete the profile and get your score online at this textbook's web site.

	YES	NO
1. I use study methods that give me feedback so that I know whether I am learning.	____	____
2. I have problems studying new information when it is not an area of genuine interest to me.	____	____
3. I have problems identifying and pulling out the information that is important to study.	____	____
4. I rearrange information into meaningful units or clusters so it is easier to learn.	____	____
5. I wait until close to test time before I practice the information that I previously read.	____	____
6. I talk out loud to myself as I study because reciting seems to help me learn.	____	____
7. I use the same method of learning information for everything I need to study.	____	____
8. I frequently use rote memory by memorizing specific details exactly as they are presented in the book.	____	____
9. I make movies in my mind about the information I am learning.	____	____
10. I take time to relate or associate new information to information I already know.	____	____

Reflection Writing 1 — CHAPTER 2

On a separate piece of paper or in a journal, do the following:

1. Discuss your profile score for this chapter. What was your score? What does it mean to you?
2. How do you feel about your memory? Is it usually vivid, strong, and accurate, or is it often unclear, weak, and inaccurate? When does your memory seem stronger, and when does it seem weaker? What do you see as your greatest memory strengths and your greatest problem areas?

The Information Processing Model

Psychologists frequently use the **Information Processing Model** to help explain how we receive, process, and learn information. The Information Processing Model consists of six main parts. Although each part has its own distinct functions, the parts do not work independently. Each part has an important role to move information through your memory system as you learn. Refer to the following diagram of the model as you read about each of its parts.

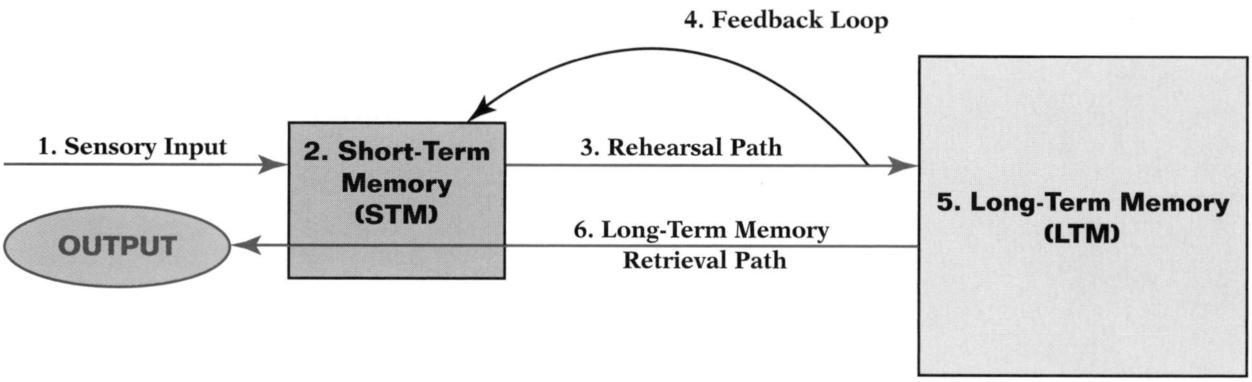

The Information Processing Model

1. Our senses take in information, or sensory input.
2. Our short-term memory receives the information and holds it briefly.
3. We rehearse the information we want to learn.
4. If we get feedback that we are not learning what we rehearse, that information goes through the feedback loop and returns to short-term memory for re-processing.
5. Information that is adequately rehearsed moves into long-term memory, where it is permanently imprinted.
6. Information stored in long-term memory is accessed through long-term retrieval, and the output shows that we have learned.

Sensory Input

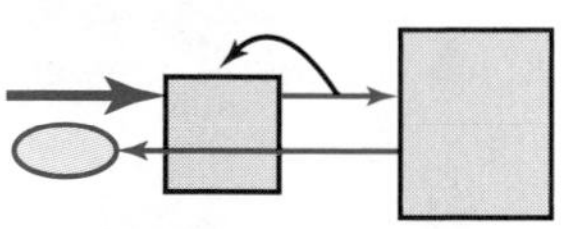

We receive information through our five senses (sight, sound, smell, taste, and touch); this information is called **sensory input**. Such input comes in the form of **sensory stimuli**, which can be letters, numbers, words, pictures, and sounds.

Short-Term Memory

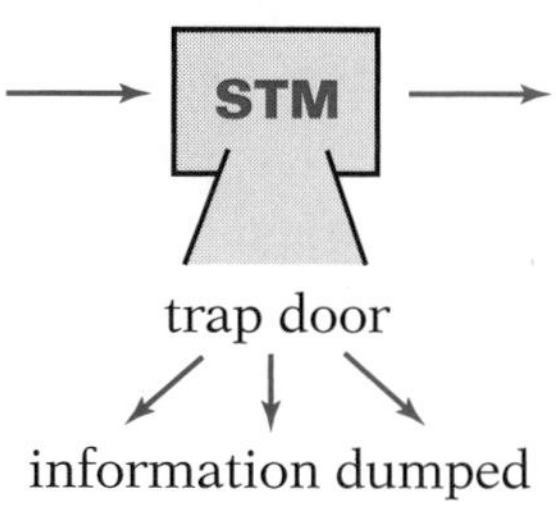

Short-term memory (STM) is a temporary *storage center* that is very limited in time and capacity (up to seven items at one time). Sensory input first moves into short-term memory and remains there for a few seconds. Within that short time, a "decision" is made by the person receiving the stimuli to dump the information or process it further. This decision may be made consciously or subconsciously. If attention is not given to the stimuli, the automatic response will be to "dump" it through an imaginary trap door. This imaginary **trap door** discards unwanted or unattended-to information before it has the chance to be processed in memory.

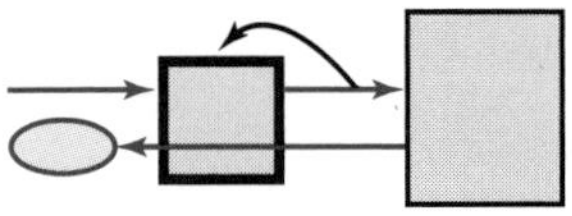

Short-term memory is the entry point to your memory system, so strengthening your short-term memory improves your overall ability to learn. **The following important strategies can help you strengthen the effectiveness of your short-term memory.**

1. *Pay attention to incoming sensory input.* This requires focusing, concentrating on, or attending to the stimuli. You need to be alert and ready. For example, if you are listening to another person, block out distractions and focus your attention on the speaker's words and ideas. If you are reading, the stimulus is in the form of words; read slowly enough to comprehend the material. Block out any distractions that disrupt your concentration.
2. *Limit the number of items and the speed with which you take in stimuli.* Remember that short-term memory has a limited capacity and duration. If you try to take in too much information too rapidly, some or all of the information will be dumped. The short-term memory system breaks down from overload. Cramming and reading complex textbooks quickly are examples of attempts to move too much information too rapidly through a memory system that begins with a limited capacity.
3. *Make it your intention to learn.* Motivation is a key factor. As you begin to receive information, remind yourself that you want to learn this information, and make a conscious decision to do so. For example, perhaps you have difficulty learning names of people at social gatherings. When you are motivated to remember the names and make a concerted effort to do so, you begin to process the information as soon as you receive the names.
4. *Find meaning or significance in the incoming information.* When you know that you have to learn new information because it is a course requirement, essential to your job, or important to you in some other way, you begin the learning process as soon as the information enters your short-term memory. If you find no value in the information, the *trap door* will automatically open and the information will be dumped. As an example, how many black cars did you pass on your way to school today? You are not likely to have an accurate answer because there was no reason to count black cars. However, if your instructor asks you to gather information for a project by recording the number of black cars you pass on your way to school, you have a reason to pay attention to the incoming stimuli.
5. *Show or create interest in the information you are trying to process into your memory.* If you automatically label something boring, you send a signal to that trap door in your memory to discard the information, for it is not significant. Being aware of your attitude toward a topic can alert you to the need to create an interest, which in turn creates an intent to learn, when your interest level is low.

What problems does the survival technique of cramming create in a student's memory system?

6. *Remove stress and negative feelings as much as possible.* Stress and negative feelings start to shut down the learning process before it has much opportunity to start. Information received may become distorted, blurry, or incomplete. As you will learn in Chapter 5, a relaxed state of mind helps you become receptive to incoming sensory information and leads to more effective processing.

Rehearsal Path

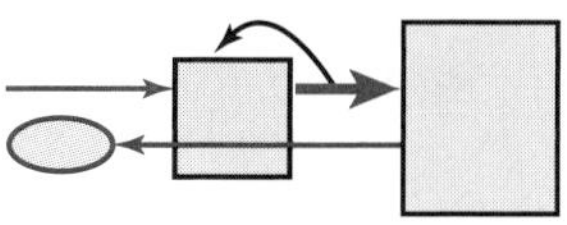

Once you decide that particular information is important to learn, that information moves on to the **rehearsal path**. It is on this path that you select effective learning techniques to move the information into your long-term memory. The rehearsal path is an *active path* where practice, comprehension, and learning take place. It carries the sensory stimuli in a coded form that long-term memory can recognize. The type of **encoding** depends on the type of information being transmitted:

1. *Linguistic coding,* also called *acoustic coding,* carries verbal information.
2. *Visual coding,* also called *imaginal coding,* carries visual images, such as pictures or diagrams.
3. *Motor coding,* also called *physical coding,* carries messages that are related to muscle movement, such as riding a bike, typing, or driving a car.
4. *Semantic coding* carries the general meaning and emotional responses of a specific experience.

The rehearsal path is an extremely important part of the information processing model, for the way you rehearse will affect how clearly, effectively, and efficiently the information will be placed in your long-term memory system. One way to rehearse information is to use **rote memory**. Rote memory involves repetition—lots of repetition—to learn the information in the *exact form* in which it was received. Rote memory often does not involve thoroughly understanding the information, its purpose, or its relationship to other things. While rote memory can be useful at times, such as when memorizing a new phone number, a spelling word, an interesting quotation, or your social security number, it often is ineffective for learning academic material. Rote memory does not provide you with adequate comprehension of the information to be able to apply it in different ways or to different situations. The results are simply too limiting.

A second and a much more powerful way to rehearse information is to use **elaborative rehearsal**. Elaborative rehearsal involves active thinking processes. Time and effort are given to understanding the information, seeing how it relates to other information, recognizing how it can be used, associating or linking it to information you know, and using multisensory approaches to learn the information accurately and thoroughly. When you learn information through elaborative rehearsal, you will be able to explain it, show you understand it, and apply it as needed.

The rehearsal path has the significant role of encoding information so it can be received, understood, and stored effectively in long-term memory. The rehearsal path is the *learning path.*

The following important strategies can help you strengthen the effectiveness of the rehearsal path.

1. *Select learning strategies that use your strongest modalities or preferences.* Your goal is to encode the information clearly and efficiently. You can often do this best by working with strategies that capitalize on your strengths and abilities.

2. *Use a variety of rehearsal strategies.* A variety of strategies, possibly including multisensory strategies, creates a strong code for long-term memory. For example, if you need to learn a new set of math formulas, you may want to make a flash card for each formula. On the rehearsal path, you could recite the cards, visualize them, and practice writing the formulas from memory. In this manner, you would not only be using your preferred learning modality, but you would be using all three cognitive modalities and three different encoding systems. This approach utilizes more than one sensory channel or path into long-term memory.
3. *Use elaborative rehearsal instead of rote memory.* Strive to comprehend the information, attach meaning to it, understand it as thoroughly as possible, and recognize its relationship to other ideas.
4. *Allow ample time to practice frequently.* To learn any skill thoroughly requires time, effort, and ample practice. If you know how to ski, play an instrument, or sew clothing, you learned through practice. The rehearsal path involves frequent practice for information to move solidly into long-term memory.
5. *Use* **self-quizzing** *for feedback so you can gauge the effectiveness of your learning strategies.* As you rehearse information, quiz yourself to ensure that you are creating a clear imprint of the information for your long-term memory. Reciting, writing, discussing, drawing or reproducing, and demonstrating understanding in other ways are self-quizzing activities you can do to get valuable feedback.
6. *Adjust your learning strategies or encoding methods after you receive feedback.* Pay attention to the feedback you receive. If you do not know the information, do not skip over it or tell yourself you will return to it later. Try a different learning strategy or learning modality to rehearse and encode the information. Move on to other rehearsal activities when you receive feedback that you know the information.
7. *Vary your approach to rehearsing.* If you get feedback that you do not know specific information, do not continue to rehearse the information in the same way. You may end up recycling through the feedback loop repeatedly without making any progress. For example, if you made a list of key terms and definitions for one of your textbook chapters but were not able to give the definitions, do not continue to work only with that list. Try a different strategy, such as making and sorting flash cards, using the terminology in your own spoken sentences, or discussing the definitions in a study group.

Feedback Loop

When you rehearse and find out that you do not understand or know the new information, you receive feedback that you need more rehearsal or practice. The information "zips" through the **feedback loop**, which is nothing more than a quick path back to short-term memory.

Following are several important points to know about the feedback loop:

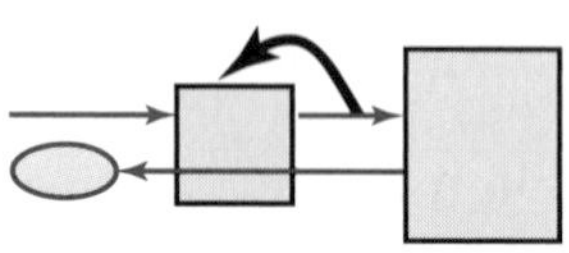

1. The feedback loop is an *inactive path.* It does nothing but immediately send the information back into short-term memory for further rehearsal.
2. An easy image to associate with the feedback loop is the suction duct that banks use to send deposits or withdrawals from the teller to the car that is in a lane away from the building. The driver of the car puts his or her money into a container and sends the container through a suction duct that drops the container at the teller window. The feedback loop works in a similar way.

Long-Term Memory

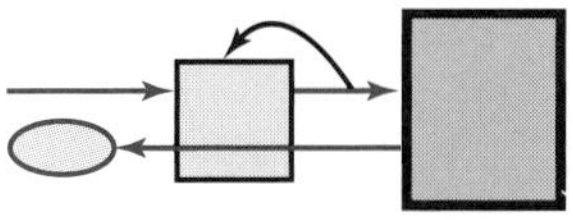

Long-term memory (LTM) is an enormous *storage system* that "files away" information. So that new information can be located when it is needed, long-term memory often stores it in clusters of related information called **schemas**. (As an interesting note, with advanced technology brain scans can actually show which sections of the brain are activated when a person learns specific kinds of information.) When you start to learn something new and unfamiliar, the learning process at first is challenging, frustrating, and full of errors. The initial learning process of an unfamiliar topic or information may be difficult because you are just beginning to construct a new schema for this knowledge. Later, after you have learned this information or skill, learning additional information is easier and smoother because a schema for that subject already exists. This concept of schemas helps explain why learning is so much easier and sometimes effortless when there is an interest, a background, and perhaps even some expertise in a specific field.

Another way to look at long-term memory is to think of your brain as a filing system with many different files and many different drawers filled with different kinds of information. When information is carefully placed in the file cabinet, you can locate it when you need it in the future. If any drawer is opened and a file stuffed in without organization or logic, the file may be difficult to find at a later time. *Elaborative rehearsal* organizes information carefully and logically, so it is easier to locate at a later time in long-term memory.

Researchers continue to study the human mind and the processes that occur in long-term memory.

The following points about long-term memory are significant:

1. Information that has been processed along the rehearsal path is carried to long-term memory by neurological impulses, or **neurotransmitters**.
2. Information that enters long-term memory is **imprinted** in your brain. The impact of the impulses marks the place in the brain in which the information is stored.
3. Because information is imprinted, long-term memory is considered to be permanent memory.
4. Long-term memory is a storage facility with unlimited capacity. It never runs out of space to store new information.
5. New information is linked or imprinted in existing schemas.

Long-Term Memory Retrieval Path

Long-term retrieval is the process of accessing, or finding, information stored in the long-term memory system. When information is retrieved along this *active path,* you are then able to show what you have learned through some form of "output." Output may mean that you are able to respond correctly by talking, explaining, writing, drawing, demonstrating, or applying the learned information in one or more ways. Practice keeps information accessible. By reviewing information on a regular basis, you strengthen the retrieval path so that you can use the information you worked hard to learn.

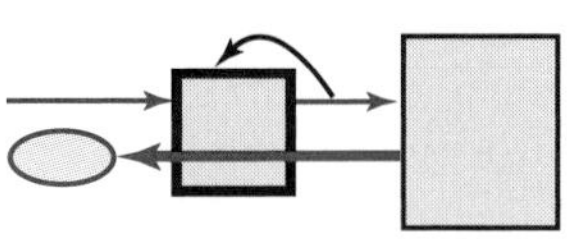

Learning a foreign language is a good example of the necessity to practice retrieval. Imagine that you spent time learning a foreign language but have not practiced it for many years, so you probably no longer speak that language fluently. You may remember the sentence structure but have probably forgotten the vocabulary needed to express your ideas. If you do not retrieve information for years at a time, you will no longer have access to that information in memory. However, by "brushing up" with a few lessons you may find that the vocabulary comes back to you fairly quickly. You will definitely "relearn" the language faster than you learned it the first time.

Retrieving information from long-term memory is a process that you use frequently. Every time you try to recall something you have learned, every time you take a test, you are using the retrieval path actively.

The following strategies can help you use your retrieval path more effectively:

1. *Review information on a regular basis.* Ongoing review provides you with practice locating and accessing information you have learned. The more you practice, the easier the process becomes to locate information in your long-term memory.
2. *Think about related categories or associations if you cannot immediately locate information in your memory.* Information is linked together and in schemas. Frequently you can locate information by thinking about something that relates to it. For example, if you cannot immediately define the term "elaborative rehearsal," but you know it is in your long-term memory, try linking it to other topics. Perhaps you would remember that it is the opposite of rote memory or that it is a positive thing that happens on the rehearsal path. You might link it to the meaning of the word "elaborative." Creating these links or logical connections can often lead you to the information.
3. *Practice retrieving information by using several different methods.* You may want to recite, summarize, discuss, draw, or reproduce the information for practice. The more varied ways you work with information, the more equipped or prepared you will be to work with the information in different forms or situations.
4. *Strive to eliminate unnecessary stress.* Just as stress can affect the input of stimuli into short-term memory, so can it affect the ability to retrieve information from memory. A calm, relaxed, emotionally-level state of mind makes retrieval easier and more efficient. Use stress-reduction strategies or work with a counselor if stress seems to be disrupting your learning process.

Output

Output is the end result or the "proof" that learning has taken place. Output occurs when each part of the Information Processing Model functions effectively. There are many ways to show outcome. Positive results on a test show that specific kinds of learning occurred. Being able to express new concepts, argue a point of view with specific details to back up your comments, or connect ideas together smoothly in a paper or an essay all demonstrate information that has been learned. Being able to apply information, such as constructing an electronics board, tuning an engine, or using a formula to solve a math problem also demonstrates positive output.

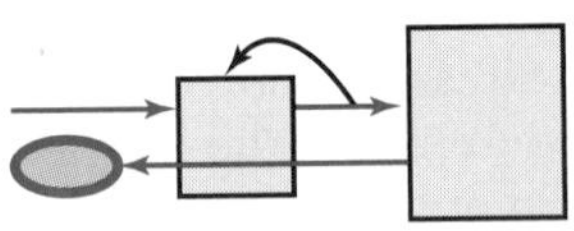

Your knowledge of the Information Processing Model can now be used to assess your own learning progress. Examine the techniques you are using to study. Are you alert to incoming sensory stimuli? Are you rehearsing effectively? Are you using techniques to give you feedback as you study? Are you organizing the information clearly around schemas? Are you taking time to practice retrieving information? With your knowledge about how learning occurs, you can now adjust your methods and fine-tune your approach to processing and learning new information.

The following points are important to know about output:

1. Output is the proof that learning has taken place.
2. Output is a demonstration of accurate details, applications, or procedures.
3. Output can be shown verbally, in writing, or through completion of a product.

Group Processing: A Collaborative Learning Activity

Form groups of three or four students. Complete the following directions.

1. On large chart paper, draw and label the parts of the Information Processing Model.
2. Without referring to your textbook or your notes, jot down key words or phrases to show what you remember about each part of the model. Accept ideas from all members of your group. You may use different pen colors for each part of the model.
3. Be prepared to explain your model to the rest of the class.

EXERCISE 2.1 Problem Identification

In a small group, with a partner, or on your own, identify the parts of the Information Processing Model that each of the following students is not *using effectively. Answer the questions that follow each student situation.*

1. Manuel had twenty new vocabulary words to learn. He read quickly through a list of the words and their definitions and was confident that he knew the terminology. A short time later, he was surprised to realize that he could not remember the meanings of many of the words.
   a. Which part of the model did Manuel not use effectively?

   b. What learning strategies could Manuel use to achieve better results?

2. Teresa spent many hours studying her biology notes for a test that would take place in three weeks. She got involved with many other activities and did not review right before the test. She was confident that she had learned the material thoroughly, but her test score was disappointingly low.
   a. Which part of the model did Teresa not use effectively?

   b. What learning strategies could Teresa use to achieve better results?

3. Leon has good rote memory skills, so when he had to learn ten new math formulas, he repeated the formulas to himself. On the test, Leon was not able to answer any of the questions that required application of the formulas because the questions did not match the way he had memorized the formulas.
   a. Which part of the model did Leon not use effectively?

   b. What learning strategies could Leon use to achieve better results?

4. Penny enrolled in an art history class to meet a graduation requirement. She has little interest in art or history, so the class was challenging for her. Penny saw no relevance in the course to her studies. During class lectures, she seldom took notes because nothing seemed to be important. She chose instead to use the time to work on other homework assignments or think about issues in her personal life. As the term progressed, her grades went downhill.
   a. Which part of the model did Penny not use effectively?

   b. What learning strategies could Penny use to achieve better results?

Exercise 2.2 Using the Information Processing Model

Complete the following tasks by using a personal learning experience.

1. In the space below, draw and label the Information Processing Model.

2. Think about a specific skill, concept, or process that you recently learned in school, in sports or recreation, or in your personal life. In your memory, trace how the learning process occurred.
   - **a.** What sensory input did you receive?
   - **b.** What happened to the information in your short-term memory?
   - **c.** What did you do to prevent the information from being dumped?
   - **d.** How was the information processed on the rehearsal path?
   - **e.** Did any of the information move through the feedback loop?
   - **f.** What do you think happened to the information in your long-term memory?
   - **g.** How did you use the retrieval path?
   - **h.** What was the output?

3. Show how the new information moved through the model above by summarizing what happened in each part of the model. Use whatever method you wish to demonstrate your learning process.

Name ______________________________ Date ______________________

EXERCISE 2.3 Memory Principles Inventory

You will soon learn about the twelve principles of memory that enhance the learning process. First, complete the following inventory by answering YES or NO to each question. The letter in the upper left corner of each box will be explained later.

S	YES	NO
1. Do you spend a lot of time studying but seem to study the "wrong information" for tests?	______	______
2. Do you get frustrated when you read because everything seems important?	______	______
3. Do you tend to highlight too much when you read textbooks?	______	______
4. Do your notes seem excessively long and overly detailed?	______	______
5. Do you avoid making study tools such as flash cards because you are not sure what information to put on the study tools?	______	______

A	YES	NO
1. Do you tend to memorize facts or ideas in isolation?	______	______
2. When you try to recall information you have studied, do you sometimes feel "lost" because there is no direct way to access the information in your memory?	______	______
3. Do you feel that you are memorizing numerous lists of information but not really understanding what they mean or how they are connected?	______	______
4. Do you "go blank" on tests when a question asks for information in a form or context different from the way you studied it?	______	______
5. Do you lack sufficient time to link difficult information to familiar words or pictures?	______	______

V	YES	NO
1. When you finish reading, do you have difficulty remembering what paragraphs were even about?	______	______
2. Do you have difficulty remembering information that appeared in a chart your instructor presented on the chalkboard or on a screen?	______	______
3. Is it difficult for you to get a visual image of printed information?	______	______
4. When you try to recall information, do you rely mainly on words rather than pictures?	______	______
5. Are the notes and study tools that you create done with only a pencil or one color pen?	______	______

E	YES	NO
1. Do you sometimes take "the easy way out" or look for shortcuts when you study?	______	______
2. Do you feel that doing problems or creating study tools that are not assigned is a waste of your time?	______	______
3. Does the term *studying* mean to basically "do the assignments" and no more—then studying is over?	______	______
4. If extra credit projects or options are available, do you tend to skip doing them?	______	______
5. Do you choose to study alone and avoid studying with other students or attending a weekly study group?	______	______

C	YES	NO
1. Do you easily get distracted or find your mind wandering?	______	______
2. Are there so many interruptions when you study that you are not quite sure what you accomplished at the end of a study block?	______	______
3. Do you miss important information during a lecture because your mind tends to wander or daydream?	______	______
4. When you are reading, do you find it difficult to keep your mind focused on the information in the textbook?	______	______
5. Do you study with the television, radio, or stereo turned on?	______	______

R	YES	NO
1. Do you feel you lack effective listening skills?	______	______
2. Do you have difficulty expressing your ideas on paper?	______	______
3. Do you have difficulty clearly explaining textbook information to another person?	______	______
4. Does your current method of studying lack techniques that give you feedback about whether you know the information?	______	______
5. Do you feel awkward or uncomfortable talking out loud to yourself?	______	______

I	YES	NO
1. Do you label the class or the textbook you are using as boring, dumb, useless, or a waste of your time?	______	______
2. Do you dislike going to class?	______	______
3. Once you are in class, do you resent being there and tend to tune out whatever is going on?	______	______
4. Do you find it difficult to complete homework assignments because you just cannot get interested in the subject?	______	______
5. Is it difficult to understand why you have to take specific courses when they do not seem to be related to your career field?	______	______

B	YES	NO
1. Do you have problems finding the main idea even though you are able to understand the individual details?	______	______
2. Do you understand general concepts but oftentimes have difficulty giving details that relate to the concept?	______	______
3. Do you need to make a more concerted effort to take the time to find the relationships between concepts and details?	______	______
4. Do your lecture notes capture main ideas but lack details?	______	______
5. Do your notes include running lists of details without a clear method of showing main ideas?	______	______

F	YES	NO
1. Do you use tests as your main means of getting feedback about what you have learned?	______	______
2. Do you keep taking in new information without stopping to see whether you are trying to learn too much too fast?	______	______
3. When you are rehearsing, do you "keep on going" even if you sense that you have not clearly understood something?	______	______
4. Do you tend to use self-quizzing only when you are preparing for a test?	______	______
5. Do you sometimes cram for tests?	______	______

O	YES	NO
1. Does the information presented in class or in the textbook seem disorganized?	______	______
2. Do you have difficulty remembering the sequence of important events, steps of a process, or details in general?	______	______
3. When you try to do a "memory search" to locate information in your memory, are you sometimes unable to find the information?	______	______
4. Do you spend most of your time trying to learn information in the exact order in which it is presented?	______	______
5. Do you feel unsure about rearranging, reorganizing, or regrouping information so that it is easier to learn and recall?	______	______

T	YES	NO
1. Do you often find it necessary to cram for tests because you simply run out of time?	______	______
2. Do you get tired when you study because you are trying to study too much at one time?	______	______
3. When you study, do you change to a second subject as soon as you complete the assignments for the first subject?	______	______
4. Are some of your study blocks more than three hours long?	______	______
5. In at least one of your courses, do you spend less time studying that subject than most other students in class?	______	______

O	YES	NO
1. Once you have completed an assignment, do you put it aside until close to the time of the next test?	______	______
2. Do you have problems remembering or recalling information that you know you learned several weeks earlier?	______	______
3. Do you need to add more review time to your weekly study schedule?	______	______
4. Do you study fewer than two hours per week for every one hour in class?	______	______
5. Do you sit down to study and feel that you are all caught up and have nothing to study?	______	______

About the Inventory

1. The letters in the upper left corner of each of the boxes on the inventory represent one of the principles of memory. Return to the inventory and label each of the boxes with the following principles of memory:

Selectivity	**C**oncentration	**F**eedback
Association	**R**ecitation	**O**rganization
Visualization	**I**nterest	**T**ime on Task
Effort	**B**ig and Little Pictures	**O**ngoing Review

2. Now look at your answers. A NO indicates you are already using the principle of memory when you study. If you gave NO answers to all the questions within one memory principle box, you are using the principle of memory consistently and effectively. A YES answer indicates that you will benefit by learning to use this principle of memory more effectively when you study. The more YES answers you have, the greater the need to add this principle of memory to your learning strategies or study techniques.

Reflection Writing 2 — CHAPTER 2

On a separate piece of paper or in a journal, summarize your results on the Memory Principles Inventory. Which principles do you use effectively on a regular basis? Which principles do you use only sometimes or only on occasion? Which principles have you not yet used effectively and need to learn to use on a more consistent basis?

Twelve Memory Principles

Learning, as you have seen, is a complex process. Many mental processes are involved in moving information into long-term memory and then retrieving that information when you need it. The following **twelve memory principles** can help you process information more efficiently through all the stages of information processing. These principles, when used consistently throughout the learning process, result in a stronger, more efficient memory. The memory words **SAVE CRIB FOTO** will help you remember all twelve principles; each letter in the words represents one of the memory principles.

Twelve Memory Principles (SAVE CRIB FOTO)

1. **S**electivity involves selecting what is important to learn.
2. **A**ssociation involves associating or linking new information to something familiar.
3. **V**isualization involves picturing in your mind the information you are learning.
4. **E**ffort on your part is essential for learning.
5. **C**oncentration is necessary when you study.
6. **R**ecitation involves repeating information verbally in your own words.
7. **I**nterest must be created if it does not already exist.
8. **B**ig and little pictures involves recognizing levels of information.
9. **F**eedback in the form of self-quizzing checks your progress.
10. **O**rganization involves logical reordering of information.
11. **T**ime on task refers to the time dedicated and scheduled for learning.
12. **O**ngoing review promotes practice retrieving information from memory.

Exercise 2.4 Learning the Basics

Before you begin reading the details about each memory principle, try learning the basic labels for each of the twelve principles of memory. This will help you "set up the schema" for the information you will be reading. Use the short clue below each line and the initial letter of the word to help you list the twelve principles of memory. Try to complete this without looking at the list of principles.

S ______________________
(Picking and choosing)

A ______________________
(Linking ideas)

V ______________________
(Seeing it in your mind)

E ______________________
(Trying hard)

C ______________________
(Focusing)

R ______________________
(Explaining out loud)

I ______________________
(Enjoying)

B ______________________
(Concepts and details)

F ______________________
(Self-quizzing)

O ______________________
(Structuring logically)

T ______________________
(Using minutes and hours)

O ______________________
(Repeated practice)

Selectivity

SAVE CRIB FOTO

Selectivity is the process of separating important main ideas and details from a larger body of information. Learning everything—every detail, every example, every word—is not possible and certainly is not reasonable. You as the learner must continually evaluate the importance of information and strive to pick out only that which is significant. Units III and IV of this book help you improve your selectivity skills as you learn to decide what to survey in chapters, what to highlight, what to write in notes, and what importance to place on various study tools. In each case, you will be honing your skills in identifying and pulling out main ideas and supporting details. The process of learning is greatly simplified when you reduce the amount of information that needs to be placed in your memory system *and* you place appropriate information into memory.

Association

sAVE CRIB FOTO

Association is the process of linking two or more items. The long-term memory system is organized around schemas or clusters of related information. This system of organization is based on interconnections or associations. Sometimes when you try to recall something from memory you can go straight to the information and have an immediate answer. More frequently, however, a **memory search** involves thinking your way to the information by associating or linking ideas. One idea serves as a **retrieval cue** for another idea.

The mnemonic (memory trick) for the twelve principles of memory is an association that uses the words SAVE CRIB FOTO. This mnemonic links the twelve principles of memory to each of the letters in the mnemonic and serves as an effective

Which Principles of Memory could a marketing expert use to prepare a polished presentation to her (his) clients?

retrieval cue for you to name all of the principles of memory. Learning the mnemonic helps you learn the twelve principles of memory more quickly.

You can use many kinds of associations in the learning process. You may link a concept or specific details to a picture that you create in your mind or a diagram that appears in your textbook. You may also link a concept or details to familiar information that you already have in schemas in your long-term memory. You can associate new information to existing schemas by asking yourself the following questions:

What do I already know about this subject?

How is the new information similar to or different from something I already know?

Frequently information that you are studying is already paired, so the association is automatic. For example, if you are studying a list of vocabulary words and their meanings, an automatic pairing exists. After sufficient rehearsal, naming one of the words works as a retrieval cue for the definition. Reverse rehearsal should also be done. When you see or hear the definition, it should work as a retrieval cue to the vocabulary word. Recognizing and studying this association will make the learning of new vocabulary words, or any paired information, much easier.

Visualization

SA**V**E CRIB FOTO

Visualization is the process of making pictures in your mind. It is a valuable skill for several reasons. Information that is mentally pictured is easier to comprehend and recall. Long-term memory is strengthened when two sensory channels (such as auditory for reciting and visual for visualizations) are processing information. Also, mental pictures are stored in one side of the brain (the right hemisphere) and words in the other (the left hemisphere). Using visualizations to aid in processing information activates your entire brain. The result is better memory skills

The process of visualization can be used with both printed words and pictures or graphic information. Some visual learners have the ability to recall or picture information in the form of printed words. These visual learners can see "in their mind's eye" the textbook page, the specific flash card, the line of notes, or the information written on a screen in the classroom. The information is recalled in the form of words, numbers, or letters such as in formulas. This printed form of visualization can be strengthened by adding colors to the words, letters, or numbers. It may then be strengthened even further by associating the information with pictures or graphics.

Visualizing images in the form of objects, scenes, or complete story line sequences, such as seeing "movies in the mind," is a valuable skill you can learn. As mentioned, you can improve both comprehension and recall by consciously using visualization. If you are just beginning to learn to visualize what you read, begin by *visualizing individual objects.* Examine the object closely; pay attention to size, color, shape, and position. Then close your eyes and try to "see the object on the inside of your eyelids." Open your eyes and compare your visual image to the actual object.

Now practice *visualizing larger pictures.* Use the technique described above to visualize a larger picture such as a photograph, a map, a graph, or a chart. Focus on visually memorizing the main features or the "skeleton." Once the skeleton image is clear, "zoom in" to work on remembering the smaller parts or details. Each time you encounter visual materials in your classes, take the time to work with creating the visual image of the material in your mind.

The final form of visualization is to *create movies in your mind.* This process works with units of information that are processed through time. Many good readers automatically start the "cameras rolling" when they begin reading. The story unfolds on the movie screen in their minds. This is the same process that you should activate when you read textbooks. The movie may not be as action filled as a movie in the mind that you create when reading a novel, but it will serve as a retrieval cue for information at a later time. For some people, visualizing during the reading process is not automatic; effort and intention are required to create the visual images. Time spent creating movies in the mind and rerunning the movies as a way to review is time well spent.

Effort

SAVE CRIB FOTO

Effort, driven by motivation and determination, is needed throughout information processing. Taking information in, rehearsing it, and retrieving it all require effort. Many of the study tools you will use to help boost your memory will not necessarily be seen by teachers or be graded. You are the one who decides whether such study tools will help you learn; you create your own learning activities for yourself, not because they are "required."

To avoid losing information during the learning process, consciously make the effort to learn and retain information. You will be rewarded with more thorough learning, a greater sense of satisfaction, and better grades.

Concentration

SAVE CRIB FOTO

Concentration, the process of focusing the mind on only one task or item, results in uninterrupted thought processes and more efficient learning. You will learn important techniques for setting the physical stage and the mental stage for good concentration (see Chapter 5). Being able to control your concentration enables you to create the ideal setting for receiving sensory information and moving it through the stages of information processing. Your mind has to be alert and focused on the task at hand. Strive to block out internal and external distractors. Concentration is an essential mental discipline that enables you to make optimum use of your valuable time.

Recitation

SAVE CRIB FOTO

Recitation is the process of verbalizing what you are learning or have already learned. When you recite, remember to use your own words in the form of complete sentences to explain the information as clearly as possible. Imagine that you are trying to explain the information to a friend who is not familiar with the subject. Pay attention to areas that seem a little "fuzzy." This is feedback to you that you need to go back to the sources of your information to check for accuracy and additional details.

Some students are uncomfortable with reciting because they are not used to talking out loud to themselves and thus feel that others will think they are "weird." Nevertheless, an increasing number of teachers and students recognize the value of reciting and encourage this process of verbalizing. Reciting is valuable in studying because it provides you with immediate feedback so that you know whether you are really understanding information. As you recite, you activate your auditory channel, which strengthens the path to your long-term memory. Reciting keeps you actively involved; active learning leads to better concentration and comprehension. As you recite in your own words, your focus is on understanding rather than on rote memory. You are personalizing the material.

Students who have difficulty expressing their ideas in class or on paper will especially find value in reciting what they are studying. Frequently, all that they need is the opportunity to put ideas together coherently when there is not a time element involved such as occurs during class discussions or tests. Practice expressing ideas in complete sentences prepares students ahead of time and increases the level of familiarity with information prior to the class discussion or test.

Interest

SAVE CRIB FOTO

Interest is exhibited through feelings of curiosity, fascination, enthusiasm, and appreciation. Learning new information about areas that you "love" is usually easy; you have genuine interest working for you. Unfortunately, you will be required to take some courses in which you have not developed an interest. Your task, then, is to generate an interest so that your learning is more enjoyable and less stressful.

You can create an interest by looking for a value or a purpose in knowing the information, by using new study techniques to learn the information, or by asking another student or several students to join you in a study group so you can learn together. You can also locate someone who is knowledgeable or works in the field you are studying and ask that person what drew him or her to the field. Checking out books, videos, or cassettes that are related to the topic you are studying may give you a new, more appealing perspective on the topic.

On a more personal level, you may wish to examine your attitude toward the subject to see if your dislike or lack of interest is related to a previous experience or past incident in the class. Take time to identify what you *do* like about the subject. Emphasize and strengthen the positive aspects rather than focusing on the negatives.

The Big and Little Pictures

SAVE CRIB FOTO

Big and little pictures is based on the understanding that learning requires the use of at least two levels of information. One level is the "big picture," which is the general concept or category of information. For example, the subject of concentration is a big picture. To really understand the concept of concentration, however, you need to know another level of information, the specific details, or the "little pictures," that together create this concept. These details include a definition, the uses of concentration, its effects, how it works, and specific strategies.

To get a sense of these two levels of information, draw a circle in the center of your paper. This circle represents the main idea or the general category of information. (This is a schema.) Surround the circle with details that relate to the topic in the center of the circle. Then categorize information into lists with the category (big picture) at the top of the list.

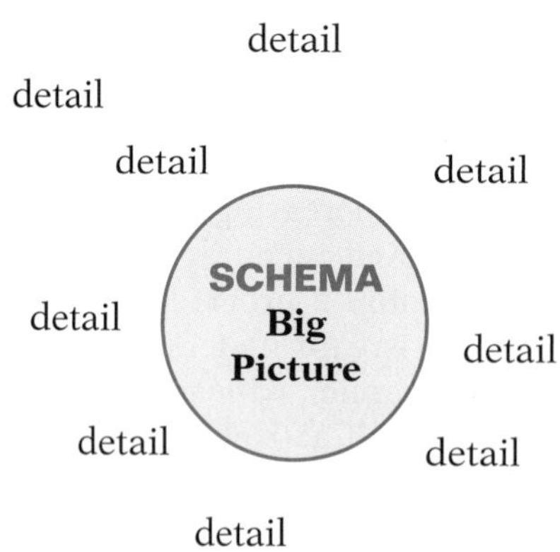

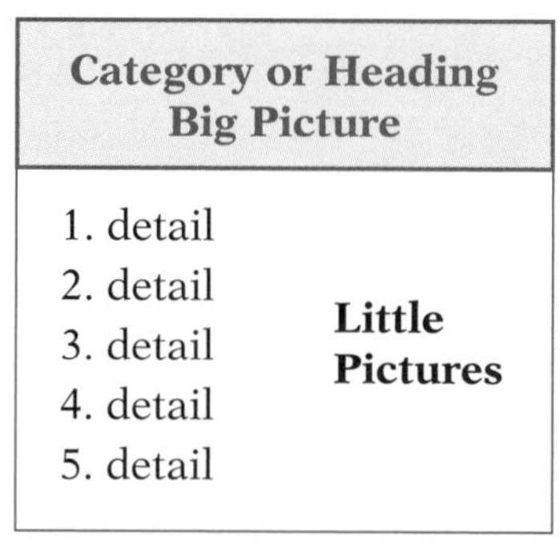

Category or Heading
Big Picture
1. detail
2. detail
3. detail
4. detail
5. detail
Little
Pictures

This principle of big picture–little pictures is sometimes also referred to as the "forest and the trees." If you focus only on seeing the forest, you miss the meaning and the beauty of the individual trees. If you focus on only a few individual trees, you do not see that all the trees create a much larger group, the forest.

Learning new knowledge is similar to the idea of the forest and the trees. If you place too much emphasis on the details, you may fail to see their relationships to each other and to larger concepts. If you focus only on finding the main ideas, you are left without the specific details that support or prove the main idea.

The principle of big picture–little pictures is used frequently when you study. Each time you highlight, take notes, rearrange information, or make mappings, hierarchies, or outlines, you are using this important principle of memory.

Feedback

SAVE CRIB **F**OTO

Feedback is the process of verifying you have learned or of recognizing that you have *not* learned specific information. The most useful feedback occurs when you use self-quizzing or self-checking when you study. If you are involved in **marathon studying** or *cramming,* you do not have sufficient time for feedback. The main feedback from cramming comes *after* you have taken a test. Feedback should occur frequently *before* test time.

Several study techniques can provide feedback as you are learning. *Reciting* is the most frequently used form of feedback. You can use reciting after you read a paragraph, underline, take notes, practice from flash cards, or use other visual study tools. *Writing summaries* can be effective feedback. At the end of a section in the chapter and again at the end of the entire chapter, practice writing a summary of what you have read (and highlighted or placed in your notes). For this to be true feedback, attempt to write your summary without looking at your notes or your book. Then check your accuracy by comparing the summary to your notes or the book.

You can also *draw mappings or pictures* without looking at your notes or the book. Compare your drawings to the original. Check your accuracy, and add any details you missed when you drew from memory. This same process can be used to reproduce the visual mappings found at the beginning of each chapter in this book. Finally, as you work through a chapter, *write your own test questions.* Once you have finished the chapter, quiz yourself. This gives you feedback that is similar to the feedback you receive during tests. If the chapter has chapter questions, sample exercises, or quizzes, complete them even if they are not assigned. This extra effort will provide you with feedback that can help you focus your attention on areas that need additional work.

Organization

SAVE CRIB F**O**TO

Organization refers to a meaningful, logical structure or arrangement of ideas. Organization as a principle of memory does not refer to organizing furniture, a study area, notebooks, or assignments.

If you sit at a computer keyboard and begin punching in random commands and information, the computer may not accept what you have entered. The mind works in much the same way. You must organize the information you want to put into your long-term memory in a meaningful, logical way if you want to access it later. When you try to retrieve information from long-term memory, your mind searches through the different "files" of information you have stored. If you "threw everything into your memory" without filing it properly, or without associating it with clusters of information, you would have difficulty locating the information you thought you had learned.

This principle of organization explains why rote memory of small, individual facts is not very reliable. **Rote memory** involves repeating a fact or detail in the exact words each time. Information learned through rote memory may be in your long-term memory but may be difficult to find. If a teacher asks you a question that is stated differently from the way you memorized the information, you will not be able to use the memorized detail effectively. You may not even recognize that the question and what you learned are related.

The order in which information is presented in a textbook or a lecture may not be the most logically organized way to study the information. **Elaborative rehearsal** often involves *rearranging* the information into more concise and logical ways.

The following six ways are often used to rearrange information for more effective studying:

1. Place the information in *chronological order* to show the sequence of events over a period of time.
2. *Categorize* the information. Look for logical groupings within the information you are studying. Rewrite the information into lists.
3. Place the information *alphabetically* in lists or groups.
4. Rearrange the information into a *visual graph* or *visual study tool.* This may include organizing the information into a visual mapping, a hierarchy, a time line, a comparison chart, or a flow chart.
5. Organize the information around a *visual graphic,* which may be any kind of picture. The picture becomes the point of focus. The words are used as labels for the visual graphic.
6. Organize the information into a set of *Cornell notes,* outlines, or flash cards. Flash cards will be discussed in Chapter 7. Cornell notes will be explained in Chapters 9 and 10.

Time on Task

SAVE CRIB FOTO

Time on task refers to the amount of time you spend involved in the learning process. There is a high correlation between the amount of time spent studying and the grade earned in a course. Students who spend too little time studying, for whatever reason, tend not to do well in the class. Students who spend ample time on the task of studying tend to show greater success. Chapter 3 discusses time-management strategies; however, one strategy that is valuable to know at this time is the **2:1 ratio**. The 2:1 ratio states that for most college courses, sufficient time on task will occur if you study two hours for every one hour in class. If your class meets for three hours a week, study six hours per week for that class.

How you spend time on task is also important. If you overload your memory system by trying to study too much information at one time or for a time period that is too long, the ability to comprehend and remember what you have read decreases. An ideal study block for adults is a fifty-minute period of concentrated studying. Then, if you wish to study for more than one hour, take a ten-minute break. Avoid studying for more than three hours in a row. **Marathon studying**, also known as **massed studying**, occurs when you try to study for more than three hours in a row. Marathon studying in most cases is ineffective. **Distributed practice**, or distributed studying, is much more effective; with this method, studying is done in several different study blocks spread throughout the week.

Ongoing Review

SAVE CRIB FOTO

Ongoing review, or practicing what you have stored in long-term memory, makes information much more accessible and easier to retrieve quickly. The 2:1 ratio is recommended because it usually provides you with "extra" time to use each week to review previously studied information. You should never be idle during a study block or be able to say, "I have nothing to study." When you apply ongoing review, information remains active and fresh in your mind, and you can avoid last-minute cramming.

Exercise 2.5 Matching Principles to Descriptions

Match the principles below with the descriptions at the right. On the line, write the letter from the list at the right to show your answer.

_______ **1.** Selectivity

_______ **2.** Association

_______ **3.** Visualization

_______ **4.** Effort

_______ **5.** Concentration

_______ **6.** Recitation

_______ **7.** Interest

_______ **8.** Big Picture–Little Picture

_______ **9.** Feedback

_______ **10.** Organization

_______ **11.** Time on Task

_______ **12.** Ongoing Review

a. I practice and review information by saying it out loud, in my own words, and in complete sentences.

b. I use self-quizzing to verify that I am learning new information.

c. If I do not have a genuine interest in the subject, I find ways to create an interest and curiosity.

d. I link new information to old information, to other concepts, or to pictures.

e. I use strategies to keep my mind focused on the material I am studying.

f. I schedule ample time to study, rehearse, make study tools, and review.

g. I practice retrieving information from memory on a regular basis.

h. I make pictures or movies in my mind for the information I study.

i. I carefully select the main ideas and important details to study.

j. I look for the larger concepts and the smaller details of information I study.

k. I personalize the learning process by rearranging information in logical, meaningful ways.

l. I am motivated and do more than the instructor assigns so I can learn information thoroughly.

EXERCISE 2.6 Critical Thinking

1. Draw and label the Information Processing Model.

2. Insert the following words in the appropriate places where they occur in the above drawing:

practice path	inactive path
schemas	outcomes
imprinting	review
sensory stimuli	unlimited capacity
self-quizzing	trap door
limited capacity	learning path

3. Use the numbers below for each of the twelve principles of memory. Place the numbers on your model to show where each memory principle is actively used. Numbers may appear in more than one place.

1. Selectivity	7. Interest
2. Association	8. Big and Little Pictures
3. Visualization	9. Feedback
4. Effort	10. Organization
5. Concentration	11. Time on Task
6. Recitation	12. Ongoing Review

EXERCISE 2.7 Case Studies

Each of the following case studies describes a student situation. Read each case study carefully, highlighting key ideas or student issues. Then answer the question that ends each case study. In your response, address the key points that you highlighted and that relate directly to the question. Use complete sentences in your answers. These case studies are also available online; you can email your response to your instructor or print a copy of your work online.

1. By the end of the week, Curtis needs to read a thirty-page chapter and be prepared to discuss it in class. Curtis does not enjoy this textbook or course, so he tends to procrastinate about the assignments. Finally, the night before class he finds two hours to spare, so he reads quickly through the chapter to get an overview. He jots down a few words, phrases, and main ideas and shoves the list in his book so he will be prepared for the class discussion the next day. Instead of a class discussion, however, the instructor gives a short quiz. Curtis answers only two out of ten questions. What principles of memory did Curtis ignore when he read the assignment?

2. Damon knows he learns best when he can discuss information with others. He will have a midterm in one of his classes in two weeks. Damon asks other students in class to join him in a study group. His enthusiasm and understanding of the subject attract many students to his study group. What principles of memory does Damon implement in this approach to prepare for his midterm?

3. Elena uses flash cards to learn the definitions for the vocabulary terms in her Anatomy and Physiology 201 course. Within the first four weeks of the class, she already has more than one hundred cards. She sets aside time each week to review all of the cards. She reads the front of each card, recites the definition, checks her answer with the back of the card, and sorts the cards into piles labelled "correct" and "incorrect." She then makes a stronger image or an association for the cards in the "incorrect" pile; she tries reciting again. Regina also makes flash cards for the class, after she reads each chapter. She puts her flash cards in an envelope so they are available when she studies right before the test. What principles of memory does Elena use that Regina does not?

Exercise 2.8 LINKS

In Chapter 1 (page 25), you learned the basic techniques for making a visual mapping. In the following visual mapping of the Information Processing Model, notice how key words or short phrases branch from each of the main ideas and how the words are on a horizontal plane instead of slanted, sideways, or upside down.

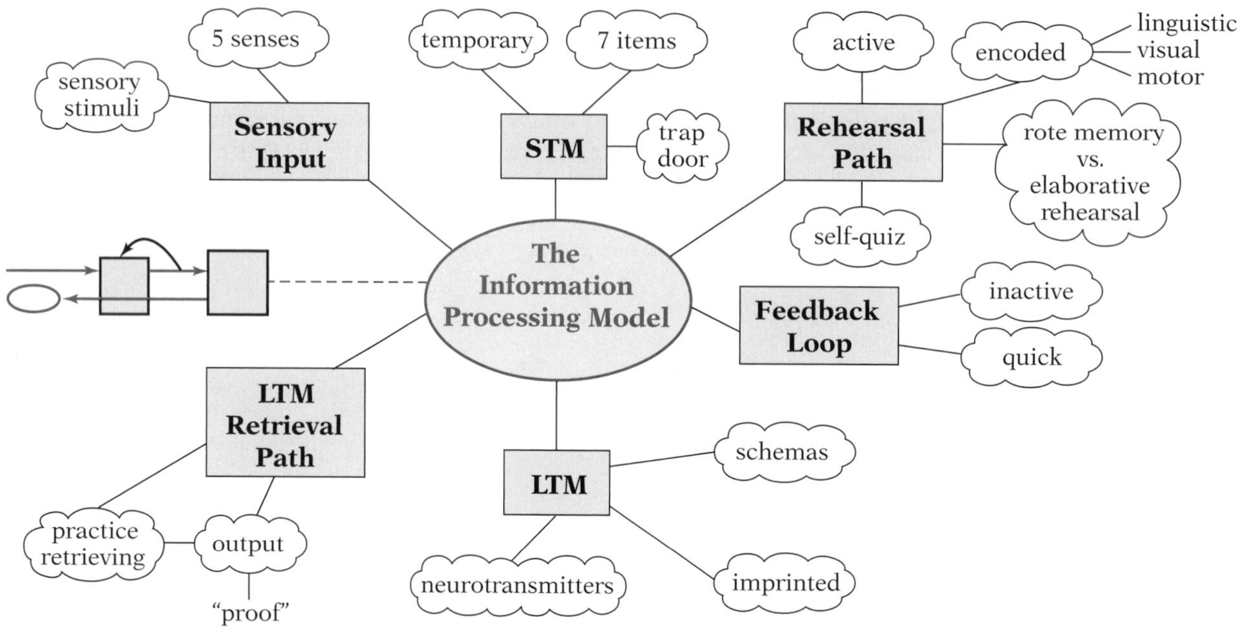

The following visual mapping uses pictures to represent each of the principles of memory. Complete this mapping by adding your own key words or phrases to branch off the main ideas (the pictures).

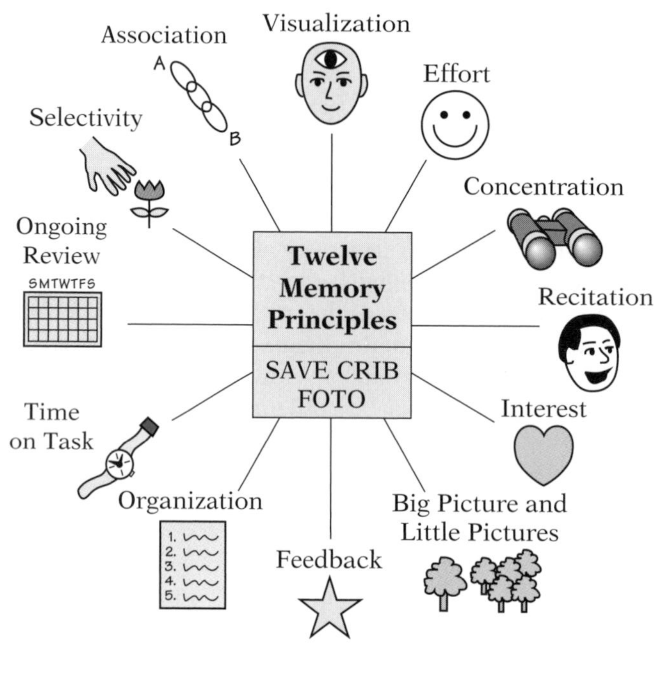

Reflection Writing 3 — CHAPTER 2

On a separate piece of paper or in a journal, discuss specific strategies you plan to use to move information across the rehearsal path and later the retrieval path. Include terminology from this course in your answer.

SUMMARY

- The six-part Information Processing Model explains how information is learned.
  1. Sensory input is received from stimuli in the environment.
  2. Short-term memory briefly stores the information.
  3. Information moves along the rehearsal path, where it is practiced.
  4. Information that is not yet learned is rerouted through the feedback loop.
  5. Effectively learned information is imprinted and stored in long-term memory.
  6. When learned information is needed, it is pulled out of long-term memory and moved along the retrieval path.
- The memory phrase SAVE CRIB FOTO is a way of remembering the twelve principles that can be used to strengthen your memory.
  1. Selectivity
  2. Association
  3. Visualization
  4. Effort
  5. Concentration
  6. Recitation
  7. Interest
  8. Big picture–little pictures
  9. Feedback
  10. Organization
  11. Time on task
  12. Ongoing review

ACE Practice Tests, which are scored online, supplementary exercises, enrichment activities, and related web site links are available online for *Essential Study Skills*, 4e. Use the following directions to access this web site:

Type: **http://college.hmco.com/collegesurvival/students**

Click on *List of Sites by Author.* Use the arrow to scroll down to Wong *Essential Study Skills*, 4e. Click on the title. If you are working on your own computer, bookmark this web site.

LEARNING OPTIONS

The following learning options provide you with opportunities to demonstrate your understanding of the topics in Chapter 2. Your instructor may assign one or more specific options or may ask you to select one or more options that interest you the most.

1. Expand the Chapter 2 mapping on page 29. Notice that the name of the chapter appears in the center and each of the chapter headings extends outward from the center of the mapping. Copy this structure on a blank piece of paper. Reread the information under each heading in your textbook. Extend branches on the mapping to show important key words or phrases for each heading. You can add pictures and colors to your mapping to accentuate the points.

2. Create an interesting brochure that explains the twelve principles of memory. Provide "helpful hints" that suggest ways students can apply the principles of memory to their courses. Include the source of the information and your name on the brochure. Your brochure should be in a finalized form; it may be printed for distribution to other students.
3. Use the Internet to locate an informative web site for any one of the following topics:

cognitive psychology	learning theories	Information Processing Model
short-term memory	long-term memory	rote memory
elaborative rehearsal	schemas	imprinting in memory
neurotransmitters	cramming	distributed practice
visualization	recitation	ongoing review

Print the information. Prepare a short presentation or a written summary of the most significant information. In your presentation or summary, explain how the contents of the web site relate to the content of Chapter 2.
4. In Chapter 1 on page 16, you learned how to make a comparison chart. Make a comparison chart for the Twelve Principles of Memory. Include the following two columns, plus any other columns you think would be valuable. You may add colors and pictures to your chart.

Principle	**Definition**	**Importance**	**?**
Selectivity			
Association			

5. For one week, keep a study log each time you study. At the end of each study session, list the Principles of Memory that you used actively during that study block. Add to your log comments that discuss any study patterns you see. Which of the Principles of Memory do you ignore or use infrequently? Which do you use often?
6. Form a study group with three or more students to meet outside class to review the content of this chapter. In addition to the review work, spend time discussing ways to implement the Information Processing Model and the Twelve Principles of Memory while studying for this course. Write a summary paper discussing the highlights of your study group.
7. Create a study tape for Chapter 2. On your tape, summarize or explain the most important points of the chapter that you need to learn. This tape will serve as an excellent review tape later in the term.

Chapter 2 REVIEW QUESTIONS

True-False

Carefully read the following sentences. Pay attention to key words. Write T *if the statement is TRUE. Write* F *if it is FALSE.*

________ **1.** Short-term memory holds all sensory stimuli until they are learned.

________ **2.** The feedback loop is used to practice retrieving information from long-term memory.

________ **3.** Practice is needed in the rehearsal and retrieval stages.

________ **4.** Information that is well organized in long-term memory is believed to be organized around clusters of related information.

________ **5.** The principle of ongoing review is needed on the retrieval path of the Information Processing Model.

________ **6.** The principle of effort is used in more than one stage of the Information Processing Model.

________ **7.** Self-quizzing should be included in study strategies used on the rehearsal path.

________ **8.** The memory principle of organization refers to having an organized work area, notebook, and class notes.

________ **9.** Relating new information to old information involves the principle of association.

________ **10.** The principle of time on task recommends that you use distributed practice when you study.

________ **11.** Marathon studying is different from mass studying because mass studying always lasts longer.

________ **12.** The principle of organization is used when information is rearranged in a meaningful, logical way.

________ **13.** If a person reads rapidly and does not remember what he or she read, his or her short-term memory system may have been overloaded.

________ **14.** The memory principles of time, effort, interest, and association are used during elaborative rehearsal.

________ **15.** When you do a *memory search,* retrieval cues in the form of words or pictures can assist you in locating information in your long-term memory.

Fill-in-the-Blank

You may refer to the list of "Terms to Know" on page 29. Write one word on each line to make an accurate and complete sentence. Do not use any word more than one time.

1. Sensory ______________________ carry messages into short-term memory.

2. ______________________ carry information into our memory systems through the form of neurological impulses.

3. When the 2:1 ratio for studying is used effectively, a student should have time each week to use the memory principles of ______________________ on task and ______________________ review.

4. ______________________-______________________ memory has a limited capacity and duration.

5. ______________________ memory occurs when understanding or meaning is not attached to information as it is memorized.

6. Information that you do not attend to in ______________________-term memory is "dumped."

7. The ______________________ ______________________ is an inactive path that returns information to short-term memory.

8. ______________________ ______________________ occurs when study blocks are spread throughout the week.

9. The memory principle of ______________________ is used when information is rewritten into categories, visual mappings, or chronological order.

10. The memory principle of ______________________ is used when a student ignores the ideas and details that are not essential for understanding the big picture.

Short Answer and Critical Thinking

Use complete sentences to answer the following:

1. Give several reasons why some sensory input never reaches long-term memory.

2. Explain the differences between rote memory and elaborative rehearsal.

3. Give at least three reasons why recitation is a powerful memory-boosting strategy.

CHAPTER 3

Managing Your Time

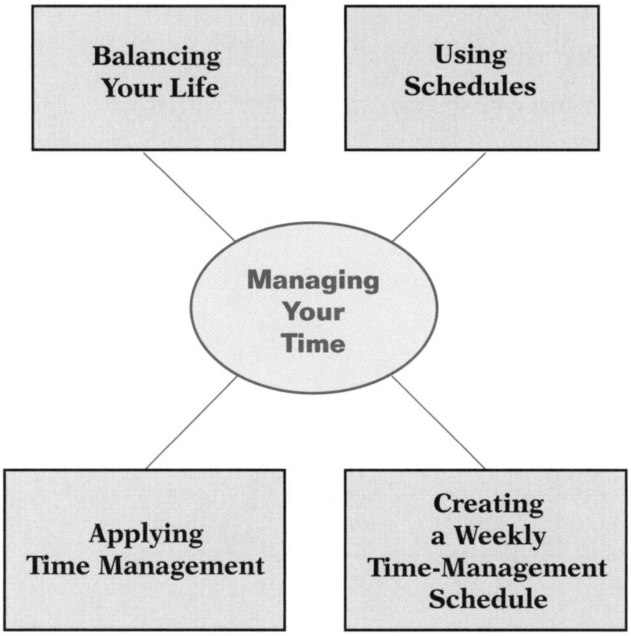

Time management, perhaps the most essential of all study skills, is an organized method for planning the use of your time to achieve goals. Learning to use time management to balance your academic, work, and leisure time leads to greater productivity, more successes, and less stress. Using four different kinds of schedules, including a comprehensive weekly schedule, puts you in control of your life.

Terms to Know

pie of life
Increase–Decrease Method
term schedule
weekly schedule
circadian rhythms
daily schedule
task schedule
2:1 ratio
distributed practice
marathon studying
massed practice
flex study blocks
trading time

CHAPTER 3: Managing Your Time Profile

DO, SCORE, and **RECORD** your profile before you read this chapter. If you need to review the process, refer to the complete directions given in the Profile for Chapter 1 on page 2.

ONLINE: You can complete the profile and get your score online at this textbook's web site.

	YES	NO
1. I use a weekly schedule to organize my studying, work, and social lives.	______	______
2. Friends and family often take priority over my study time.	______	______
3. I try to make each scheduled day different so I do not get bored.	______	______
4. I often study for three hours or more in a row so I can stay current with my reading and homework assignments.	______	______
5. I usually study two hours during the week for every one hour in class.	______	______
6. I schedule specific times to study during the weekend.	______	______
7. I know the times during the day when I am the most mentally alert.	______	______
8. I study my least favorite subjects at night.	______	______
9. I avoid time management because I prefer to be spontaneous.	______	______
10. I have a consistently established routine that is easy for me to follow.	______	______

Reflection Writing 1 — CHAPTER 3

On a separate piece of paper or in a journal, do the following:

1. Discuss your profile score for this chapter. What was your score? What does it mean to you?
2. How do you currently feel about time management? What successes and problems have you had with time management? Give details.

Balancing Your Life

As a student you will need to continually balance three main areas in your life: school, work, and leisure. *School* includes attending classes; completing homework assignments; studying on your own, with a partner, with a tutor, or in a study group; developing study tools; using ongoing review; and preparing for tests. School may also include involvement with athletics, student government, or student organizations. *Work* includes a part- or full-time job, volunteer work, and any personal responsibilities such as parenting, household chores, and running errands. *Leisure* includes time with family and friends, recreational activities, personal hobbies, or personal time to relax or pursue special interests. How you spend your time in these three main areas depends on your goals, needs, and interests. Feeling confident, fulfilled, happy, challenged, and in control are signs that you have achieved an effective balance in your life. Frequent bouts with negative feelings, self-doubt, resentment, or a sense of a lack of control are signs that you need to examine and rebalance the three areas of your life.

Pie of Life

The **pie of life** is a graphic representation that shows how much time you dedicate to each of the three main areas of your life: school, work, and leisure. A balanced pie is not necessarily divided into three equal parts; the amounts of time dedicated to school, work, and leisure vary according to an individual's circumstances, goals, and values. A student who is not working or not living with family members will have a different pie of life than a student who has a job or family responsibilities. The first circle below shows a pie of life divided into three equal parts. Divide the second circle into a pie that shows the estimated amount of time you spend per week in each of the three areas of life. In the last circle, adjust the lines to show your ideal pie of life.

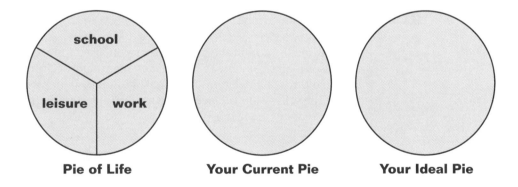

Pie of Life — Your Current Pie — Your Ideal Pie

Achieving your ideal pie of life requires a willingness to examine the ways you currently use time and a commitment to try new strategies that will improve your time management and goal-setting skills. Change is not always easy, but the benefits of having a more balanced life make it rewarding.

Increase–Decrease Method

There are only so many hours in a week. If your pie is unbalanced, you have two choices. First, you can learn new strategies to use your time more efficiently. The study strategies you will learn to use in this textbook can result in more effective studying, thus reducing or eliminating time-consuming, ineffective techniques. You can use this same concept to look for ways to perform tasks such as shopping, household chores, or errands more effectively and efficiently. Second, you can use the **Increase–Decrease Method** to change the boundaries in the pie of life by expanding or increasing any section of the pie that needs more time. To do this, you will need to decrease one or both of the remaining sections of the pie. The following chart provides you with options for adjusting the boundaries of your pie of life and helping you get closer to the balance you seek.

Using the Increase–Decrease Method to Balance Your Pie

Problem	Possible Solutions
Too Little Time for Family or Friends	1. Reduce the amount of time spent on other leisure activities. 2. Explore reducing or changing work hours, if possible. 3. Reduce the hours spent on chores by seeking more help from other members in the household or by using goal setting to do chores more efficiently. 4. Reduce school hours by taking fewer classes, if possible. 5. Reduce time spent studying by learning more efficient study techniques.
Too Little Time for School	1. Reduce social time; make school a greater priority. 2. Maintaining some social time is important, but consider creating more "meaningful" or "quality" social time and eliminating the less significant time spent with friends or family. 3. Reduce work hours, if possible, to make more time for studying. 4. Consider applying for scholarships, financial aid, grants, and/or loans to replace income if you reduce your work hours. 5. Reduce the number of classes you are taking so you have enough time to do well in fewer classes. 6. Examine the combination of classes you are taking; consider alternative classes if all your classes have heavy reading or writing requirements. 7. Learn time-management techniques to make better use of your time. 8. Use the self-discipline needed to study during study blocks allocated on your time-management schedule.
Too Much Leisure Time	1. Increase school time by adding another class. 2. Increase work hours, if possible, or volunteer your time at a local agency or community program. 3. Pursue new hobbies or set new goals. 4. Get involved with campus or community organizations.

Name ____________________ Date ____________

Exercise 3.1 Estimating How You Spend Your Time

Estimate the number of hours you spend on the following activities during the school week (Monday through Friday) and on the weekend (Saturday and Sunday). For activities that fit in more than one category, count them in only one of the possible categories to avoid duplication.

Monday Through Friday	Estimated hours	Saturday and Sunday	Estimated hours
Daily routines			
1. Getting ready in the morning	______	1. Getting ready in the morning	______
2. Commuting	______	2. Commuting	______
3. Preparing and eating meals	______	3. Preparing and eating meals	______
4. Sleeping	______	4. Sleeping	______
5. Other: ____________	______	5. Other: ____________	______
Total hours:	______	Total hours:	______
School			
1. In class	______	1. In class	______
2. Reading and studying	______	2. Reading and studying	______
3. School activities/sports	______	3. School activities/sports	______
4. Special meetings	______	4. Special meetings	______
5. Other: ____________	______	5. Other: ____________	______
Total hours:	______	Total hours:	______
Work			
1. Employment	______	1. Employment	______
2. Household chores	______	2. Household chores	______
3. Volunteer work	______	3. Volunteer work	______
4. Child care	______	4. Child care	______
5. Errands	______	5. Errands	______
6. Other: ____________	______	6. Other: ____________	______
Total hours:	______	Total hours:	______
Leisure			
1. Socializing with friends	______	1. Socializing with friends	______
2. Family time	______	2. Family time	______
3. Talking on the phone	______	3. Talking on the phone	______
4. Watching television	______	4. Watching television	______
5. Using the Internet	______	5. Using the Internet	______
6. Recreation/exercising	______	6. Recreation/exercising	______
7. Quiet, personal time	______	7. Quiet, personal time	______
8. Hobbies/special interest	______	8. Hobbies/special interest	______
9. Listening to music/playing video games, etc.	______	9. Listening to music/playing video games, etc.	______
10. Other: ____________	______	10. Other: ____________	______
Total hours:	______	Total hours:	______

Summarize your total hours for each of the following categories. Note: We all have 168 hours in a week. Your hours for the weekdays should not total more than 120; your hours for the weekend should not total more than 48.

	Weekdays	Weekend	Total
Daily routines	_____ hours	_____ hours	_____ hours
School	_____ hours	_____ hours	_____ hours
Work	_____ hours	_____ hours	_____ hours
Leisure	_____ hours	_____ hours	_____ hours

EXERCISE 3.2 Recording Time Expenditures

Keep a log of the way you spend your time for seven days. Use the same categories that appear in Exercise 3.1. Compare your actual use of time to your estimated use of time. Compare the results of Exercises 3.1 and 3.2 in a short summary paper. (A form to use for logging your time expenditures for the week is available on the Chapter 3 web site for this textbook.)

Using Schedules

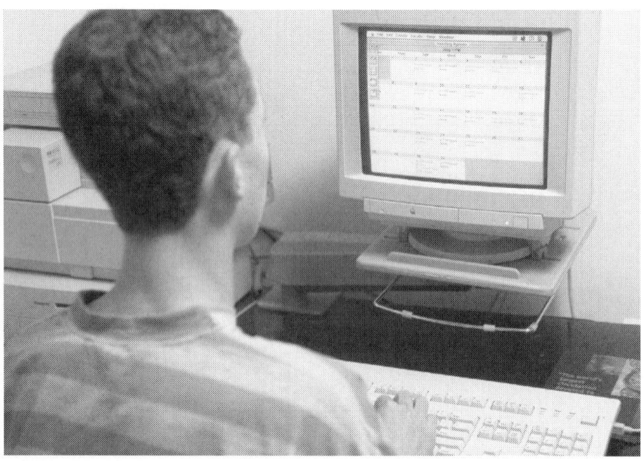

Which kinds of time-management schedules could you create on a computer? What are the advantages of creating your schedule on a computer?

Well-designed schedules serve as road maps to guide you through the term, through the week, and through each day. Rather than being at the mercy of time, you take control of it. With schedules, *you* create goals and plans for how you wish to spend your time. If you like to be spontaneous and unstructured, you can schedule leisure times without any specific plans in mind. When you reach your leisure time on your weekly schedule, you can do whatever you feel like doing at that moment; it is *your* time for spontaneity. If you like to structure and work with detailed plans, on your weekly or daily schedule you can specifically name the tasks or activities that you plan to complete in areas such as chores, social life, work, or school. Even though your time-management schedules can reflect your individual preferences, goals, and lifestyle, they have one thing in common: they are plans for managing and controlling time in order to achieve greater personal success.

Four Types of Time-Management Schedules

1. A *term schedule* provides you with an overview of important dates for the entire term.
2. A *weekly schedule* provides you with a plan that allocates time blocks for school, work, and leisure activities.
3. A *daily schedule* provides you with a quick reference guide for the day that may be more specific than the weekly schedule.
4. A *task schedule* provides you with a goal or goals to achieve during a specific block of time.

Term Schedule

A **term schedule** is a month-by-month calendar that shows important events and deadlines for the entire term. You can use a regular calendar or a monthly planner, or you can create a monthly calendar on a computer and run enough copies for each month in the term. At the beginning of each term, create your term schedule by adding the following items to your calendar:

1. Important deadlines, special events, and holidays that appear on your campus calendar
2. Dates for special projects, lab assignments, writing assignments, or reports that appear on all of your course syllabi
3. Scheduled tests, midterms, and final exams that appear on all of your course syllabi
4. Special meetings, workshops, or conferences on or off campus
5. Times available for tutors, study groups, or other kinds of support services
6. Personal appointments, birthdays, or other special events

Keep the term calendar in the front of your notebook so you can refer to it on a regular basis. Update the calendar throughout the term with deadlines for new assignments or significant events. A term calendar is an effective tool that provides you with an overview of the term, reduces the chances that you will overlook or forget an important date, and serves as a guide when you create your weekly schedule.

EXERCISE 3.3 Term Schedules

Use your campus calendar, the syllabus from each of your courses, and your personal calendar of events to create a term schedule. Include the six items listed in the previous section on creating term schedules. If your instructor does not provide you with calendar pages, use any month-to-month calendar, planner, or computer software program.

Weekly Schedule

Your **weekly schedule** is a detailed plan designed to bring balance to your life in school, work, and leisure activities. For many students, the weekly schedule is their guide or anchor to help them maintain a focus, keep their priorities straight, and stay on track even when a week may be hectic. With a weekly schedule, you will not only be able to plan how to spend your time, but you will also be more equipped to monitor and regulate your time and your activities. Following a weekly schedule requires careful, realistic planning and then motivation and self-discipline. Though following a weekly schedule may sound like a lot of work at first, many students find that following the schedule quickly creates a comfortable, manageable routine in which they can be productive and lead more balanced lives. With careful planning, you may be able to find more time for studying, for socializing or spending with your family, for other leisure activities, or for work. Being your own time manager becomes a lifelong skill that will bring you many rewards.

The example of a weekly schedule on page 72 shows many characteristics of an effective time-management schedule. It is organized logically and realistically so it is easy to follow. When you design your weekly schedule, incorporate as many as possible of the following characteristics of an effective schedule:

1. *The schedule reflects a realistic pie of life balance for you in the areas of school, work, and leisure.* By planning seven days at a time, you can schedule sufficient study and review time throughout the week; you can *plan* how much to study rather than studying only when you have an assignment or a test. You can incorporate your work schedule into your weekly

schedule by setting aside blocks of time for household chores and errands. You can let your family and friends know when you are available for leisure time. The five steps for planning a schedule (pages 68–71) will guide you through this process.

2. *The schedule includes time for specific goals you wish to achieve.* When you have goals that you want to achieve, time to work on those goals is essential. For example, if you want to jog three times a week, write letters once a week, meditate twenty minutes every day, or spend time in the park with your children twice a week, demonstrate the importance of the goal and your commitment to it by scheduling it each week.
3. *The schedule provides time for meals, adequate sleep, and exercise.* To keep your energy high and your physical and emotional health strong, plan to slow down to enjoy three meals a day. Put everything else aside and treat yourself to relaxed meals rather than meals on the run. Establish a routine time to go to bed so your internal clock and your sleep-awake patterns are stable and you get adequate rest each night. Plan some form of exercise for several days each week or even daily. Look for ways to include more exercise in your daily routine; for example, park on the outer aisles of parking lots and walk greater distances to your classes, to work, or to stores; or take the stairs instead of elevators.
4. *The schedule has strong patterns that can easily become routine.* Consistent patterns for certain days of the week or times of the day make learning a weekly schedule much easier. The following examples show several kinds of patterns that create consistency:
   a. Monday, Wednesday, and Friday follow one pattern; Tuesday and Thursday follow another pattern.
   b. Study blocks for a specific class occur at the same time each day or on alternating days; for example, *study writing* occurs from 2:00 to 3:00 P.M. Monday through Thursday, or *study math* occurs from 8:30 to 10:00 A.M. Monday, Wednesday, and Friday.
   c. Consistent times for meals and family time appear on the schedule so other family or household members can understand and adapt to the routine.
   d. Consistent blocks of time for social, leisure, or recreational activities appear on the schedule.
5. *The schedule reflects the individual's learning styles, preferences, and lifestyle.* For example, if a student is an *interactive learner,* time to work in study groups, with a "study buddy" or partner, or with tutors should appear on the weekly schedule. If a student has young children at home or children coming home from school in the afternoon, the schedule should include study times on campus between classes or when the children are in school or daycare, followed by time set aside to be with the children. When possible, the study schedule should reflect study blocks during an individual's high alertness hours. An ideal schedule reflects effective use of these energy and alertness patterns, known as *circadian rhythms.*

Circadian rhythms are the physical and behavioral patterns that people follow during a 24-hour period. They are biologically triggered by the brain. Circadian rhythm patterns involve body temperature, blood pressure, and other bodily functions. The most frequently discussed circadian rhythms are the awake–sleep cycles and the alert, high-energy times versus the slumping, low-energy times of the day.

1. *Awake–Sleep Patterns.* Some people are larks; they go to bed early and rise early. They are most alert and focused early in the day; they may prefer to use quiet, early morning hours for studying. Larks function well in today's society, which typically begins the work or school day in the morning hours. Owls are those people who prefer to stay up and wake up late. Even though the owls may function well at night, their circadian pattern often does not blend well with their work or school schedules, so they may need to adjust their awake–sleep pattern and study hours to fit into the typical work or school schedule.
2. *Peak Alertness–Slump Patterns.* Circadian rhythms include peak-energy and low-energy patterns (slumps) during the day. When possible, schedule tasks that require a high level of concentration during your high–energy times and tasks that do not require high energy or concentration during your low-energy times of the day. You can explore your high- and low-alertness patterns by completing Exercise 3.4.

Daily Schedule

A **daily schedule** is a specific list of tasks that you plan to achieve over the course of a day. This list can include specific homework and review activities; chores or errands; and family, social, recreational, or leisure activities. A simple index card works well to plan a daily schedule, or you may prefer to use a daily planner or organizer. Each night before you go to bed, take a few minutes to prepare your daily schedule for the next day's activities. Keep the schedule in a convenient place for quick reference.

TO DO WED:

8–9:00 A.M. Study Psy.
Read & notes for
pages 95–116

CLASSES—Regular schedule

1–3:00 P.M. Study Algebra
—Redo Ex. 6 #2–5
—Do Ex. 7 odd numbers
—Make study flash cards

3–5:00 P.M. —Start laundry
—Grocery shop
—Read mail
—Finish laundry

Task Schedule

A **task schedule** is a step-by-step plan for achieving a specific task in a specific block of time. You may use a task schedule to complete household chores more efficiently, plan an hour of work at your place of employment, or study productively. For example, if you plan to study math from 10:00 to 11:00 A.M., in one or two minutes at the beginning of the study block you can create a plan of action—a task schedule—for the study block. Your task schedule becomes your goal for the hour. (A *goal* is a well-defined plan aimed at achieving a specific result.)

WED. 10–11:00 A.M. Study Math

1. Review class notes.
2. Rework class problems.
3. Read pages 26–32. Highlight key points.
4. Do even-numbered problems on p. 33.
5. Check answers with answer key. Study and rework any incorrect answers.

Creating a task schedule is equivalent to setting a goal. You identify specific steps or tasks to complete within the block of time. If you are not able to complete all the tasks you scheduled during the study block, you can transfer the remaining tasks to your next study block or use a flex block of time (see pages 70–71). Task schedules are effective for several reasons:

1. They provide structure for the block of time so you do not waste time trying to decide what to do or where to start.
2. They give you a purpose and motivate you to stay on task to achieve your goals.
3. They help you learn to estimate more accurately the amount of time required to complete specific kinds of tasks.
4. They provide a form of immediate feedback at the end of the block of time. Your confidence, sense of accomplishment, and feeling of being in control increase when you are able to check off the study tasks you completed successfully.

Group Processing: A Collaborative Learning Activity

Form groups of three or four students for this brainstorming activity.

1. Divide a large chart into two columns. In the left column write all the problems the members of your group have encountered with managing time. List as many different ideas as possible.
2. After you have a list of common problems, brainstorm to find possible solutions. Write the possible solutions in the right column. You may provide more than one possible solution for each problem.
3. Be prepared to share your list of problems and possible solutions with the class.

Exercise 3.4 Discovering Your Peaks and Slumps

The chart on the right shows typical blocks of time in a day. Below is a list of activities. Decide when during the day you prefer to do each activity. Write the activity number on the chart in the correct time slot. You may place an activity in more than one time slot.

When would you prefer to

1. concentrate on memorizing
2. work on hard math problems
3. sit and relax
4. take a nap
5. do creative writing
6. do household chores
7. sit and talk with a friend
8. write a speech or plan a class presentation
9. exercise or work out
10. do easy review work
11. do problem solving kinds of homework
12. type or copy notes
13. move around (to avoid becoming too restless or sleepy to sit)
14. eat a meal or snacks
15. organize your notebook, notes, or study materials

5:00 A.M.– 7:00 A.M.
7:00 A.M.– 9:00 A.M.
9:00 A.M.–10:00 A.M.
10:00 A.M.–12:00 noon
12:00 noon–1:00 P.M.
1:00 P.M.– 3:00 P.M.
3:00 P.M.– 5:00 P.M.
5:00 P.M.– 7:00 P.M.
7:00 P.M.– 9:00 P.M.
9:00 P.M.–11:00 P.M.
11:00 P.M.– 1:00 A.M.

Looking for Patterns

1. Place a symbol on each number in the chart that you completed above.

On your chart, **STAR:**	**1, 2, 5, 8, 11**	These activities require peak alertness and concentration. These times are good for you to do the "serious studying."
On your chart, **CIRCLE:**	**10, 12, 15**	These activities require a lower level of concentration but could still be used for some studying.
On your chart, **BOX IN:**	**3, 4, 6, 7, 9, 13, 14**	These activities require little concentration. These are your "slump" hours for studying; try to avoid scheduling study blocks at this time of day.

2. Look for patterns. If a time block has all stars or stars and circles, it could potentially be an effective study block for you. If a time block has all boxes, it might be better to use that time for something other than studying. If a time block has a mixture of symbols, it could be an effective study block if you use effective concentration strategies to keep your mind focused on studying. The pattern you identify can help you plan your weekly schedule; however, classes, work schedules,

or personal responsibilities may not always make it possible for you to use your most ideal time blocks for studying.

3. What are the times with high levels of concentration? ______________________

What are the times with medium levels of concentration? ______________________

What are the times with low levels of concentration? ______________________

Creating a Weekly Time-Management Schedule

Each Sunday spend a few minutes planning your schedule for the upcoming week. Keep this schedule in the front of your notebook. Refer to this schedule whenever you wish to make new plans or set up appointments. By using the following steps to create your weekly schedule, you can feel confident that you will have a more balanced weekly routine.

Creating a Weekly Time-Management Schedule

1. Write in all your fixed activities.
2. Write in your fixed study times for each class.
3. Add several flexible study blocks.
4. Add time for specific goals and other responsibilities.
5. Schedule leisure, family, and social time.

Step 1: Write your fixed activities. Fixed activities are those activities that do not change from week to week, as well as special appointments that cannot easily be rescheduled. On your weekly calendar, write the following fixed activities in the appropriate time blocks:

1. Class times
2. Work schedule (employment)
3. Meals
4. Special appointments
5. Sleep

Step 2: Write your fixed study times. After learning about the importance of the memory principles of time on task and ongoing review, you should understand the importance of making study blocks a high priority on your weekly schedule. By using the following time-management techniques for scheduling fixed study times, you will be able to allot sufficient time to complete your reading and homework assignments, create study tools, use elaborative rehearsal, and practice retrieving information through ongoing review.

1. *Use the* **2:1 ratio**, *which recommends studying two hours for every hour in class, for all of your classes that require reading and homework assignments.* For example, if your writing class meets for three hours each week, schedule six hours of studying *for the writing class* each week. When you first begin using the 2:1 ratio, you may think it gives you too many study hours per week. Remember, however, that studying in college means much more than just doing the reading or the assignments. You want to build in time each week to reflect on your work, add quality to your work, create original study tools, and use ongoing review. Any time you sit down to study for

a given subject and find that you have completed all of the assignments, you will be able to enjoy time to self-quiz on previous work and review, review, review. This process eliminates later test anxiety or stress and the need to cram.

How should these athletes schedule their practice time for the term? Do you think athletes should consider athletics as part of school, work, or leisure?

On some occasions you may have classes that truly do not require the use of the 2:1 ratio; you can perform well in the classes and have sufficient study and review time with fewer fixed study hours. You may also on occasion have classes that require more than the 2:1 ratio; perhaps you will need a 3:1 ratio for an extremely demanding class. In other words, the 2:1 ratio is a standard college expectation for the amount of *quality* time you spend studying, but the ratio is not necessarily the most appropriate for all classes.

2. *On your weekly schedule, label each study block to indicate specifically the course you intend to study during that time block.* Simply labeling a block of time "study" does not provide you with a plan that supports your goal of using the 2:1 ratio for each class. Instead, that vague label tends to result in simply studying what needs to be done at that given time. "Study English," "Study math," and "Study photography" will provide you with a more effective plan of action each time you sit down to study.
3. *Plan to study one subject for about a fifty-minute block of time.* You will become more involved with the subject matter if you stay with the subject for fifty minutes; you create a "mindset" for the material, establish a good level of concentration, and allow time for the information to consolidate or register in your memory. Switching to two or more subjects in a fifty-minute time period is often ineffective and reduces your recall or retrieval ability later. After a fifty-minute block of time with one subject, take a ten-minute break before either continuing with that subject or changing to a new subject.

4. *Try to schedule at least one study block every day of the week.* Balancing your *pie of life* is easier if each day you give yourself time to study, to work, and to enjoy leisure activities.
5. *Use* **distributed practice**, *which involves distributing your study time over several different time periods and days of the week.* For example, instead of studying for your health course only on the weekends, plan to study for that class on Monday, Wednesday, Friday, and Sunday. By using distributed practice, you avoid the need to cram.
6. *Unless you are working on a project that involves creativity, avoid* **marathon studying**, *also known as* **massed practice**. Marathon studying or massed practice occurs when you study more than three hours in a row. After three hours, productivity, concentration, retention, and effectiveness decrease. You will see better results by studying for two or three hours and then leaving to do something other than studying. The break will often work to your advantage; your mind will continue to mull over, work with, and process the information when you step away from studying. You may find it difficult to leave projects, such as painting, constructing a model, or writing a research paper after three hours and then come back and "step into" the same channel of creativity. In situations such as these, which require a flow of creativity, using marathon studying may actually be a better course of action than leaving the project after two or three hours.
7. *Study during your alert times of the day whenever possible.* Concentration is easier to achieve during your high-energy, high-alert times of the day when you tend to be more productive and task oriented. When studying at your alert times is not possible due to other scheduling conflicts, using effective concentration techniques can increase your levels of productivity and alertness.
8. *Study your hardest or your least-liked subjects early in the day.* Often the tendency is to delay studying for these classes until the end of the day when you are likely to be more physically tired, less interested, and less motivated.
9. *When possible, study right* before *a class in which you are expected to discuss information or participate in group activities.* For example, studying right before a foreign language class or a speech class creates a mindset for the course, refreshes your memory of new words, and provides you with time to rehearse a speech. This time prepares you to perform at a higher level in class. *Study right* after *a lecture or a math class.* Work with your lecture notes and work on problem sets or math assignments while the information is fresh in your mind.
10. *When possible, create study schedule patterns so your schedule is easier to remember and becomes habitual.* For example, perhaps you could study math every day from 2:00 to 3:00; for your computer class Tuesday, Thursday, and Saturday from 3:00 to 5:00; and for your reading class between classes on Monday, Wednesday, and Friday, from 11:00 to 12:00, and three hours on the weekend. Creating strong patterns and planning your study blocks carefully may result in a study schedule that you can use consistently for the entire term.

Step 3: Add several flexible study blocks. Identify two or three hours each week that you can hold in reserve in case you need additional time to study for a specific class, prepare for a test, or complete a special project. On your weekly schedule write *flex* for these time blocks. Unlike fixed study blocks, which you should use each time they appear on your schedule, **flex study blocks** are flexible blocks of time that you use only when you need them. Flex blocks are *safety nets* for extra study time. If you do not need flex blocks, convert them to free time.

Step 4: Add time for specific goals and other responsibilities. Any important goals should have time allotted on your weekly schedule so you can work on them. If you do not specifically set aside time, you may find yourself postponing the goals and dabbling at them instead of making steady progress. The same is true for any other personal responsibilities.

Step 5: Schedule leisure, family, and social time. After you complete steps one through four, the remaining time on your schedule can be labeled *family, social,* or *leisure.* You can include specific plans, such as "family skating," "movie," or "go fishing," or you can leave the time open and flexible to whatever you are in the mood to do at that time. Having family, social, and leisure time is important for mental and physical health and strong relationships. If you do not have adequate time on your schedule for these activities, look for ways to use the Increase–Decrease Method to find a more comfortable balance in your week.

In the schedule on page 72, the student uses the five steps for planning a weekly schedule. Notice how the student organizes the week and the study blocks for these classes: a math class (4 credits), a reading class (3 credits), a P.E. class (1 credit), a career planning class (1 credit), and a computer class (3 credits).

Exercise 3.5 Creating Your Weekly Schedule

1. Make several copies of the time-management form on page 73. (An additional form is available in Appendix B.)
2. Complete the five steps below to create a weekly time-management schedule. Use a pencil at first so you can rearrange time blocks as needed to create a manageable and realistic schedule.

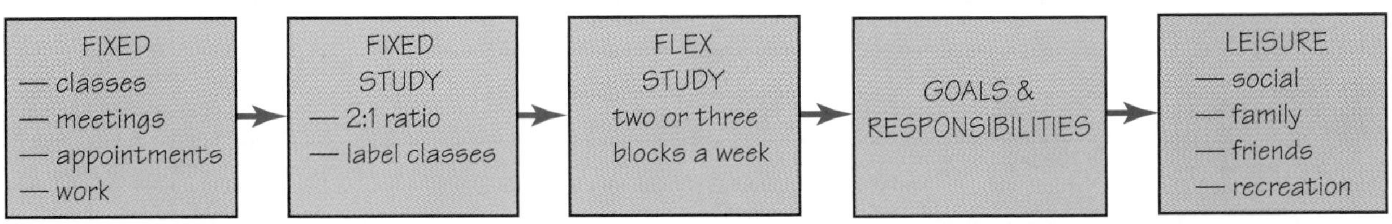

3. Mentally walk through each day on your schedule to determine whether it is realistic. Then answer the questions on the Weekly Time-Management Checklist (page 74). Adjust your schedule if you discover areas that you can strengthen or improve.
4. Color code your schedule so it is easier to see at a glance. Use one color for your classes; another for study times; and a third for leisure, family, and social time. Use a fourth color for work or leave it without color coding.
5. Begin following your schedule as soon as possible. Several times during the day, indicate on your schedule how often you followed it as planned. Create a code system, such as stars for blocks that worked as planned and checks for blocks that you did not follow according to the plan.
6. Use your schedule for a full seven days. After that, be prepared to turn in your first schedule and the Weekly Time-Management Checklist.

WEEKLY TIME-MANAGEMENT SCHEDULE

For the week of ________________

Time	Monday	Tuesday	Wednesday	Thursday	Friday	Saturday	Sunday
12–6 A.M.	**SLEEP** →						
6–7:00	**SLEEP** →						
7–8:00	**Get up, get ready, eat breakfast** →					**SLEEP**	**SLEEP**
8–9:00	**Commute to school** →					**Get up**	**Get up**
9–10:00	**PE Class**	**Study Math**	**PE Class**	**Study Math**	**PE Class**	**breakfast**	**breakfast**
10–11:00	**Math Class**	**Math Class**	**Math Class**	**Math Class**	**Study Math**	**Career Class**	**Get ready**
11–12 NOON	**Study Math**	**LUNCH**	**Study Math**	**LUNCH**	**with TUTOR**	**Study Career**	**CHURCH**
12–1:00	**LUNCH**	**Computer Class**	**LUNCH**	**Computer Class**	**LUNCH**	**ERRANDS**	**CHURCH**
1–2:00	**Reading Class**	**Computer Class**	**Reading Class**	**Computer Class**	**Reading Class**	**LUNCH**	**LUNCH**
2–3:00	**Study Reading**	**Lab-Study Computer**	**Study Reading**	**Lab-Study Computer**	**Study Reading**	**CHORES**	**LEISURE**
3–4:00	**Study Reading**	**Lab-Study Computer**	**FLEX**	**Lab-Study Computer**	**FLEX**	**CHORES**	**LEISURE**
4–5:00	**Commute home** →					**CHORES**	**LEISURE**
5–6:00	**DINNER** →						**LEISURE**
6–7:00	**LEISURE**	**LEISURE**	**LEISURE**	**LEISURE**	**WORK**	**WORK**	**DINNER**
7–8:00	**Study Reading**	**WORKOUT** ↓	**Study Math**	**WORKOUT** ↓	**WORK**	**WORK**	**Study Computer**
8–9:00	**Study Reading**		**Study Math**		**WORK**	**WORK**	**Study Computer**
9–10:00	**LEISURE**		**LEISURE**		**WORK**	**WORK**	**FLEX**
10–11:00	**LEISURE**		**LEISURE**		**WORK**	**WORK**	**PLAN WEEK**
11–12 A.M.	**SLEEP** →				**WORK**	**WORK**	**SLEEP**

WEEKLY TIME-MANAGEMENT SCHEDULE

For the week of ______________________________

Time	Monday	Tuesday	Wednesday	Thursday	Friday	Saturday	Sunday
12–6 A.M.							
6–7:00							
7–8:00							
8–9:00							
9–10:00							
10–11:00							
11–12 NOON							
12–1:00 P.M.							
1–2:00							
2–3:00							
3–4:00							
4–5:00							
5–6:00							
6–7:00							
7–8:00							
8–9:00							
9–10:00							
10–11:00							
11–12 A.M.							

Weekly Time-Management Checklist
Use this checklist to evaluate your weekly time-management schedule and to strengthen it by adding any items that you may have overlooked. Write *Y* for yes or *N* for no.

Study Blocks

_______ Do you have enough study blocks set aside to study for each class? (Use the 2:1 ratio when it is appropriate.)

_______ Do you specifically label "study" and name the class?

_______ Are your study blocks spread throughout the week?

_______ Are you spending some time studying on the weekends?

_______ Do you avoid marathon studying so that you do not study more than three hours in a row?

_______ Do you avoid studying late at night?

_______ Do you include flex time in your schedule?

Fixed Activities

_______ Do you schedule time for three meals each day?

_______ Do you schedule sufficient time to sleep each night?

_______ Do you keep a fairly regular sleep schedule throughout the week?

Balancing Your Life

_______ Do you plan time specifically to be spent with your family and friends?

_______ Do you plan time for exercise, hobbies, or special interests such as clubs, organizations, and recreational teams?

_______ Do you plan specific time to take care of household chores and errands?

_______ Do you plan time to work on specific goals?

Will the Schedule Work?

_______ Can you "walk through each day" in your mind and see that your schedule is realistic?

_______ Are your peak energy times used wisely?

_______ Do you feel that your life would be more balanced if you followed what you have planned on your weekly schedule?

Other

_______ Have you used color codes in the schedule?

_______ Have you referred to the term schedule for special deadlines or events?

Reflection Writing 2 — CHAPTER 3

1. For three weeks in a row, create and use a weekly schedule. After you use your first week's schedule, note any time blocks that were difficult to follow. Consider modifying and strengthening your schedule for the second and then the third weeks. If your first schedule was effective, copy the schedule but include any minor changes such as special appointments, social activities, or work schedules. Save all three schedules so you can turn them in with this reflection writing.
2. On a separate piece of paper, answer the following questions.
   a. Draw your original *pie of life* and your current *pie of life*. How has your *pie of life* changed? Be specific.

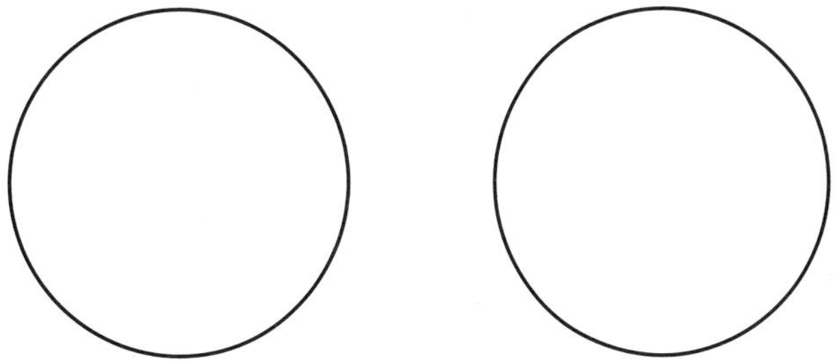

Original Pie of Life **Current Pie of Life**

   b. What are the most difficult times of the day for you to "stay on schedule"? Why are these times more difficult than others? What strategies are you using to overcome tendencies to abandon your schedule during these times?
   c. Discuss the effectiveness of your study blocks. Did you use the 2:1 ratio? Did you have adequate time to study and review each week? Did you need to use your flex blocks? Did you use a task schedule for your study blocks?
   d. Was time management effective for you? What were the benefits? What were the drawbacks? Will you continue to use a weekly schedule this term? Why or why not?

Applying Time Management

Time management is a highly prized skill in both the work force and the academic world. Learning to manage time effectively will help you meet your goals, be productive, and achieve success in many different avenues of your life. The following strategies will help you apply your time-management skills more effectively and consistently.

Time-Management Strategies

1. Be flexible with change; time management requires time, commitment, and patience.
2. Inform others of your commitment to time management.
3. Use trading time sparingly.
4. Seek solutions to time-management problems you encounter.
5. Modify time-management strategies for independent study and online courses.
6. Incorporate goal setting into your time-management strategies.

Be Flexible

Change is not always an easy process. Self-doubt, frustration, resistance, lack of motivation, or unexpected barriers sometimes crop up when a person attempts to change behavior patterns that have existed for years. Flexibility on your part can make the process of change easier. Be willing to relax your old patterns or ways of doing things, be willing to try new approaches, and be willing to give something new a chance to succeed. Be patient with yourself. As soon as you recognize that you are wandering from your time management plan, do not be hard on yourself or discard the schedule for the remainder of the day. Simply start in with the task you planned and move forward. The longer you strive to use time management on a daily basis, the easier and more habitual it becomes.

To alter the way you see and handle time, commit to using your schedule for three weeks. During the times when you do not follow your schedule, examine the reasons or the situations. Was there an emergency or situation that was beyond your control that took precedence over your schedule? Did you abandon your schedule by choice? What swayed you from the schedule? Were there other ways you could have dealt with the situation and still followed your schedule? Learning to observe, understand, and monitor your choices is part of learning to use time management successfully. To know the true value and benefits of time management, strive to follow your plan as closely as possible for three weeks. After that time, use what you learned about yourself, about managing your time, and about achieving your goals to decide how you wish to continue managing your time.

Inform Others of Your Commitment to Time Management

Inform family members, roommates, partners, or friends about your goals to organize your time more effectively. Members of your household are often more supportive if they are aware of your goals and priorities and see how you plan to allocate your time. Posting a copy of your schedule on the refrigerator helps them know when you are available and when you have set aside special time just for them. Involving family members in the creation of your schedule each week can also add structure to the week and can strengthen communication about activities and events that are important to each person. Developing a weekly schedule in their presence often becomes motivation for them to create a schedule as well.

Use Trading Time Sparingly

Trading time is a time-management technique that gives you some flexibility without compromising your daily goals. You can trade time slots on a specific day in order to participate in an activity that becomes available on short notice or unexpectedly. For example, the weekly schedule on page 72 shows 2:00 to 6:00 on Sunday as leisure time and 7:00 to 10:00 P.M. as time to study for the computer class and flex time. Let us assume that the student receives an invitation to go out to dinner and a movie. By *trading time,* the student moves the two hours of studying and the one hour of flex time to the afternoon leisure time blocks and converts the evening blocks to leisure. The activities for both time blocks occur, but at different times. Switching time blocks gives you some flexibility to respond to unexpected opportunities or activities; however, use trading time sparingly. If you begin to trade time blocks too frequently, you will lose the sense of having a schedule and your self-discipline may decline. For ordinary unexpected activities, saying "no" and sticking with your plan of action may be more beneficial than trading time too frequently.

Seek Solutions to Time-Management Problems

Some students find that their lives have specific circumstances that make creating a weekly time-management schedule difficult. Be resourceful and seek solutions to your scheduling conflicts. Discuss your circumstances with your instructor or with other students; frequently they will be able to suggest solutions. The following problems and solutions are commonly presented by students who are learning to create weekly time-management schedules.

1. *Rotating work schedules.* If your work schedule varies each week, you should not have a problem because you are developing a schedule each week. Write your work schedule first as a fixed activity. Adjust your study blocks and other goals and responsibilities around your work schedule.
2. *Different sleep–awake patterns.* Before you photocopy the weekly time-management schedules, block out the times that are shown in the left-hand column. Write in the times that will fit your awake hours. This is a common situation for people who work swing or graveyard shifts.
3. *Young children at home.* Young children require and deserve your time and attention. Their schedules are important and you should accommodate them when you create your schedule. Consider changing your sleep patterns by getting up earlier in the morning before they are awake. If your children attend child care, consider extending the child care an hour or two and stay on campus to study during that time. Use all available time between classes to complete as much studying on campus as possible so that more of your time at home can be devoted to your children's needs.
4. *Not on campus five days a week.* Students who attend classes only two or three days a week have the intention of studying on the days they are not on campus, but many times they find they are not as productive as they had anticipated. Consider coming to campus even on days on which you do not have classes. You will probably study more effectively and have access to instructors, tutors, the library, computer labs, and other resources. If you chose your classes so you could have two or three days off from school, next term consider registering for classes on all five days of the week. The days at school for classes will be less intense, and you will have more time and energy to prepare for classes if they are distributed more effectively over five days.

Modify Strategies for Independent Study and Online Courses

You can use many of the same time-management techniques discussed in this chapter for independent study or online courses. With these alternative delivery systems, you still have reading and homework assignments and some form of testing or assessment requirements. However, you do not have the physical structure of a classroom or the face-to-face contact with the instructor or students. Many students find independent study and online courses appealing; they like the concept of working on their own and at whatever time they prefer. However, many students learn how difficult it is to maintain the self-discipline, dedication, and time commitment that are required to successfully complete independent study or online courses.

To avoid the common pitfalls of independent study and online courses, you can use the following modified and new time-management techniques to achieve greater success in your independent study or online courses.

1. Create a term calendar. Use the course syllabus to identify due dates for papers, homework assignments, and tests. If the course materials do not include a time line with due dates, create your own by identifying the number of assignments, modules, or units you need to complete to pass the course. On your term calendar, assign completion dates for each component. Also include any orientation, onsite testing, or individual meetings you are required to attend.
2. On your weekly schedule, write specific times you need to be available to view a telecast program, such as a distance learning lesson via television, or

times you need to be on the computer to participate in a real-time group discussion.

3. Commit yourself to work on the course during specific time blocks each week. To calculate the number of hours you must dedicate to each course, count the number of hours that a similar class would meet in a classroom setting, figure the 2:1 ratio for studying, and add one to three additional hours. Independent study and online courses often have components that require more time than those included in a classroom approach. To avoid problems with completing a course due to lack of sufficient time or lack of time-management skills, schedule more time to complete these courses than you would a classroom course. For example, assume you are enrolled in a three-credit online sociology course; students enrolled in this course in a regular classroom meet three times a week. You would want to schedule more than nine hours of study time for this course *each week*.

"classroom equivalent hours"	=	3 hours
study time using the 2:1 ratio	=	6 hours
additional independent study time	=	1–3 hours
Total hours for an independent or online course:		10–12 hours per week

4. During your study block, limit your use of the television or the computer to the course material you are studying. If you are watching a telecourse, avoid cruising the stations to get a glimpse of other television programs. To keep your mindset tuned in to the course and your thought patterns focused on the tasks waiting for you, turn off the television and continue to study when you finish viewing the telecourse. If you are working online, resist using your study time to check your email from people not enrolled in the course, and resist the temptation to surf the Internet for topics unrelated to the course content. If you are in online study or discussion groups, strive to keep your contributions related to the topic under discussion. Too much time can vanish with discussions that wander or fail to address the discussion topic. Because many people can spend endless hours on the computer and roaming through cyberspace, monitoring your use of the computer during online course time is critical.
5. Make a task schedule each time you sit down to work on your independent study or online course. Create a roadmap for yourself so you have a clear picture of the goals you intend to achieve during the study block. Be vigilant about the passage of time, including the amount of time required to complete various types of assignments.

Incorporate Goal Setting into Your Time-Management Strategies

Time management and goal setting go hand in hand. Once you have organized your day into time blocks and scheduled specific topics in each time block, the next step is to decide how to use those blocks most effectively. The task schedule discussed on page 66 are goals for your study block. In Chapter 4, you will learn to combine time management and goal setting to manage term-long projects, create five-day study plans for tests, and bring greater success to all areas of your life.

EXERCISE 3.6 Case Studies

Work in a small group, with a partner, or on your own to answer the following questions. Use information from this chapter to support your answers. Use complete sentences for each answer. These case studies are also available online; you can email your response to your instructor or print a copy of your work online.

1. Cindy always seems to be caught off guard. She is surprised when she arrives in class and hears that a specific assignment is due that day. She seldom has her assignments done on time. Sometimes she does not remember them and other times she runs out of time. She prefers to do all her studying on the weekends, so when something is due in the middle of or at the end of the week, she never has it completed. What suggestions would you give to Cindy so she might modify her approach to her assignments?

2. Raymond is frustrated by college. He is used to a busy life that includes a variety of activities with his friends. None of his friends are going to college, so they just do not seem to understand. Raymond does not feel like he has time for the things he really loves doing. This frustration is affecting his overall attitude toward school. What strategies could help Raymond?

3. Lydia is a night owl who has to begin her day at 6:30 A.M. She is busy during the day taking classes and working thirty hours a week. She arrives home each day at four o'clock and tends to the needs of her three young children. By the time everyone is fed and tucked into bed, it is ten o'clock at night. Too many nights she finds herself falling asleep on her books. She is behind in all her classes and has no energy left for studying or for herself. How can Lydia use the Increase–Decrease Method to examine ways to solve some of these issues?

Exercise 3.7 LINKS

In a group or with a partner, answer the following questions about the links or relationships between time management and the concepts you learned in Chapters 1 and 2. Use the space below each question to take notes and write a response. Be prepared to discuss your ideas in class.

1. The memory principle big picture–little pictures refers to learning different levels of information: large concepts and small details. Sometimes the principle is referred to as "seeing the forest and seeing the trees." Which aspects of time management could be considered "the forest" and which could be considered "the trees"?

2. Which of the three main cognitive learning modalities do you actively use when you create a weekly time-management schedule?

3. What is the relationship between the 2:1 ratio for studying and elaborative rehearsal? Can you have one without the other?

4. Which of the four kinds of time-management schedules help students apply the memory principle of time on task most effectively?

Reflection Writing 3 CHAPTER 3

On a separate piece of paper or in a journal, do the following:

1. Discuss how learning and using time-management skills can affect your life. What are the benefits? What changes will you make as a result of learning how to manage your time?
2. What areas of time management are most difficult for you? What strategies can you use to overcome these difficulties?

SUMMARY

- Learning time-management skills helps you achieve balance in your pie of life in three main areas: school, work, and leisure.
- The Increase–Decrease Method stresses the need to adjust the boundaries that reflect the amount of time you spend in the three areas of your pie of life.
- Using term, weekly, daily, and task schedules helps you organize and control your time. A term schedule outlines important dates on a monthly calendar. A weekly schedule shows specific times for fixed activities; study blocks; flex blocks; goals and responsibilities; and leisure time, which includes friends, family, and recreation. A daily schedule provides a roadmap for the day. A task schedule sets goals for a specific block of time.
- An effective weekly schedule promotes distributed practice rather than marathon studying or massed practice; makes use of your circadian rhythms; and strives to create a balance in the way you use your time for school, work, and leisure.
- Numerous time-management strategies, including trading time, help you improve your time-management skills and achieve your goals.

ACE Practice Tests, which are scored online, supplementary exercises, enrichment activities, and related web site links are available online for *Essential Study Skills*, 4e. Use the following directions to access this web site:

Type: **http://college.hmco.com/collegesurvival/students**

Click on *List of Sites by Author*. Use the arrow to scroll down to Wong *Essential Study Skills*, 4e. Click on the title. If you are working on your own computer, bookmark this web site.

LEARNING OPTIONS

The following learning options provide you with opportunities to demonstrate your understanding of the topics in Chapter 3. Your instructor may assign one or more specific options or may ask you to select one or more options that interest you the most.

1. Copy the Chapter 3 mapping on page 57 onto a blank piece of paper. Expand the mapping by extending branches to show key words or phrases for each heading. (See Chapter 1, page 25, for an example.) You can add pictures and colors to your mapping to accentuate the points.
2. Create a term-long schedule and a weekly schedule using a software program on your computer. Add color coding or shading to your schedules; add graphics if you wish.

3. Use the library or the Internet to locate three or more articles that provide additional tips for managing time. Copy or print the sources of your information. Compile the information into a brochure, a flyer, or a poster that can be shared with your classmates.
4. Form a study group with three or more students to meet outside class to review the content of this chapter. In addition to the review work, spend time discussing your homework and reflection assignments. Write a summary paper that discusses the highlights of your study group.
5. Before you go to bed each night for a week, create a schedule for the following day. Include specific details for your study blocks and your work blocks. At the end of the day, check off the tasks you completed as planned. Compile the seven daily schedules; write a short summary about the successes and problems you encountered with your daily schedules.
6. Determine which of your classes has the most assignments over the course of one week. Create a task schedule at the beginning of each study block for this class. At the end of each study block, check off the tasks you completed as planned. Compile the task schedules; write a short summary that discusses the effectiveness of the task schedules and your ability to estimate the amount of time required for the individual tasks within each study block.
7. Interview three people who have three different professions. Create a standard set of questions to ask them about the kinds of time-management problems they encounter in their work, the time-management strategies they find effective, and the importance of time management in their line of work. Summarize your findings in the form of a chart or in a paragraph. Include the interview questions and responses.

CHAPTER 3 REVIEW QUESTIONS

Multiple Choice

Choose the best *answer for each of the following questions. Write the letter of the answer on the line.*

_______ **1.** Using time management effectively
- **a.** instills a sense of being in control of your free time.
- **b.** balances the three areas in your *pie of life:* school, social, and family.
- **c.** frees up your weekends for social, leisure, and recreational time.
- **d.** provides you with a roadmap to be more productive and in greater control of the main areas of your life.

_______ **2.** When you use a fifty-minute study block effectively, you should
- **a.** spend time reviewing each of your courses.
- **b.** create a mindset that focuses on only one subject.
- **c.** take a short break every twenty minutes.
- **d.** begin by identifying which class has an assignment due the next day.

_______ **3.** An effective weekly time-management schedule includes
- **a.** eight hours of studying on weekends.
- **b.** adequate time to use the 2:1 ratio, elaborative rehearsal, and distributed practice.
- **c.** three or more flex blocks, three or more times to trade time, and adequate time for massed practice.
- **d.** all of your study blocks during your peak hours of alertness.

_______ **4.** Marathon studying
- **a.** is an acceptable practice when you are engaged in creative projects.
- **b.** occurs when you study for more than three hours in a row.
- **c.** is the same as massed practice.
- **d.** All of the above

_______ **5.** Which one of the following suggestions should you *not* use when you plan your study blocks on a weekly schedule?
- **a.** Label each study block by naming the class you will study so you can ensure that you are using the 2:1 ratio each week.
- **b.** Take a short break every thirty minutes to stretch, let the information settle in your mind, and get a nutritious snack.
- **c.** Study your most difficult or your least favorite subject earliest in the day.
- **d.** Create patterns in the week so your schedule is easier to learn.

_______ **6.** The primary purpose of the Increase–Decrease Method is to
- **a.** help you find ways to increase your social time each week.
- **b.** find a more satisfying and productive balance in your *pie of life.*
- **c.** move you toward having a *pie of life* that shows an equal amount of time each week for school, work, and leisure.
- **d.** All of the above

_______ **7.** A task schedule is
- **a.** a step-by-step plan to achieve a specific task during a specific block of time.
- **b.** a step-by step plan that should be used specifically for study blocks.
- **c.** an approach for planning weekend study blocks.
- **d.** a plan of action for flex blocks on a weekly schedule.

_______ **8.** The fixed study blocks on your weekly time management schedule should
a. provide you with ample time to complete assignments and use ongoing review.
b. not be converted to free time when assignments are done.
c. identify which course you plan to study during that time block.
d. All of the above

_______ **9.** Which of the following is *not* an effective strategy for planning study blocks on a weekly schedule?
a. Study during your most alert times of the day when possible.
b. Study right before a class in which you are expected to discuss information or participate in class activities.
c. Study right before a class that mostly involves lectures and requires extensive note taking.
d. Place a different kind of activity on your schedule after two or three straight hours of studying.

_______ **10.** Flex blocks
a. provide you with blocks of time reserved for extra study time that might be needed to complete assignments or study for tests.
b. can be converted to free time if they are not needed.
c. should appear two or three times on your weekly schedule.
d. All of the above

Short Answer and Critical Thinking

Answer the following questions using terminology and information from this chapter. Answer in complete sentences.

1. Assume that a student named Mark only studies when he has an assignment due. Another student named Rudy has a weekly schedule that uses the 2:1 ratio for each of his classes. What benefits will Rudy likely have that Mark will not?

2. Why should you use trading time sparingly?

3. What are the main benefits of creating and using each of the following kinds of schedules?

a. term schedule

b. weekly schedule

c. daily schedule

d. task schedule

CHAPTER 4

Setting Goals

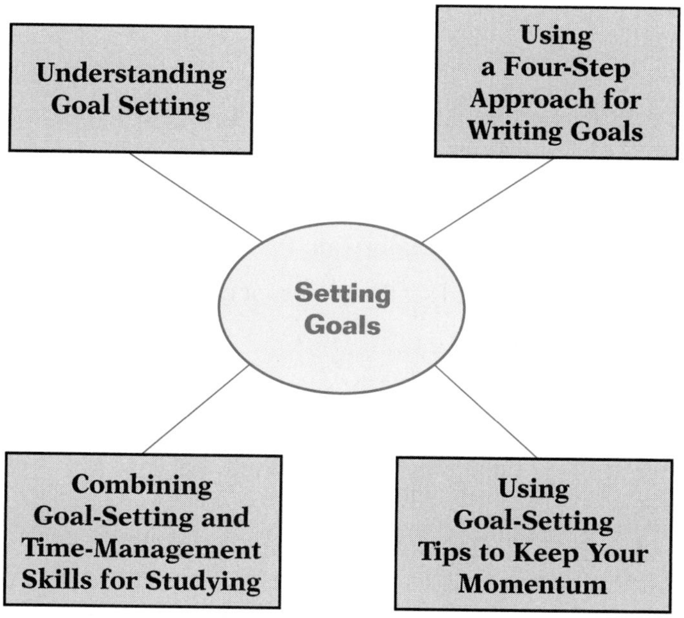

Terms to Know

goals
motivation
long-term goals
intermediary goals
short-term goals
immediate goals
procrastination
extrinsic reward
intrinsic reward
goal organizer
visualization
affirmations
task schedule
five-day study plan
summary notes
term-long project

Goals—well-defined plans aimed at achieving a specific result—can be long-term, intermediary, short-term, or immediate. Setting goals can help people achieve success in all areas of their lives. The four-step goal-setting process includes identifying a specific goal, target date and time, specific steps, and an internal or an external reward. When working on achieving specific goals, you can use a variety of strategies to keep up your momentum and motivation to succeed. Goal setting and time management work in a close partnership; both sets of skills can be used effectively to set academic goals for study blocks, test preparation, and term-long projects.

CHAPTER 4 Setting Goals Profile

DO, SCORE, and **RECORD** your profile before you read this chapter. If you need to review the process, refer to the complete directions given in the Profile for Chapter 1 on page 2.

ONLINE: You can complete the profile and get your score online at this textbook's web site.

	YES	NO
1. I set goals for myself each week.	______	______
2. I write goals, but I leave the time to complete the goals open-ended so I can work on the goals at my own pace.	______	______
3. It is difficult for me to know specifically what goals I want to reach.	______	______
4. I use visualization to see myself achieving the goals I really want to reach.	______	______
5. I break term-long assignments into smaller steps and set time lines for each step.	______	______
6. I tend to set too many goals and then feel overwhelmed.	______	______
7. I sometimes lack sufficient motivation to follow through on goals that I set.	______	______
8. I identify a reward for myself when I reach a goal, and I deny myself the reward if I do not reach the goal.	______	______
9. I always plan my goals in my head and do not feel a need to write them down.	______	______
10. I set goals for myself at the beginning of each study block on my weekly schedule.	______	______

Reflection Writing 1 — CHAPTER 4

On a separate piece of paper or in a journal, do the following:

1. Discuss your profile score for this chapter. What was your score? What does it mean to you?
2. In what areas of your life have you used goal setting successfully?
3. In what areas of your life has goal setting not worked effectively?

Understanding Goal Setting

Goals are well-defined plans aimed at achieving a specific result. Goals are your roadmap to where you want to go in life. They reflect your values and priorities about what is truly important to you in various areas of your life, perhaps including your education; finances; health; physical condition; career; social, family, or community life; and emotional or spiritual development. Goals provide the avenue for you to become the person you want to be and to create the life you want to live. When you plan a course of action to achieve a goal and then successfully complete that goal, you feel a sense of pride and accomplishment. You feel more in control of your time, your choices, and your personal life.

Motivation is an integral part of goal setting. **Motivation** is the feeling, emotion, or desire that moves a person to take action. Motivation helps people make changes, learn something new, perform at a higher level, overcome procrastination, and persevere to complete a goal. Motivation is often the factor that begins the process of goal setting. Interestingly, once a person achieves a goal, the accomplishment generates new motivation to tackle other challenges and create new goals. The result is an upward spiral of personal growth, confidence, and success.

Different Kinds of Goals

Goals can be categorized in a variety of ways; categorizing goals according to the length of time involved to achieve each goal is one common method for discussing different kinds of goals. **Long-term goals** may take months or even several years to achieve. Long-term goals become more realistic when they are perceived as a series of **intermediary goals**, or goals that link the present to a more distant future. Intermediary goals serve as signposts or benchmarks to reach along the way to achieving the more comprehensive long-term goal. **Short-term goals** are goals that you plan to attain within a short period of time, such as a term, a month, or a week. **Immediate goals** are those that will begin and end within a few hours, the same day, or over the course of two days at the most. For example, for a student who is planning to complete a four-year degree, graduation from a university is his or her *long-term goal.* This student's *intermediary goal* is to complete a two-year degree at a community college. The student needs to achieve many *short-term* and *immediate goals* to succeed at the intermediary goal. He or she needs to complete required and elective courses successfully each term, as well as complete tests and homework assignments with passing grades. The following graphic shows how the long-term goal is the "big picture" to achieve. The intermediary, short-term, and immediate goals are "the smaller pictures," each a subgoal for a higher level. As a student achieves each subgoal, the long-term goal is closer to becoming a reality.

What long-term planning goals does this student need to make in order to plan a spring break vacation?

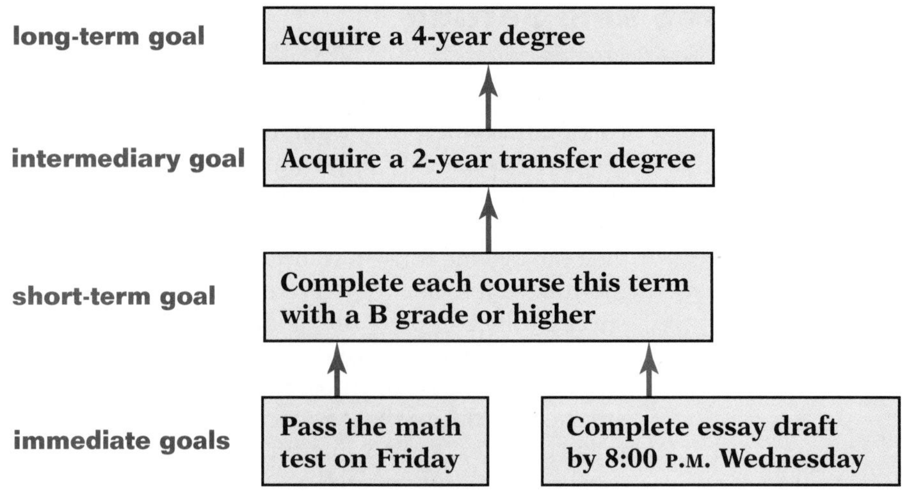

Some short-term or immediate goals are not always directly linked to a higher level or more long-term goal. For example, you may want to create a goal to clean your bedroom thoroughly, create an effective study area, sort your boxes of photographs, recycle old clothing, change the oil in your car, clean the garage, or plant a vegetable garden. Short-term or immediate goals such as these can be planned, implemented, and achieved within a relatively short period of time without being part of a larger intermediary or long-term goal.

Group Processing: A Collaborative Learning Activity

Form groups of three or four students. Complete the following directions.

1. Divide a large piece of paper into two columns. Label the left column *Reasons goals fail.* Label the right column *Reasons goals succeed.*
2. Brainstorm together to make a lengthy list of reasons why some people fail to achieve their goals. Write your ideas in the column on the left.
3. Brainstorm together to make a lengthy list of reasons why some people succeed at achieving their goals. Write the reasons in the column on the right. What are common characteristics, attitudes, or behaviors for goal achievers?
4. Discuss how the ideas in the right column could be used to address the problems listed in the left column. Be prepared to share your group work with the class.

Reasons Some People Do Not Set Goals

If setting goals has so many personal benefits, why do some people shy away from goal setting? The reasons vary, but the following reflect common reasons why some people do not set goals for what they value in their lives.

1. *They are unclear about what they want in their lives.* In other words, they have not taken the time to do a personal inventory on where they want to go and what they want to achieve. When some people go through a major life transition, such as moving away from home for the first time, losing a job and needing retraining, or starting a new life after a divorce or the death of a loved one, they experience a time of confusion and uncertainty. They feel the need to explore and have new experiences before focusing on specific goals. More than ever, times of transition are perfect times to conduct a personal inventory to identify values and priorities and begin to lay

the foundation for a new direction. For people dealing with life without major transitions, moving through time without goals may create feelings of aimlessly wandering that often lead to feelings of dissatisfaction, lack of purpose, and frustration with life that does not change in positive ways. Regardless of the situation, becoming clear about what you want in your life can get you on the path of setting and achieving meaningful goals. (See Exercise 4.1, Identifying Your Goals, page 91.)

2. *They believe goal setting is too restricting and requires too much commitment.* Some people shy away from making commitments, even when the commitments are in their best interest. This thinking may be linked to past experiences when goals were set for an individual by someone else and the goals were intended to meet someone else's expectations. Setting goals that are right for you, based on your values and priorities, is the opposite of restricting—it is liberating. Setting and achieving goals does require planning, motivation, work, and commitment, but when the commitment is to yourself, the priority shifts from meeting other people's expectations and needs to meeting your own.
3. *They fear failure.* Perhaps they believe that it is better to not try than to try and not succeed. Perhaps they tried setting goals in the past but became discouraged and frustrated when they failed to achieve their goals. Not achieving a goal, however, can provide valuable insights into better goal-setting techniques. Was the goal that was set unrealistically high? When a goal is unrealistically high, without proper attention to other factors or techniques for setting achievable goals, the goal setter is liable to fail. If the person does not believe from the start that the goal is achievable, he or she lacks adequate motivation and commitment to turn the goal into a reality. Was the goal set too low? When a goal is set too low, the person feels a lack of challenge or purpose to achieve the goal. The goal simply fades. Was the goal based on an outcome of being "the highest achiever or the very best performer" rather than on skills, knowledge, or performance on an individual level? Outcome-based goals in which you compete with others often lead to a sense of failure; even your personal best may not be perceived as success if someone else performed at a higher level. Setting goals based on your individual performance or acquisition of skills is more effective. You can overcome the fear of failure by learning to set realistic goals that express values, skills, and priorities that you yearn to achieve in your life and by using the steps for setting effective goals.
4. *They set too many goals and become overwhelmed.* People who are not used to setting goals may get so excited about setting goals that they "go overboard" by setting too many goals—usually short-term goals—at one time. Rather than move forward on one or two significant short-term goals, they try to work simultaneously on too many goals. Taking time to prioritize goals is the solution. Select the top two or three short-term goals that will receive your full attention every day. As you progress with those goals, you can add additional goals to your schedule. Recognize, however, that many of your short-term goals are steps to achieving some of your long-term goals. Taking time to see how the short-term goals fit into the larger picture of your long-term goals can help to minimize your sense of feeling overwhelmed.
5. *They do not know how to set goals.* Goal setting is more than wishful thinking or dreaming of what could be. Effective goal setting involves a systematic approach and plan of action to achieve a specific outcome. If you have always wanted to set goals but did not know how, the goal-setting steps and techniques in this chapter can guide you through the process.

6. *They are procrastinators.* **Procrastination**, the act of putting things off for a later time, is a learned behavior that can establish itself as a habit. Procrastinators may establish goals, but they seldom follow through and complete the steps to achieve those goals. The learned pattern of procrastinating can be unlearned; procrastinators can learn to be action oriented. (Chapter 5 discusses strategies to reduce or eliminate procrastination.)
7. *They do not understand the connection between cause and effect.* In *The Magic Lamp—Goal-Setting for People Who Hate Setting Goals,* Keith Ellis explains the relationship of cause and effect this way:

> No effect occurs without a cause; the cause must always precede the effect. Simple, inescapable, it's the easiest natural law to understand, and the easiest to forget. Who would stand in front of a wood stove and demand heat without first filling the stove with wood? Who would expect to make a withdrawal from a savings account before first making a deposit? Who would stand before a patch of barren earth and demand vegetables without first planting a garden? Life teaches us that we have to put wood in a wood stove *before* we get heat; we have to make a deposit *before* we can make a withdrawal; we have to plant seeds, water them, weed them, and nurture them before we can harvest our first ear of corn or pick our first tomato. Too often, we don't apply this knowledge to the way we run our lives.
>
> When you desire a specific effect in your life—like a more meaningful relationship, a better job, or an important accomplishment—you must *first* set in motion the cause of that effect. If the cause is missing, the effect will be missing as well. If the effect is missing, you can be certain that you have neglected to set in motion the appropriate cause. The most important decision you will ever make in life is this: *Do you choose to be a cause or an effect?* When you choose to be a cause, you make things happen. When you choose to be an effect, you settle for whatever happens to you. When you choose to be a cause, you become the star quarterback of your own life. When you choose to be an effect, you just watch from the stands. The difference between being a cause and being an effect is the difference between being a hammer and being a nail. One acts; the other is acted upon.
>
> [Source: http://www.keithellis.com/sample.html; a sample chapter from *The Magic Lamp,* by Keith Ellis.]

Reflection Writing 2 — CHAPTER 4

On a separate piece of paper or in a journal, do the following:

1. **Explain your long-term educational goals. What certificate or degree do you plan to obtain?**
2. **What are the requirements for your program? Locate a printed page of a catalog or brochure that shows the sequence of classes and requirements you need to complete.**
3. **Use the information from step 2 or information you have received from your adviser to develop a plan to reach your long-term goal. List the courses you plan to take each term and any program modifications you plan to implement to finish your certificate or degree.**

Name ________________________________ Date ____________

Exercise 4.1 Identifying Your Goals

Five-Year and Two-Year Goals

What goals do you want to achieve in the following areas five years *and* two years *from now? The two-year goals may be intermediary goals or "stepping stones" to your five-year goals. Be as specific as possible.*

	Five-Year Goals	Two-Year Goals
Education		
Finances		
Health		
Physical condition		
Career		
Social life		
Family life		
Community life		
Emotional well-being		
Spiritual growth		
Other:		
Other:		

What short-term goals do you want to achieve this term? *For categories that are not a priority for this term, simply state "none at this time." For the other categories, be as specific as possible.*

Short-Term Goals for This Term

Education	
Finances	
Health	
Physical condition	
Career	
Social life	
Family life	
Community life	
Emotional well-being	
Spiritual growth	
Other:	
Other:	

Using a Four-Step Approach for Writing Goals

Many people have good intentions and a strong desire or motivation to succeed by achieving their goals; however, many of these same people fall short of making their goals reality. Frequently the inability to achieve goals begins with the lack of a sound process or strategy to write effective goals. You can learn to set and achieve all kinds of goals that will enhance your performance, increase the balance in your life, and move you closer to being the person you want to be and to achieving the things you would like to have in your life by using the following four-step process for writing effective goals.

Four Steps for Writing Effective Goals

1. Set **S**pecific, clear, and realistic goals.
2. Set a specific **T**arget date and time to complete each goal.
3. Identify the individual **S**teps involved in reaching the goal.
4. Plan a **R**eward for yourself when you reach the goal.

Step 1: **Set Specific Goals** When your goal is clear, specific, and realistic, you have an exact picture of what you wish to achieve. To simply say "I will do better" or "I want something new" results in vague goals whose achievements are not easily measured. To say "I will be a millionaire tomorrow" is not realistic for most people. Before you commit to a goal, evaluate whether the goal is clear, specific, and realistic for you.

Step 2: **Set a Specific Target Date and Time** Procrastinators (people who put off doing something) seldom achieve goals. You can reduce or eliminate procrastination by setting a specific target date (deadline) and even a specific time to finish the steps involved in reaching your goal. The target date works as a form of motivation to keep you moving forward and on time.

Step 3: **Identify Steps** Careful planning of the steps involved in achieving a goal makes it possible for you to allocate enough time to complete each step. Take time to think through the individual steps required. List these steps on paper. If several steps are involved, list specific target dates for completing each step. When you use this method of breaking one large goal into several smaller ones, a goal that extends over a long period of time can be treated as a series of smaller goals to be accomplished on their own time lines.

Step 4: **Plan a Reward** You can celebrate the completion of a goal with a reward. You can also use that same reward as an incentive—a motivation—to meet your goal. There are two kinds of rewards you can include in your goal-setting plan: extrinsic rewards and intrinsic rewards.

Extrinsic rewards are material things or activities that you will give yourself after you reach your goal. The following are examples of extrinsic rewards: buy a tape, buy a new shirt, go to a movie, go out to dinner, plan a short trip.

Intrinsic rewards are the emotions or feelings you know you will experience when you reach a goal. Many people can be motivated just by recognizing that when the goal is reached, they will enjoy feelings such as increased self-esteem, pride, relief, joy, more confidence, or immense satisfaction.

A reward is a strong motivator only if you use it *after* you reach the goal. You must also withhold the reward if you do not reach the goal. For rewards to work as motivators, select rewards that truly represent what you *want* and can look forward to receiving.

Example of the Four Steps in Goal Setting

Step 1—Specific goal: Organize my desk to create an ideal study area

Step 2—Target date and time: Have it done by this Sunday at 4:00

Step 3—Specific steps:

1. Separate my bills and mail from the other things on my desk. Put them in a separate basket.
2. Sort my notes and homework assignments according to my classes.
3. For each class, put current assignments and notes into my notebooks in chronological order. Put all other into file folders. Label each folder.
4. Organize my textbooks, dictionary, and other references. Find bookends to use to stand them up.
5. Organize my supplies into a box or into the drawer.
6. Get rid of any remaining clutter. Empty wastepaper basket.

Step 4—Reward: Extrinsic: Go out for pizza and a movie with friends.

Using Goal-Setting Tips to Keep Your Momentum

Have you ever started working toward a well-planned goal with great enthusiasm and conviction, only to find yourself quitting before reaching the goal? There are many distractions and obstacles that can move you off your course of action. The following tips can help you stay motivated and keep the momentum moving toward the completion of your goal.

Tips for Reaching Goals

1. Use a goal organizer.
2. Evaluate and prioritize your goals.
3. Monitor your progress on a daily or weekly basis.
4. Break larger goals into a series of smaller goals.
5. Visualize yourself reaching your goal.
6. Use affirmations to reinforce your goal.
7. Acknowledge and praise yourself.

Use a Goal Organizer

Begin by clarifying your values, your purpose, and your general approach to achieving a specific goal. You can use this goal organizer for long-term, intermediary, short-term, and immediate goals. A **goal organizer** helps you:

- think seriously about your goal
- plan a course of action to achieve the goal
- predict possible obstacles
- prepare a strategy to deal with the obstacles

Goal Organizer

1. What is your goal?	
2. What benefits will you gain by achieving this goal?	
3. What consequences will you experience by *not* achieving this goal?	
4. What obstacles might you encounter while working on this goal?	
5. How can you deal with the obstacles effectively if they occur?	
6. What people or resources could help you with achieving this goal?	

Evaluate and Prioritize Your Goals

If you are having difficulty with a specific goal, ask yourself the following questions:

1. *Is this goal still important or relevant?* Goals, especially long-term goals, can become outdated. Life circumstances change and more significant goals can replace old goals. If a goal is no longer of value to you, abandon it. Do not, however, abandon a goal because it is more difficult to achieve or requires more from you than you had anticipated.
2. *Are other goals more important?* If you feel overwhelmed, you may be trying to achieve too many goals at one time. Make a list of the goals you are working on and then prioritize them. Pay attention to target dates so you begin lower-priority goals *after* you finish higher-priority goals.

Monitor Your Progress

For immediate or short-term goals, monitor your progress on a daily or weekly basis. Begin each day by asking yourself what actions or steps you will take that day to move forward with your goals. You may want to write your goals on index cards and then place the cards in several locations in your house and in your notebook. Documenting the progress you make each day in a daily journal is another way to monitor your progress and recognize the work you are doing to make your goals a reality. As you write in your daily journal, ask yourself whether there are better ways to work on the goal and whether you are pleased with that day's results.

Break Larger Goals into a Series of Smaller Goals

Any time a goal seems too overwhelming, think of the goal as a series of steps. Each step is a subgoal, but you can treat each step as a goal by itself. Every time you complete one of the smaller goals, move to the next step or subgoal. You can work your way to completing the larger goal with less stress and fewer feelings of being overwhelmed.

Visualize Yourself Reaching Your Goal

Close your eyes and try to visualize yourself achieving your goal. How do you feel? How does it change your life? How does it affect others? **Visualization**, the process of picturing or imagining information or events in your mind, is a powerful tool for learning and goal setting. If you have difficulty visualizing yourself achieving a goal, the goal may not be realistic or right for you. Ask yourself these questions: *Did I set this goal for myself or was the goal imposed by someone else or to please someone else? Why did I choose the goal in the first place? Does this goal express what I truly want to achieve or do I need to rethink what I want to achieve? Is the goal no longer appropriate for my given situation?*

Use Affirmations

Affirmations are positive statements used as motivators. Affirmations help change your basic belief systems, your self-image, and the direction you are moving to make changes in your life.

Use the following guidelines to write effective affirmations and then repeat the affirmations several times daily:

1. *Use positive words and tones.* Avoid using words such as *no, never, won't.* Say, for instance, "I complete my written work on time," not "I will never turn in a paper late again."
2. *Write in the present tense.* Present tense in verbs gives the sense that the behavior already exists. When you think and believe in the present tense, your actions begin to match your beliefs. Say, for example, "I am a non-smoker," rather than "I will stop smoking soon."
3. *Write with certainty and conviction.* Say, for instance, "I exercise for thirty minutes every day," not "I want to exercise more each day."
4. *Keep the affirmation short and simple.* Brief, simple affirmations are easier to remember and repeat.

Use these guidelines to practice writing affirmations for yourself.

____

____

____

____

____

____

Acknowledge and Praise Yourself

You can be your best cheerleader, supporter, and motivator. Practice acknowledging your accomplishments and your daily successes by praising yourself and giving yourself a pat on the back. For example, when you successfully rework a math problem from class, tell yourself, "Good job; you got that one right." When you complete a step in one of your goals, tell yourself, "Well done; you're on your way to succeeding." Positive words to yourself reinforce your positive actions and provide a steady stream of intrinsic motivation.

Name ____________________ Date __________

✎ EXERCISE 4.2 Reflecting on Tips for Reaching Goals

Complete the following directions to show how you could use the seven tips for reaching goals.

1. Select any one of the short-term goals that you wrote in Exercise 4.1 for this term. With that goal in mind, complete the following goal organizer.

Goal Organizer

1. What is your goal?	
2. What benefits will you gain by achieving this goal?	
3. What consequences will you experience by *not* achieving this goal?	
4. What obstacles might you encounter while working on this goal?	
5. How can you deal with the obstacles effectively if they occur?	
6. What people or resources could help you with achieving this goal?	

2. Make a list of five goals that are *not* related to school work and that you would like to accomplish this week. Use the numbers 1 through 5 to prioritize these goals, with 1 the most important and 5 the least important.

3. What method do you prefer to use to monitor your progress?

4. In the column on the left, give an example of one of your goals that seems too overwhelming to begin. On the right, rewrite the goal as a series of several smaller goals.

Large Goal ____________________ Smaller Goals ____________________

5. Describe the picture in your mind that appears when you visualize yourself reaching your goal.

6. Write a meaningful affirmation that you would like to use on a regular basis.

7. When is the last time you acknowledged an accomplishment or gave yourself praise? Briefly explain the circumstances and describe how you patted yourself on the back.

EXERCISE 4.3 **Achieving an Immediate Goal**

Use the four goal-setting steps to tackle a small task that you would like to accomplish but keep putting off doing. For example, you could set a goal to organize an area in your house; clean a specific closet, cupboard, or room; perform a minor repair on your car; weed a garden; mend some clothes; organize a notebook; or arrange a study area in your home. Select an immediate goal, one that can be completed within the next few days. (If the goal is larger, such as clean the garage, *break it down into smaller goals; then, for this exercise, select one of the smaller goals, such as* organize the workbench area.*) Complete each step below unless your instructor asks you to write your responses on a separate piece of paper.*

1. What is the *specific* goal? ____________________

2. What are the *target date* and *time* to complete this goal? ____________________

3. What are the individual *steps* you must complete to achieve the goal? List each step.

4. What is your reward? ____________________

5. Did you achieve your goal by the target date and time? ____________________

   If yes, explain what contributed to your success. If no, describe the obstacles that interfered with the process. ____________________

Combining Goal Setting and Time-Management Skills for Studying

What goal-setting strategies do you think these students used in order to take their tests with minimal stress?

You can combine the four steps for writing effective goals with your time-management skills. The relationship between goal setting and time management is strong. Without time management, you might not find adequate time to work on your goals. Without goal setting, you might not use your time wisely or productively. You can use this combination of goal setting and time management effectively for academic work in three ways.

Ways to Combine Goal Setting with Time Management

1. Write immediate goals for study blocks.
2. Create a five-day study plan to prepare for a test.
3. Develop a long-term goal for a term-long project.

Immediate Goals for a Study Block

On page 66 you learned to create a task schedule. A **task schedule** is a list of immediate goals to achieve during a specific block of time. If the block of time is a study block, your task schedule shows the specific activities you plan to complete during the study block. Your task schedule is step 3 of the four-step process for setting goals. To convert a task schedule into a four-step goal, recognize that the goal and the target date and time are built into the task schedule. All you need to add to the task schedule is your intrinsic or extrinsic reward for completion of the steps in the study block. The following example shows a plan for an immediate goal for a study block.

A Study Block Goal

Step 1—Specific goal: Review math class and do math homework pp. 26–33.

Step 2—Target date and time: Wednesday, 10:00–11:00

Step 3—Specific steps:

1. Review class notes.
2. Rework class problems.
3. Read pages 26–32. Highlight key points.
4. Do even-numbered problems on p. 33.
5. Check answers with answer key. Study/rework any incorrect answers.

Step 4—Reward: Extrinsic: Watch my favorite show on television.

A Five-Day Study Plan to Prepare for a Test

A **five-day study plan** helps you organize your materials and time to review for a major test, such as a midterm or a final exam. This plan promotes distributed practice and ongoing review and reduces tendencies to procrastinate, cram, or suffer test anxiety. Recall, or the ability to retrieve information from long-term memory, occurs more comfortably. The same four steps that you use to write other kinds of goals can be used in writing a five-day study plan.

Step 1: Be specific and realistic.

Begin by making a list of all the topics that you need to review for the test. List the chapters, class lecture notes, homework assignments, lab reports, group projects, or any other materials covered in the class.

Step 2: Set target times and dates.

Days 1, 2, 3, and 4, with specific time blocks, are organized review sessions. Schedule day 5 the day before the test; on day 5 plan to dedicate all of your study time to reviewing the special notes you created in step 3, below. Mark these days and times on your calendar or your weekly schedule.

Five-Day Study Plan

Monday review:	Wednesday review:	Friday	Saturday	Sunday
8–9:00 A.M.	8–9:00 A.M.	8–9:00 A.M.	10:00 A.M.–12:00 P.M.	2:00–4:00 P.M.
3–4:00 P.M.	3–4:00 P.M.	3–4:00 P.M.	4:00–6:00 P.M.	7:00–9:00 P.M.

Step 3: Identify the steps involved.

This step requires careful planning and completion of four processes:

First, refer to the list of materials you need to review. Group the items in four logical categories; you will review one category of information on each of the first four days of your five-day schedule.

Second, to avoid wasting precious review time, create a pattern or plan for reviewing in your mind or on paper. Perhaps you always want to begin by reading the chapter summary, reviewing your textbook notes, reviewing your class notes, reviewing your homework assignment, and reviewing terminology.

Third, to use your time efficiently, select one or more forms of summary notes to use as you review each chapter. **Summary notes** are special notes that you make for only the materials that need to be reviewed one final time before the test. If you have used effective learning strategies and ongoing review throughout the term, you will already know many concepts and terms; these do not need to appear in summary notes. The following formats are commonly used for summary notes. (These formats will be discussed further in Chapters 9 and 11.)

Fourth, indicate on your five-day plan what you will review each day. See the example of the five-day study plan on page 102.

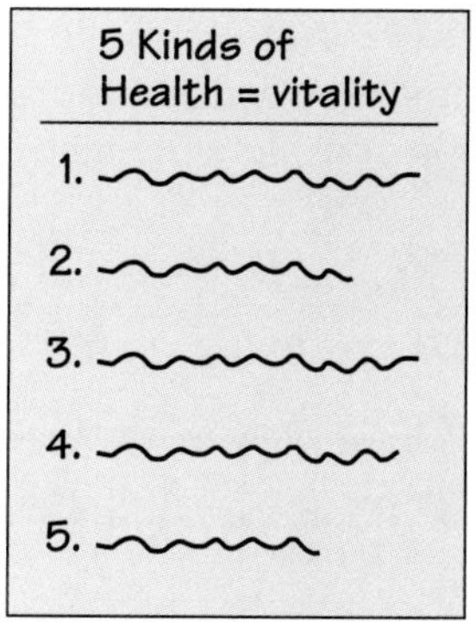

Lists/Categories of information to remember

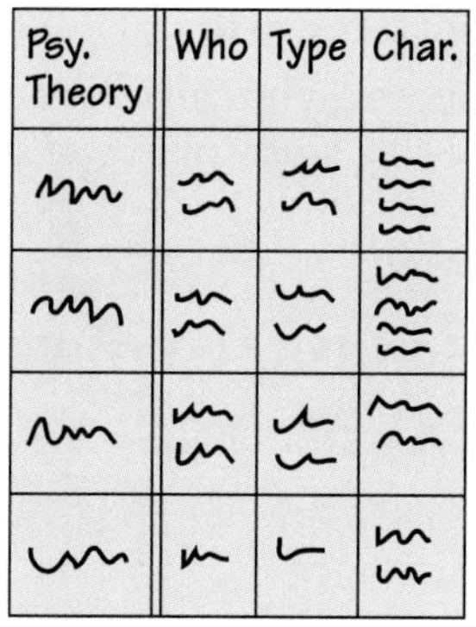

Comparison charts to compare or contrast different subjects studied

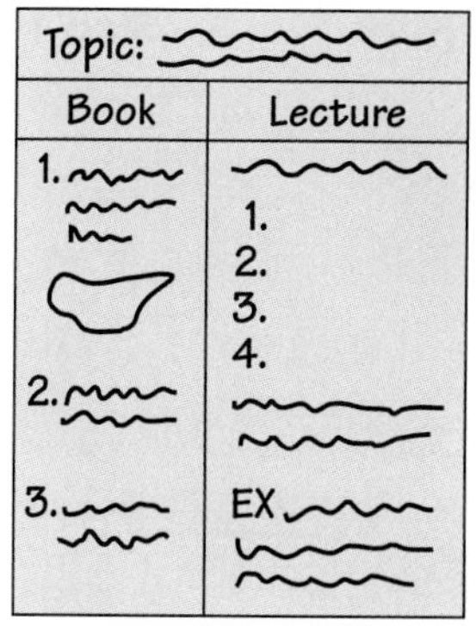

Notes based on topics that include textbook and lecture information

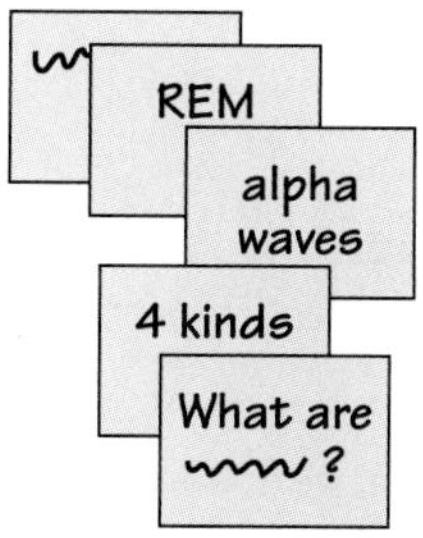

Flash cards of categories and terminology

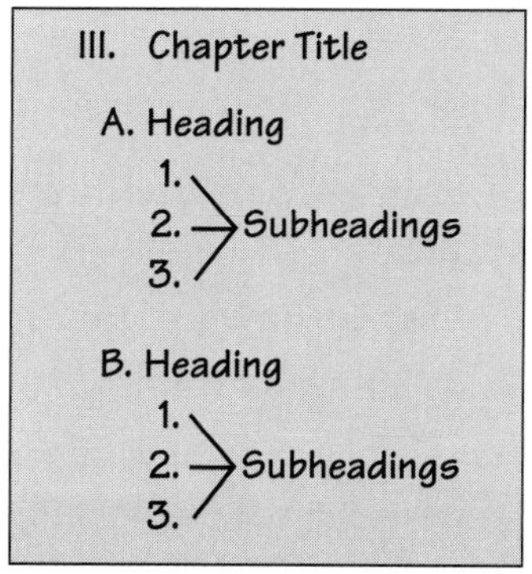

Chapter outlines made by using headings and subheadings

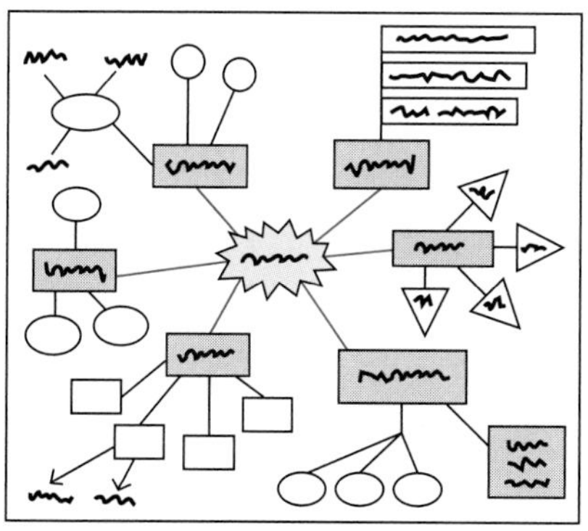

Visual mappings for individual chapters or topics that appear in several different chapters

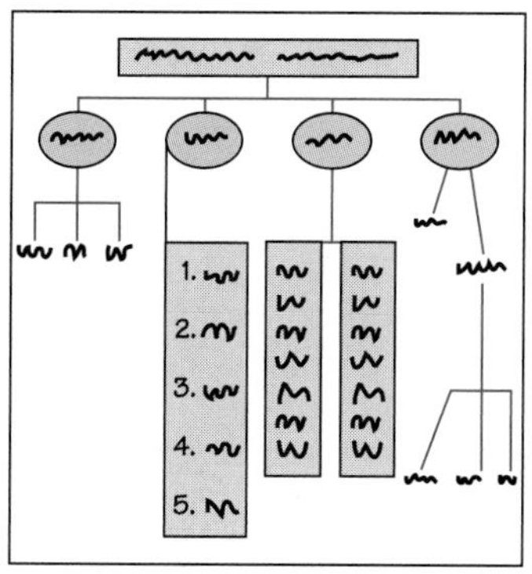

Large hierarchies made on poster paper to include several topics or chapters

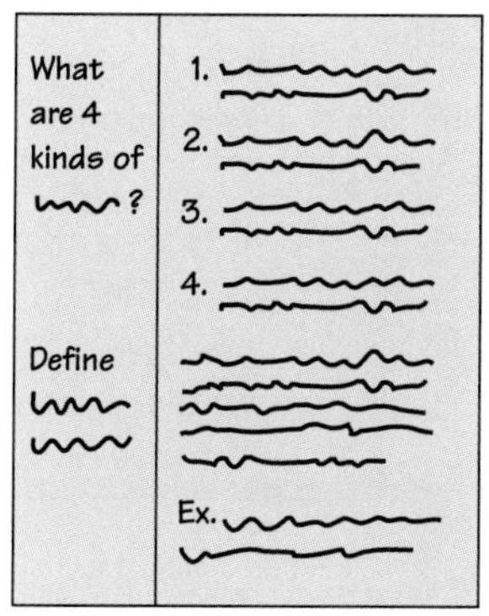

Cornell notes with study questions on the left for self-quizzing (see Chapter 9).

Step 4: Plan a reward.

Choose an intrinsic or an extrinsic reward for yourself *after* you complete your five-day study plan *and* after you complete the test.

Goal for a Five-Day Study Plan

Step 1—Be specific and realistic: Prepare for the midterm in sociology scheduled for Monday by reviewing:

Chapters 1–4	The two short papers	Homework questions
Terminology (study guides)	Notes from guest speaker	Notes from video
Lecture notes	Textbook notes	

Step 2—Set target dates and times to study.

Mon. 8–9:00 A.M. 3–4:00 P.M.	Wed. 8–9:00 A.M. 3–4:00 P.M.	Fri. 8–9:00 A.M. 3–4:00 P.M.
Sat. 10–12:00 P.M. 4–6:00 P.M.	Sun. 2–4:00 P.M. 7–9:00 P.M.	

Step 3—Identify the steps involved: *Process: Review class work first, then textbook work. Make flash cards for things I need to review again.*

Step 4—Reward: At the end of each daily review time, use the intrinsic reward: the satisfaction that the studying is under control. After the test, use the extrinsic reward: a day trip to the coast next Saturday.

Monday	Wednesday	Friday	Saturday	Sunday
8-9:00 A.M. (Ch. 1) class study guide homework Q handouts	8-9:00 A.M. (Ch. 2) study guide homework Q video notes	8-9:00 A.M. (Ch. 3) class study guide handouts homework Q	10-12:00 P.M. (Ch. 4) study guide (no handouts) homework Q 2 short papers	2-4:00 P.M. Review summary notes; self-quiz on Ch. 1 & 2
3-4:00 P.M. (Ch. 1) lecture notes textbook notes Notes-Guest speaker	3-4:00 P.M. (Ch. 2) lecture notes textbook notes	3-4:00 P.M. (Ch. 3) lecture notes textbook notes	4-6:00 P.M. (Ch. 4) lecture notes textbook notes	7-9:00 P.M. Review summary notes; self-quiz on Ch. 3 & 4

Long-Term Goals for Term-Long Projects

Some instructors assign at the beginning of the term a project that is not due until the middle or the end of the term. Many students get a false sense of time; rather than start right away, they put off the assignment until too close to the due date. Unnecessary stress is added, plus study times for other classes often have to be neglected so that the project can be finished. As soon as you are assigned a **term-long project**, begin planning a schedule for that project.

For example, assume that you receive the following assignment in week 3 of the term. The final project is due week 9:

> Assignment: *Select one of your favorite American poets. Do research in the library or on the Internet to learn about the life of this author. Summarize significant information about the author that influenced his or her work. Select two of the author's poems. Write a paragraph or two to discuss the structure and meaning of each poem.*

The following steps can guide you through the process of completing the assignment on time.

1. *Break the assignment into specific tasks.* What are the actual tasks you will need to work through from the beginning to the end of the project? Analyze the project carefully until you can identify the individual tasks involved. List these tasks or steps on paper.
2. *Estimate the time needed for each task.* Estimate the number of hours you think you will need to complete each task. Base this estimate on your past experiences with similar projects.
3. *Double the estimated time needed for each task.* You do not want to run out of time. To avoid any tendency to underestimate the amount of time you will need, double your estimate. In that way, you are giving yourself extra time in case you run into unforeseen problems or find that you have to change directions.

Step 1: List the Tasks	***Step 2: Estimated Time***	***Step 3: Doubled Time***
1. Review lists of American poets. Select one I like.	1 hr.	2 hrs.
2. Do library or Internet research on his or her life.	3 hrs.	6 hrs.
3. Read several of the author's poems. Find some that reflect influences of the author's life.	2 hrs.	4 hrs.
4. Write a draft of the summary of the author's life.	1 hr.	2 hrs.
5. Select two specific poems.	½ hr.	1 hr.
6. Write about the structure and the meaning of poem 1 (draft).	2 hrs.	4 hrs.
7. Write about the structure and the meaning of poem 2 (draft).	2 hrs.	4 hrs.
8. Revise the drafts and integrate into the final paper.	4 hrs.	8 hrs.
9. Proofread. Revise as needed.	1 hr.	2 hrs.
10. Assemble the final project. Include the poems, the research notes, and a bibliography.	½ hr.	1 hr.
Time to plan for project:		34 hrs.

4. *Record due dates on your term calendar for each task.* Consider the amount of hours needed for each task and the study block times (and flex times) you have available on your weekly schedules. Set a goal to complete each

task by a specific date. Each week when you make your weekly schedule, check this term calendar and add the tasks to your weekly schedule.

Week 3: Do Steps 1 and 2 (8 hours).
Week 4: Do Steps 3 and 4 (6 hours).
Week 5: Do Steps 5 and 6 (5 hours).
Week 6: Do Step 7 (4 hours).
Week 7: Do Step 8 (8 hours).
Week 8: Do Steps 9 and 10 (3 hours).
Week 9: I completed the project last week!

5. *Begin right away.* Do not waste time procrastinating. If you finish a task ahead of schedule, it is because you did not need the "doubled time" you allocated. Begin the next task immediately. If you finish your project ahead of schedule, you will have time to revise it again if you wish, and you will be able to breathe a sigh of relief!

Your Planning Sheet for a Long-Term Project

Step 1: List the Tasks	Step 2: Estimated Time	Step 3: Doubled Time
Time to plan for project:		

Exercise 4.4 Case Studies

Each of the following case studies describes a student situation. Read each case study carefully; highlight key ideas or student issues. Answer the question that ends each case study. In your response, address the key points that you highlighted and that relate directly to the question. Use complete sentences in your answers. These case studies are also available online; you can email your response to your instructor or print a copy of your work online.

1. Betty wants to be more efficient and productive. She sets weekly goals, but invariably things happen to disrupt her plans to complete her goals. When these unexpected events crop up, she gets frustrated and says that the goal was not that important. She has more uncompleted goals than she does successfully completed goals. What strategies can Betty use to change this pattern?

2. Ronnie is a "supermom" who "does everything for everyone." She feels she is able to do so much because she is an organized goal setter. Every Sunday she writes a new list of goals for the week. She adds more goals on a daily basis. At the end of each day, she often finds that she has to move the goals that are most important to her list for the next day. How can Ronnie improve her approach to writing and implementing goal setting?

3. This is Joel's fifth term in college. He has changed his major four times. His adviser wants him to create a long-term plan, but Joel keeps making excuses, saying he will do it "sometime soon." He resists the idea of goal setting because it makes him uncomfortable. What are some possible reasons why Joel avoids using goal-setting strategies?

Exercise 4.5 LINKS

Refer to the Terms to Know *on page 85. Work with a partner to recite the definitions of the terms out loud, in your own words, and in complete sentences. Alternate reciting the definitions. Circle any words you are unable to define. Return to one or more chapters that you have already studied. Repeat the process with the* Terms to Know *for those chapters.*

EXERCISE 4.6 Making Flash Cards

Making flash cards (index cards) for the terms and lists of items for each chapter provides you with study tools to use for review and for test preparation. If you had difficulty explaining any terms in Exercise 4.5, write each of those terms on the front of an index card and the definition on the back of the card. In addition to definition cards, you can also use the index cards to make review lists, such as the steps for writing effective goals or the two kinds of rewards. For review lists, write the category on the front and the list of steps on the back. To use your cards for review, read the front of the card. Recite the information out loud and then check your accuracy by looking at the back of the card. Sort the cards into two piles: terms and lists you know and terms and lists you need to study further.

Flash Cards for Definitions
(Definition Cards)

front	back
intrinsic rewards	Rewards in the form of emotions or feelings you receive when you complete a goal; pride, relief, joy, or satisfaction

Flash Cards for Lists
(Category Cards)

front	back
Steps for effective goal setting	1. Specific goal 2. Target date and time 3. Steps 4. Rewards

Reflection Writing 3 CHAPTER 4

On a separate piece of paper or in a journal, do the following:

Discuss which topics or strategies in this chapter are potentially the most valuable or important to you. Explain why and how you will benefit from this information.

SUMMARY

- Goals are well-defined plans aimed at achieving a specific result in any area of your life. Long-term, intermediary, short-term, and immediate goals vary in the length of time required to achieve the final result, but all four kinds of goals are well-defined plans to achieve success.
- Motivation is the feeling, emotion, or desire that moves a person to take action. Motivation is an integral part of goal setting.
- A systematic four-step approach can be used to write effective goals for all areas of your life:
  1. Set **S**pecific, clear, and realistic goals.
  2. Set a specific **T**arget date and time to complete each goal.
  3. Identify the individual **S**teps involved in reaching the goal.
  4. Plan a **R**eward (intrinsic or extrinsic) for yourself when you reach the goal.
- Tips for keeping your momentum and reaching your goals include using a goal organizer, evaluating and prioritizing your goals, monitoring your progress on a regular basis, breaking larger goals into smaller goals, using visualization and affirmations, and acknowledging and praising yourself.
- Time management and goal setting work in a close partnership. For academic work, you can use goal setting for study blocks, to prepare for tests, and to complete term-long projects.
- You can convert a time-management task schedule to an immediate goal for a study block by listing the individual tasks you want to complete during a study block and identifying a reward.
- You can use the four steps for writing goals to create a five-day study plan to prepare for a major test. Days 1 through 4 are review days for specific chapters and materials and time to create special summary notes. Day 5 of this plan is set aside to review the summary notes and materials you generated on review days 1 through 4.
- You can use the four steps for writing goals to organize and plan a term-long project. After you identify the specific tasks that you need to do to complete the project, estimate the hours you think you will need for each task. Then double your estimated times and write target dates for each task on a term calendar.

ACE Practice Tests, which are scored online, supplementary exercises, enrichment activities, and related web site links are available online for *Essential Study Skills*, 4e. Use the following directions to access this web site:

Type: **http://college.hmco.com/collegesurvival/students**

Click on *List of Sites by Author*. Use the arrow to scroll down to Wong *Essential Study Skills*, 4e. Click on the title. If you are working on your own computer, bookmark this web site.

LEARNING OPTIONS

The following learning options provide you with opportunities to demonstrate your understanding of the topics in Chapter 4. Your instructor may assign one or more specific options or may ask you to select one or more options that interest you the most.

1. Expand the Chapter 4 mapping on page 85. You can add pictures and colors to your mapping to accentuate the points. (See the example in Chapter 1, page 25.) Use the chapter mapping as your guide to write a short summary paragraph that converts the information on your mapping into sentence and paragraph form.
2. For one week, write an immediate goal or a task schedule for every study block for any one of your classes. If you would like, you can create a form that shows the individual steps. Record your work in a journal. At the end of each study block, write a short statement to pat yourself on the back, use positive self-talk, or comment on the effectiveness of the task schedule for that study block.
3. Use the Internet or the library periodicals (magazine) section to locate meaningful information about goal setting. Print or copy the information. Prepare a short presentation or a written summary that discusses the information and its significance. In your presentation or summary, explain how the contents of the web site relate to the content of Chapter 4.
4. Create a plan for a term-long project, or create a five-day study plan for a major upcoming test. Include specific details for each step of your plan. Refer to pages 102 and 103 for the steps and the examples. As you move through the plan, keep notes to show your progress and any obstacles that you encounter.
5. Create an inspirational poster that depicts various people who have achieved success by setting goals. Use your library periodicals (magazine) and newspaper sections, as well as any magazines you may have, to locate stories about personal achievements. On your poster, you may photocopy, draw, or use published pictures from magazines you own. Include information about the individuals' goals and accomplishments.
6. On paper or on the computer, enlarge the goal organizer on page 95 and make three copies. Complete the goal organizer for three separate goals: an immediate, a short-term, and a long-term goal. These goals may apply to your personal life, your academic life, or your work life. Be specific and give sufficient detail to show that you put serious thought into your goal organizers.
7. Create a study tape for yourself for Chapter 4. On your tape, summarize or explain the most important points of the chapter that you need to learn. This tape will serve as an excellent review later in the term.

Chapter 4 REVIEW QUESTIONS

True–False

Carefully read the following statements. Write T if the statement is true and F if it is false.

_______ 1. Setting a specific target date to complete a goal can help reduce or eliminate procrastination.

_______ 2. Extrinsic rewards involve positive feelings, a sense of pride, and renewed motivation to tackle new goals.

_______ 3. Visualizing yourself completing a goal is a technique that helps you keep up your momentum and motivation to achieve success.

_______ 4. Affirmations should include words such as *no, never,* or *won't* so you have a constant reminder of the negative things you want to avoid in your life.

_______ 5. If a goal seems too overwhelming, you should discard it and write only immediate goals that you can achieve in one day.

_______ 6. A person who sets too many goals may benefit from prioritizing the goals so he or she can dedicate time to the goals that are the most important.

_______ 7. A goal organizer helps a person identify the benefits of achieving and the consequences of not achieving a goal, anticipate possible obstacles, and create a plan to deal with obstacles individually or with the help of other people or resources.

_______ 8. To make a large goal more manageable, you can break it into a series of smaller goals, each with its own target date, steps, and reward.

_______ 9. In a five-day study plan, you should create summary notes on the last day of the plan so you have something to review quickly an hour or two before a major test.

_______ 10. When you plan a term-long project, you should double the estimated time to complete each step of the project to compensate for underestimating the time needed to complete individual tasks successfully.

Definitions

Write two or three sentences to define and explain the following terms.

1. intermediary goal

2. extrinsic reward

3. summary notes

Short Answer and Critical Thinking

Answer the following questions using information and terminology from this chapter. Answer in complete sentences.

1. If a student tries to shorten the four-step process for writing effective goals by omitting one of the steps, the process will be weakened and therefore less effective. Discuss negative outcomes that might occur by eliminating any *one* specific step of the process. Identify the step and then the outcomes if the step is omitted.

2. Discuss any two reasons some people shy away from setting goals. Briefly add suggestions or strategies these people could use to change their attitudes toward setting goals.

3. What is the relationship between goal setting and motivation?

CHAPTER 5

Increasing Concentration; Decreasing Stress and Procrastination

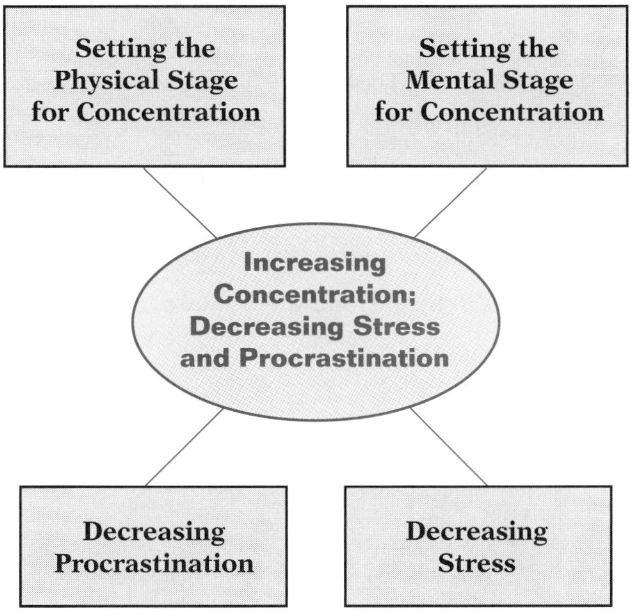

Setting the physical stage for concentration involves creating an ideal study area that promotes learning. Setting the mental stage for concentration involves creating a state of mind that is receptive to learning and capable of blocking out different kinds of distractors. Stress, which is wear and tear on our bodies, needs to be monitored and managed before it becomes excessive. A variety of techniques can reduce the cognitive, physical, and emotional effects of stress. Procrastination, the process of delaying what needs to be done, is a self-defeating behavior that can be reduced or eliminated through a variety of effective strategies.

Terms to Know

concentration
ideal study area
active learning
task schedule
chunking
study ritual
warm-ups
external distractors
internal distractors
take charge
say *no*
no need
red bow
checkmark
mental storage box
tunnel vision
mental rehearsal
emotional *e* words
positive self-talk
affirmations
stress
visualization
perfect place
soothing mask
relaxation blanket
breathing by threes
deep breathing
deep muscle relaxation
procrastination
motivation
fear of failure
self-efficacy
seeing success

CHAPTER 5 Increasing Concentration; Decreasing Stress and Procrastination Profile

DO, SCORE, and **RECORD** your profile before you read this chapter. If you need to review the process, refer to the complete directions given in the Profile for Chapter 1 on page 2.

ONLINE: You can complete the profile and get your score online at this textbook's web site.

	YES	NO
1. My study area has two sources of light, a low noise level, an adequate work surface, and an availability of materials and supplies.	______	______
2. I often study with the radio, stereo, or television turned on.	______	______
3. I set individual goals for study blocks before I begin studying.	______	______
4. I stop studying when I become uninterested, unmotivated, or bored.	______	______
5. I use specific concentration strategies on a regular basis to help me keep my focus when I study.	______	______
6. I have difficulty getting started on assignments when I sit down to study.	______	______
7. My level of stress often reduces my performance or ability to concentrate.	______	______
8. When I feel overwhelmed, I break large assignments into a series of smaller, more manageable tasks or steps.	______	______
9. I tend to procrastinate when faced with unpleasant or uninteresting tasks.	______	______
10. I put my greatest amount of effort into my work at the last minute because I work best under pressure.	______	______

Reflection Writing 1 — CHAPTER 5

On a separate piece of paper or in a journal, do the following:

1. Discuss your profile score for this chapter. What was your score? What does it mean to you?
2. What do you see as your greatest problems with concentration, stress, and procrastination?

Setting the Physical Stage for Concentration

Concentration is the ability to block out distractions so you can focus your mind on one specific item or task. Concentration is a flighty process; you can concentrate one minute and then easily become distracted and lose that concentration the very next. Concentration is a mental discipline that requires a concerted effort to train your mind to keep focused. As discussed in Chapter 2, concentration is also a memory principle, a key element in the process of learning.

To increase your ability to concentrate, give careful attention to your physical environment. The noise level, lighting, and work space can directly affect your ability to concentrate. An **ideal study area** has few or no distractions that will affect that concentration.

An Ideal Study Area

1. The noise level is conducive to studying.
2. The lighting includes two or more sources of light.
3. The work space promotes concentration.

The Noise Level

Studying, comprehending, and thinking critically involve complex thought processes. An environment filled with noise disrupts the thought processes and mental focus. The following three types of students show how tolerance levels for noise and perceived levels of concentration vary.

1. People with short attention spans or attention deficit disorder (ADD) often need a quiet, motionless environment. Their ideal study area is a quiet room, such as a bedroom, an office, or a small space in a library with few or no distractions.
2. People with longer attention spans can block out minor noises and distractions. They have a wider choice of study areas at school and at home. They are able to concentrate in open spaces, such as a lab area, the library, or various rooms at home. Minor movement does not create distractions.
3. People who are used to an environment with a lot of noise and movement say that they can concentrate and study effectively in noisy, busy areas. They believe they concentrate best with music playing, the television turned on, people talking in the background, or foot traffic passing by. However, research shows that excessive noise and music with words and frequent variations in rhythm interrupt thought processes and brainwave patterns. Though these people may feel they are concentrating, their concentration more likely turns on and off and on and off in split-second intervals because the brain processes only one item at a time. Trying to study with excessive noise in the environment is a time waster; removing the noise and movement in the environment often leads to more efficient studying in less time.

As you strive to increase your ability to concentrate, use any of the following suggestions to create an environment that has a level of noise conducive to effective studying:

1. Use earplugs or a headset to create silence if you work best in a quiet environment.

2. Turn on a small fan or play soft, classical music if you are distracted by silence. These gentle sounds create a buffer between you and the rest of the environment. Research shows that soft, classical and instrumental music (especially Baroque music) is conducive to learning; the music positively alters brainwave patterns (alpha waves) and assists the learning process by creating a relaxed, receptive state of mind.
3. If you are in the habit of studying with the television turned on, replace the sound (and visual stimulus) with soft, classical background music. The visual and verbal stimuli emitted by television force the brain to tune in, tune out, tune in, tune out to the point where you do not retain either the entire contents of the television program or what you are studying. Studying with the television on is simply not time efficient. Television is more effective as an extrinsic reward *after* you complete your study block.
4. If you are in the habit of studying in a cafeteria, restaurant, coffee shop, lounge area, or in an area that is the center of family or household activity, seek a new study location that has less noise and traffic. Students who move from noisy, busy environments to locations with less stimuli often find that they become more productive and retain information more effectively and efficiently.

The Lighting

Proper lighting is important in any study area. If you have too little light, your eyes can easily become strained and tired. Some lighting can create shadows or glare on your books. To avoid many of the problems created by poor lighting, have two sources of light in your study area. This may inlcude an overhead light and a desk lamp or two lamps in different locations. Two sources of lighting may seem like a minor detail, but sometimes ignoring small details leads to big problems.

Many students have the choice to live in campus dorms or off-campus in their own apartments. What factors might affect the study areas in either of these locations?

The Work Space

Attention to your work space at home and at school results in the most effective and productive use of your study time. The following techniques can help you create an ideal work space to promote concentration:

1. Sit on a comfortable chair at a table or desk that has a work surface with enough room to spread out your books, notebook, paper, and necessary supplies. Sitting on a couch, in a recliner, or on a bed is not conducive to the

level of concentration needed for effective studying; handling the textbook, taking notes, and completing homework assignments becomes awkward and ineffective.

2. If you work at a kitchen table, remove all items unrelated to studying. This breaks the subconscious association with meals and eating; you will reduce the tendency to stop work and get up for snacks or beverages.
3. Take time to remove clutter from your work surface. A table or desk that is cluttered with bills, correspondence, or materials for hobbies creates instant distractions.
4. To avoid having to get up, equip your study area with basic supplies for studying. Organize your study area at home using file folders for important papers and small boxes, trays, or drawers for items such as pens, pencils, highlighting pens, a calculator, a spell checker, a stapler, index cards, and paper clips. Organize your study area at school by equipping your backpack with the same essential supplies.

EXERCISE 5.1 My Ideal Study Area

In the middle column in the chart below, describe your typical study areas at home and at school. In the right column, describe the changes you could make to create a more ideal study area.

Home	**Current Study Area**	**Ideal Study Area**
Noise		
Movement nearby		
Lighting		
Chair		
Work surface		
Supplies		
School		
Noise		
Movement nearby		
Lighting		
Chair		
Work surface		
Supplies		

Setting the Mental Stage for Concentration

Concentration is a mental process affected by your external environment and your physical, emotional, and attitudinal states. Creating the ideal study area helps you control the effects of the external environment on your concentration. The following strategies will help you create the ideal state of mind for increased concentration and effective studying.

Strategies for Setting the Mental Stage

1. Be an active learner.
2. Use goal-setting techniques.
3. Do warm-ups at the beginning of each study block.
4. Use techniques to deal with internal and external distractors.

Be an Active Learner

Active learning (the opposite of passive learning) means you are actively involved in the learning process. You can combat many internal distractors such as feeling sleepy, bored, uninterested, or unmotivated by becoming more of a participant in the learning process. Unlike reading without remembering what you have read, or working in a mechanical way, active learning promotes critical thinking, multisensory learning, and greater comprehension. All of the following learning strategies are used by active learners:

1. Have a pen in your hand when you study. Take notes, write questions, or jot down lists of information you need to learn.
2. Use markers to highlight important information in the textbook or in your notes.
3. Talk out loud (recite) as you study to activate your auditory channel and improve both concentration and comprehension.
4. Write summaries or make other kinds of study tools such as visual mappings, hierarchies, flash cards, or comparison charts.
5. Quiz yourself on the material you are studying. Write or recite questions and answers.

Use Goal-Setting Techniques

Goal-setting techniques help you organize and prioritize your tasks, focus your mind, and create a plan of action. All of these benefits of goal setting lead to setting an effective mental stage to be productive and effective.
To increase your level of concentration, use the following goal-setting techniques:

1. Create a **task schedule** at the beginning of each study block (see page 66). Identify what needs to be done during the study block; organize the tasks or assignments in order of priority. Create a motivational reward for yourself upon successful completion of the study block.
2. For large assignments, or assignments that will require several study blocks to complete, use the **chunking** technique, which involves breaking an assignment into sections. With chunking, longer or more detailed assignments become manageable. Rather than feeling frustrated or overwhelmed, you will become more motivated and confident that the situation is under control.
3. Create a **study ritual** or routine to use each time you study. Having a ritual can save time and confusion by allowing you to get started quickly. A study ritual helps you move directly into the mindset needed to study. For example, your ritual might be to use a quick relaxation or visualization technique, create a task schedule, and do a warm-up. Establishing a goal to create a study ritual takes only a few minutes!

Do Warm-Ups at the Beginning of a Study Block

Warm-ups are used at the beginning of a study block to create a mindset and a focus on the topic you intend to study. Warm-ups, which require only 5 or 10 minutes of your time, include *previewing* and *reviewing* information:

1. *Preview:* Skim through the new chapter or assignment. If you plan to read a new chapter, survey it by looking through the key elements of the chapter

before you begin to read (see Chapter 7). If you plan to work on a homework assignment, glance over the entire assignment, including the directions and your class notes about the assignment. Previewing gets your mind ready for the new information it will receive and gets you interested in the upcoming material.

2. *Review:* Take a few minutes to review your class notes, a previous assignment, or study tools you have already created. You can also reread a chapter summary for a chapter you have already studied. Reviewing gets your mind focused on the subject and stimulates associations that you have already created in your long-term memory.

Use Techniques to Deal with Internal and External Distractors

Distractors are elements that break your concentration. **External distractors** are caused by things in your physical environment, such as noises, people, television, enticing weather, clutter, and lighting. **Internal distractors** are disruptions that occur inside you. Worries, stress, anxiety, depression, sickness, hunger, pain, daydreams, and anticipation of upcoming events are examples of internal distractors that reduce your level of concentration. When you find yourself distracted and concentrating difficult, the first step is to analyze the situation to determine the source of your distraction. Once you realize the source, try using one or more strategies consistently to reduce or eliminate distractions.

Experiment with the following strategies to deal with distractors:

1. **Take charge:** Accept responsibility for the distraction by taking charge of your situation. If you cannot control the noise level around you, rather than blame others, *take charge* by moving to another location. If the distraction is the phone, the television, or an uncomfortable work space, *take charge* by altering your environment. Let the phone ring, unplug it, or turn on an answering machine. Turn off the television. Choose a more comfortable work space or take time to make the existing space comfortable.
2. **Say *no*:** Sometimes ridding yourself of a distraction is as easy as saying *no*. When friends or family members ask you to drop your study schedule and participate in an activity with them, show your assertiveness by simply saying *no*. Inform them of the times that you *are* available. This technique can also be used to tell yourself to resist the urge to participate in a distraction: no snack, no television now, no daydreaming, or no phone calls.
3. **No need:** For minor noises or movement, you can use the *no need* technique to train yourself not to look up and not to break your concentration to attend to minor occurrences that are familiar. For example, if you study in the library, you know that occasionally someone will walk by, pull out a chair, or turn the pages of a book. Without looking, you know the source of the distraction, so force yourself to keep your eyes on your own work. Tell yourself, "There is *no need* to look."
4. **Red bow:** Frequently other people are distractors. They interrupt your studying and break your concentration. On your door or in your study area, place a red bow or any other item or symbol to signal to others that you are studying and you want privacy. Ask them to respect your request for no interruptions unless an emergency occurs.
5. **Checkmark:** Each time you lose your concentration, make a checkmark on a score card you keep on your desk. At the end of your study block, count the number of checks. Set a goal each time you study to reduce the number of checkmarks.

6. **Mental storage box:** Before you begin studying, identify any concerns, worries, or emotions that might interrupt your concentration. Place them inside an imaginary box. Put the lid on the box and mentally shove the box aside for the time being. Tell yourself that you will deal with the contents of the box at a more appropriate time, and then do so.
7. **Tunnel vision:** Picture yourself at the beginning of a tunnel that has a yellow line running down the middle. You want to stay on the middle line. As soon as your mind starts to wander, picture yourself swiftly getting back to the middle line before you bump against the walls.
8. **Mental rehearsal:** Use visualization skills to mentally rehearse your actions and performance. Mental rehearsal is effective because it gives you the opportunity to see yourself responding or performing in advance of the actual situation. Many athletes use mental rehearsal to elevate performance; they picture themselves making the perfect shot at the free throw line, catching and maintaining control of the football, or reading the green correctly for a perfect putt. Any time you feel apprehension, self-doubt, or lack of confidence, use mental rehearsal to create in your mind a movie that shows you performing effectively. Picture yourself beginning an assignment without effort, writing answers to a test with confidence, or using your entire study block without encountering distractions.
9. **Emotional *e* words:** Attitude plays an important role in concentration and learning. Any time you find yourself dealing with negative emotions toward studying a specific subject or an assignment, combat those emotions by refocusing your mind on words with positive energy. Quickly brainstorm and say out loud positive words that begin with *e*. For example, you might say *effortless, enthusiastic, excited, energetic, eager, effective, efficient, essential, excelling, excellent, expert, exhilarating,* or *educated.* In your mind, attach an image of yourself exhibiting these qualities. The result is an attitude adjustment that is more conducive to concentration and learning.
10. **Positive self-talk** and **affirmations:** Self-talk—the little comments you say to yourself in your head—can be positive or negative. When you hear yourself using negative self-talk, quickly turn your thoughts into positive statements. Positive self-talk involves statements that show optimism, confidence, determination, and control. A positive self-talk statement that you choose to repeat frequently becomes an affirmation. (See Chapter 4, page 96, for more information about affirmations.) Both positive self-talk and affirmations increase your level of concentration and motivation, adjust your attitude, and reduce stress and procrastination.

What relaxation techniques do you practice?

As you can see, there are many strategies to deal with internal and external distractors. Experiment with these techniques and then select those that work most effectively for you. The more frequently you use the techniques, the more comfortable you will be activating them when the need arises. *Stress* and *procrastination* are two internal distractors that affect many students. The following sections discuss techniques designed specifically to deal with these distractors.

Group Processing: A Collaborative Learning Activity

Form groups of three or four students for this brainstorming activity.

1. Divide a large chart into two columns. In the left column, write as many different internal and external distractors as possible in a ten-minute period.
2. After you have a list of distractors, brainstorm techniques to use to combat each distractor. List the techniques in the right column. You may provide more than one technique for each distractor. You may refer to the *Terms to Know* list on page 111.
3. Be prepared to share your list of distractors and techniques with the class.

Decreasing Stress

Stress is a reaction or a response to events or situations that threaten to disrupt our normal patterns or routines. It is the wear and tear on our bodies due to physical, emotional, and cognitive responses. We may experience stress due to work, finances, personal relationships, health conditions, course assignments, tests, or other unexpected events or emergencies. Some stress is normal and should be anticipated as we move through life making decisions and changing directions in our personal, work, and academic lives. In some situations, stress is beneficial and contributes to positive change. Healthy stress can compel us to take action to move in new directions. It can increase adrenaline levels and help us perform on a higher level.

In other situations, however, as stress increases, our ability to deal with and control the stress decreases. Headaches, backaches, insomnia, fatigue, anxiety attacks, mood swings, depression, forgetfulness, carelessness, and irritability are early warning signs that stress is becoming more intense and is moving into the range of excessive. Excessive stress hinders performance and affects our cognitive abilities. Recall from Chapter 2 that excessive stress can affect our ability to move stimuli through short-term memory and later to retrieve information from long-term memory. It also reduces our ability to concentrate, to recall information accurately, to use problem solving effectively, and to make wise decisions. Excessive stress from unresolved issues has physical consequences as well: an increased pulse rate; faster breathing; higher blood pressure; a weakening of the immune system; and a decrease in the production of endorphins, the neurochemicals that make us feel happy and content. Excessive, prolonged stress can lead to ulcers, heart attacks, strokes, and clinical depression. Learning to manage stress is a lifelong skill that will not only improve the quality of our lives, but may also add more years to our lives.

Stress Management Techniques

How you *perceive* and *handle* external situations—rather than the situations themselves—is the cause of stress. People who handle stress best are those individuals who actively look for solutions and use techniques to alter their perception of external situations. The following techniques can help you take control of stress before it becomes excessive or prolonged. (See Exercise 11.1 in Chapter 11 for additional coping strategies.)

Stress-Management Techniques

1. Use time-management and goal-setting techniques.
2. Interact with others.
3. Redirect your emotions.
4. Become more active.
5. Take time to center yourself.
6. Go on mental vacations.
7. Express and process your feelings.
8. Choose a healthy lifestyle.
9. Practice relaxation techniques.

Use Time-Management and Goal-Setting Techniques Identify your stressors and then group them into two categories: the stressors that you can do something about and the stressors over which you have no control. Take time to create goals for the stressors that you can do something about; create a plan of action either by yourself or with the help of a counselor, a support group, or local resources. Your plan of action may include the following:

1. *Use a goal organizer (page 95) and create a plan of action.* This approach turns an external situation that you previously felt was hopeless into a situation you can control. The goal organizer helps you see the benefits of your plan and allows you to organize it.
2. *Create term, weekly, daily, and task schedules to organize your time and your activities.* Stress for many people is the result of trying to do too many things and taking on too many responsibilities without a plan of action. (See Chapter 3, pages 63–66.)
3. *Prioritize the things you need to do and let go of the rest.* Shed the image of superman or superwoman, the idea that you need to do everything for everyone. Say *no* to people and things that are not top priorities. This often requires setting firmer boundaries with your time and your commitments. Lighten up your social calendar by spending your time on social activities that are the most rewarding to you. Seek ways to delegate tasks so the workload is distributed more evenly. Strive to reduce your own expectations of yourself and any tendencies for perfectionism in areas where less than perfect suffices.

Interact with Others Many research studies recognize the importance of social interaction in reducing stress, improving overall health and the immune system, stimulating mental faculties, and staving off depression. Participation in a student or community organization, a church, or a study group can shift your attention from your stress to more positive emotions. Making time to spend with a close network of friends or creating new friendships opens up doors of opportunity for laughter, bonding with others, and finding a zest for life. Creating this time to interact socially moves you closer to achieving a balanced pie of life (page 59).

Redirect Your Emotions Engaging in activities that create positive emotions provides you with the opportunity to reduce the intensity of your emotional reactions to stress. Take time out to redirect your emotions by spending time on a favorite hobby or craft, listening to music, playing an instrument, singing, dancing, baking, playing a video game, or watching a movie. Continuously dwelling on a negative situation intensifies your emotions; substituting those emotions with positive ones can dissipate the negative energy and lead to an altered perception of the stressor. Redirecting your emotions serves to balance them. When you revisit the problem or issue later, you may see the situation differently and be able to seek solutions more calmly and rationally and with a less emotional response.

Become More Active Physical activity reduces the physiological effects of stress. Plan 20 to 30 minutes a minimum of three times a week to exercise (walk, run, swim, bike, lift weights, do aerobics, or play basketball, baseball, soccer, or golf). For more structure, sign up for a physical education course, an intramural sport, or a community exercise program, or work out with a regularly televised exercise program. In addition to reducing your stress level and giving yourself a mental break from thinking about the stressor, the benefits of regular exercise are many:

1. Exercise gets oxygen moving more smoothly to your brain; your concentration levels will increase, and information will enter and move through your memory system more efficiently.
2. Exercise improves your cardiovascular system, thus reducing your risk of more serious health conditions that may result from prolonged stress.
3. Exercise strengthens your body, making it more resistant to the physical and emotional effects of stress. Your body becomes better equipped to handle stress when stress does occur.

Take Time to Center Yourself Engage in a mind-calming activity, such as meditation, yoga, prayer, or biofeedback, to center yourself and return to a state of calmness and serenity. Sitting in a sauna, a hot tub, or a warm bath with your focus solely on the physical experience can also be a mind-calming activity. Centering activities provide a way to block out the rest of the world and temporarily shield yourself from your reactions to outside events. Taking time to center yourself shows that you are taking time to make yourself the center of attention; your priority is on you and your emotional well-being.

Go on Mental Vacations In Chapter 4, you learned about **visualization** (pages 95–96). **Perfect place** is a visualization technique that integrates your imagination with a breathing exercise and takes you on a mental vacation. To practice this technique, close your eyes and breathe in slowly. Start creating a perfect place in the world where you feel relaxed, confident, safe, comfortable, and content. Breathe out slowly as you continue to let the perfect place unfold in your imagination. Continue the slow breathing process as you add sensations to your picture: sounds, smells, sights, tastes, and tactile feelings. Tune in to the way your body feels in this perfect place. Practice this technique several times until you can create the setting and the sensations consistently. Then, take a mental picture of this setting. When you feel stressed, close your eyes and bring back the mental picture. Through the power of association, the calming sensations of your perfect place appear with the mental picture. (This technique is also a centering technique.) You can use other techniques as well for a mental vacation. Again, relax and close your eyes. Reminisce about a wonderful vacation you had, or visualize a relaxing vacation you would like to take in the future. Taking mental vacations separates you in a healthy way from stress and stressful situations.

Express and Process Your Feelings As previously mentioned, your perception and method of handling a situation, rather than the situation itself, are often the source of stress. Trying to understand and deal with a stressful situation in isolation, without the input or perception of others, or trying to hide your reactions to stress often compounds your stress. Bottling up your emotions or burying your feelings like a secret is only a temporary solution; the emotions will continue to dwell in you and eventually will resurface. The following techniques show more constructive ways to deal with the powerful emotions often linked to stress:

1. *Discussing your situation with others may thwart the tendency to make a mountain out of a molehill.* Talking to friends, creating a support network, or working with a counselor provides you with the opportunity to express and process your feelings, listen to their suggestions, receive their support, and feel connected. When under stress, many people exaggerate the extent of a problem or the hopelessness of a solution. Expressing your feelings with others often helps you process and handle the experience more effectively.
2. *Writing in a journal may provide you with insights and solutions.* Taking time to write in a private journal allows you to identify your source of stress, describe your feelings and reactions, and tap into some of your innermost thoughts in a nonthreatening way. Putting your emotions on paper often reduces the intensity of the emotions, disperses some of the negative energy, and gives you an opportunity to analyze the situation more rationally. Keeping a journal also provides you with an ongoing record of your forward progress and the strategies you used successfully to control your stress and make shifts in the direction of your life. There are no right or wrong ways to keep journals; some people find that writing random thoughts and expressions of their feelings works best. Others prefer a more structured approach, such as the following:
   - **a.** What is the stress? What is bothering me?
   - **b.** How exactly do I feel about this? What are my specific emotions or reactions?
   - **c.** Why do I feel this way? What's really below the surface?
   - **d.** How could I have reacted differently? What would the situation look like if I could redo the "scene" with a different response or reaction?
   - **e.** What do I want to happen now? What changes do I want and need to make?

Choose a Healthy Lifestyle In addition to regular exercise, nutrition and adequate sleep play a role in reducing and coping with stress. Frequently people experiencing stress turn to fast foods and snacks that are high in sugar and fat. Foods high in sugar often produce a surge in energy as they increase blood sugar in the body. However, the increased blood sugar quickly drops, thus leaving the individual feeling less energetic than before eating the high-sugar foods or snacks. Stress may also lead to poor sleep and a disruption in normal sleep patterns. The results are fatigue and low energy.

The following guidelines can help you make choices as part of a healthier lifestyle:

1. Instead of eating foods loaded with sugar, choose foods that break sugars down more slowly and release energy over a more sustained period of time. Complex carbohydrates, such as those found in grains, cereals, rice, pasta, bread, and potatoes, protect blood levels from the roller coaster effect of highs and lows.
2. Consume three to four helpings of fruits and vegetables each day. In addition to providing you with essential vitamins and minerals, these foods increase your brain's production of serotonin, a brain chemical that stabilizes mood swings and promotes a sense of happiness. Multivitamins can supplement your dietary needs for vitamins and minerals, although they are not a substitute for good eating.

3. Limit your use of nicotine, caffeine, alcohol, and drugs. People often use more of these products when under stress, but they are not effective ways to cope with stress, and their health consequences may lead to more serious problems.
4. Set aside 15 to 30 minutes three times a day to sit down and enjoy a relaxing meal. Put work and other distractions aside so meals become a quiet time to enjoy and digest the food, or a time to socialize with others.
5. Get your sleep pattern on a regular schedule. During times of stress, people's sleep patterns become irregular and often resemble a roller coaster ride. Individuals experience *insomnia,* the inability to fall asleep, their hours of restful sleep are too few, or they do not reserve enough hours per night to get a good night's sleep. Strive to eliminate poor sleep patterns by establishing consistent sleep and waking times. If you experience insomnia, use the time to relax in a prone position. You may want to listen to soft music or spend the time visualizing or practicing relaxation techniques. Resetting your body's time clock requires training and often three or more weeks of scheduling consistency. Your goal is to create a pattern that gives you about eight hours of sound sleep, which results in your awaking each morning refreshed and ready to begin a new day.

Practice Relaxation Techniques Relaxation techniques can help you reduce your stress levels and improve your emotional health. The goal behind relaxation techniques is to create a state of mind and body that perhaps can best be described as "Ahhhhhhh." In this state, the body is not tense and the mind is not wandering; you are open and ready to receive new information or expand on previously learned information. Relaxation techniques are effective in a wide variety of emotional situations: when you feel anxious, nervous, tense, stressed, apprehensive, hyperactive, restless, defeated, frustrated, or overwhelmed.

The following relaxation techniques are easy to learn and require only a few minutes of your time:

1. *Soothing mask* Close your eyes. Place your hands on the top of your head. Slowly move your hands down your forehead, down your face, and to your neck. As you do this, picture your hands gently pulling a **soothing mask** over your face. This mask removes other thoughts, worries, fears, or stresses from your mind. Keep your eyes closed for another minute. Feel the soothing mask resting on your face. Block out thoughts or feelings that are not related to your soothing mask. As you practice this technique, you will be able to do it without using your hands. Your imagination can take you through the same process of pulling the mask over your face.
2. *Relaxation blanket* Sit comfortably in your chair. Close your eyes. Focus your attention on your feet. Imagine yourself pulling a soft, warm blanket up over your feet. Continue to pull this blanket up over your legs, lap, and chest until the blanket is snuggled around your shoulders and against your neck. Feel how your body is more relaxed now that it is covered with the blanket. This **relaxation blanket** feels like a security blanket, keeping you warm, confident, and comfortable. Keep your eyes closed for another minute as you enjoy the warmth and comfort of the blanket.
3. *Breathing by threes* This technique can be done with your eyes opened or closed. Inhale slowly through your nose as you count to three. Gently hold your breath as you again count to three. Exhale slowly through your nose as you count to three. Repeat this several times. Often you can actually feel your body begin to slow down and relax when you are **breathing by threes**.

4. *Deep breathing* Take a deep breath to fill your lungs. You may think your lungs are full, but there is room for one more breath of air. Inhale once again. Now slowly exhale and feel your body relax. Repeat this **deep breathing** several times. If you feel lightheaded or dizzy after trying this exercise, you might want to select one of the other options.
5. *Deep muscle relaxation* Stress is often felt in one or more of these muscle groups: shoulders, arms, lower back, legs, chest, fingers, or face. Take a minute to notice the amount of tension you feel in the various locations throughout your body. Then make a clenched fist tight enough that you can feel your fingers pulsating. Breathe several times and feel the tension in your fingers and your hands. Then breathe slowly and uncurl your fists until they are totally relaxed. Pay close attention to the different sensations as you go from tense to relaxed. Continue this with other muscle groups. Let the feelings of **deep muscle relaxation** and the feelings that the tension is washing away spread throughout your body. Feel the difference!
6. *Yoga* Sign up for a class or work with someone who knows yoga to learn this Eastern practice, which blends stretching, flexibility, breathing exercises, and meditation. Besides enjoying a sense of calm and relaxation, followers of yoga believe yoga helps the body heal, alleviates various forms of pain, reduces hypertension, and soothes the nervous system.

Reflection Writing 2 — CHAPTER 5

On a separate piece of paper or in a journal, do the following:

1. Think of one specific stressor that you are experiencing now or experience on a fairly regular basis. Take a personal inventory of the ways this stressor is affecting you physically and emotionally. Do *one* of the following and then respond to the second question:
   a. In your journal, simply state that you have identified a stressor and recognize the physical and emotional effects it is having on you. You do not need to give any detail.
   b. In your journal, discuss the stressor and its effects on you.
2. Identify specific techniques discussed in this chapter that you could use to deal with your stressor more effectively. Explain each technique in your own words and tell how you will use it. The combination of techniques you select creates a "stress reduction plan" that you can begin to implement to gain greater control over your source of stress.

Name ______________________________ Date ______________

EXERCISE 5.2 Making a Comparison Chart

A comparison chart is a form of note taking that shows key characteristics of several different topics. To create a comparison chart, list individual topics (subjects) in the left column. At the top of each column, write the categories of information you want to summarize in the chart. To complete the chart, use only key words, short phrases, or short sentences to write important points in the cells (the boxes in the chart). The first topic is done as an example.

Increasing Concentration and Decreasing Stress

Topic	Techniques	Special Notes
Physical Stage	1. appropriate noise level 2. two sources of light 3. organized work space	These create an ideal study area. Fewer distractions increase concentration.
Mental Stage		
Dealing with Internal and External Distractors (Mental Stage)		
Stress Management		
Relaxation Techniques (Stress Management)		

EXERCISE 5.3 Case Studies

Each of the following case studies describes a student situation. Read each case study carefully; highlight key ideas or student issues. Answer the question that ends each case study. In your response, address the key points that you highlighted and that directly relate to the question. Answer in complete sentences. These case studies are also available online; you can email your response to your instructor or print a copy of your work online.

1. Katlin feels that her life is spinning out of control. She simply cannot find enough time to do quality work in her classes. She feels that she is slapping her work together haphazardly. She makes more mistakes on her assignments than she did in previous terms. She is annoyed with herself and then gets caught up in a lot of negative self-talk. She is too embarrassed about her feelings and stress to talk with anyone. In fact, she finds herself avoiding even her closest friends. She does not know how much longer she can "put on a happy face" in public. What can Katlin do to break this negative pattern?

2. Lynn tries to study at the kitchen table since it is the largest work surface in her apartment. She takes a long time getting short assignments done because of all the annoying disruptions and distractions. The humming sound of the refrigerator bothers her, as do the sounds that come from outside. Every time she gets distracted, she feels compelled to get up, move around, and get something to drink or to snack on. As long as she is up and around, she often stops to throw some laundry in the washing machine or empty the dishwasher. Needless to say, she feels that she is getting nowhere fast. What strategies can Lynn use to deal with her external distractions more effectively?

3. José has a lot of friends and enjoys a wide variety of activities outside school. He was an excellent student in high school but is finding it hard to do well in college. No one told him how much more demanding college would be. His friends come by often to see how he is doing. They usually end up inviting him to go out for a while, and he goes. He tries studying when he gets home later at night. By then he has trouble concentrating. He wastes a lot of time trying to settle down and get assignments started. He feels pressured to do so many things that he has problems deciding where to begin. What strategies can José use to adjust his approach to the demands of college and college-level work?

4. Debbie worked hard to create a weekly schedule with sufficient time to study for each of her classes. She has disciplined herself to sit down to study during the scheduled blocks of time. Frequently, however, an hour passes and she will have accomplished nothing. Her assignments seem long and tedious. She knows she needs to do them, but she cannot seem to gain the momentum, the interest, or the motivation to use her time blocks effectively. What strategies would you recommend Debbie use when she sits down to study?

EXERCISE 5.4 Partner Discussion

Discuss with a partner ways both of you can use each of the following techniques in your life. Be prepared to summarize your discussion with the rest of the class.

1. Active learning
2. Warm-ups
3. Say *no*
4. Red bow
5. Checkmark
6. Mental rehearsal
7. Breathing by threes
8. Study ritual

Decreasing Procrastination

Procrastination is the process of putting off something until a later time. (You were introduced to procrastination in Chapter 4, page 90.) Procrastinators choose low-priority tasks over high-priority tasks. Procrastination is a learned behavior that can be reduced or eliminated by understanding the reasons for procrastinating and then activating effective strategies to modify the self-defeating behavior. Reducing or eliminating procrastination results in a more productive use of time, improved performance, less stress, and new opportunities and successes.

Recognizing When You Procrastinate

Any time you find yourself avoiding a specific task or making statements such as *I'll do it when I am in the mood; I have plenty of time to do it later; I can let it slide a few more days;* or *I will wait because I work better under pressure,* recognize that you are procrastinating. Become aware of your procrastination patterns by answering the following questions.

1. Are there specific kinds of tasks involved when you procrastinate? For example, do you plan and follow through with studying for your computer class, but procrastinate with your writing or your math class? Do you plan and follow through with specific household chores but procrastinate when faced with the laundry? Identify the specific kinds of tasks that you avoid most frequently; for those tasks, you will want to activate strategies to change your momentum.
2. Do you tend to procrastinate beginning a specific task, or do you begin a task enthusiastically but then procrastinate in the middle of working on the task? For example, do you struggle with setting time aside and sitting down to begin writing a paper? Do you make excuses for not beginning the paper? Or do you begin the paper but lose interest or motivation halfway through the process of writing the paper? Do you almost have the task or the goal accomplished but find yourself quitting close to the end of the task? For example, do you put off typing the final version of the paper even though you have finished writing the paper? Understanding *when* in the process of a task you procrastinate can help you select strategies to complete tasks or goals more consistently.
3. Do you start multiple tasks, jumping from one to another, and make less important tasks seem more important or urgent? This behavior is a

common sign of the onset of procrastination. Procrastinators can get so caught up in this whirlwind behavior that they do not realize all the busy work is a mask for avoiding specific tasks. When you find yourself scurrying around, sometimes aimlessly keeping busy, take time to identify the task you are avoiding.

Recognizing Reasons for Procrastinating

Procrastination occurs for various reasons. In order to select appropriate strategies to reduce or eliminate procrastination, begin by pinpointing the causes of procrastination.

The following are common reasons why people procrastinate.

1. *Lack of motivation, interest, or purpose:* Starting and completing a task is difficult when you harbor negative attitudes and perceive the task as boring, uninteresting, or meaningless. **Motivation**—the feeling, emotion, or desire that moves a person to take some form of action—is the direct result of showing interest in a task and attaching a purpose, a reason, or importance to completing a task. Using strategies to increase your interest level and give meaning and purpose to your task will increase your level of motivation.
2. *Fear of failure:* Sometimes people use **fear of failure** to procrastinate as a way to avoid a possible failure. Rather than experience a failure, they make verbal excuses, such as the following: *I did not have enough time to do it; I had to take care of more important things; my boss asked me to work more hours; I lost the assignment;* or *I had a family emergency.* In the mind of the procrastinator, the verbal excuses are a way to "save face" and protect the ego and self-esteem. This approach may also be used when there is a fear of disappointing someone else. These excuses create an impression that if the person had only attempted the task, it would have been completed successfully.
3. *Lack of self-efficacy:* **Self-efficacy** is the belief one has in his or her own abilities to perform various tasks. People who lack self-efficacy are filled with doubts and apprehension. They feel inadequate and incapable of succeeding. They "know" that they do not have enough time, that the situation is hopeless, that they cannot meet the level of expectation, or that they do not have the right skills; consequently, they make no attempt to tackle the task. They claim defeat rather than attempt the challenge.
4. *Task too difficult or complex:* Some tasks, especially those that involve unfamiliar information or new skills, are perceived as being too difficult or too complex. The thought of beginning the task is too unpleasant, overpowering, or overwhelming. Procrastination is the result of frustration and lack of a solid approach to break the task into smaller, more manageable sections and identify the skills, materials, or information needed to begin and complete the task.
5. *Inaccurate perception of time:* Some people have difficulty estimating the amount of time needed to complete various kinds of tasks. For example, students may delay starting a term project because they believe there is still plenty of time in the term to start and complete the assignment. Other students may lack motivation to begin a project because they inaccurately assess the time needed for a project. They may put off reading a new sociology chapter because they falsely believe that the assignment will take five or six hours and it is best to wait until larger blocks of time are available. In reality, they may need only two hours to read the chapter and could easily complete it during one or two study blocks.

6. *Overextended and overcommitted:* People who take on too many activities and responsibilities use procrastination as a way to shield themselves from more. They do not feel that they can manage what is currently "on their plate," so they have no desire to add more stress to their lives with more tasks to complete. Procrastination in this situation becomes an attempt to refrain from adding more stress to an already stressful pattern. However, the consequences of ignoring specific tasks that need to be completed can actually add more stress and create new problems.
7. *Unclear about the task or expectations:* Lack of momentum to act may be due to lack of strategies, understanding, or clarity. In this state of confusion, people lack problem solving or analytical skills to examine the task to determine what needs to be done or which steps to use to tackle the task. To avoid feeling embarrassed or uncomfortable, they shy away from asking for clarification or help.
8. *Perfectionism:* Perfectionists are not happy unless their work is—in their view—perfect. They can be excessively critical of their own work or performance, so they may use delay tactics to avoid tasks that will be difficult to complete or they may create excuses for their work before anyone even evaluates it. They may say things such as, "I had to do this in a hurry; it is not my best work." They strive desperately to preserve their self-image as a person who is the "best" and to maintain their high standards even when those standards are unrealistic.
9. *Unconducive environment:* Some people procrastinate because their work or study environment creates problems and frustrations, and they are not productive. It is difficult to be motivated to work on a task when clutter covers your work surface, lights hurt your eyes, furniture is too uncomfortable, or you are plagued by interruptions from other people. Trying to work in a less than ideal situation becomes too much of a struggle, so tasks are postponed until later.
10. *Habitual pattern:* People who procrastinate frequently to avoid starting all kinds of tasks have created a behavioral and cognitive pattern that is ingrained in their way of "doing life." They accept and even boast about being procrastinators; they pride themselves on being able to do things quickly, at the last minute, and under pressure. They often wait for a "push," a threat of a specific consequence, a crisis, or some outside force to get the momentum to do what needs to be done. Their focus is on completing the task and not necessarily on the quality of the final product. Habitual procrastinators benefit from learning new techniques, such as time management and goal setting, that can replace old, less effective behavioral and cognitive patterns.

Reasons for procrastinating vary for different tasks, situations, and individuals. In some cases procrastinating will not have any serious consequences. For example, procrastinating about moving a stack of magazines to the garage or putting your compact discs back in their cases has no dire consequences other than the clutter of magazines or disorganized or scratched compact discs. In many other cases, procrastinating leads to increased stress and additional problems. Procrastinating about paying your bills, studying for a test, or filling your tires with air will have more serious consequences, some of which could alter your goals or course for the future. Learning to reduce or eliminate procrastination can empower you, enhance your self-esteem, strengthen your self-discipline, and put you in greater control of your life.

EXERCISE 5.5 Looking at Yourself

On the following chart, identify five tasks you recently procrastinated doing. In the middle column, write the reason why you procrastinated. You can use one or more of the ten reasons discussed on the previous pages, or you can add new reasons. In the last column, tell the status of the task: Did you finally complete the task? If so, what motivated you? Is the task still unfinished? If so, why? You may be asked to discuss your responses in class or in a small group.

Task	Reason	Status

Strategies to Decrease Procrastination

Many time-management, goal-setting, concentration, and stress-reduction strategies that you have already learned can be used to tackle problems with procrastination. The following chart provides you with numerous strategies to deal with procrastination. As you read each strategy, think of problems with procrastination that you have previously experienced that you could have dealt with more effectively by using that strategy.

Strategies to Decrease Procrastination

Strategy	Explanation
Create a plan of action.	As soon as you recognize that you are procrastinating, end the inertia by writing a specific goal with a target time and date. List the steps in your plan of action. Plan a reward that you will enjoy only when you achieve the goal.
Create an interest.	Create an interest and increase your motivation by engaging another person to work with you, such as an assistant or a study group. Seek alternative sources of information such as an informative video or Internet search to find a new perspective on the topic. Realize that interest also develops once you begin to get involved with the task.
Identify a purpose.	When tasks seem meaningless or useless, focus on the relationship of the task to a larger, more meaningful goal. Use a goal organizer (page 95) to identify advantages of completing the task and consequences of avoiding the task. Attaching greater significance to the completion of a task improves your motivation.
Face your fear of failure.	Focus on your positive traits, your accomplishments, and your talents. Use: ■ Positive self-talk and praise. Plan to increase your self-efficacy and self-image as a person who is in control and taking steps to succeed. ■ Mental rehearsal to practice working through the specific steps of the task with ease, confidence, and success. By mentally rehearsing several times before you begin the task, you reduce your fear and belief that you will fail. ■ **Seeing success**, which is another type of visualization. Instead of focusing on yourself *doing* the steps as in mental rehearsal, create a mental picture of yourself succeeding at the task. Focus on how you feel working on and completing the task. What are the benefits? What emotions will you experience? Seeing success helps sweep away images of failure.
Keep a journal.	Express your feelings through an "anti-procrastination journal." Discuss your feelings about procrastinating, the steps you are taking, problems you are encountering, and, most important, the successes—both minor and major—you are experiencing. Watch for procrastination patterns; create plans to change those patterns of behavior.
Change negatives to positives.	Each time you get involved in self-criticism, negative thinking, self-doubting, or statements of frustration, put a halt to the negatives by replacing them with positive thoughts and images. Adjust your attitude and commit to a new plan of positive action. Use: ■ Emotional *e* words ■ Affirmations ■ Positive self-talk

(continued)

Break a difficult or complex task into smaller, more manageable steps.	Use stress-reduction techniques to reach a peaceful state of mind. Then take a problem-solving approach to identify the problem areas. Use *chunking* to identify the individual parts of the task and the individual steps needed to achieve your goal. Plan to work on one step at a time.
Ask for help or guidance.	Make good use of other people as resources. Recognize there is no reason to be embarrassed about asking questions, asking for clarification, or seeking help in tackling the task.
List your priorities.	When you feel overwhelmed or overextended with things you need to do and responsibilities you need to meet, make a list of tasks. Prioritize the tasks. Focus your time on the most important tasks; let go of those that consume your time but are not your top priorities.
Set your boundaries.	Identify your boundaries and protect those boundaries by learning to say *no* to distractors and people who make demands on your time when the demands are not your priorities.
Relax your personal standards.	If you tend to be a perfectionist, examine your standards or expectations for yourself to determine whether they are unrealistically high. Find a more comfortable and realistic set of standards that still produces quality work but does not require you to be "the best" at a specific task.
Create an environment conducive to work.	Remove the elements in your environment that affect your motivation or ability to perform a task. *Take charge* by organizing or rearranging your space so you can be more motivated and productive.
Be willing to try new approaches.	Explore ways to break old patterns and habits. Just because you have "always done things this way" does not mean that your current way is the most efficient or effective. Listen to yourself. If you are rationalizing or using delay tactics that are past patterns, be willing to discard those habits and replace them with new ones.
Make a contract with yourself.	When you hear yourself making verbal excuses for your behavior, take time to make a contract with yourself to complete a specific task. Push yourself to "just do it." The hardest barrier at times is beginning; once the task is started, forward progress is easier.
Ask for support.	Explain your desire to move forward and end your procrastination on a specific task. Tell your friends or family members of your intent. Seek their support and encouragement.
Work on a task a few minutes each day.	Set aside time each day to chip away at the task. Before long, you will be on your way to completing the task.
Use your time-management skills.	After you create a plan of action, schedule time throughout the week for the task. During the time block for the task, avoid making excuses or using delay tactics. Use some of the previous techniques to plunge into the task and work diligently on it for the allocated block of time.

Exercise 5.6 LINKS

With a partner, in a small group, or on your own, find the relationships within the following paired topics. If you are working with a partner or a small group, discuss the relationships. If you are working on your own, explain the relationships in writing on a separate piece of paper.

Paired Topics	How are these items related?
goal setting and time management	
time management and procrastination	
procrastination and stress	
procrastination and motivation	
motivation and goal setting	

Reflection Writing 3 — CHAPTER 5

On a separate piece of paper or in a journal, discuss the strategies examined in this chapter that you feel will be most effective for increasing your concentration, decreasing your stress, and decreasing your patterns of procrastination.

SUMMARY

- Concentration requires that you set a positive physical stage conducive to maintaining a mental focus. An ideal study area addresses noise, lighting, and work space issues.
- Concentration requires that you set a positive mental stage by being an active learner, using goal setting, doing warm-ups, and using techniques to deal with internal and external distractors. *Take charge, say* no, *no need, red bow, checkmark, mental storage box,* and *tunnel vision* are techniques that reduce or eliminate distractors.
- Stress is a reaction or a response to events or situations that threaten to disrupt normal patterns or routines. Healthy stress can motivate us to move forward and change. Excessive stress has cognitive, physical, and emotional consequences.
- Stress-management techniques can help you take control of stress before it becomes excessive.
- *Soothing mask, relaxation blanket, breathing by threes, deep breathing, deep muscle relaxation,* and *yoga* are six relaxation techniques that reduce stress.
- Procrastination, a learned behavior, is the process of putting off something until a later time.
- For procrastinators, lower-priority tasks take precedence over higher-priority tasks.
- People procrastinate for a variety of reasons. Lack of motivation, fear of failure, lack of self-efficacy, perfectionism, and habitual patterns are five of the ten common reasons for procrastinating.
- A variety of strategies can help you tackle the problem of procrastination. Many of the strategies are similar to those strategies used for time management, goal setting, and concentration.

ACE Practice Tests, which are scored online, supplementary exercises, enrichment activities, and related web site links are available online for *Essential Study Skills*, 4e. Use the following directions to access this web site:

Type: **http://college.hmco.com/collegesurvival/students**

Click on *List of Sites by Author.* Use the arrow to scroll down to Wong *Essential Study Skills*, 4e. Click on the title. If you are working on your own computer, bookmark this web site.

LEARNING OPTIONS

The following learning options provide you with opportunities to demonstrate your understanding of the topics in Chapter 5. Your instructor may assign one or more specific options, or may ask you to select one or more options that interest you the most.

1. Expand the Chapter 5 mapping on page 111. Notice that the name of the chapter appears in the center and each of the chapter headings extends outward. Copy this structure on a blank piece of paper. Reread the information under each heading in your textbook. Extend branches on the mapping to show important key words or phrases for each heading. You can add pictures and colors to your visual mapping. (See pages 25, 52, and Chapter 11 for additional information.)
2. Use index cards to create a set of flash cards for the terms listed at the beginning of this chapter (page 111). Write the terms on the fronts of the cards and the definitions and explanations on the backs.
3. Use the Internet or the periodicals (magazine) resources in your library to locate an informative web site for the topic of *concentration, stress management,* or *procrastination.* Print the information. Prepare a short presentation or a written summary of the most significant information. In your presentation or summary, explain how the contents of the web site relate to the content of Chapter 5.
4. Design an informative brochure that could be given to students outside this class. Explain *one* of the following: ways students can improve concentration, ways students can decrease stress, or ways students can overcome procrastination.
5. Interview five or more adults to find out the kinds of stresses they face in their everyday lives and the strategies they use to reduce their stress levels. Write a separate summary for each of your interviews. Include the list of questions you used in the interviews.
6. Create a humorous poster that uses one of the following titles: *How to Create Stress in Your Life* or *How to Become a Habitual Procrastinator.* On the poster, list techniques to become stressed or a habitual procrastinator. Students who see your poster should be able to understand that effective strategies to reduce stress or procrastination are the *opposite* of the strategies on your poster.
7. Create a plan of action for increasing concentration, decreasing stress, or decreasing procrastination. Write your plan of action as a goal; use the four steps for effective goal setting (page 93). Keep a daily journal or record of your progress for seven or more days. At the end of seven days, evaluate your success. Discuss any problems you had following your plan of action and how you handled those problems.

CHAPTER 5 Review Questions

Multiple Choice

Choose the best answer *to complete each of the following statements and write its letter on the line.*

_______ **1.** Concentration is
- **a.** the ability to block out distractions and focus on only one item or task.
- **b.** one of the twelve principles of memory.
- **c.** a mental discipline that involves training your mind to keep a focus.
- **d.** All of the above

_______ **2.** Poor concentration may stem from
- **a.** stress about personal relationships, worries, or fears.
- **b.** a lack of motivation.
- **c.** internal and external distractors.
- **d.** a noisy studying environment.

_______ **3.** External distractors can include
- **a.** sunshine, noises, and lighting.
- **b.** smells, noises, and worries.
- **c.** negative self-talk, clutter, and people.
- **d.** the checkmark technique, the red-bow technique, and framing.

_______ **4.** When you hear yourself involved in negative self-talk, it is best to
- **a.** calmly listen to it and add other reminders of past disappointments.
- **b.** replace it with positive statements or affirmations that recognize your good qualities.
- **c.** turn on the television, radio, or stereo to distract your thought processes.
- **d.** All of the above

_______ **5.** Which techniques would work best for a student who wanted to stop wasting the first half hour of a study block trying to "get started" on studying?
- **a.** Warm-ups, chunking technique, and setting goals
- **b.** Perfect place, red-bow, and reviewing
- **c.** Breathing by threes and relaxation blanket
- **d.** Tunnel vision, soothing mask, and take charge

_______ **6.** Active learning
- **a.** occurs when you use a lot of energy reading a textbook nonstop for several hours.
- **b.** requires a person to walk, pace, or move around the room while studying.
- **c.** is a type of passive learning in which learning becomes automatic.
- **d.** requires the learner to use study strategies that require active participation in the learning process.

_______ **7.** Procrastination
- **a.** may stem from lack of interest, fear of failure, or perfectionism.
- **b.** occurs when low-priority tasks take the place of high-priority tasks.
- **c.** is a learned pattern that can be altered by using effective strategies.
- **d.** All of the above

_______ **8.** Which of the following strategies are *not* designed to adjust a person's attitude from negative to positive?
- **a.** Tunnel vision, intrinsic rewards, and deep breathing
- **b.** Mental rehearsal and positive self-talk
- **c.** Affirmations and emotional *e* words
- **d.** Seeing success and strategies to increase self-efficacy

_______ 9. Which of the following statements is *not* true about stress?
- **a.** Stress is normal and can help people move in new directions.
- **b.** Prolonged stress can have physical, emotional, and cognitive consequences.
- **c.** Excessive stress requires prescription medications in order to avoid physical damage to the body.
- **d.** Excessive stress may affect the functioning of short-term and long-term memory.

_______ 10. Which of the following helps a person decrease or eliminate the habit of procrastinating about doing important tasks?
- **a.** Taking time to understand *when* and *why* procrastination occurs
- **b.** Using weekly schedules and task schedules
- **c.** Using effective time-management and goal-setting techniques
- **d.** All of the above

Short Answer and Critical Thinking

Answer the following questions. Answer in complete sentences using details and terminology from this chapter.

1. What are the differences between an active and a passive learner?

2. When normal stress becomes excessive, changes occur in cognitive functioning. Discuss how excessive stress affects our ability to process information through the Information Processing Model.

3. Identify one reason why some people procrastinate. Then discuss three or more strategies that these procrastinators could use to end this form of procrastination.

Boosting Your Memory and Preparing for Tests

CHAPTER 6

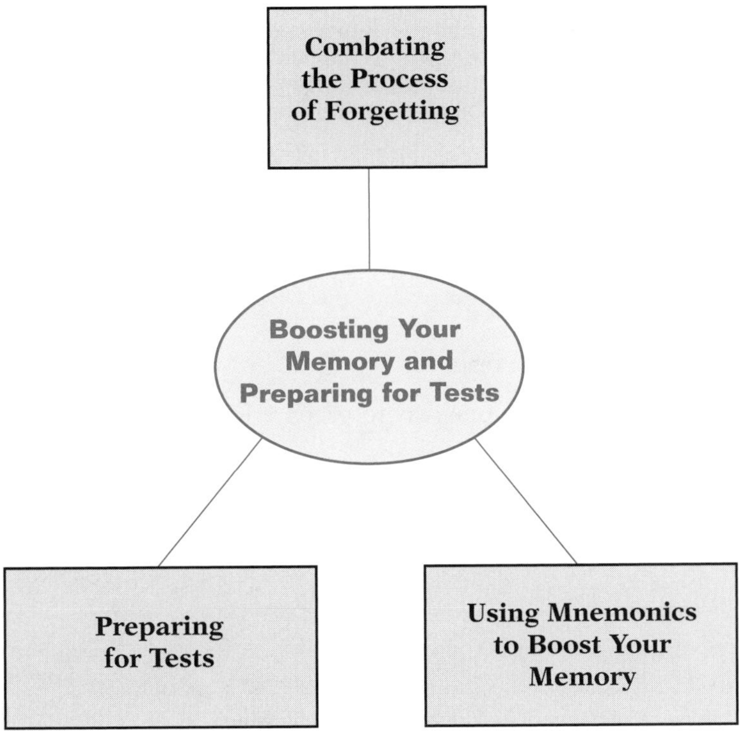

Forgetting is a natural process that occurs throughout the memory system. Five Theories of Forgetting explain why you must strive to use effective study skill strategies to combat the process of forgetting. In addition to an array of study skills strategies, you can use mnemonics (memory tricks) to boost your memory and your ability to recall information that is otherwise difficult to retrieve. Tests in college are a standard method to assess your understanding of course material. In this chapter, you will learn effective strategies to prepare for tests and reduce the occurrence of test anxiety.

Terms to Know

Five Theories of Forgetting
Decay Theory
Displacement Theory
Interference Theory
Incomplete Encoding Theory
Retrieval Failure Theory
mnemonics
acronyms
acrostics
associations
rhythms, rhymes, and jingles
stacking
loci
peg systems
rhyming peg system
number shape peg system
cramming
five-day study plan
summary notes
Bloom's Taxonomy
stress
test anxiety
locus of control
internal locus of control
external locus of control
systematic desensitization

CHAPTER 6 Boosting Memory and Preparing for Tests Profile

DO, SCORE, and **RECORD** your profile before you read this chapter. If you need to review the process, refer to the complete directions given in the Profile for Chapter 1 on page 2.

ONLINE: You can complete the profile and get your score online at this textbook's web site.

	YES	NO
1. When I take tests, I tend to forget information I have studied.	______	______
2. I usually feel prepared and confident about upcoming tests.	______	______
3. I am often nervous, feel sick, or have physical problems (headache, stomachache, clammy hands) right before a test.	______	______
4. I sometimes use memory tricks (mnemonics) to help me learn specific information.	______	______
5. I try to find out as much information as possible about a test before it is given.	______	______
6. Difficulties I have on tests are usually due to factors that are beyond my control.	______	______
7. I make special summary notes before every major test.	______	______
8. I make a five-day study plan before major tests.	______	______
9. I use the survival technique of cramming for most tests.	______	______
10. I practice predicting and writing test questions as one way to prepare for tests.	______	______

Reflection Writing 1 — CHAPTER 6

On a separate piece of paper or in a journal, do the following:

1. Discuss your profile score for this chapter. What was your score? What does it mean to you?
2. Discuss reasons why you would benefit from learning strategies to boost your memory. In what areas do you feel you have the most difficulty remembering information?

Combating the Process of Forgetting

The process of forgetting, unfortunately, occurs quite naturally in the human memory system. In Chapter 2 you learned that sensory stimuli enter short-term memory, which is a temporary storage system with limited capacity and duration. If you do not make a conscious effort or decision to process the information from the sensory stimuli, more likely than not the information will be dumped out of the memory system rather than processed and imprinted in your long-term memory. As discouraging as it sounds, forgetting is not limited to short-term memory. Forgetting can occur as you rehearse information, and it can occur when you attempt to retrieve information from schemas in your long-term memory. Because forgetting is quite a natural process, being aware of the different types of forgetting can help you select strategies designed to boost your memory and overpower the process of forgetting.

Five Theories of Forgetting

The Twelve Principles of Memory (SAVE CRIB FOTO) discussed in Chapter 2 enhance your ability to learn new information. *Selectivity, association, visualization, effort, concentration, recitation, interest, big and little pictures, feedback, organization, time on task,* and *ongoing review* strengthen your ability to imprint information accurately and efficiently in your long-term memory. These memory principles also facilitate the process of retrieving information from long-term memory so you can use or apply it as needed. However, the human memory system is extremely complex; even when you use the twelve principles, you will still experience situations in which you forget information. The **Five Theories of Forgetting** explain different types of forgetting that you might experience.

The **Decay Theory** occurs in short-term memory. When some stimuli reach short-term memory, they are simply too weak to be processed. The information decays or fades away before it can be sorted or processed. Stimuli often grow weak when you do not give adequate attention or assign importance to the incoming information. Because the information is never processed, it is never really "learned."

The **Displacement Theory** also occurs in short-term memory. This theory states that if too much information comes into short-term memory too rapidly, some of the information that is already in this limited storage center will be shoved aside or displaced to make room for the new incoming stimuli. Ample time was not available to process or move the displaced information through the memory system. Consequently, this information also was never learned.

The **Interference Theory** applies to the confusion that can occur between old and new information in long-term memory. One type of confusion occurs when the new information you are learning interferes with your ability to recall or retrieve information that you learned previously. For example, if you once knew how to speak Portuguese but are now studying Spanish, you may have a hard time locating in your memory words that you once knew in Portuguese because your newly acquired Spanish language skills interfere with your recall of Portuguese words. This type of interference occurs more frequently when the new and the old information are similar in nature. A reverse type of interference may also occur: old information interferes with learning new information. The old information is so thoroughly imprinted that it is recalled or retrieved instead of the new information. Using the same example of two languages, you might have difficulty learning or correctly using Spanish vocabulary because your tendency is to automatically retrieve and use Portuguese words, which are more familiar and more firmly imprinted as part of your memory system.

Forgetting due to interference occurs frequently. Consider the confusion you would likely experience if your current math instructor were to require a different series of problem-solving steps than did your previous instructor. Or consider the confusion you might experience in a history class that teaches a more culturally sensitive and accurate portrayal of historical events than you previously learned in traditional history textbooks. When old and new information contradict each other or are so similar that you have difficulty distinguishing the finer details between the subjects, interference may occur and result in a weakened memory system and forgetting.

The **Incomplete Encoding Theory** applies to information as you rehearse it. Some information is only partially learned because you did not encode it clearly during the rehearsal or practice stage. If you do not self-quiz or use techniques that provide you with feedback as you learn, you may be under the assumption that you have learned the new information. When you attempt to retrieve the information from your long-term memory, however, you find that the information is vague or incomplete. Incomplete encoding may occur when inadequate attention is given to the specific details or when rote memory is used instead of elaborative rehearsal.

The **Retrieval Failure Theory** occurs when you are not able to find information in your memory bank. Even though you previously learned the information and you know that it is imprinted, you "go blank." Failure to locate information in memory may be attributed to a weak organizational system for storing or filing information. The information is not firmly attached to a schema. This often occurs when you use rote memory to learn individual facts; the facts are stored in memory but are difficult to locate if understanding, relationships, or meaning are not attached to them. Retrieval failure may also be attributed to lack of use or ongoing review. To get a clearer picture of this form of forgetting, imagine a rusty access door that does not allow you to open the information, or a cobweb covering information that you have not used for quite some time. Retrieval failure may also occur when thought processes are disrupted due to test anxiety, stress, or other emotional reactions.

Each of the Five Theories of Forgetting shows that you can forget information during several different stages of the Information Processing Model. In this chapter you will learn new strategies and review previously learned strategies for taking in, rehearsing, storing, and retrieving information in ways that reduce or eliminate the effects of the Five Theories of Forgetting.

Group Processing: A Collaborative Learning Activity

Form groups of three or four students.

1. On a large piece of paper, write the Five Theories of Forgetting. (You may organize your work in a category chart or in lists.)
2. Brainstorm study strategies that you can use to combat each of the five kinds of forgetting. What steps or techniques can you use to reduce or eliminate each kind of forgetting? Compile all your ideas on paper. You may be asked to share your ideas with the class.

Using Study Skills to Combat the Process of Forgetting

A primary goal of learning effective study skills is to increase your learning potential, which includes combating the process of forgetting. In the first five chapters of this textbook, you have already learned an array of skills that will boost your memory and facilitate the process of learning. The following chart summarizes many of the techniques that you have already learned to enhance memory. Later chapters will cover additional techniques for learning information presented in your textbooks and in lectures.

	Study Skills Strategies to Combat Forgetting and Boost Memory
Chapter 1	Using multisensory learning strategies for three cognitive learning styles Using strategies for global and linear learners Using strategies for structured, interactive, and independent learning Using your multiple intelligences
Chapter 2	Processing information through short-term memory Rehearsing information Using self-quizzing for feedback Retrieving information from long-term memory Using the Twelve Principles of Memory to strengthen your memory
Chapter 3	Using term, weekly, daily, and task schedules to manage time effectively Using distributed practice and avoiding marathon studying or massed practice
Chapter 4	Setting long-term, intermediary, short-term, and immediate goals Using a four-step approach for writing effective goals Using a goal organizer to create a plan of action Using goal setting for study blocks Creating a five-day study plan Developing a long-term goal for term-long projects Creating summary notes Making flash cards or index cards as study tools
Chapter 5	Creating an ideal physical stage for increasing concentration Creating an ideal mental stage for increasing concentration Using strategies to reduce or eliminate internal and external distractors Using strategies to decrease stress and procrastination

Application of these study skills requires a commitment on your part to change the way you meet the demands of college-level work. The more consistently you use these strategies, the more quickly they become habitual. With practice, you will find that your confidence level for learning new information increases and that you will experience greater academic success. In the following section, you will learn to use mnemonics—memory techniques—to add interest to the process of learning while boosting your memory.

Using Mnemonics to Boost Your Memory

Mnemonics are memory techniques or memory tricks that serve as bridges to help you recall specific facts or details that for whatever reason are difficult for you to remember. Mnemonics provide you with an extra clue to help trigger your memory so you can recall information more easily. In this textbook, *SAVE CRIB FOTO* is a mnemonic designed to help you recall the Twelve Principles of Memory accurately. You have probably used mnemonics to some extent before. For example, have you ever met someone and then used some type of memory trick to remember that person's name? Perhaps you associated that person's name to another person you know with the same name or to some object or picture that would help you recall the name at a later time. Maybe you created a rhyme or a short phrase to help you remember the name. For another example, think back to a time when you received a new license plate for your car. Do you remember creating a memory trick to learn the new license plate number?

Mnemonics serve an important role in memory, but they have limitations and should be used sparingly. If you use mnemonics too extensively, they become cumbersome and can add confusion to your learning process. If you do not study the mnemonics accurately, they hinder rather than help you recall information accurately. The following chart shows the advantages and disadvantages of using mnemonics.

Advantages of Using Mnemonics	Disadvantages of Using Mnemonics
1. They provide a memory bridge to help you recall information that otherwise is difficult to remember. 2. They involve rearranging or reorganizing information, which also helps you personalize the information and be a more active learner. 3. They add interest to studying by providing you with new ways to work with information. 4. When used properly, they allow you to spend less time retrieving information from your long-term memory.	1. They must be recited and practiced in a precise manner in order to work correctly. 2. They require time to create, learn, and practice. 3. They can become "crutches" and can give you a false sense of security that you know the information. 4. They rely more on rote memory than on elaborative rehearsal, so your actual understanding of the concepts may be inadequate. 5. Overuse of mnemonics can result in confusion and an excessive expenditure of time reviewing all the mnemonics.

Some students use mnemonics quite naturally and on a regular basis. Others shy away from mnemonics because they are foreign or unfamiliar and seem to require too much extra work. However, as with all the other study skills in this textbook, after you learn how to create and study from the following kinds of mnemonics, using them when you study or in your personal life becomes an option that you can use selectively to boost your memory.

Mnemonics

1. Acronyms and acrostics
2. Associations
3. Rhythms, rhymes, and jingles
4. Pictures or graphics
5. Stacking
6. Loci (location)
7. Peg systems

Acronyms and Acrostics

Acronyms and acrostics are mnemonics designed to help you learn a list of items in either a fixed or a random order. An **acronym** is a *word or group of words* made by taking the *first letter of the key words in a list of items* and using those letters to create a new word or phrase. The new word or phrase, such as SAVE CRIB FOTO, is the mnemonic or memory bridge that helps trigger your memory to recall something, in this case the Twelve Principles of Memory. The following example shows the steps in creating and memorizing acronyms.

1. Make a list of the items you need to remember—for example, the five Great Lakes in the northern United States:

   Lake *Superior*

   Lake *Huron*

   Lake *Erie*

   Lake *Ontario*

   Lake *Michigan*

2. If any item in your list consists of more than one word, underline *one* key word that would help you remember the item. Do not choose two key words for an item, or you will end up trying to remember more items than are actually there.
3. Write the *first letter of each key word* on the side or bottom of your paper. For the Great Lakes, the letters would be *S H E O M.* If you have difficulty creating a word or a phrase, try listing the vowels on one line and the consonants on a second line below the vowels. For the Great Lakes, the letters could be lined up as follows:

       E   O
   S   H   M

4. Rearrange the letters until you can form a word or group of words. For the Great Lakes, the letters can be rearranged to create the acronym HOMES.
5. Practice memorizing the acronym. Then practice translating the acronym accurately by reciting what each letter represents: *H* (Huron), *O* (Ontario), *M* (Michigan), *E* (Erie), *S* (Superior).

Keep these important tips in mind when you create acronyms:

1. Every word needs at least one vowel *(a, e, i, o, u),* so if none of the words in your list of key words begins with a vowel, you cannot create an acronym. Your next option would be to create an acrostic (see below). For example, assume you wanted to create an acronym for six relaxation techniques: soothing mask, relaxation blanket, breathing by threes, deep breathing, deep muscle relaxation, and yoga. Even though *y* sometimes works as a vowel, you do not have other vowels to work with. Instead you have a choice of consonants: *s* or *m* (soothing mask), *r* or *b* (relaxation blanket), *b* or *t* (breathing by threes), *d* or *b* (deep breathing), *d* or *m* or *r* (deep muscle relaxation), and *y* (yoga).
2. A real word is easier to recall than a nonsense word, so strive to rearrange the letters to create real words.

3. If you must recall the key items in your list in an exact order, chances are slim that the first letter of the key words in your list of items will automatically form a word.
4. Acronyms are easier to create when you can reorder the items versus having to recall them in a fixed order.
5. If an item in your list consists of more than one word, select *one* of the words to use. If you have difficulty creating an acronym, return to the key words and select a different key word for an item on the list. For example, with the memory principle of *ongoing review,* you could work with the *o* or the *r.*
6. You cannot add additional letters to create an acronym. Adding letters that do not reflect key words in your list will confuse you when you try to recall the key words represented by the items in the acronym.

An **acrostic** is a *sentence* made by using the *first letters of the key words in a list of items* to create words that form a sentence that helps trigger your memory to recall the items in the list. The following example shows the steps in creating and memorizing with acrostics.

1. Make a list of the items you need to remember: For example, suppose you need to remember the order of operations in a math problem. They are:

   parentheses
   exponents
   multiplication
   division
   addition
   subtraction

2. If there is more than one word per item, underline *one* key word that would help you remember the item.
3. Write the *first letter of each key word* on the bottom of your paper. Leave space after each letter.

   P______ **E**______ **M**______ **D**______ **A**______ **S**______

4. Make a sentence using the letters in order. Sometimes it is easier to remember a sentence if it is *silly, bizarre,* or *significant to you.* An acrostic for the order of mathematical operations is as follows:

   Please excuse my dear Aunt Sally.

5. Memorize the sentence. Then practice translating the mnemonic by reciting what each word represents.

Keep these important tips in mind when you create acrostics:

1. Humorous or bizarre sentences are often easier to remember. If you can create a picture in your mind of the information in the sentence, that may help also.
2. You cannot add additional words to create a sentence. Each word in the sentence must begin with a letter that corresponds to the first letter of the key words in your list to memorize.
3. If more than one word in your list of items to remember begins with the same letter, try using words that begin with the *first two letters of the key words.* For example, in the Twelve Principles of Memory, there are two principles that begin with the letter *o*—organization and ongoing review. In an acrostic you could use words that begin with *or* and *on.*

EXERCISE 6.1 Working with Acronyms and Acrostics

1. *The mnemonic SAVE CRIB FOTO is an acronym that has been used throughout this book.* For any mnemonic to be effective, you must practice naming what each letter represents. *In the space below, tell what each letter represents.*

   SAVE CRIB FOTO is a mnemonic for: ____________________

S = ____________	**C** = ____________	**F** = ____________
A = ____________	**R** = ____________	**O** = ____________
V = ____________	**I** = ____________	**T** = ____________
E = ____________	**B** = ____________	**O** = ____________

2. Create acronyms for the following items. The letters to use appear before the space to write your acronym. In some cases, you have a choice of letters to use for key items; remember, however, to use *one*—not both—of the letters.

   a. A pediatrician's advice for food a child should eat when he or she has a stomach flu: *bananas, applesauce, toast, rice.*

   Letters to use: **b a t r**

   Acronym: ____________________

   b. What you should do to treat sudden muscle injuries: *compress, elevate, use ice,* and *rest.*

   Letters to use: **c e u** *or* **i r**

   Acronym: ____________________

   c. The four voices in a quartet: *alto, bass, tenor,* and *soprano.*

   Letters to use: **a b t s**

   Acronym: ____________________

   d. Ten body systems in humans: *skeletal, digestive, muscular, endocrine, circulatory, nervous, reproductive, urinary, respiratory,* and *integumentary.*

   Letters to use: **s d m e c n r u r i**

   Acronym: ____________________

3. Create acrostics for the following items. The letters to use to begin words in a sentence appear below; however, if the items do not need to appear in order, you may rearrange the letters.

   a. Four levels of response in order for test questions: *immediate, delayed, assisted,* and *educated guessing*

   I ________ d ________ a ________ g ________.

   b. Steps for writing goals: *Set* ***specific*** *goals, set specific* ***target*** *date and time, identify* ***steps,*** and *plan a* ***reward***

   S ________ t ________ s ________ r ________.

   c. Maslow's Hierarchy of Needs: *physiological, safety, social, esteem,* and *self-realization*

   P ________ s ________ s ________ e ________ s ________.

d. Types of contemporary views on motivation: *Equity Theory, Expectancy Theory, Reinforcement Theory,* and *Theory Z*

E ________ e ________ r ________ z ________.

e. The names of the five lines of the treble clef in the music staff are *E, G, B, D,* and *F.* A famous acrostic for these lines is: *Every good boy does fine.* Create a new acrostic for the lines in the treble clef.

E ________ g ________ b ________ d ________ f ________.

Associations

Oftentimes an item can be remembered when you associate it to something that is familiar or has a similar characteristic. For example, if you want to remember someone's name and the person has the same name as your aunt, connect the person to your aunt. When you see the person again, you think about your aunt and remember this person's name. You can also link the person to an object. If the person's last name is Carpenter, picture the person wearing a carpenter's apron and holding a hammer in one hand.

The following examples show other kinds of **associations** that have been created to remember specific information:

- How high is Mount Fuji in Japan? You can remember the height by stringing the number of months in a year to the number of days in a year and then adding 24 hours: 12,365 + 24 = 12,389 feet.
- Do you enjoy a nice "dessert" or a nice "desert" after dinner? After dinner, you want dessert, the word with two *S*'s. Just remember this mnemonic that has two *S*'s: *s*o *s*weet.
- You must remember to get your gym clothes out of the dryer tomorrow before you go to school. Since you always start coffee in the morning, go to bed with a clear mental picture of your gym clothes stuffed inside the coffee pot. The association occurs in the morning when you see the coffee pot.
- Do you frequently confuse the spelling of two homonyms: principal and principle? You can use this mnemonic to avoid further confusion. A princi*pal* is your pal; he is also the princi*pal* (main) administrator in the school. The only time you use the *-ple* spelling is when you are referring to a ru*le* or a standard. So you study *principles* of accounting; you live your life based on your *principles*. However, you pay the *principal* on a loan; you have the *principal* role in a play.

Rhythms, Rhymes, and Jingles

Auditory learners and those with strong language or musical skills enjoy learning through **rhythms, rhymes, and jingles**. Such individuals can use their creativity by rhyming words, attaching a catchy tune or rhythm, creating a rap, or thinking up a jingle. Any time you find yourself singing a commercial or repeating an advertising slogan, marketing experts have succeeded in getting information into your long-term memory. When you use this form of mnemonic, you are using your verbal and musical strengths to boost your memory. The following examples demonstrate the use of rhythms, rhymes, and jingles as mnemonics to learn information.

Many companies have memorable jingles or slogans. What company or product slogans do you know?

- Use *i* before *e* when you hear a *long e* except after *c* (chief, believe, receive, sleigh, eight).
- Use *i* before *e* except after *c* or when sounded as *a* as in *neighbor* and *weigh.*
- In fourteen hundred and ninety-two, Columbus sailed the ocean blue.
- Spring forward; fall back (daylight saving time).
- Thirty days hath September, April, June, and November. All the rest have thirty-one (except February).
- Who invented dynamite? *Alfred Nobel had quite a fright when he discovered dynamite.*
- Which way should you turn to open a jar or tighten a bolt? *Righty tighty, lefty loosy.*
- Stalactites are icicle-shaped deposits that hang down from the roof of a cave. Stalagmites are deposits in a cave that build up from the floor. *When the mites go up, the tights come down.*

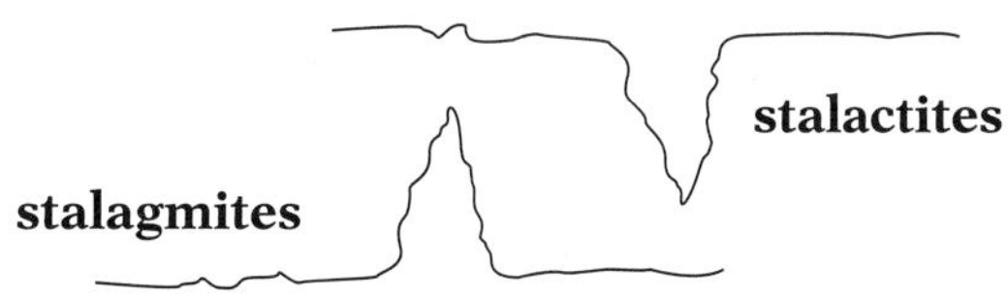

Pictures and Graphics

Pictures and graphics are stored differently than words in long-term memory. Visual learners and students with artistic talents often find that converting information into pictures or graphics and using a variety of colors in their study tools help them remember and recall information more efficiently.

To boost your memory, you can add pictures and graphics to study tools such as mappings, hierarchies, category charts, Cornell notes, or index cards. Linking pictures and colors with words often creates a stronger imprint of information in long-term memory. Notice how the combination of words and pictures in the Chapter 2 Links exercise, page 52, facilitates the process of learning the Twelve Principles of Memory; if you are not able to recall the words, you can shift your attention or memory search to the pictures that appear on the study tool. As you experiment with the impact of detailed pictures, whimsical cartoons, basic stick figures, or colorful borders or patterns in your study tools, you create opportunities to add creativity and interest to your work. The following examples show creative ways to combine pictures with information you may need to learn.

- Three cognitive learning modalities

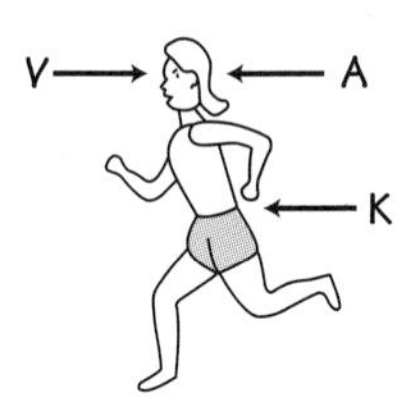

■ Eight intelligences

Visual-spatial	Bodily-kinesthetic
Linguistic	Intrapersonal
Music	Interpersonal
Logical math	Naturalist

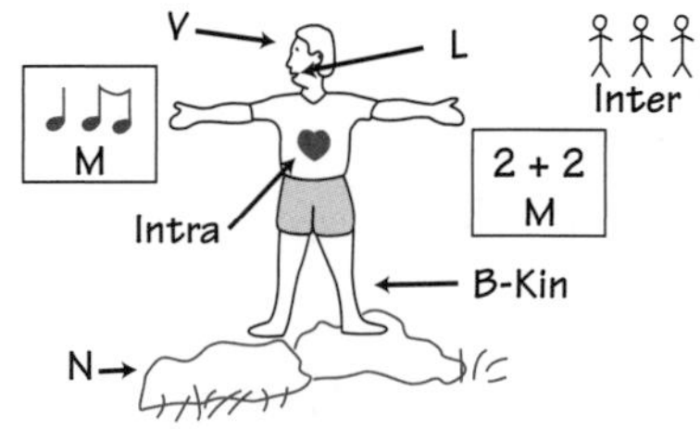

■ Do you sometimes forget which direction is *latitude* and which is *longitude* on a map or globe? Say each word and exaggerate your mouth as shown in the pictures. Notice when your mouth is *long?* Say "latitude" with your mouth smiling (going *around* the globe).

■ Is the Tropic of Cancer north or south of the equator? Which is the Tropic of Capricorn? Well, when you have *corns* on your feet, are they on the northern or the southern half of your body? The picture helps with the visual image.

Stacking

The **stacking** type of mnemonic uses pictures and associations to remember a list of items. To create a stacking mnemonic, begin by listing the items you need to remember. Then create a strong visual image of the first item on the bottom of the stack. In your mind, add the next item. Visually review the first item and then the second item before you add the third item. Continue this process of reviewing the previous items before you add a new item. Practice reciting the items from your visual memory. In addition to using this technique for lists of items from one of your courses, you can practice strengthening your visual memory by using the technique for a shopping list. You can then go to the store and complete your shopping without carrying a written list of items. The following stacking shows a shopping list with ten items.

Exercise 6.2 LINKS

1. The following pictures represent the Five Theories of Forgetting. Write the name of each theory under the relevant picture.

5 Theories of Forgetting

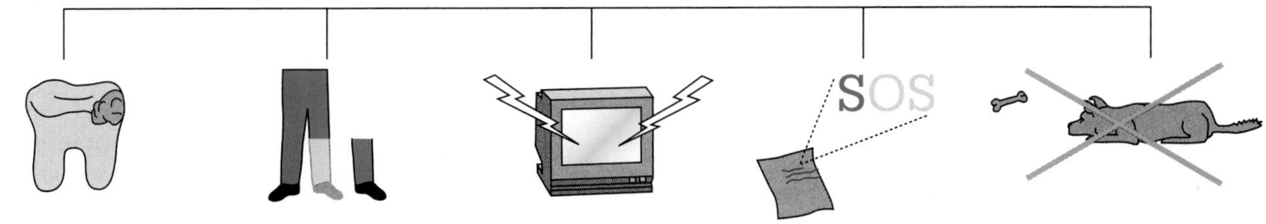

2. List the Five Theories of Forgetting and one letter for each key word. Create an acronym.

List the Five Theories	Write the Letters	Create Your Acronym
a. ______	______	______
b. ______	______	
c. ______	______	
d. ______	______	
e. ______	______	

3. Create your own pictures for each of the Five Theories of Forgetting. Present them in the form of a *stacking.*

4. Draw the Information Processing Model. On the model, show where each theory of forgetting occurs. Organize your work in a way that is easy to read and understand.

Loci

Loci, which means *locations*, is a mnemonic that dates back to the early times of Greek orators, who could deliver lengthy speeches without any written notes. Instead orators made mental notes by associating parts or topics of their speeches with familiar rooms or locations in a building. In their minds, as they walked through each room, they visualized items in the rooms that they associated to the topic to be discussed. With this technique they were able to deliver organized, fluent speeches to their audiences.

For example, you may want to picture the first floor of a building on your campus. The following drawing shows *front doors, hallway, cafeteria, lounge area, hallway, lecture hall, foreign language lab,* and *restrooms*. For each of these locations, you could mentally attach a picture that represents the topic you would like to present in a speech, or you could attach pictures that represent a specific event in a sequence of events.

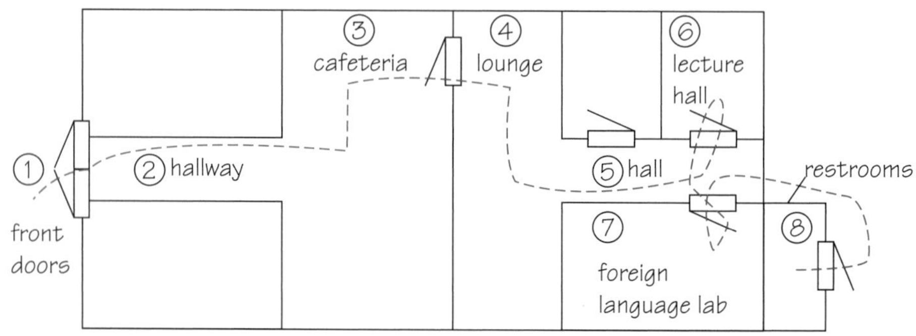

For example, assume that you are going to give a speech or write an essay for a history class about the end of the economic boom in the 1970s. You need to discuss these topics: 350% increase in oil prices; Arab oil embargo; high retail prices; slump in auto industry and manufacturing; high unemployment; easy credit; high costs of health, safety, and pollution controls; and massive government spending. You can picture the following images at each location in the building:

1. At the front door, picture a poster that says "350% increase in oil prices."
2. In the hallway, picture a row of oil barrels with large Xs painted on them.
3. In the cafeteria, picture food prices: hamburgers $4.50, milk $3.00.
4. In the lounge, picture posters on the walls of closed factories.
5. In the hall, picture people lined up for job interviews.
6. In the lecture hall, picture credit card companies handing out high interest credit cards to students.
7. In the foreign language lab, picture a filthy, unsafe, polluted room with a sign that says, "Too expensive to meet standards."
8. In the restrooms, picture outrageous price tags hanging on fixtures that bear a label that says, "Government property."

Use the following steps to create and learn from a loci mnemonic.

1. Make a list of the items you need to remember.
2. Draw a floor plan of a familiar location.
3. On paper or mentally, attach a picture of the first item you need to remember. Place this picture inside the first location or room on your floor plan. You can exaggerate the size or shape of the pictures or hang them in unusual positions to make them stand out in your memory.
4. Continue walking through the floor plan, attaching one item in each room.
5. Visually practice walking through all the rooms and reciting the important information associated to the items in the rooms.

EXERCISE 6.3 Using Loci

1. Select one of the following situations to use with the loci mnemonic technique:
   a. You need to have an important discussion with your roommate concerning five issues.
   b. You have an appointment with your instructor to discuss four topics about the class and your work.
   c. You need to remember the sequence of events or steps for information from one of your courses. There are at least four events or steps in this information.
2. Draw a floor plan of a familiar building. In each room, attach a picture that symbolizes the item you need to discuss or name.
3. Practice mentally walking through your building and reciting the information represented by the pictures in each room. Your instructor may ask you to recite your information in class.

Peg Systems

Several kinds of **peg systems** can be used to help you remember a list of items. With each peg system, you must first learn a set of pegs that never changes. Each peg is a word represented by a picture. The items on your list that you need to remember are "hung" or attached to the pegs. Pictures that are bizarre, humorous, or exaggerated are easier to remember. By rehearsing the pegs and the attached pictures frequently, you can recall an item by remembering the peg.

The **rhyming peg system** uses a picture that rhymes with a number word from one to ten. This picture is the peg that never changes. In your mind, create a picture for each of the following:

one	= bun	six	= sticks
two	= shoe	seven	= heaven
three	= tree	eight	= gate
four	= door	nine	= vine
five	= hive	ten	= hen

What memory techniques might a motivational speaker use in order to present a speech without reading directly from a set of notes?

Assume you want to use the rhyming peg system to remember eight secondary defense mechanisms discussed in psychology: *displacement, projection, identification, rationalization, intellectualization, substitution, fantasy,* and *regression.* Your task, then, is to link the first mechanism with the *bun.* Continue to create the visual links; review each peg and defense mechanism before you add a new one to the visual image. The examples on the following page show associations you could make to learn the eight secondary defense mechanisms.

Peg Picture	Defense Mechanism	Picture You Create with the Peg
bun	displacement	a hamburger bun being thrown into a garbage can (displaced)
shoe	projection	a shoe thrown through the air as a projectile
tree	identification	a person with a magnifying glass examining a tree
door	rationalization	an opened door with someone being kicked out; the word *but* is written numerous times on the door
hive	intellectualization	surround the hive with "intellectual" facts related to bee hives: drones, worker bees, queen bee, honey
sticks	substitution	show a hand replacing a brown stick with a red stick
heaven	fantasy	show a person fantasizing about life in heaven
gate	regression	show a person walking backward out of a gate

A **number shape peg system** uses a picture in the shape of the number for each peg. A number peg system can go beyond ten pegs. If you have ever seen a stage performer memorize fifty or one hundred items that the audience calls out, chances are that the performer used a number shape peg system to memorize the items quickly. A person with sharp visual memory skills can quickly recall items in numerical order or out of sequence. Memorize the first twelve pegs that commonly appear in this system.

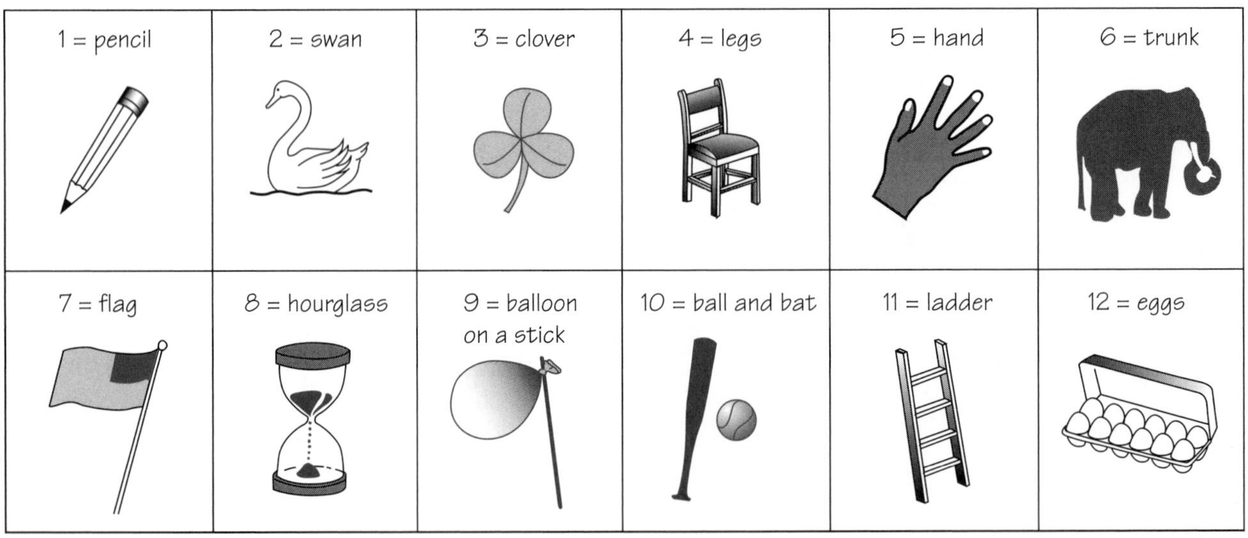

You can use this number peg system for a list of items in one of your courses, or you can use it for everyday convenience, such as remembering a list of items while grocery shopping or a list of weekend tasks you need to accomplish. For a list of eight weekend tasks, begin by memorizing the first eight pegs. Then take the first task and associate a mental picture to the pencil. In the following example, your first task is to start the laundry. You could picture a washing machine with an enlarged shirt and a pencil in its pocket as it is about to enter the machine. The funnier your picture is, the easier it will be to remember. After you see the picture clearly, work with the second item. Review items one and two mentally. Proceed to add one item at a time. With practice, you can hang items quickly on the pegs. The following example demonstrates visualizing eight different tasks on the first eight pegs.

EXERCISE 6.4 Creating Mnemonics

Use any of the seven kinds of mnemonics listed on page 142 to create a mnemonic for each of the following:

1. Planets in order: Mercury, Venus, Earth, Mars, Jupiter, Saturn, Uranus, Neptune, Pluto

2. Eight parts of speech: noun, pronoun, verb, adverb, adjective, preposition, conjunction, interjection

3. The seven coordinating conjunctions used in compound sentences: for, and, nor, but, or, yet, so

4. Skeletal (bone) structure of the arm: humerus, ulna, radius, carpals, phalanges

5. Elisabeth Kübler-Ross's stages of facing death: denial, anger, bargaining, depression, acceptance

6. Four types of cloud structures: cumulus, stratus, nimbus, cirrus

7. Five extinct species or races of humans: Java Ape, Peking, Heidelberg, Neanderthal, Cro-Magnon

EXERCISE 6.5 Checking Your Memory

How much do you remember from this chapter? (Some mnemonics are provided as hints.) Answer as many as possible of the following questions without looking back at the text.

1. What are the names of the five Great Lakes? (HOMES)

   ________ ________ ________ ________ ________

2. What is the order of operations in a math problem? (Please excuse my dear Aunt Sally.)

   ________ ________ ________ ________ ________ ________

3. What should you feed a child with stomach flu symptoms?

   ________ ________ ________ ________

4. What are the ten human body systems? (*Nicer drums*, or your own acronym)

   ________ ________ ________ ________ ________

   ________ ________ ________ ________ ________

5. If you want to loosen a lid on a jar, do you turn it to the right or the left? ________________
6. Do stalagmites point up or down? ________________
7. What are the Five Theories of Forgetting?

   ________ ________ ________ ________ ________

8. Is the Tropic of Cancer north or south of the equator? ________________
9. What are the first four secondary defense mechanisms in psychology? (bun, shoe, tree, door)

   ________ ________ ________ ________

10. What are the four voices in a quartet?

    ________ ________ ________ ________

11. Do longitude lines run north and south or east and west? ________________
12. What picture represents each of the following numbers in a number peg system?

    8 = ________ 3 = ________ 6 = ________

    11 = ________ 1 = ________ 7 = ________

Reflection Writing 2

CHAPTER 6

On a separate piece of paper or in a journal, do the following:

1. **What is your reaction to the various types of mnemonics you can create for information you need to learn? Do you enjoy using mnemonics? Why or why not? What are the benefits? What are the drawbacks?**
2. **What mnemonics have you learned elsewhere? Do you remember any from elementary, junior high, or high school? What mnemonics have you learned or created in other college courses?**

Preparing for Tests

In college tests are a way of assessing your understanding of information presented in your courses. Tests also indicate how well you have prepared, the effectiveness of your study methods, and how well you can take tests. (Chapters 12 and 13 provide you with specific test-taking strategies for objective, recall, math, and essay tests.) Students who do not apply study skills on a regular basis often need to resort to cramming. **Cramming** is an attempt to learn large amounts of information in a short period of time. Cramming is a survival technique that often backfires; frequently, students who cram become even more aware of how much *they do not know.* Feeling underprepared can create test anxiety and lead to poor test performance. As discussed in Chapter 2, the brain needs time to process information, form associations or connections between information, and assign meaning to concepts and details. Cramming does not provide the brain with time to learn information thoroughly and accurately. Effective study strategies, including the following test-preparation strategies, will help you prepare for tests and increase your test performance.

Test-Preparation Strategies

1. Make a five-day time management plan to prepare for major tests.
2. Make summary notes as you review chapters and sections of materials.
3. Find out as much as you can about the upcoming test.
4. Predict test questions.
5. Write and answer practice test questions.
6. Participate in a review session.
7. Deal with sources of test anxiety before the test.

Five-Day Plan

Review the **five-day study plan** to prepare for tests (Chapter 4, pages 100–102). For smaller tests, use the same steps but shorten the time period. Perhaps you will do all of the steps in two days instead of five. The important point is to allow some time to review the information and then some time both the night before the test and the day of the test to review summary material one last time.

Make Summary Notes

Summary notes are a special set of notes that you create specifically to study for tests. These are the notes that you will review the day before the test (day 5) and immediately before the test. Frequently when you begin the review and test preparation process, you become aware of how much you have learned. Information that was once foreign now seems to be "obvious, logical, or common sense." After reviewing this information and feeling confident that you know it, you do not need to spend any more time reviewing it. Move on to the next set of information. The information that you identify as needing to be reviewed further should be placed in some form of summary notes. Summary notes are also valuable if you know specific kinds of questions that will appear on the test. For example, if the teacher clearly tells you that there will be an essay on a specific topic, as you review you will want to create summary notes that pull together information that can be used in that essay. Review formats for summary notes in Chapter 4, page 101.

Find Out About the Test

Take the time and make the effort to find out as much as you can about the upcoming test. Some teachers make previous tests available for review. Some teachers will provide you with details about the types of questions and which areas to study. Knowing the kinds of questions, the number of questions, and the areas of emphasis often has a calming effect because you are better able to predict what you will encounter when you receive the test. Sometimes talking to students who have already completed the course is helpful, especially if the teacher provides you with little information. Former students may be able to give you suggestions for ways to study for a particular teacher's tests and the kinds of tests to expect. However, teachers change their tests and their test formats, so do not become overconfident based on information received from former students.

Predict Test Questions

Predicting test questions is an excellent method for preparing for tests and reducing test anxiety. Predicting test questions is even easier after you have taken one or two tests from a specific teacher and have a sense of the types of tests he or she uses. Understanding types of test questions is the first step. The following chart shows test formats that are common in college courses.

Kind of Question	Level of Difficulty	Includes	Requires
Recognition (objective)	Easiest	True-False Multiple-Choice Matching	Read and recognize whether information is correct; apply a skill and then recognize the correct answer.
Recall	More demanding	Fill-in-the-Blanks Listings Definitions Short Answers	Retrieve the information from your memory.
Essay	Most difficult	Essays	Retrieve the information from memory, organize it, and use effective writing skills.

Effective test preparation should include studying all the important material thoroughly so you are well prepared for any type of test question. However, many students prefer to modify their test-preparation strategies to reflect specific testing formats when the formats are announced in advance. The following chart provides you with a summary of the types of material you should focus on and practice strategies to include in your review time.

If You Predict . . .	Study This Kind of Information:	Practice May Include:
Objective Questions	• Definitions of key terms • Category flash cards • Details: names, dates, theories, rules, events	• Writing true-false questions • Writing multiple-choice questions • Writing matching questions • Working with a study partner to exchange practice questions
Recall Questions	• Information presented in lists • Definition cards —say and spell words on the fronts for fill-in-the-blank tests —three-part definitions on the backs of cards for definition and short-answer tests • Category cards • Cornell recall columns (Chapter 9) • Questions created in the *Q* step of SQ4R (Chapter 7) • Summaries at the ends of chapters (Chapter 8) • Details on visual notetaking systems (Chapter 11)	• Reciting information in full sentences and in your own words • Writing a short summary to practice expressing ideas on paper • Writing answers to the questions created in the *Q* step of SQ4R • Writing your own questions for fill-in-the-blank questions, listings, words to define, and short answers • Working with a study partner to exchange practice questions
Essay Questions	• Themes • Relationships • Major concepts	• See Chapter 13 for strategies.

Write and Answer Practice Test Questions

Writing and answering practice test questions is an excellent way to prepare for an upcoming test. You can refer to your textbook and your lecture notes to write objective, recall, and essay questions. If you have a study partner, each of you can practice writing test questions and then exchange questions so you can practice writing test answers. If you do not have a study partner, you can practice answering your own test questions.

On your tests, you will encounter a variety of types of questions. In 1956, a psychologist named Benjamin Bloom developed a classification system with colleagues for levels of questions commonly used in educational settings. This classification system, known as **Bloom's Taxonomy**, begins with the lowest level of questions (recall or recognition of knowledge) and ends with the highest or most complex level of questions (evaluation). The following chart shows the skills that each type of question demonstrates and *question cues* or direction words that each level of question uses. When you write your practice questions, strive to include questions for each of these categories.

Bloom's Taxonomy

Levels	Skills Demonstrated and Question Cues
Knowledge	• observation and recall of information • knowledge of dates, events, places • knowledge of major ideas • mastery of subject matter • *Question Cues:* list, define, tell, describe, identify, show, label, collect, examine, tabulate, quote, name, who, when, where, etc.
Comprehension	• understanding information • grasp meaning • translate knowledge into new context • interpret facts, compare, contrast • order, group, infer causes • predict consequences • *Question Cues:* summarize, describe, interpret, contrast, predict, associate, distinguish, estimate, differentiate, discuss, extend
Application	• use information • use methods, concepts, theories in new situations • solve problems using required skills or knowledge • *Question Cues:* apply, demonstrate, calculate, complete, illustrate, show, solve, examine, modify, relate, change, classify, experiment, discover
Analysis	• seeing patterns • organization of parts • recognition of hidden meanings • identification of components • *Question Cues:* analyze, separate, order, explain, connect, classify,arrange, divide, compare, select, explain, infer
Synthesis	• use old ideas to create new ones • generalize from given facts • relate knowledge from several areas • predict, draw conclusions • *Question Cues:* combine, integrate, modify, rearrange, substitute, plan, create, design, invent, what if?, compose, formulate, prepare, generalize, rewrite
Evaluation	• compare and discriminate among ideas • assess value of theories, presentations • make choices based on reasoned argument • verify value of evidence • recognize subjectivity • *Question Cues:* assess, decide, rank, grade, test, measure, recommend, convince, select, judge, explain, discriminate, support, conclude, compare, summarize

*Adapted from: Bloom, B. S. (Ed.) (1956) Taxonomy of educational objectives: The classification of educational goals: Handbook I, cognitive domain. New York, Toronto: Longmans, Green. [Source: http://www.coun.uvic.ca/learn/program/hndouts/bloom.html]

Participate in Review Sessions

Review sessions are a powerful way to receive immediate feedback about both the topics you understand clearly and those that you need to review further. Review sessions often provide you with the opportunity to verbalize information, which again is an excellent form of feedback. Actively listening to other students explain information or answer practice test questions can be a rewarding learning experience. If the teacher has not organized a review session, take the initiative to invite another student or a small group of students to meet with you to review. Frequently, review sessions are more productive if one person suggests a review approach to use. Here are a few possibilities:

- Each member writes a specific number of practice test questions to bring to the group.
- Each member is responsible for summarizing a specific chapter and facilitating a discussion on that chapter.
- Each member brings some type of study tool to the group to use for reviewing. This may be a set of index cards, or lecture, textbook, or visual notes.

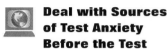

Deal with Sources of Test Anxiety Before the Test

Understanding anxiety begins by first understanding stress. **Stress** is defined as your reaction or response to events or situations that threaten to disrupt your normal pattern or routine. With normal stress, a person is aware of the stress and aware of the source of the stress. The person is also still able to control his or her reaction or responses. A student may feel stress related to an upcoming test. That stress actually helps to motivate the student to work hard to try to do his or her best. *Anxiety* occurs when the level of stress is excessive to the point that it hinders one's ability to perform well. During a bout with anxiety, a person no longer recognizes the source of the excessive stress, no longer has control of the situation, and is reactionary rather than problem-solving oriented.

Test anxiety is excessive stress that may occur before or during a test. Test anxiety hinders performance and immobilizes thinking abilities. A student may "go blank," make excessive careless mistakes, mark answers in the wrong place, or quit due to frustration. Symptoms of test anxiety may appear in physical or emotional forms, as shown in the chart below.

Physical Symptoms of Anxiety	Emotional Symptoms of Anxiety
Rapid heartbeat Increased blood pressure Upset stomach, nausea Shakiness Abnormal nervousness Headaches Tight muscles, tension Clammy palms, sweating Blurred vision	"Going blank" Sense of confusion, disorientation Panicky feelings Depression Procrastination Short temper Continuous negative self-talk Crying, sobbing Misdirected attention, focus on other things Feelings of "fight or flight" Fixating on one item too long Exaggeration of consequences Feelings of frustration, anger

Test anxiety is a *learned behavior.* As such, it can be unlearned. The first step is to analyze the situation and your feelings to identify when the behavior begins and what triggers the anxiety.

There are four common sources of test anxiety:

1. *Underpreparedness* Knowing that you have not put enough time and effort into reading and homework assignments or ongoing review is one source of test anxiety. Using effective study skills consistently each week throughout the term can eliminate this source of test anxiety.
2. *Past experiences* Some test anxiety may stem from past experiences that affected a person's belief system, self-esteem, and confidence. Negative self-talk may occur, telling the person that he or she never does well on tests, does not understand the material, or will not pass the course. Test anxiety rooted in past experiences sometimes is complex and difficult to resolve. Seeking guidance from a counselor is one way to address the deep-seated issues. For milder cases, using affirmations, positive self-talk, goal-setting, and concentration strategies, such as *seeing success,* may be the key to letting go of past beliefs and attitudes that cause the test anxiety. Using effective study strategies, working in study groups with ample feedback, and successfully completing daily assignments will also build confidence levels and reduce test anxiety.
3. *Fear of failure* Placing undue emphasis on one test may be tied to the fear of failure. Students with this type of test anxiety may fear disappointing someone else (parents, a partner, or an instructor), losing a scholarship or eligibility in an athletic program or financial aid, or not being able to live up to their own personal standards. These students have the tendency to link their grades to their self-worth. If they do poorly on a test, they label themselves *dumb* or *no good.* They exaggerate the importance of one test and fail to see that one test or one grade is only a measure of performance at that one moment in time and for that one specific course. To overcome this type of test anxiety, students can look at the variety of methods used to calculate their grades in a course. They can gain a more realistic look at their overall performance by talking with their instructors or developing a plan of action to boost their grades in the areas of assessment that are not based on tests (such as completion of homework, class participation, attendance, or extra credit projects). Dealing with the fear of failure early in the term will prevent this type of belief system from escalating.
4. *Poor test-taking skills* Some students are prepared for tests and know the course content, yet still feel test anxiety. These students may lack test-taking skills or strategies. Chapters 12 and 13 provide the necessary skills to learn *how* to take different kinds of tests and boost test performance.

Besides the study skills and test preparation skills already discussed, you can use two additional anxiety-reducing strategies to reduce or eliminate test anxiety. **Locus of control** is a concept that refers to a person's sense of control. An **internal locus of control** means that the individual feels that he or she has the power to control his or her circumstances. An **external locus of control** means that the individual relinquishes control and sees other people or other situations as having the power. Low self-esteem, low confidence in one's abilities, and high levels of frustration blamed on what other people are doing to cause a person's situation are results of an external locus of control. To reduce test anxiety, the locus of control needs to shift to the individual, to become an *internal* locus of control. A person who has an internal locus of control has self-confidence and perceives that he or she has the ability to perform well and succeed. The central focus or source of power is in accepting responsibility for events. Notice the difference in power between external and internal centers of control in the following chart.

External Locus of Control	Internal Locus of Control
I did not do well because the teacher does not like me. This test is totally unfair. I could not study because of my children. All the questions were trick questions. I failed the test because it was poorly written. The teacher did not even take the time to try to understand what I wrote. The teacher did not understand my situation.	My negative attitude is affecting my work. I was not prepared for this test. I did not remember to study the charts. I need to find more time to myself to study. I need to strengthen my test-taking skills. I need to add more review time. I need to improve my writing skills. I did not know the answer to the essay question. I should join a study group.

Systematic desensitization is the second anxiety-reducing strategy that you can use before the day of a test. This strategy involves a series of exercises or activities designed to reduce strong negative emotional reactions to upcoming tests. With this strategy, you replace fear-based thoughts with positive thoughts that emphasize the successes you have already experienced. *Seeing success* is one desensitization activity in which you replace the image of failure with the image of success. Systematic desensitization can also be used in the following ways:

1. Make a list of specific situations or words that trigger your test anxiety. For example, words such as *There will be a test next Monday on chapters 2 through 5* may trigger early test anxiety. After you have your list of *trigger situations or words,* take time to visualize yourself reacting in a different manner. Perhaps you could visualize your response as *Good. I have time to make a five-day plan,* or *I have stayed current with my work, so I can be ready for this test.* Basically you are creating and rehearsing a script that emphasizes a constructive, positive behavior.
2. Predict and write practice test questions. Decide on an appropriate amount of time to answer the test questions. Create a test environment as close as possible to the real thing. If the classroom in which you will take a test is empty, be in that room when you take your practice test. Use relaxation techniques and other study skills you know to work through the test without a strong negative reaction.

The two following exercises, 6.6 and 6.7, will help you analyze additional information about yourself and your test-preparation skills. The insights you gain from these two exercises can help you unlearn ineffective behavior and attitudinal patterns and learn new behaviors and attitudes to improve your overall test-taking performance.

EXERCISE 6.6 Academic Preparation Questionnaire

What was the last test you took in one of your classes? ___________________
Think back to the days prior to that test. Check YES or NO for the following statements. Be honest with your answers.

	YES	NO
1. I had all the reading assignments done on time.	______	______
2. I had all the homework assignments done on time.	______	______
3. I reviewed the work on my homework assignments when they were returned.	______	______
4. I asked questions about information I didn't understand.	______	______
5. I worked with a tutor or a study partner for review.	______	______
6. I recited information that I was studying on a regular basis.	______	______
7. I followed my time-management schedule and used the 2:1 ratio.	______	______
8. I spent time reviewing each week.	______	______
9. I attended classes regularly.	______	______
10. I was an active learner and used a variety of study methods.	______	______
11. I used active reading techniques and took notes.	______	______
12. I created study tools that I have found to be effective.	______	______
13. I found enough time to read and highlight the textbook carefully.	______	______
14. I made a special study schedule for the days prior to the test.	______	______
15. I used study techniques that gave me feedback.	______	______
16. I was an active listener and participant in class.	______	______
17. I was able to stay fairly motivated about the class and the work.	______	______
18. I was organized and was able to find the materials I needed to study.	______	______
19. I avoided cramming the night before the test.	______	______
20. I can honestly say that I gave it my best.	______	______

If you answered yes *to all or most of the above questions, you used effective study techniques and should have been well prepared for the test. All of the* no *answers indicate a need to improve your study methods. Analyze the* no *answers to determine which study techniques you need to strengthen. Review the specific skills you need to learn to utilize more effectively.*

EXERCISE 6.7 Test Anxiety Indicator

Check the response that seems to best *describe you this term.*

	NEVER	SOMETIMES	ALWAYS
1. I procrastinate so much about studying that I am always behind in my assignments.	❒	❒	❒
2. I found it necessary to cram for the last test I took.	❒	❒	❒
3. I read the textbook, but I do not highlight or take any other kind of textbook notes.	❒	❒	❒
4. I have trouble sleeping the night before a test.	❒	❒	❒
5. I fear the consequences of failing a test.	❒	❒	❒
6. I can't help but remember what happened on the last test: I really blew it.	❒	❒	❒
7. My negative voice is quick to tell me what I can't do.	❒	❒	❒
8. I can feel a lot of tension in my shoulders, arms, or face on the day of a test.	❒	❒	❒
9. My heart beats fast during a test.	❒	❒	❒
10. I feel hot, clammy, or downright sick during a test.	❒	❒	❒
11. I am much more hesitant to enter the classroom on a test day.	❒	❒	❒
12. I try to find excuses not to go to school on the day of a test.	❒	❒	❒
13. I am irritable, snappy, impatient, and sometimes even rude right before a test.	❒	❒	❒
14. I make careless mistakes on the test. Sometimes I can't believe the answers that I marked.	❒	❒	❒
15. As soon as I leave the classroom after taking a test, I remember answers that I didn't know during the test.	❒	❒	❒
16. My mind goes blank, but I know that I know the answers.	❒	❒	❒
17. I get distracted and annoyed by the littlest things others do in class during a test.	❒	❒	❒
18. I always worry about not having enough time to complete tests.	❒	❒	❒
19. Without knowing why, I panic and start changing answers right before I turn the test in.	❒	❒	❒
20. I get stuck on one question and become stubborn. I don't want to move on until I remember the answer.	❒	❒	❒
21. I hurry to get out of the room and out of the test as quickly as possible.	❒	❒	❒
22. Enough is enough. I don't even want to think about going back to check my answers or proofread.	❒	❒	❒
23. I turn in tests that are incomplete even when I have more time.	❒	❒	❒
24. I find myself blaming the teacher, my family, or my friends for the fact that I am not prepared for tests.	❒	❒	❒
25. I did not find time to make summary notes or review effectively.	❒	❒	❒

Answers in the NEVER column = No problem; not indicators of test anxiety
Answers in the SOMETIMES column = Possible indicators; seek ways to alter your behavior
Answers in the ALWAYS column = Sources of test anxiety; seek strategies to reduce these

Exercise 6.8 Case Studies

Each of the following case studies describes a student situation. Read each case study carefully; highlight key ideas or student issues. Answer the question that ends each case study. These case studies are also available online; you can email your response to your instructor or print a copy of your work online.

1. Adolpho has not been in school for fifteen years. He was never taught how to study or take tests. He works hard and is able to respond in class and in study groups to questions that are related to the current assignment. However, when it is time to take tests that cover several chapters of information, he freezes and goes blank. What test-preparation and test-taking strategies would you recommend for Adolpho?

2. Jellison does not study much for her communications class because she is taking the class for pass/no pass rather than a grade. As the end of the term approaches, she realizes that she may not have enough points to pass the class. She intends to deal with the situation the way she usually deals with tests—cramming in the day or two before the final exam. What test-preparation strategies would you suggest she use during the last two weeks of the term?

3. Richard enjoys creating mnemonics. He has made more than forty index cards with mnemonics for his biology class. As he prepares for a midterm exam, he starts to panic. Information from one mnemonic is interfering with information from other mnemonics. He is frustrated because his mnemonics no longer seem to be working. What strategies can Richard use to reduce his frustration and prepare more effectively for the midterm exam?

Reflection Writing 3 — CHAPTER 6

On a separate piece of paper or in a journal, consider which strategies discussed in this chapter for boosting your memory and preparing for tests would be most beneficial for you to learn. Summarize your ideas.

SUMMARY

- Five Theories of Forgetting help explain why you may forget information during the learning process: Decay Theory, Displacement Theory, Interference Theory, Incomplete Encoding Theory, and Retrieval Failure Theory. Effective study strategies can combat each type of forgetting.
- Mnemonics—when used selectively—are helpful for remembering information. Mnemonics provide a bridge when you do memory searches. The following mnemonics may be incorporated into your study skills strategies:

acronyms	pictures or graphics
acrostics	stacking
associations	loci
rhythms, rhymes, and jingles	peg systems

- Cramming is a survival technique in which you attempt to learn large amounts of information in a short period of time. To avoid cramming you can create a five-day time management plan, as well as summary notes to review.
- To prepare effectively for tests, you should find out as much about an upcoming test as possible.
- Predicting test questions and writing a variety of practice test questions helps you prepare for tests and reduces test anxiety.
- When you write practice test questions, use direction words from each of the levels of Bloom's Taxonomy. Bloom's levels of questions, from most basic to most complex, will prepare you for the kinds of questions you may encounter on tests: knowledge, comprehension, application, analysis, synthesis, and evaluation.
- Test anxiety, defined as excessive stress, hinders performance and immobilizes thinking abilities. Test anxiety is a learned behavior stemming from underpreparedness, past experiences, fear of failure, or poor test-taking skills.
- In addition to the use of effective study skills strategies, developing an internal locus of control and using systematic desensitization can reduce or eliminate test anxiety.

ACE Practice Tests, which are scored online, supplementary exercises, enrichment activities, and related web site links are available online for *Essential Study Skills*, 4e. Use the following directions to access this web site:

Type: **http://college.hmco.com/collegesurvival/students**

Click on *List of Sites by Author*. Use the arrow to scroll down to Wong *Essential Study Skills*, 4e. Click on the title. If you are working on your own computer, bookmark this web site.

LEARNING OPTIONS

The following learning options provide you with opportunities to demonstrate your understanding of the topics in Chapter 6. Your instructor may assign one or more specific options or may ask you to select one or more options that interest you the most.

1. Expand the Chapter 6 mapping on page 137. Copy this structure on a blank piece of paper. Reread the information under each heading in your textbook. Extend branches on the mapping to show important key words or phrases for each heading. You can add pictures and colors to your mapping to accentuate the points. (See pages 25, 52, and Chapter 11 for additional information.)
2. Create a colorful and informative poster that explains the Five Theories of Forgetting. On the poster, include study strategies to combat each type of forgetting.
3. Use the Internet to search for informative web sites for *one* of the following topics: forgetting, mnemonics, or test preparation. Print the web pages that you find to be the most valuable and informative. Prepare a short presentation or a written summary of the most significant information. Include the web site addresses.
4. Create a set of index study cards for the terminology in Chapter 6. (See Chapter 4, page 106, to review techniques for creating comprehensive index cards.)
5. Create a portfolio of mnemonics for one of your courses. Use each type of mnemonic shown in the box on page 142.
6. Form a study group with three or more students to meet outside of class to review the content of this chapter. In addition to the review work, spend time discussing specific strategies you can use to prepare for a test in this course. Write a summary paper that discusses the highlights of your review.
7. With a partner, prepare a set of twenty-four test questions that cover the content of Chapters 1 through 6 of this textbook. Write *four* questions for *each* of the six categories of questions in Bloom's Taxonomy.

CHAPTER 6 REVIEW QUESTIONS

Multiple Choice

Choose the best *answer for each of the following. Write the letter of your answer on the line.*

______ **1.** Effective use of mnemonics involves
a. creating mnemonics only for information that is otherwise difficult to recall.
b. creating acronyms and acrostics for every chapter in your textbook.
c. limiting the use of mnemonics to information that appears in lists.
d. All of the above

______ **2.** Mnemonics work effectively when you
a. memorize them with 100 percent accuracy.
b. practice converting them into the information they represent.
c. use them as bridges to conduct memory searches for specific information.
d. All of the above

______ **3.** The Memory Principle of Association is used
a. when you create pictures or graphics for information you need to learn.
b. in all of the types of mnemonics designed to boost your memory.
c. each time you create an acronym or use the stacking method.
d. when you associate a peg to an object you need to recall at a later time.

______ **4.** Effective test-preparation skills
a. reduce the necessity to cram for tests and use rote memory techniques.
b. include time-management and goal-setting techniques.
c. involve working with the information by making summary notes, predicting test questions, and writing practice questions.
d. All of the above

______ **5.** In Bloom's Taxonomy
a. recognition questions frequently use knowledge level questions.
b. application questions are more complex than evaluation questions.
c. eight levels of questions are organized by their degree of complexity.
d. the third and fourth levels of questions appear most frequently on college tests.

______ **6.** Test anxiety can stem from
a. fear of failure.
b. underpreparedness and past experiences.
c. poor test-taking skills.
d. All of the above

______ **7.** Cramming
a. is a survival technique used for underpreparedness.
b. uses most of the memory principles.
c. processes large amounts of information efficiently.
d. can be effective when used the day before a test.

______ **8.** A person with an external locus of control
a. accepts responsibility for external situations that happen to him or her.
b. shows a strong sense of self-confidence and control.
c. blames others for his or her lack of success.
d. would likely make the following kind of statement: *I need to modify my approach to taking tests so I can increase my test performance.*

Comparison

Complete the following comparison chart by listing the Five Theories of Forgetting, briefly describing each theory, and then providing one *study strategy to combat each form of forgetting.*

Forgetting Theory	Brief Description	One Study Skills Strategy

Short Answer and Critical Thinking

On a separate piece of paper, write one or two paragraphs to answer each of the following questions.

1. Explain the relationship between the Displacement Theory of Forgetting and cramming.
2. Summarize the four main sources of test anxiety. For each source of anxiety, name at least two study strategies to reduce or eliminate the source of anxiety.
3. List ten different techniques you can use to boost your memory.

Using a Reading System

CHAPTER 7

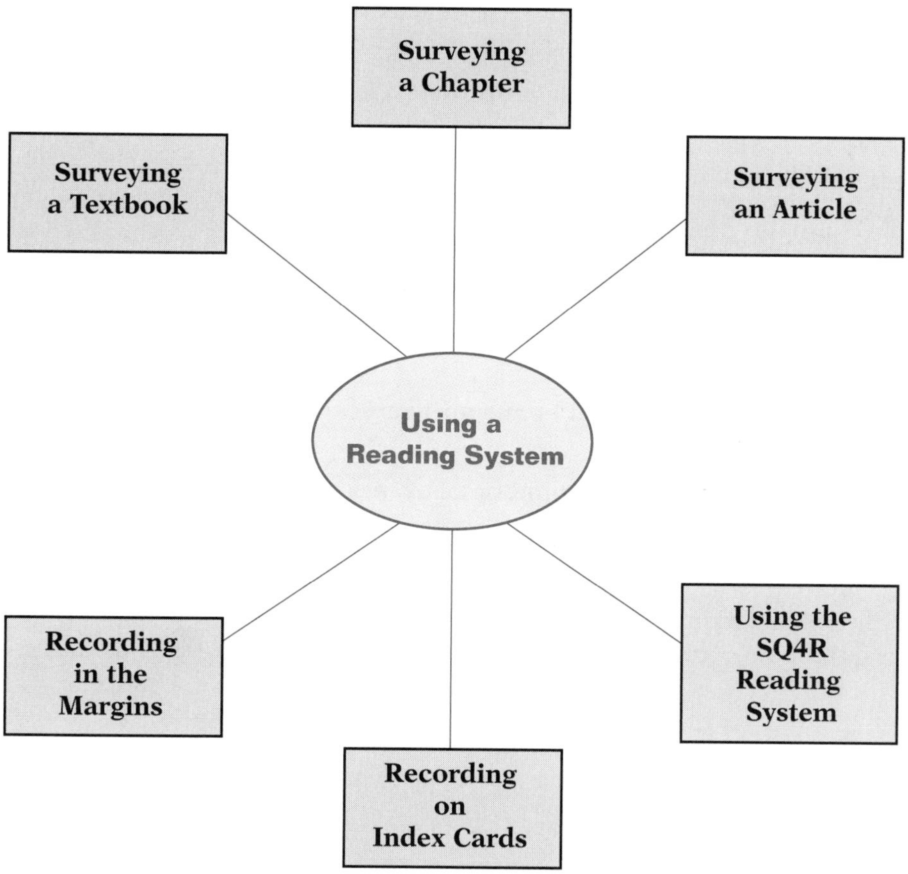

Using an effective reading system helps you comprehend and master your college textbooks. Surveying, a process that provides you with an overview of the material you plan to read, can allow you to familiarize yourself with an entire textbook, a specific chapter, or an individual article before you begin the in-depth process of reading. SQ4R, which begins with the process of surveying, is a powerful, effective six-step approach that promotes comprehension, learning, and retention of textbook information. Recording, which is another term for notetaking, is part of the SQ4R reading system. Recording notes on index cards and in the margins of your textbook are two notetaking options that you can learn to use effectively.

Terms to Know

- survey
- title page
- copyright page
- table of contents
- introductory materials
- preface
- appendix
- glossary
- references/bibliography
- index
- marginal notes
- SQ4R system
- Survey Step
- Question Step
- Read Step
- automatic pilot
- Record Step
- Recite Step
- read-record-recite cycle
- Review Step

CHAPTER 7 Using a Reading System Profile

DO, SCORE, and **RECORD** your profile before you read this chapter. If you need to review the process, refer to the complete directions given in the Profile for Chapter 1 on page 2.

ONLINE: You can complete the profile and get your score online at this textbook's web site.

	YES	NO
1. I skim through or preview the front and back sections of new textbooks before I begin the first reading assignment.	______	______
2. I only use the glossary of a book when I need a quick definition of a word.	______	______
3. When I begin reading a new chapter, I open the book to the first page and read straight through to the end of the chapter.	______	______
4. I read the chapter review questions and the summary before I start reading the chapter.	______	______
5. I write my own study questions for each heading and subheading in the chapter.	______	______
6. I read all the information under one complete heading before I stop to think about what I have read.	______	______
7. I often finish reading a chapter only to find out that I remember very little of what I have just read.	______	______
8. After I read a short section, I stop to highlight, underline, or take notes.	______	______
9. When I study, I am quiet because I do all my practicing or reviewing in my head.	______	______
10. I know how to use index cards to record information and how to make concise marginal notes in the textbook.	______	______

Reflection Writing 1 — CHAPTER 7

On a separate piece of paper or in a journal, do the following:

1. Discuss your profile score for this chapter. What was your score? What does it mean to you?
2. Describe the system or approach you currently use to read a new chapter. Be specific.

Surveying a Textbook

To **survey** reading material means to preview or skim through information to get an overview or a *big picture* of the content of a book, a chapter, or an article before you begin reading. Surveying a complete textbook before you begin reading specific chapters acquaints you with the book's philosophy, organization, and special features. Often in this overview, you will find suggestions for using the book more effectively, and you will become familiar with sections of the textbook that will enable you to use the book more efficiently. Surveying a textbook, a process that usually requires less than thirty minutes of your time at the beginning of the term, appears as one of the Quick Start suggestions in the front of this textbook on page xix. The following chart summarizes the Quick Start information by listing the parts of a textbook to include in the survey process.

Surveying a Textbook

1. Title page, copyright page, and table of contents
2. Introductory information
3. Appendix
4. Glossary
5. References or bibliography
6. Index

Title Page, Copyright Page, and Table of Contents

The **title page** provides you with the name of the book, the author, the edition, and the publishing location. It may also show you the author's affiliation to an organization, university, or corporation; this information, if provided, appears below the author's name. If the book is in its first edition, no reference to an edition appears below the author's name. Each revision number indicates that the book has been updated, so textbooks that have been published in multiple editions have a track record of success.

The **copyright page** appears on the back of the title page. With a quick glance, you can learn the publication date of the textbook. The copyright date is important when you need to know whether the material in the book is current. The copyright page also states the publisher's policy for copying content from the book and the book's Library of Congress catalog number (or ISBN, International Standard Book Number).

The **table of contents** provides you with an overview of the topics in the textbook, the organization of the topics (chronological or thematic), chapter headings and subheadings, page numbers, and other textbook features. When you are planning a time-management schedule, the table of contents is a quick way to check the length of chapters so you can begin to estimate the time you will need to work with each chapter.

Introductory Information

The **introductory materials** may include sections titled *Preface, Introduction, To the Teacher* (or *To the Instructor*), and *To the Student*. The **preface** (pronounced pref′is, not pre-face′) or the *introduction* provides insight into the philosophy, objectives, and structure of the book. It may also include background information about the author. The section titled *To the Instructor* provides instructors with information on the teaching/learning approach used by the author, the goals and objectives of the textbook, and suggestions for using the book effectively. The section titled *To the Student* is one of the most important sections for you to read carefully, for it provides you with valuable suggestions, study strategies, and explanations of textbook features that will help you learn the textbook content and use the book effectively.

Appendix

The **appendix**, located in the back of the textbook, contains supplementary materials for various chapters. The appendix may include useful information that would break the flow of the chapter or disrupt its structure. In a history textbook, for example, the Bill of Rights and the Constitution are important documents; due to their length, however, they might be found as supplementary materials in the appendix. The appendix might also include answer keys; additional exercises; practice tests; supplementary readings; or important tables, graphs, charts, or maps. For textbooks with a wide variety of supplementary materials, there may be more than one appendix. Because these materials are significant, becoming familiar with the content of the appendix at the beginning of the term can help you throughout the term.

Glossary

The **glossary** is a course-specific mini-dictionary located after the appendix. Definitions in a glossary are limited to the word meanings used in the textbook. (Use a standard college dictionary to locate multiple meanings of terminology.) Most textbooks use bold, italic, or colored print within textbook chapters to indicate which words appear in the glossary. Even though glossaries are useful tools for students, not all textbooks include glossaries. If your textbook does not have a glossary, you might want to create and update your own glossary as you study each chapter. If your textbook does have a glossary, you can benefit by using the following strategies:

1. Each time you see words in special print in a chapter, take time to review the glossary definitions; sometimes they provide you with more details or more directly clarify the terminology.
2. As you encounter new terms during the reading process, place a star next to the terms or highlight them in the glossary. When you study for tests, you can use the glossary as a review tool.
3. Make separate flash cards or study sheets with the definitions of key terms that you need to review to prepare for tests. (See page 106.)

References or Bibliography

The **references** or **bibliography** section in the back of the book cites the titles and authors of books, magazines, or articles that the author used in writing the textbook. (The term *bibliography* comes from the Greek word roots *biblio-*, which means *book,* and *-graphy,* which means *written record.*) If you are working on a paper or a speech, or if you want to pursue a specific topic further, you can use the information in this section to locate the original sources of information.

Index

The **index**, one of the most frequently used sections in the back of a textbook, is an alphabetical listing of the textbook's significant topics. By using the index, you can quickly locate pages throughout the textbook that refer to a specific topic. Some textbooks may have more than one index; for example, you might find a *subject index,* an *author index,* or an *index of illustrations.* Frequently, topics are cross-referenced so they appear in more than one place in the index. For example, if you look up *Theory of Multiple Intelligences,* you may find it listed alphabetically under *Theory,* under *Intelligences,* and under *Multiple Intelligences.* The following strategies will help you use the index effectively:

1. If you are not able to find a term in the index, think of alternative wordings. For example, if you cannot find the term *body rhythms,* try looking under *rhythms,* or look for the more formal wording, *circadian rhythms.*
2. During a class discussion or lecture, you may hear others use an unfamiliar word. Write the word in your notes or in the margin of your textbook. After class, use the index to locate the page or pages that explain the term in context. Read the information carefully and then relate the information from the book to the discussion or lecture.
3. When you are assigned a specific topic for a research paper, an essay, any type of writing assignment, a project, or a test, begin by locating the topic in the index. Then turn to the page numbers provided in the index and read or review the information.

EXERCISE 7.1 Surveying This Textbook

Take 15–30 minutes to survey this textbook. Then answer the following questions. Your instructor may ask you to respond on separate paper.

1. Read the chapter titles; which chapters contain the skills you feel you most need to learn or improve?

   ____

   ____

2. What helpful information did you learn from the preface? ______________________

   ____

3. Did you read the *To the Student* section before you began working in this book? ________ If yes, how did the information in this section help you? If no, how could this information have helped you use this textbook if you had read it earlier? ______________________

   ____

4. *To the Student* provides suggestions on how to start each chapter. Which of these suggestions have you been using each time you began a new chapter? ______________________

   ____

5. What kind of information appears in the appendices? ______________________

   ____

6. This textbook does not have a glossary. Have you started any kind of glossary or system for learning definitions of terminology yourself? Explain. ______________________

   ____

7. How have you made use of the index so far this term? ______________________

EXERCISE 7.2 Using the Table of Contents

The following Contents in Brief *is a condensed table of contents for* Introductory Chemistry *by Darrell D. Ebbing and R.A.D. Wentworth. (In the textbook, a comprehensive table of contents follows this condensed version.) Survey the* Contents in Brief *and then answer the questions that follow.*

Contents in Brief

1. Based on this table of contents and generally speaking, what does the study of chemistry entail?

____

____

2. What are the basic concepts that lay the foundation for the study of chemistry?

____

____

3. What are the three states of matter? ______________________________

____

4. What are three different fields of study in the area of chemistry? ______________________________

____

5. Assume that you preview several pages in the textbook and notice that each page is dense with information. You estimate that you will need at least eight minutes per page to read, take notes, and understand the content on each page. Then you notice the length of an average chapter. How will this information help you plan study blocks for chemistry?

____

____

6. What will you find in the appendix of this textbook? ______________________________

Surveying a Chapter

You can also use surveying to look through or preview a chapter. Surveying a chapter before beginning the process of careful, thorough reading is a *warm-up* activity you can use at the beginning of a study block to help you focus your mind and create a *big picture* of the chapter. (See Chapter 5, pages 116–117.) Surveying also enhances your motivation, increases your interest in the chapter, breaks inertia or the tendency to procrastinate, and boosts confidence in your ability to master the material. By surveying, you will have a general idea about the length and difficulty of the chapter; with this understanding, you will be better equipped to set realistic goals and manage your time more effectively.

The benefits of surveying a chapter are numerous, yet doing so generally requires fewer than twenty minutes. For longer chapters, you can modify the process by surveying as many pages of the chapter as you think you can realistically cover in one or two study blocks. Plan to survey the remaining pages at the beginning of a future study block in which you also plan to complete the chapter. The following chart shows the parts of a chapter to include in surveying.

Surveying a Chapter

1. Read the introductory materials carefully.
2. Read the headings and the subheadings.
3. Look at visual materials, such as charts, graphs, or pictures.
4. Read marginal notes.
5. Skim over terminology or information in special print.
6. Read the end-of-chapter materials, including any conclusion, summary, or chapter review questions.

Introductory Materials

Read the title of the chapter carefully; take a moment to relate this topic to previous topics and information you already know about the topic. Read any lists, paragraphs, or visual materials that state the objectives for the chapter or introduce the chapter's content.

Headings and Subheadings

Headings and subheadings appear in larger, bolder, or special print. Take time to identify the format the author uses to indicate the main headings and the minor headings (subheadings). Begin moving through the chapter by glancing over the headings and subheadings; this step of surveying shows you the "skeleton" structure of the chapter. Later, if you want, you can write the headings and subheadings on paper to make a chapter outline or visual mapping. You may be surprised by the amount of information you obtain when you read the headings and the subheadings in the order in which they appear in the book.

Visual Materials

Visual materials include charts, graphs, diagrams, illustrations, cartoons, and photographs. Read the information that appears next to, above, and below the visual materials. A picture—or in this case, visual materials—may be worth a thousand words, so take time to gather information about the topic by examining the visual materials.

Marginal Notes

Marginal notes may be brief explanations, short definitions, lists of key points or objectives, or study questions that appear in the margins of the textbook pages. Marginal notes are designed to draw your attention to important information or to summarize key points. Taking time to read marginal notes during the process of surveying can provide you with background details that will be helpful when you engage in more thorough reading.

Terminology and Special Print

As previously mentioned, terminology (words whose definitions you will need to know) often appears in special print. During the surveying process, skim over the terminology to get a general idea of the number of terms you will need to learn and to gain some familiarity with these key words. Do *not* take the time during surveying to read about the words in bold print or to look for their definitions.

End-of-Chapter Materials

Carefully read the end-of-chapter materials, which may include a conclusion, a summary, a list of key concepts, or chapter review questions. These materials highlight or summarize the important concepts and information you should know and understand after you have read and studied the chapter.

EXERCISE 7.3 Surveying This Chapter

Use the steps on page 175 to survey this chapter. Then answer the following questions. Write your answers on separate paper.

1. How did reading the introductory material help you begin to formulate a *big picture* of this chapter?
2. How long did it take you to survey the entire chapter? If you spent more than fifteen minutes surveying the chapter, did you get sidetracked and begin some in-depth reading?
3. Though cramming is strongly discouraged, sometimes students find themselves in situations in which cramming is necessary. If you had to cram, would surveying the different parts of a chapter be an effective cramming technique? Explain why it would or would not be effective.
4. When you surveyed this chapter, which parts of the chapter provided you with the most information and helped you become most familiar with the content?
5. What do you find are the benefits of surveying a chapter before you begin in-depth reading?

Surveying an Article

You can also use surveying to preview an article from a newspaper or a magazine or an excerpt from a book. Surveying an article requires a minimal amount of time but can provide you with valuable information. Always begin by reading any introductory paragraphs that appear before the main body of the article. The *thesis statement,* the main point of the article, often appears in the introductory paragraph along with background information about the subject or the author that will help you understand the article more clearly. Continue the process of surveying with the following steps:

1. Read the entire introductory paragraph. The thesis statement frequently appears in this paragraph. The thesis statement tells the purpose of the article or the main point the author wants to make.
2. Skim through the rest of the article by reading headings, subheadings, and marginal notes (also called *sidebars*).
3. Read the concluding paragraph. The concluding paragraph often restates the thesis statement and summarizes the main ideas in the article.

Group Processing: A Collaborative Learning Activity

Form groups of three or four students. Complete the following directions.

1. Individually, think of the last complete chapter that you read in any one of your textbooks. On a piece of paper, make a list of things you do when you read a chapter. Try to explain in chronological order how you go about completing a chapter.
2. Put all the lists together so you and the members of your group can compare them. Do any of you use the same process? What do the lists have in common? Which approach seems most comprehensive? Be prepared to share your discussion with the rest of the class.

Using the SQ4R Reading System

One of the first textbook reading systems, SQ3R, was developed by Francis P. Robinson in 1941. This system acquired its name by using the first letter of each step in the system: survey, question, read, recite, and review. Other systems have been developed for reading textbooks, but they all basically contain the same essential steps found in SQ3R. The **SQ4R system** in this chapter is based on SQ3R, with a fourth R added for the "record" step. The SQ4R system thus becomes a six-step approach to reading and comprehending textbooks.

As with any approach, skipping a step weakens the system. To gain the most benefit from this system, use all six steps on a regular basis. Not only will you comprehend information more readily, you will not waste precious time rereading chapters to learn new information.

The Steps of SQ4R

1. *Survey* the chapter.
2. Write *Questions* for each heading and subheading.
3. *Read* the information, one paragraph at a time.
4. Select a form of notetaking to *Record* information.
5. *Recite* the important information from the paragraph.
6. *Review* the information learned in the chapter.

Step One: Survey the Chapter

Use the steps for surveying a chapter given on page 175. When you do the **Survey step**, you will use the introductory materials, headings, subheadings, visual materials, marginal notes, terminology, and end-of-chapter materials to create an overview of the chapter.

Step Two: Write Questions

During the **Question step**, formulate a question for each heading or subheading in the chapter. Use the words *which, when, what, why, where, how,* or *who* to turn each heading or subheading into a question. Writing the questions, which often takes less than ten minutes, will improve your comprehension as you read and will provide you with valuable study questions to use when you review the chapter. Because the process of learning should be tailored to strategies that work best for you, several options for the question step are available for you to try:

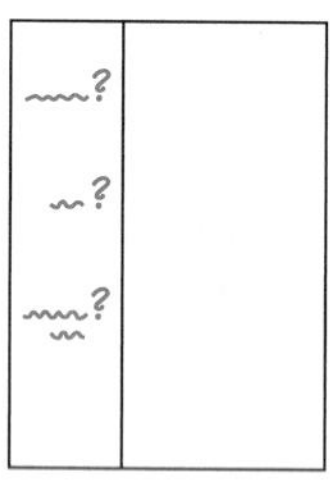

- Write the questions in your book next to each heading and subheading.
- Write the questions on notebook paper. Make a $2\frac{1}{2}$- or 3-inch column on the left. Write your questions in this column. Leave several lines between each question so you have room to write answers to your questions in the right column during the review step.
- Write the questions on index cards, one question per card.
- If the chapter is longer than twenty pages and you cannot possibly read it in one or two study blocks, write questions only for the number of pages that you surveyed in Step 1.

Writing your own study questions has several advantages:

1. The questions give you a *purpose for reading*. Natural curiosity then leads you to read so that you can answer your questions.
2. Your *curiosity can help you concentrate* on what you are reading.
3. With increased concentration, you gain *increased comprehension*.
4. Your questions help *prepare you for future tests*. You can prepare for a test by answering your own questions during the review step of SQ4R.

Step Three: Read Carefully

Some students feel that they should be able to "read fast" to get through the chapter. Others read the chapter, only to find at the end of the chapter that they do not remember much of what they have just read; consequently, they must reread at least one more time. The **Read step** of SQ4R encourages you to read *carefully*. For most textbooks, you should read *one paragraph at a time* and stop so that you can concentrate and comprehend each paragraph. With careful reading, you will not need to spend valuable study time rereading chapters.

If the textbook is written on an easy-to-read level and does not contain large amounts of details in each paragraph, you can read more than one paragraph at a time before you stop for the next step. For a very difficult, technical textbook, you may find that you need to read and stop after several sentences rather than at the end of the paragraph. Reading carefully requires this flexibility; the

How does textbook reading differ from leisure-time reading of magazines or paperback books?

amount you read at a time should be determined by your reading skills and the level of difficulty of the material.

Reading college textbooks involves *active reading*. When you read your textbooks, concentrate on the meanings of individual words, especially course-specific terminology, the meanings of sentences, and the meaning of the paragraph as a whole. Reread individual sentences if they are initially unclear. Circle words in special print (terminology) and confirm that you understand their meaning; refer to a glossary or a dictionary for additional understanding of unfamiliar words if necessary. Active reading also involves identifying both the main ideas and the supporting details for each paragraph. (Chapter 8 will provide you with active reading techniques to strengthen your comprehension and your critical thinking skills.)

In mathematics textbooks, in addition to understanding paragraphs with instructional material and explanations, you need to read and comprehend numerous math problems and examples that appear throughout each chapter. Because math is based on sequential learning, reading carefully and comprehending the math concepts presented in each chapter are crucial steps, for those skills lay the foundation for later chapters and higher-level math concepts. In addition to learning new math concepts, you will need to learn a language of symbols so you can read mathematical equations and express information in mathematical terms. As you read through each new chapter, take the time to compare the written words and explanations to the examples that are written as equations or algebraic expressions. (The *record* and *recite* steps of SQ4R provide you with additional practice reading mathematical statements with symbols.) Your goal is to be able to read the examples, solve the problems, and express your work in English words as well as in mathematical equations or algebraic expressions with numerals, letters, and symbols. Notice in the following list how reading the algebraic expression would be impossible if a student did not learn to associate the symbols to their English words.

Algebraic expressions	*English words*
$9 > x$	Nine is greater than x.
$x + 8$	Eight more than x.
$x/6$	Quotient of x and 6.
$2(x + 5)$	Two times the sum of x plus 5.
$\{1, 3, 5, \ldots\}$	The set of odd counting numbers.
$\sim(p \wedge q)$	Both p and q are not true.

Reading carefully helps you in several ways:

1. Your *mind stays focused* on the information. Reading too quickly or carelessly puts your mind into "**automatic pilot**," where little or no information registers in your memory.
2. By keeping a stronger focus, you can attain accuracy and higher levels of concentration. The result is *better comprehension*.
3. This approach gives your *memory time to process new information* before you start demanding that it take in even more information. You also have time to think about information and understand it with greater accuracy.
4. It *promotes critical thinking*, an essential skill for college students.

Step Four: Record Information

Reading comprehension involves finding main ideas and recognizing important supporting details. After you read a paragraph carefully, it is time to use the **Record step** by taking notes of the important information you will need to learn. You have eight basic choices of notetaking or recording systems to use for the important information:

- Notes on index cards
- Notes in the margins of the book
- Underlining or highlighting (see Chapter 8)
- The Cornell format for taking notes on paper (see Chapter 9)
- Visual mapping or hierarchies (see Chapter 11)
- Comparison charts (see Chapter 11)
- Formal outlines (see Chapter 11)
- Three-column notes (see Chapters 9 and 11)

After you learn to use all eight options, you may find that you prefer one or two of them. If the textbook you are reading is not too difficult, usually one form of notetaking is sufficient. You may find, however, that you prefer to use a combination of two or more systems to help you study and learn. Your goal is to learn to use all eight options and apply them in a way that you feel is most appropriate for the situation.

For math or science materials with formulas, copy the example problems or formulas on paper. Label each step to show the process used to solve the problem or apply the formula.

Recording can benefit you in several ways:

1. It gives you a *reduced or condensed form of the information* that you need to learn.
2. Because writing is involved, you are *actively involved* in the learning process. Your automatic pilot, a passive form of studying, does not have the opportunity to turn on.
3. The *writing process* also involves fine motor skills, which form another channel into your memory system.

Step Five: Recite

Before you move on to the next paragraph, stop and use the **Recite step**. Recite the information you wrote in your notes. Speak out loud using your own words, and in complete sentences. For math or science chapters with formulas, recite the steps used to solve problems or apply formulas. Convert symbols in equations to English words.

Once you have finished reciting the information just covered, continue to move through the chapter by reading the next paragraph (or section) carefully, recording main ideas and important supporting details, and reciting the new information. As you move through the chapter with this method, your reading is thorough, detailed, and accurate. Your mind is alert, challenged, active, and focused. By devoting time and effort to this careful method of reading, you do not need to reread the chapter. When you have completed this cycle for the entire chapter, move on to the final step of SQ4R.

Reciting, one of the twelve memory principles, is valuable for these reasons:

1. Reciting requires you to *explain the information clearly.*

2. Reciting provides you with *important feedback*. If you are not able to recite the information, then you know that you did not understand it very well. Glance back at your notes for clues.
3. Reciting leads to *active learning,* which increases your level and length of concentration.
4. Reciting *activates the auditory channel* to your brain. The more senses you can use in the learning process, the stronger will be the paths to your memory.
5. Reciting in your own words helps you *avoid rote memorization*. You are giving meaning to the information by using your own words.
6. When you finish the **read-record-recite cycle** for the paragraph, you have the *paragraph's ideas fresh in your memory.* You can then connect these ideas to the new information that you will be taking in as you read the next paragraph.

Step Six: Review

After you have finished surveying, questioning, reading, recording, and reciting, you do the last step—reviewing. The **Review step** can be accomplished in a variety of ways. The following activities are helpful for both immediate and ongoing review:

- Answer any questions at the end of the chapter.
- Answer the questions that you wrote in the question step.
- Study and recite from the notes that you took in the record step.
- Write a summary of the information in the chapter.
- Personalize the information by asking yourself additional questions: How can this information be used? How does the lecture from class fit in with this information? Why is this important to learn?
- Create additional study tools, such as index cards, study tapes, or visual mappings.
- For math and science textbooks with math problems and formulas, copy the problems from the book. Work the problems; compare the steps you used and your answers with those in the textbook.

Reviewing is a vital step for several reasons:

1. An immediate review of information *summarizes what you just learned.* It provides you with the "big picture" supported by important details.
2. The process of memory involves putting information into your long-term memory and being able to retrieve it from this memory storage when needed. To be able to *retrieve information efficiently,* you must practice it by reviewing it frequently.
3. Frequent ongoing review *keeps information fresh in your memory.* You have less need to cram or feel unprepared for tests.
4. When information is reviewed and understood clearly, you can more easily *associate new information* with information already in your long-term memory schemas.
5. Making time for immediate and ongoing review *builds confidence* and creates a sense of satisfaction in *being prepared* and *managing time* efficiently.

EXERCISE 7.4 Knowing the Six Steps

The following chart shows the steps of SQ4R. Fill each box with the name of the step. Then, with a partner, practice explaining each step of the process. Include as many details as you can remember without looking back in the book.

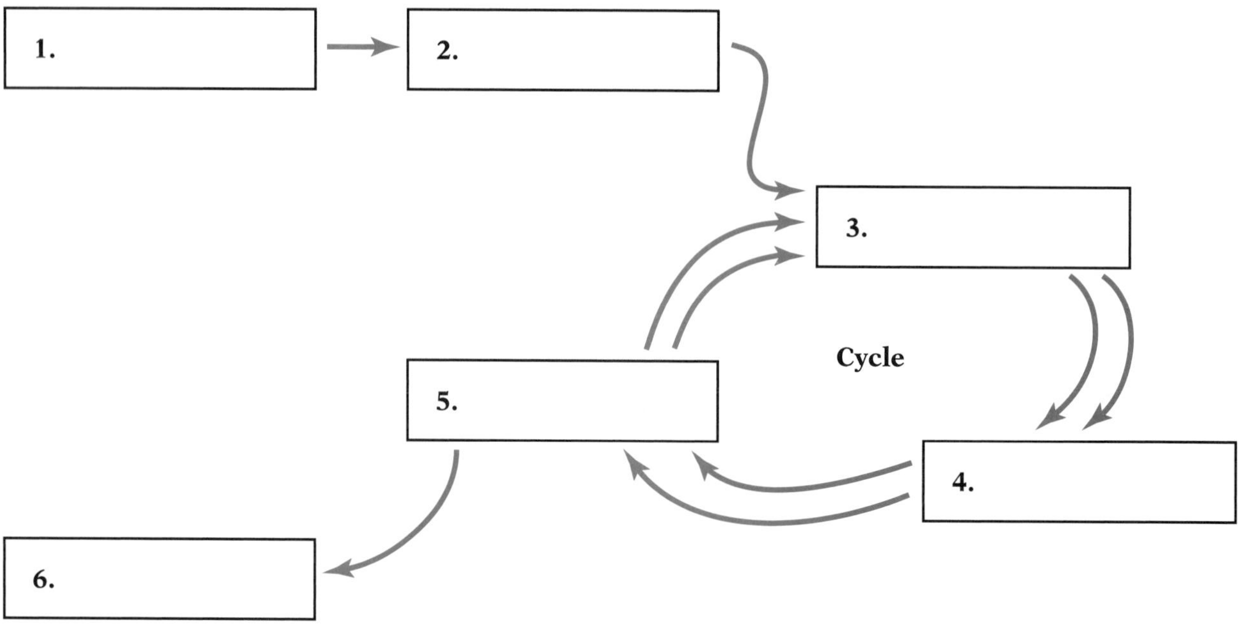

Reflection Writing 2 — CHAPTER 7

On a separate piece of paper or in a journal, do the following:

1. Discuss your approach to reading a new chapter before you learned about SQ4R.
2. Discuss the changes you will make in your reading approach now that you know SQ4R.

Recording on Index Cards

You can use index cards (3 × 5 or 5 × 7) to record important information that you will need to know. In Chapter 4, page 106, you learned to use index cards to make flash cards for lists of information and terminology. With this notetaking system, you write the category of information on the front side of the card and the list of items on the back, or you write the vocabulary word on the front side of the card and the definition on the back. You can expand your use of flash cards to include cards with a study question on the front and the answer on the back.

Critical thinking and learning occur while you create index notetaking cards. However, creating the cards is not enough; you need to study and review from the cards. Effective use of your cards will occur by involving yourself with the following activities.

Learning Activities for Index Notetaking Cards

1. Study by reciting from the fronts and the backs of the cards.
2. Use reflect activities by sorting, summarizing, and grouping.

Study from Index Cards

Once you have prepared your index cards, you must use them for studying or they will have little impact on your learning. To study effectively from your cards, plan to *study from both the front side and the back side.* The more practice you have working with these cards, the more confident you will feel about knowing the information.

Study from the Front Work from the front of each card as follows:

1. Begin by stacking the cards with the words, categories, or questions facing you. Read the front of the card out loud.
2. Recite what you know about the word, category, or answer to the question. Do *not* look at the back of the card.
3. After you have finished reciting, turn the card over for feedback. If you gave the correct information, place the card in a "Yes, I know these" pile.
4. If your feedback indicated that you still don't know the information on the back of the card, read the back out loud slowly. Think about the information. Try to visualize it. Turn the card over and try reciting again. Put the card in an "I need to study these more" pile.
5. Review the "I need to study these more" pile once again.
6. Use ongoing review for the complete set of index cards.

Study from the Back When you work from the back of the cards, you challenge your memory in new ways. Use the following steps to study from the back:

1. If the back gives a definition, read the definition, say aloud the vocabulary word you think is on the front, and then write the word on paper. Turn the card over. Check the accuracy of your answer and the spelling of the word.
2. If the back of the card gives a list of items, read that list out loud. Think of the category word or phrase that appears on the front of the card. Turn over the card to check your accuracy.
3. If the back of the card is an answer, read it out loud. Respond as though you are playing the game of *Jeopardy!*: pose a question that matches the answer. Turn over the card to check the accuracy of your answer.

In what ways are index cards more flexible to use for notetaking than marginal notes? When would index cards not be the best option to use for notetaking?

Reflect with Index Cards

Many students enjoy working with index cards because they can be used in so many different ways. One obvious advantage is that you can make piles of cards that you know and piles of cards that you need to work with more. A second advantage is that you can use the cards for reflect activities.

The following activities provide you with a multisensory approach to studying. You *see* the information, you *recite* the information, and you use a *hands-on* approach to manipulate the cards. You also incorporate critical thinking skills as you creatively find new ways to categorize and organize the information.

1. Shuffle all your cards. Go through them one by one, sorting the cards into categories that show likeness. Be creative in identifying your categories. For example, if you have made cards all term, you may have the following categories:

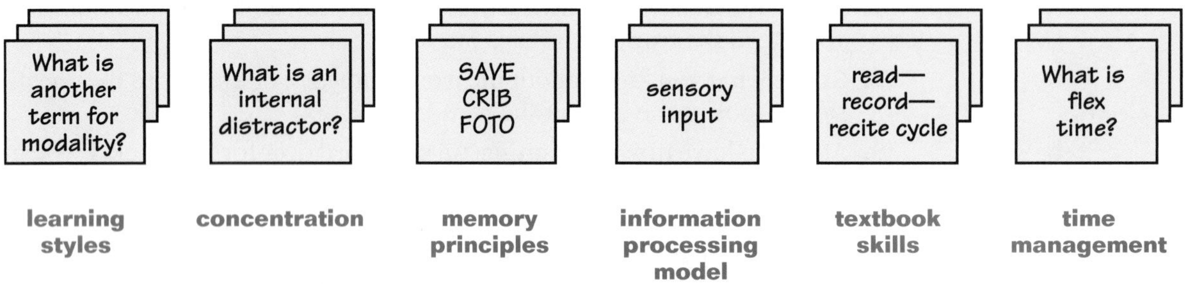

2. Select one category of cards above. Lay all the cards in the category word- or question-side up on the table. Try to give a verbal or written summary by using all the information on the cards. This is excellent practice for essay tests.
3. Shuffle all your cards. Make a mapping on the table similar to the mapping found at the front of each chapter in this book. Again, you will be grouping and categorizing the various cards according to related topics.

Recording in the Margins

You can use many forms of recording or notetaking for Step 4 of SQ4R. Recording notes of important information on index cards is one highly effective system. Recording brief notes in the margins of your textbook next to each paragraph is another method that is effective for textbooks with ample space to the left of the text and for textbooks that do not contain large amounts of new information in each paragraph. When you make these **marginal notes**, keep the notes brief to avoid cluttering the page and to make review work easier. (See Chapter 8, pages 219–221, for more information about marginal notes.) The following kinds of marginal notes provide you with short summaries that you can use when you review the textbook and study for tests:

- lists of key points
- key words or terminology
- short definitions
- personal comments
- questions to ask in class
- study questions
- diagrams or pictures

In the following example, notice how the marginal notes help clarify the content of the paragraph.

Sign mind
—logical, right order
—controls
—judges
—supervises
—strangles creativity

Design mind
—creative
—imagination
—artistic
—curious
—playful
—clustering to generate ideas

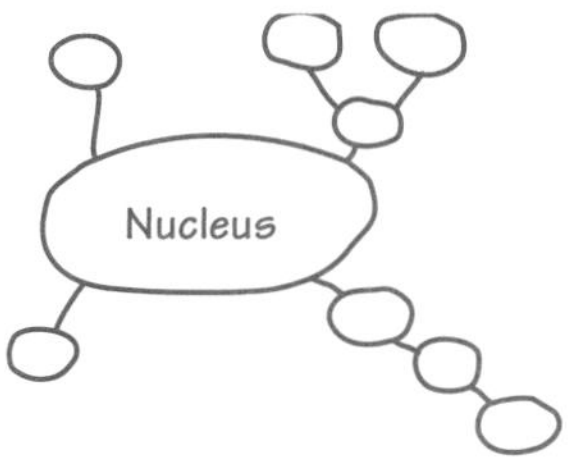

In her book *Writing the Natural Way,* Gabrielle Rico explains the method she devised to help her students get in touch with the creative, inventive part of themselves. Rico calls the part of ourselves that is always trying to be logical and put things in the right order the "Sign mind." The other creative part of ourselves that is longing to express our well-hidden imagination and artistic ability she calls the "Design mind." Rico's Sign mind . . . controls, judges, and supervises. To get out from under this watchdog, who tends to strangle our creative impulses in their early stages, Rico suggests the strategy she calls clustering as a way of giving your playful, curious Design mind free rein to generate ideas.

Begin with a nucleus word circled on an empty page. Then go with any connections that come into your head, writing each down in its own circle. Connect each new word or phrase with a line to the previous circle. "As you cluster," Rico warns, "you may experience a sense of randomness or, if you are somewhat skeptical, an uneasy sense that it isn't leading anywhere. . . . Trust this natural process, though. We all cluster mentally throughout our lives without knowing it; we have simply never made these clusterings visible on paper."

Exercise 7.5 Surveying, Questioning, Reading, and Recording

Step 1: Survey the following excerpt from a psychology textbook.

Step 2: Use each heading and subheading to formulate a study question. Write the question in your book next to the heading or subheading.

Step 3: Carefully read the excerpt one paragraph at a time.

Step 4: After you read each paragraph, make brief marginal notes.

(*Note:* If your instructor assigns Exercise 7.6, you will use another method for recording information that involves making a set of index cards.)

Approaches to Psychology

Suppose you are a psychologist trying to understand some aspect of the behavior and mental processes we have reviewed. Perhaps, like Morris and Peng, you are interested in cross-cultural differences in thought processes; or maybe you want to identify the origins of aggression, pinpoint the causes of schizophrenia, or solve the riddle of drug abuse. Where would you look for answers? In brain cells and hormones? In inherited characteristics? In what people have learned from their parents? The direction of your research efforts will be determined largely by your *approach* to psychology—that is, by the set of assumptions, questions, and methods that you believe will be most helpful for understanding the behavior and mental processes you wish to explore.

Whereas some psychologists adopt one particular approach, many others are *eclectic,* combining features of two or more approaches because they believe that no single perspective can fully account for all aspects of psychological phenomena. . . . Some of these approaches are more influential than others, but we will briefly review the essential features of all of them in order to give you a better understanding of why psychologists over the years have conducted their research as they have. . . .

The Biological Approach Investigating the possibility that aggressive behavior or schizophrenia, for example, might be traceable to a hormonal imbalance or a brain disorder reflects the biological approach to psychology. As its name implies, the biological approach assumes that behavior and mental processes are largely shaped by biological processes. Psychologists who take this approach study the psychological effects of hormones, genes, and the activity of the nervous system, especially the brain. Thus, if they are studying memory, they might try to identify the changes taking place in the brain as information is stored there.

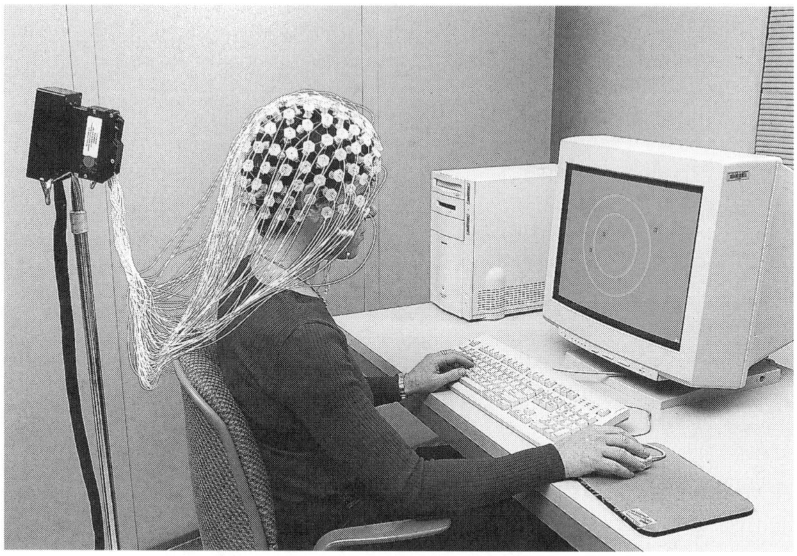

Recording Brain Waves
The biological approach to psychology seeks to understand how behavior and mental processes relate to internal bodily events and activities. Here, researchers record the brain waves of a person who is performing a task similar to that of an air traffic controller (ATC). Psychologists in the Navy and elsewhere are working on systems that could warn ATCs and radar/sonar operators that they are failing to attend to important information.

Or if they are studying thinking, they might look for patterns of brain activity associated with, say, making quick decisions or reading a foreign language. . . .

The Evolutionary Approach Biological processes also figure prominently in the evolutionary approach to psychology. The foundation for this approach was English naturalist Charles Darwin's book, *The Origin of Species.* Darwin argued that the forms of life present in the world today are the result of evolution—of changes in life forms that occur over many generations—and, more specifically, that evolution occurs through *natural selection.* Darwin believed that natural selection operates at the level of individuals, but most contemporary evolutionists maintain that it operates at the level of genes. At either level, the process is the same. Those genes that result in characteristics and behaviors that are adaptive and useful in a certain environment will enable the creatures that possess them to survive, reproduce, and thereby pass these genes on to subsequent generations (Buss & Kenrick, 1998). Genes that result in characteristics that are not adaptive in that environment will not be passed on to subsequent generations because the creatures possessing them will not be able to survive and reproduce. Thus, evolutionary theory says that many (but not all) of the genes we possess today are the result of natural selection.

Scientists who study animal behavior in the natural environment—called ethologists—have identified the effects of natural selection not only in inherited physical characteristics, such as the camouflage coloration that helps animals escape predators, but also in instinctive or, more properly, *species-specific* behaviors that aid survival.

In psychology, the evolutionary approach holds that the behavior of animals and humans today is the result of evolution through natural selection. Psychologists who take an evolutionary approach therefore try to understand (1) the adaptive value of behavior, (2) the anatomical and biological mechanisms that make it possible, and (3) the environmental conditions that encourage or discourage it. The evolutionary approach has generated a growing body of research (Buss & Kenrick, 1998). You will read about its influence in later chapters in relation to topics as diverse as helping and altruism, mental disorders, temperament, and interpersonal attraction.

The Psychodynamic Approach The psychodynamic approach offers a different slant on the role of inherited instincts and other biological forces in human behavior. Rooted in Freud's psychoanalysis, this approach asserts that all behavior and mental processes reflect the constant and mostly unconscious psychological struggles that rage within each person. Usually, these struggles involve conflict between the impulse to satisfy instincts or wishes (for food, sex, or aggression, for example) and the need to abide by the restrictions imposed by society. From this perspective, hostility and aggression reflect the breakdown of civilizing defenses against the expression of primitive urges, whereas anxiety, depression, or other disorders are the overt signs of inner turmoil.

The psychodynamic approach is reflected in a number of the contemporary theories of personality, psychological disorders, and treatment. However, the orthodox Freudian perspective is far less influential in psychology now than in the past (Robins, Gosling, & Craik, 1999). Most psychologists today who take a psychodynamic approach prefer one of the many revised versions of Freud's original theories. For example, they may focus on how people's relationship with their parents forms a template for intimate relationships later in their lives (e.g., Baldwin, 1992).

The Behavioral Approach The behavioral approach to psychology stands in stark contrast to the psychodynamic, biological, and evolutionary approaches. As founded by John Watson, the behavioral approach characterizes behavior and mental processes as primarily the result of *learning.* From Watson's point of view, biological, genetic, and evolutionary factors provide the raw material on which rewards, punishments, and other experiences act to shape each individual. Thus, whether the topic is aggression or drug abuse, self-confidence or helping, behaviorists seek to understand it in terms of an individual's learning history, especially the patterns of reward and punishment the individual has experienced. They also believe that people can change problematic behaviors, from overeating to criminality, by unlearning old habits and developing new ones.

Today, many behaviorists have come to endorse a variation on behaviorism. The *cognitive-behavioral* view (also called the social-cognitive view) adds the study of reportable mental processes to the traditional behavioral emphasis on observable actions (Beck & Weishaar, 1995; Ellis, 1995). The cognitive-behavioral approach explores how learning affects the development of thoughts and beliefs and, in turn, how these learned cognitive patterns affect overt behavior.

The Cognitive Approach Recognition by many behaviorists of the importance of cognitive factors reflects the influence of a broader cognitive approach to psychology. The cognitive approach focuses on how people take in, mentally represent, and store information; how they perceive and process that information; and how cognitive processes are related to the integrated patterns of behavior we can see. In other words, the cognitive approach guides psychologists to study the rapid series of mental events—including those taking place outside of awareness—that accompany overt behavior. Consider, for example, how an incident in which one person shoves another in front of a theater might be analyzed cognitively: The aggressor (1) perceives that someone has cut into the theater line, (2) uses stored memories and concepts to decide that this act is inappropriate, (3) attributes the act to the culprit's obnoxiousness, (4) considers possible responses and their likely consequences, (5) decides that shoving the person is the best response, and (6) executes that response.

Psychologists taking the cognitive approach are interested in discovering how people process information in domains ranging from decision making and interpersonal attraction to intelligence testing and group problem solving, to name but a few. Some of them work with researchers from computer science, the biological sciences, engineering, linguistics, philosophy, and other disciplines in a multidisciplinary field called *cognitive science,* which analyzes intelligent systems. Cognitive scientists attempt to discover the building blocks of cognition and to determine how these components produce complex behaviors such as remembering a fact, naming an object, or writing a word (Azar, 1997a; Medin & Ross, 1997).

The Humanistic Approach Another view of the role of mental events in psychology is provided by the humanistic approach (also known as the phenomenological approach). From the humanistic perspective, behavior is determined primarily by each person's capacity to choose how to think and act. And humanistic psychologists see these choices as dictated, not by instincts, biological processes, or rewards and punishments, but by each individual's unique perceptions. If you perceive the world as a friendly place, you are likely to feel happy and secure. If you view it as dangerous and hostile, you will probably be defensive and anxious. So, like cognitively oriented psychologists, humanists would see aggression in a theater line as stemming from a perception that aggression is justified.

However, unlike those who take a cognitive approach, humanistic psychologists do not search for general laws that govern people's perceptions, judgments, decisions, and actions. Instead, the humanistic approach celebrates immediate, individual experience. Many of its proponents assert that behavior and mental processes can be fully understood only by appreciating the perceptions and feelings experienced by each individual. Humanistic psychologists also believe that people are essentially good, that they are in control of themselves, and that their main innate tendency is to grow toward their highest potential.

The humanistic approach began to attract attention in North America in the 1940s through the writing of Carl Rogers (1902–1987), a psychologist who had been trained in, but later rejected, the psychodynamic tradition. . . . The humanistic approach also shaped Abraham Maslow's (1943) influential hierarchy-of-needs theory of motivation. . . . Today, however, the impact of the humanistic approach to psychology is limited, mainly because many psychologists find humanistic concepts and predictions too vague to be expressed and tested scientifically.

IN REVIEW

APPROACHES TO PSYCHOLOGY

Approach	Characteristics
Biological	Emphasizes activity of the nervous system, especially of the brain; the action of hormones and other chemicals; and genetics.
Evolutionary	Emphasizes the ways in which behavior and mental processes are adaptive for survival.
Psychodynamic	Emphasizes internal conflicts, mostly unconscious, which usually pit sexual or aggressive instincts against environmental obstacles to their expression.
Behavioral	Emphasizes learning, especially each person's experience with rewards and punishments.
Cognitive	Emphasizes mechanisms through which people receive, store, retrieve, and otherwise process information.
Humanistic	Emphasizes individual potential for growth and the role of unique perceptions in guiding behavior and mental processes.

Source: Adapted from Bernstein, *Psychology,* pp. 12–16.

EXERCISE 7.6 Recording Information on Index Cards

Return to Exercise 7.5. Create a set of index cards for important information in the excerpt. You may include vocabulary cards, category cards with lists of information, and study question cards for main points of the excerpt. Be sure to complete both the front and the back of each card. Practice reciting the information on the cards.

EXERCISE 7.7 Case Studies

Each of the following case studies describes a student situation. Read each case study carefully; highlight key ideas or student issues. On separate paper, answer the question that ends each case study. In your response, address the key points that you highlighted and that directly relate to the question. Answer in complete sentences. These case studies are also available online; you can email your response to your instructor or print a copy of your work online.

1. Justine reads her textbooks the way she reads paperback books. She begins at the beginning of the chapter and does not stop until she reaches the end of the chapter. She often finds that she needs to reread chapters two or three times before she can retain the information. What methods can Justine use to comprehend the textbook chapter better and spend less time rereading?
2. The instructor spent half the class time talking about a concept that was unfamiliar to Simon. Simon had not had a chance to read the last three chapters, so he thought perhaps the concept appeared in those chapters. When he sat down to work with a study partner, Simon started flipping through the chapters page by page, and eventually located the section of information. What strategies would help Simon be a more efficient reader and student?
3. Lily is enrolled in a medical terminology class that requires her to learn about fifty new medical terms a week. Unfortunately, her textbook does not have a glossary. What methods should Lily use to help her learn the new terminology each week?

Exercise 7.8 LINKS

With a partner or in a small group, discuss which of the Twelve Principles of Memory (SAVE CRIB FOTO) you use in each *of the steps of SQ4R. Copy an enlarged version of the following chart. Complete the following chart by listing the principles and brief explanations. Be prepared to share your results with the class.*

Steps in SQ4R	Principles of Memory Used
S	
Q	
R	
R	
R	
R	

Reflection Writing 3 CHAPTER 7

Complete the following directions. Write your results on a separate piece of paper or in a journal.

1. Use the six steps of SQ4R to read a new chapter in any one of your textbooks. Write the name of the textbook, the chapter, and the course that uses this textbook.
2. Briefly explain what you did for each of the six steps of SQ4R.
3. Evaluate the effectiveness of using SQ4R for the chapter you read. Be specific.

SUMMARY

- Surveying means to preview or skim information to get an overview. You can use the process of surveying to get an overview of a textbook, a chapter, or an article before you begin the process of careful reading.
- To survey a textbook, read the title page, copyright page, table of contents, and introductory matter. Locate and become familiar with the contents in the appendix, glossary, references or bibliography, and index.
- To survey a chapter, read the introductory materials carefully. Read the headings and subheadings; examine visual materials and marginal notes. Skim over any terminology in special print. Read the end-of-chapter materials carefully. Surveying a chapter is a warm-up activity that provides you with important information about the basic structure and contents of a chapter.
- The SQ4R reading system is a highly effective six-step approach to improving comprehension. Careful, thorough, and accurate reading results when you use the six steps of SQ4R: survey, question, read, record, recite, and review.
- After you spend what is usually less than twenty minutes surveying the chapter and less than ten minutes converting headings and subheadings into study questions, the process of careful, thorough reading begins. Read one paragraph at a time and then stop. Record important information and quickly recite what you recorded. Continue the read-record-recite cycle until you finish the chapter. The goal is to comprehend the information in the chapter through this thorough-reading approach so you can focus your time and attention on studying your notes, and not have to read the chapter multiple times. Use ongoing review to reinforce the learning process.
- You can use index cards to record (take notes) on important information. Your index cards can include categories with lists of important information, definition cards for key terminology, and study cards with questions and answers. For the cards to be most effective, study from the fronts and the backs of the cards, recite the information and check your accuracy, and use reflect activities to increase your understanding of the material.
- You can record information in the margins of your textbook. Marginal notes may include lists of key points, terminology, definitions, personal comments or questions, study questions, and diagrams or pictures.

ACE Practice Tests, which are scored online, supplementary exercises, enrichment activities, and related web site links are available online for *Essential Study Skills*, 4e. Use the following directions to access this web site:

Type: **http://college.hmco.com/collegesurvival/students**

Click on *List of Sites by Author*. Use the arrow to scroll down to Wong *Essential Study Skills*, 4e. Click on the title. If you are working on your own computer, bookmark this web site.

LEARNING OPTIONS

The following learning options provide you with opportunities to demonstrate your understanding of the topics in Chapter 7. Your instructor may assign one or more specific options or may ask you to select one or more options that interest you the most.

1. Expand the Chapter 7 mapping on page 169 by extending the branches on the mapping to show important key words or phrases for each heading. (See the example in Chapter 1, page 25.) Add pictures and colors to your mapping to accentuate the points. Below the visual mapping or on a separate piece of paper, write a one- or two-paragraph summary that discusses the highlights of the chapter. Use the information in your mapping as a guide for the content of your summary.
2. Create a category chart for *Surveying a Textbook, Surveying a Chapter,* or *Using SQ4R.* List the categories of information in the left column. Create categories of information for at least two more columns or use two or more of the following categories: *do what, how, why, importance,* or *benefits.*
3. Use the Internet to locate an informative web site for the topic of *textbook reading.* Find an alternative textbook reading approach. Print the information. Prepare a short presentation or a written summary of the steps involved in this alternative approach to textbook reading. Then write one or more paragraphs that compare the textbook reading approach to SQ4R. How are they similar? How are they different? Which system seems the most comprehensive?
4. Select a chapter from one of your textbooks. Apply the SQ4R reading system. Create a set of index (notetaking) cards to record important information from the chapter. In your set of cards, include category cards that have lists of information on the back, vocabulary cards that have definitions on the back, and study question cards with questions on the front and answers on the back. Create a title card that indicates the name of the textbook, the name of the chapter, and the name of the course in which you use this textbook.
5. On a piece of paper, formulate study questions for each of the headings and subheadings in this chapter. Leave five or six lines between the questions. Then, without referring to your textbook, write answers to your study questions. Your answers should reflect your own words, not direct wording from the textbook pages.
6. On your own, make marginal notes next to each paragraph in Chapter 7. Remember that marginal notes must be brief and concise. Then meet with another student who also used this learning option. Compare your marginal notes. Write a short summary that identifies your partner for this learning option and discusses what you learned about your marginal notes when you compared them to your partner's notes.
7. Create a mobile (a three-dimensional model that can hang from a ceiling or a light fixture) that shows the steps of SQ4R. Your mobile must be informative and instructional so students who are not familiar with the SQ4R textbook reading system will be able to identify the steps of this reading system and understand what to do in each step.

Chapter 7 REVIEW QUESTIONS

True-False

Carefully read the following statements. Write T *if the statement is true and* F *if it is false.*

________ **1.** Surveying always refers to looking at the information in the front and the back of a new textbook.

________ **2.** Often students can learn how to use a new textbook effectively by reading the information in the appendix and the index.

________ **3.** Surveying a chapter before you begin the process of careful reading is a warm-up activity that you can use to focus your mind, increase your interest, and plan efficient use of your time.

________ **4.** You can omit the fourth step of SQ4R without weakening this reading system.

________ **5.** Step 2 of SQ4R provides a purpose for reading, improves concentration, and results in the creation of meaningful study tools in the review step of the process.

________ **6.** For most college textbooks, you should first read through the entire chapter and then reread the chapter, stopping at the end of each page to take notes.

________ **7.** Several options are available for students to use to complete the *question, record,* and *review* steps of the SQ4R reading system.

________ **8.** Reciting involves speaking out loud, using your own words, and speaking in complete sentences.

________ **9.** If you need lengthy, detailed notes to review key information in a textbook, marginal notes are not the best option.

________ **10.** In Step 4 of SQ4R, your goal is to use highlighting, marginal notes, visual mappings, index cards, or other notetaking options to capture the main ideas and important supporting details on paper so you can use your notes to study and review the information.

Short Answer and Critical Thinking

1. SQ4R is a structured reading approach that uses six steps in a specific order. If you were to change the sequence of the steps from *read-record-recite* to *read-recite-record,* would the system be weakened? Explain your answer.

2. How can you use the SQ4R system for reading math or science textbooks that have mathematical problems, equations, or formulas?

3. Explain how to read a textbook without letting your mind slip into automatic pilot, where little or no information registers in your mind as you read.

4. What are the benefits of the following SQ4R steps?
   a. Step 2—Questioning

   b. Step 5—Reciting

CHAPTER 8

Strengthening Comprehension and Critical Thinking Skills

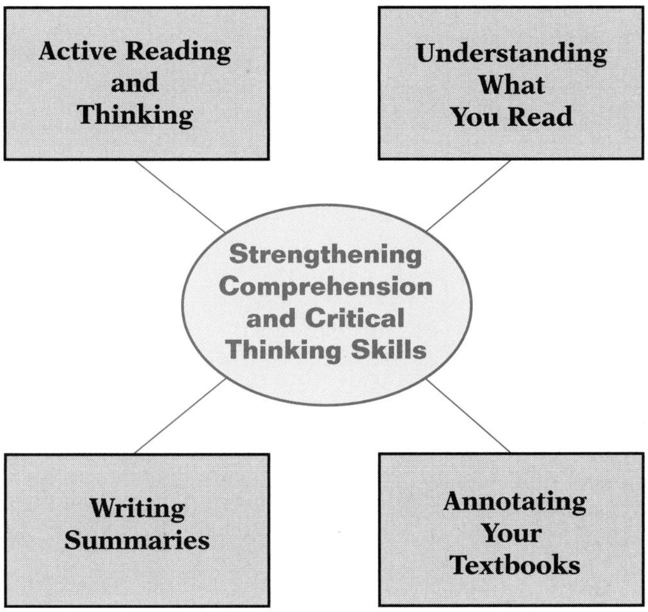

Active reading and active thinking are essential skills for college students that require students to go beyond reading the words printed on textbook pages. You can use many strategies to understand textbook information more thoroughly. Some relate to reading habits, while others relate to vocabulary development and paragraph structure. Annotating, or marking, textbooks helps you comprehend the material more thoroughly and provides study tools for further studying and reviewing. This chapter ends with a discussion of writing summaries, a strategy that promotes the expression of ideas in full paragraph form. Strengthening reading comprehension and critical thinking skills is an ongoing process; you will need to continually apply effort and the strategies in this chapter to meet the challenges presented by textbooks of varying complexity.

Terms to Know

active reading/thinking
critical thinking
verbalizing
punctuation clues
word clues
word structure clues
prefixes and suffixes
base words or roots
context clues
synonyms
antonyms
contrast
comparison
analogies
topic
main idea
topic sentence
implied main ideas
organizational patterns
chronological pattern
comparison pattern
contrast pattern
definition pattern
examples pattern
cause/effect pattern
annotating
highlighting
supporting details
bullets
transition paragraph
ordinals
place holder words
marginal notes
stringing ideas
reciting
paraphrasing
summaries

CHAPTER 8 Comprehension and Critical Thinking Profile

DO, SCORE, and **RECORD** your profile before you read this chapter. If you need to review the process, refer to the complete directions given in the Profile for Chapter 1 on page 2.

ONLINE: You can complete the profile and get your score online at this textbook's web site.

	YES	NO
1. When I read a new chapter, I take time to think about the information in the chapter, analyze it, and work with it in a variety of ways.	______	______
2. If I encounter a difficult or confusing paragraph, I skip over it and move to the next paragraph, which may be easier to understand.	______	______
3. I use the structure of words and sentences as well as context clues to discover the meanings of unfamiliar words that I encounter.	______	______
4. I often highlight or underline several complete sentences that are difficult to read in each paragraph in my textbooks.	______	______
5. I reread chapters thoroughly at least three times when I am preparing for a test.	______	______
6. After I have read a paragraph in one of my textbooks, I am usually able to identify the main idea and the most significant supporting details.	______	______
7. I use the margins in the textbook to write brief notes or draw diagrams.	______	______
8. When I write summaries, I include only the main chapter headings, which summarize the topics of the chapter.	______	______
9. I can usually recognize the primary method a textbook author uses in a paragraph to organize the supporting details.	______	______
10. I cannot study from my textbook notes because they are too disorganized and difficult to read.	______	______

Reflection Writing 1 — CHAPTER 8

On a separate piece of paper or in a journal, do the following:

1. **Discuss your profile score for this chapter. What was your score? What does it mean to you?**
2. **What are your greatest challenges or difficulties in the area of understanding the information in your textbooks?**

Active Reading and Thinking

Reading and learning from college textbooks requires both active reading and active thinking skills. In Chapter 5, page 116, you learned that *active learning* involves taking notes, writing questions, marking your textbooks by highlighting, reciting to activate your auditory channel, making study tools, writing summaries, and quizzing yourself on the information you are studying. *Active reading* and *active thinking* are components of active learning.

Active readers

1. use a reading system, such as SQ4R, to process the content of college textbooks.
2. recognize levels of information (thesis, major concepts or themes, main ideas, and supporting details).
3. recognize organizational patterns in the text (chronological, cause-effect, definition, comparison or contrast, or examples).
4. use word structure clues, context clues, glossaries, and dictionaries to understand unfamiliar words.
5. interact with the textbook by annotating passages (highlighting, marking, and making marginal notes).
6. reorganize information and elaborate important points by making study tools (visual mappings, hierarchies, index cards, or separate notes).
7. integrate the new information with information already learned.
8. actively think about the information by questioning, interpreting, evaluating, or applying the information to new situations.

Active thinkers

1. identify the important *knowledge* they need to learn. They can define, describe, label, list, match, name, and recognize important main ideas and facts (supporting details).
2. *comprehend* or grasp the meaning and significance of the information they read. They can classify, discuss, explain, interpret, restate, and summarize concepts and facts in their own words.
3. *apply* the information they learn to new situations. They can illustrate examples, solve problems, and demonstrate uses or show applications of the information.
4. *analyze* information by identifying its individual components. They can categorize, compare, contrast, diagram, distinguish characteristics of different bodies of information, identify patterns or trends, and show relationships between different parts of the whole.
5. *synthesize* or integrate information to see the big picture, concepts, or major themes. They can collect relevant information, compose original ideas, create generalizations based on individual facts, draw logical conclusions, formulate questions, organize information in new ways, and personalize information so it relates to their own experiences.
6. *evaluate* the logic, authenticity, accuracy, and objectivity or subjectivity of information. They can argue, assess, judge, defend, or support a position, perspective, or decision. They can predict logical sequences of events and outcomes.

When you use **active reading** strategies, you focus your attention on comprehending (attaching meaning and significance to) the information you read. You become engaged in the learning process by applying strategies that move you beyond merely reading the printed words. You read with a desire and a goal of understanding the information clearly and accurately and processing the information into your long-term memory system.

In Chapter 6, page 158, you learned about *Bloom's Taxonomy,* a system that categorizes cognitive levels of questioning and thinking. **Active thinking**, also known as **critical thinking**, improves your understanding of what you read and builds a stronger foundation to learn higher-level concepts. Active thinking moves you beyond rote memory and helps you internalize the information for future use. The Active Thinker's chart, based on Bloom's Taxonomy, shows common characteristics of active thinkers.

This chapter introduces active learning strategies that will help you strengthen your reading comprehension and critical thinking skills so you can learn textbook information more thoroughly and efficiently. It is important, however, to recognize that reading comprehension and critical thinking are complex processes that occur on many levels. As a result, many colleges and universities offer term-long courses designed to strengthen reading comprehension and critical thinking skills. You may want to consider enrolling in a college reading or critical thinking course next term to boost your skills beyond those you will learn in this chapter.

Group Processing: A Collaborative Learning Activity

Form groups of three or four students. Complete the following directions.

1. Discuss what *reading comprehension* means to you. As a group, formulate a definition of *reading comprehension.*
2. Brainstorm a list of reading difficulties you have encountered with some of your college textbooks. Be prepared to share with the rest of the class.

Understanding What You Read

As you already know, college textbooks vary in complexity; some are easy to read and comprehend while others require more time and effort to understand and master. Understanding textbook information begins with the first step of SQ4R—surveying. Surveying helps you form a big picture of the chapter and begin to set up schemas for the information in the chapter. Each additional step of SQ4R (question, read, record, recite, and review) provides you with active learning strategies to comprehend and master textbook information. The following strategies will help you unlock the meaning of difficult paragraphs or passages and thus increase your comprehension of the material.

Strategies to Unlock the Meaning of Text

1. Reread, verbalize, and visualize.
2. Use clues in words and sentences to learn meanings of unfamiliar words.
3. Substitute familiar words for unfamiliar words.
4. Use the natural flow or progression of information.
5. Identify main ideas.
6. Identify the organizational pattern or patterns used for the supporting details.
7. Draw a picture of the paragraph.

Reread, Verbalize, and Visualize

Reread the information more slowly and with the intent of grasping the message presented in the paragraph. On occasion, you may find yourself rushing the reading process and reading too quickly for your mind to grasp the concepts presented. Unlike the leisure reading of magazines, newspapers, or paperback books, textbook reading requires your focused attention and alertness to details. You may find that your comprehension increases simply by reading at a slower pace.

Your reading comprehension may also be enhanced by **verbalizing** what you read. In other words, read out loud. By saying the words and hearing the words, you give yourself extra assistance in understanding a difficult paragraph. When you read out loud and when you speak, you usually group information into natural phrases, which makes the information easier to understand. When you use this technique, read out loud slowly, enunciate clearly, and concentrate on hearing the words and the phrase they form.

Weak comprehension sometimes occurs when a person reads too quickly for the information to be processed effectively and accurately. Taking the time to **visualize** the information and create a "movie in your mind" carries a stronger image into your memory system. Some readers automatically visualize as they read; others need to apply more effort and intention to activate the visualization process. When you are having difficulty comprehending (or remembering) what you are reading, evaluate your approach to see if you are taking the time necessary to create the visual images. If you did not create pictures, try reading the paragraph more slowly and force the visual images to develop as you read.

Use Clues in Words and Sentences to Understand Unfamiliar Words

Many readers with comprehension problems have the tendency to skip over unfamiliar words. If you skip some words or read words but do not know their meanings, your weak comprehension of the paragraph may be tied to its vocabulary. Specialized or course-specific vocabulary may be unclear, or words that are not set off in special print may be the source of the problem.

Use the following strategies to unlock the meanings of the unfamiliar words.

1. Look for a glossary in the back of your textbook. Words in bold or special print will usually be defined in the glossary. You can learn the meanings of words that are *not* in special print by using a dictionary or an electronic handheld spell checker with a dictionary and thesaurus.
2. Use **punctuation clues** to identify definitions of terminology within the sentence or surrounding sentences. *Commas, dashes, parentheses,* and *colons* are forms of punctuation that signal definitions. Notice how the *punctuation clues* in the following examples signal the definitions of the circled words.

commas— The use of a **quality circle**, *a group of employees who meet on company time to solve problems of product quality*, is one way that auto makers are implementing this strategy at operations level.

dash— Instead, Aristarchus propounded the **heliocentric theory**—*that the earth and the planets revolve around the sun.*

parentheses— Credibility problems can occur from improper or careless **enunciation** (*the way you articulate and pronounce words in context*).

colon— An **empirical formula** is the simplest formula for a compound: *the formula of a substance written with the smallest integer subscripts.*

3. Use **word clues** that signal definitions within the sentence and link the vocabulary terms to their definitions. The following word clues are used frequently to define terminology.

also	defined as	referred to as	known as	called
is/are	to describe	mean/means	which is	or

Often, the term is presented first and then followed by the definition. However, the order can be reversed; the definition may be given first, followed by the naming of the term. Notice how word clues are used in the following sentences to signal the definitions:

> A dialect is *a particular speech pattern associated with an area of the country or a cultural or ethnic background.*

> When we talk about culture, we mean *the customary traits, attitudes, and behaviors of a group of people.*

4. Use **word structure clues** to get a general idea about the meaning of unfamiliar words. Because many words contain **prefixes** (units of meaning attached to the beginnings of words) and **suffixes** (units of meaning that follow the base word and indicate a specific part of speech, such as a noun, verb, adjective, or adverb), by learning the meanings of prefixes and suffixes, you can determine basic information about unfamiliar words. (You can find lists of prefixes and suffixes with their meanings on this textbook's web site.) For example, the word *electroencephalogram* can be broken into its structural parts. *Electro* refers to "electrical," *enceph* refers to the brain, and *gram* refers to a graph. Basically, it is "an electrical brain graph." The glossary definition in a psychology textbook states that an electroencephalogram is "a recording of the electrical signals produced by the nerve cells of the brain, obtained through electrodes attached to the surface of the skull."

Base words are words in English that can stand by themselves. **Roots** are units of meaning, also often from Greek or Latin, that do not form English words until other roots, prefixes, or suffixes are attached to them. For example, *ject* means "to throw"; however, we do not use it until we add additional word parts, such as in the words *inject, reject,* or *project.* (See the web site for a list of roots and their meanings.)

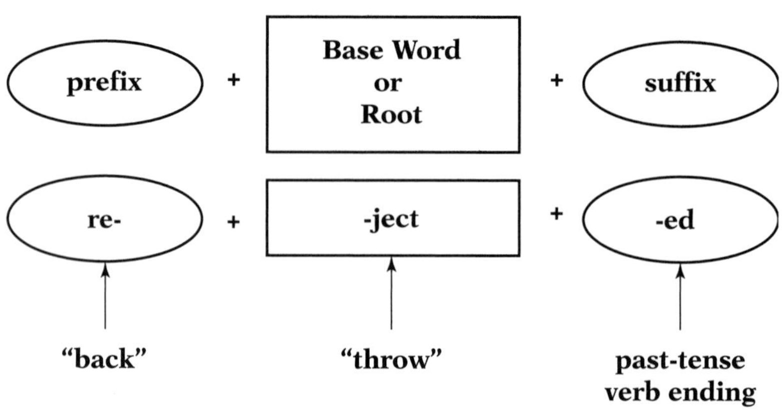

Defining a word solely by using the structural clues often does not provide a complete definition. After you have a general idea of a word, you can always use a dictionary or the glossary in your book to expand the basic meaning with a full definition.

5. Use **context clues** for hints about the general meanings of unfamiliar words. The term *context* refers to the words and sentences that surround a specific term or concept. By carefully reading the sentence with the unfamiliar word and then rereading the surrounding sentences, you can often pick up clues about the meaning of the word through words with similar meanings *(synonyms),* words with opposite meanings *(antonyms),* or words or images that indicate a likeness or difference between the unfamiliar word and some other concept. The following chart summarizes kinds of context clues and provides you with an example of each.

Context Clue	Definition	Strategy	Example Sentence
Synonyms	words with exact or similar meanings	Try substituting a familiar word (a synonym) for the unfamiliar word.	*probity:* The judge has a keen sense of recognizing a person's honesty and integrity. For that reason, the *probity* of the witness was not questioned.
Antonyms	words with opposite meanings	An unfamiliar word is understood because you understand its opposite.	*impenitent:* Instead of showing shame, regret, or remorse, the con artist was *impenitent.*
Contrasts	words that show an opposite or a difference	Look for words such as *differ, different, unlike,* or *opposite of* to understand the differences.	*thallophyte:* Because the fungi is a *thallophyte,* it differs from the other plants in the garden that have embedded roots and the rich foliage of shiny leaves and hardy stems.
Comparisons or **Analogies**	words or images that indicate a likeness or a similarity	Look for the commonality between two or more items.	*cajole:* I sensed he was trying to *cajole* me. He reminded me of a salesman trying to sell me a bridge.

Context clues sometimes are not as specific as synonyms, antonyms, or analogies. The meaning of unfamiliar words may simply be "sensed" by relating the information in the surrounding sentences to common sense, personal experience, or a variety of examples. To use these, and all kinds of context clues, the reader must keep a focused mind, concentrate, and search for useful context clues. Reading quickly without time to think, digest the information, and actively be involved with the printed word will leave many unfamiliar words undefined.

Substitute Familiar Words for Unfamiliar Words

Once you have identified the meaning of an unfamiliar word, you can use this strategy to convert formal textbook language into a less formal, more personal conversational tone. Above each of the words that was unfamiliar to you, write a more common or familiar word. Then reread the paragraph but substitute the common or familiar word for the unfamiliar word. The following example shows how this technique of substituting words adds clarity and improves comprehension of a difficult paragraph.

puzzling
Few if any philosophies are as enigmatic as *Daoism*—the teachings of
the Way (Dao). The opening lines of this school's greatest masterpiece,
morality associated with
The Classic of the Way and *Virtue* (*Dao De Jing*), which is ascribed to the
famous challenge
legendary Laozi, immediately confront the reader with Daoism's
contradiction walked lasting
essential paradox: "The Way that can be trodden is not the enduring
and the unchanging Way. The name that can be named is not the
claims
enduring and unchanging name." Here is a philosophy that purports
at the same time
to teach *the* Way (of truth) but simultaneously claims that the True
exceeds Contained
Way transcends human understanding. Encapsulated within a little book
resists rejects
of some five thousand words is a philosophy that defies definition, spurns
reason, and rejects words as inadequate.

Andrea, *The Human Record,* p. 93.

Use the Natural Flow or Progression of Information

A paragraph is defined as a group of sentences that support a main idea. Paragraphs are grouped to support a heading or a *thesis statement* (the overall purpose of the combined paragraphs). Therefore, when you have difficulty with one paragraph, sometimes you can determine the meaning or significance of the paragraph by placing it in the context of the surrounding paragraphs. Reread the preceding paragraph; read the paragraph that follows the difficult paragraph. Look for the pattern of information and the natural flow or progression of information through the series of paragraphs.

What techniques can individuals use to be sure they understand the language of a legal contract before signing the agreement?

Exercise 8.1 Rereading, Verbalizing, and Visualizing

Read the following excerpt at your normal reading pace. Then reread the paragraph out loud *to yourself. As you read, create a* movie in your mind *about the information. Answer the questions that follow the excerpt.*

Tax Evasion

Tax evasion involves deliberately and willfully hiding income, falsely claiming deductions, or otherwise cheating the government out of taxes owed. It is illegal. A waiter who does not report tips received and a baby-sitter who does not report income are both evading taxes, as is a person who deducts $150 in church contributions but who fails to actually make the donations. Tax avoidance, on the other hand, means avoiding taxes by reducing tax liability through legal techniques. It involves applying knowledge of the tax code and regulations to personal income tax.

Tax evasion results in penalties, fines, excess interest charges, and a possible jail sentence. In contrast, tax avoidance boosts your after-tax income because you pay less in taxes; as a result, you will have more money available for spending, saving, and investing.

1. What are the differences between *tax evasion* and *tax avoidance?* ______________________

____

____

2. What three examples are given to explain tax evasion? ______________________

____

____

3. Why does the government impose penalties, fines, interest charges, and sometimes jail time on tax evaders? ______________________

____

____

4. What differences did you notice in your reading comprehension when you read the paragraph out loud (verbalized)? ______________________

____

____

5. Without referring back to the paragraph, what images or "movies in your mind" can you recall about the content of this paragraph? ______________________

____

____

EXERCISE 8.2 Defining Words

Read the following excerpt carefully. Answer the questions that follow.

Personal Power

Three sources of power stem from characteristics or behaviors of the power actor: expert power, referent power, and prestige power. All are classified as personal power, because they are derived from the person rather than from the organization. Expert power and referent power contribute to charisma. Expert power is the ability to influence others through specialized knowledge, skills, or abilities—for example, like a marketing manager who is adept at identifying new markets. Referent power is the ability to influence others through desirable traits and characteristics.

Another important form of personal power is prestige power, the power stemming from one's status and reputation. A manager who has accumulated important business successes acquires prestige power. Executive recruiters, for example, identify executives who could readily be placed in key CEO positions because of their excellent track records.

1. What is *personal power?*

2. Define *prestige power.*

3. How are *expert power* and *referent power* alike?

4. How are *expert power* and *referent power* different?

5. Explain how you could use *word structure clues* to understand the term *referent.*

6. What is *charisma?*

EXERCISE 8.3 Substituting Common or Familiar Words

For some students, the words in italics in the following paragraph may be unfamiliar, leading to poor comprehension. Above each italicized word, write a more familiar word. Then read the paragraph out loud, using your substituted words.

From Germany to the Balkans, hostility is again breaking loose among the ***mosaic*** of ethnic minorities that live cheek by ***jowl***. The ***enmities*** are the same as those that ***enfeebled*** the Austro–Hungarian and Ottoman Empires and helped start World War I in 1914 and that Hitler manipulated in the years leading up to World War II in 1939. Such ***enmities*** will continue to threaten world peace in the twenty-first century. A ***corollary*** of this is the changed nature of war. Formerly war was an interstate affair in which organized armies met in combat. Today, ***ferocious*** civil war is the norm. The military historian Martin van Crevald writes: "The characteristics of the new kind of warfare, of which Bosnia is an example, are that sophisticated modern weapons play little role. . . . But although sophisticated weapons are scarcely used, these new wars tend to be very bloody because there is no distinction between armies and peoples, so everybody who gets in the way gets killed."

Mansbach, *The Global Puzzle*, p. 17.

Identify Main Ideas

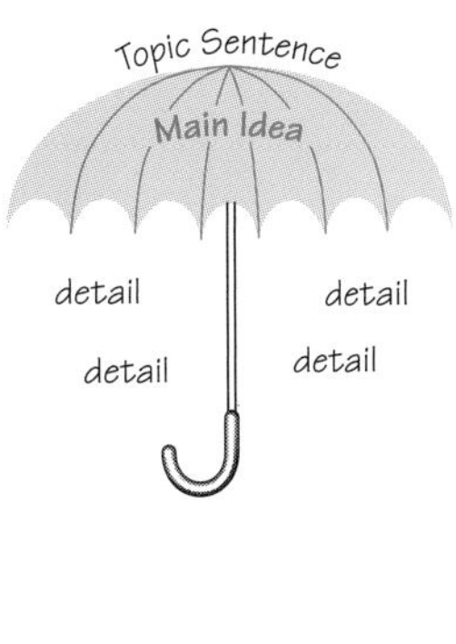

Every paragraph has a *topic*. The **topic** is the subject of the paragraph. You can easily identify the topic by asking yourself, *In one word or one phrase, what is this paragraph about?* The **main idea** of a paragraph is the main point the author intends to develop in the paragraph. Unless it is *implied* (not directly stated), the main idea is expressed in the **topic sentence**. The topic sentence is like an umbrella. It needs to be broad enough for all of the other information or details in the paragraph to "fit under" it. In a well-written paragraph, each sentence relates to or supports the topic sentence.

Unlocking the meaning of a paragraph begins by identifying the main idea. You can identify the main idea by analyzing the paragraph and locating the topic sentence.

Use the following strategies to identify the main idea or the topic sentence.

1. Ask yourself and answer the following questions to identify the topic sentence:
   - What is the topic (subject) of this paragraph? Is there a "big picture" or "umbrella sentence" that contains this topic word?
   - What is the main idea of this paragraph, the idea the author wants to make about the topic?
   - Which sentence is large enough to encompass the content of the paragraph?
2. Use the following positions of sentences to evaluate sentences that may be the topic sentence with the main idea:
   - Does the first sentence capture the overall content of the paragraph? In textbooks, the first sentence of a paragraph often states the main idea.
   - If the first sentence is not the "umbrella sentence," check the last sentence. Sometimes the details are presented first; the last sentence summarizes the main points, and thus states the main idea.
   - If the first and the last sentences do not state the main idea, carefully examine each sentence in the body of the paragraph.

In the following paragraph, the main idea is expressed in the second part of the first sentence. The last sentence restates or summarizes the first sentence.

> The main forms of plant and animal life may at first glance appear chaotic, but the biologist sees them in a high degree of order. This order is due to an elaborate system of classification. All life is first grouped into a few primary divisions called phyla; each phylum is in turn subdivided into small groups called classes; each class is subdivided into orders; and so on down through the family, the genus, the species, the variety. This system brings order out of chaos, enabling the biologist to consider any plant or animal in its proper relationship to the rest.
>
> Louise E. Rorabacher.

In the next paragraph, the first sentence introduces the topic but does not state the main idea. When this occurs, the next step is to check the last sentence. In this example, the last sentence states the main idea and the topic, which is *marketing mix*. This sentence is also an example of the natural progression of information; it serves as a lead-in to the next paragraph, which will define and explain the idea of marketing mix more thoroughly.

Creating a Marketing Mix

A business firm controls four important elements of marketing that it combines in a way that reaches the firm's target market. These are the *product* itself, the *price* of the product, the means chosen for its *distribution,* and the *promotion* of the product. When combined, these four elements form a marketing mix.

Pride, Hughes, Kapoor. *Business,* p. 363.

On occasion, you will encounter paragraphs that do not directly state the main idea—the main idea is *implied.* In paragraphs with **implied main ideas,** the assumption is that after careful reading, you will be able to state the main idea in your own words. The supporting details in the paragraph should supply you with sufficient information to draw your own conclusion about the main idea. In the following paragraph, the first sentence is not the "big picture" or the umbrella sentence. If it were the topic sentence, the entire paragraph would be dedicated to examples of civilizations that left written records that we cannot yet decipher. The last sentence cannot work as the topic sentence because it is an example of mysterious people for whom we have yet to uncover written records. After examining the body of the paragraph, notice how none of the sentences captures the "big picture" of the entire paragraph. After reading the paragraph carefully and thinking about its content, you can formulate a main idea, such as *some of the world's earliest civilizations did not leave written records or written records that can be deciphered,* or *we do not have written records to use to learn about some of the world's earliest civilizations.*

Some of the world's earliest civilizations have left written records that we cannot yet decipher and might never be able to read. These include India's Harappan civilization, which was centered in the Indus valley from before 2500 to some time after 1700 B.C.E.; and the Minoan civilization of the Aegean island of Crete, which flourished from roughly 2500 to about 1400 B.C.E.; and the African civilization of Kush, located directly south of Egypt, which reached its age of greatness after 800 B.C.E.; but with much earlier origins as a state. For many other early civilizations and cultures we have as yet uncovered no written records. This is the case of mysterious peoples who, between approximately 6000 B.C.E. and the first century C.E., painted and carved thousands of pieces of art on the rocks of Tassili n'Ajjer in what is today the central Saharan Desert. It is also true of the Olmec civilization of Mexico, which appeared around 1200 B.C.E.

Andrea/Overfield, *The Human Record,* p. 34.

EXERCISE 8.4 Identifying Main Ideas and Topic Sentences

By yourself, with a partner, or in a small group, read each of the following paragraphs carefully. Highlight or underline the sentence that you think is the topic sentence for each paragraph. If the paragraph has an implied main idea, use your own words to write the main idea next to the paragraph.

1. Global politics, then, has many kinds of issues. Some, such as U.S.–Russian arms negotiations or Syrian–Israeli peace negotiations, involve the quest for security. Others, such as negotiations on trade barriers, focus on economic questions. Still others, such as controversies about acid rain, are about threats to the environment. In other words, the enormous range of issues in global politics covers diverse topics. Increasingly, the global agenda is attracting nontraditional issues that either produce cooperation or necessitate collaboration if disaster is to be avoided.

Mansbach, *The Global Puzzle,* p. 19.

2. In a family with two adults and children, for example, one of the adults may already have a job and the other may be choosing between working at home or working outside the home. This decision may be very sensitive to the wage and perhaps the cost of child care or consuming more prepared meals. In fact, the increased number of women working outside the home may be due to the increased opportunities and wages for women. The increase in the wage induces workers to work more in the labor market. Economists have observed a fairly strong wage effect on the amount women work.

Taylor, *Economics,* pp. 327, 329.

3. To understand leadership, it is important to grasp the difference between leadership and management. We get a clue from the standard conceptualization of the functions of management: planning, organizing, directing (or leading), and controlling. Leading is a major part of a manager's job, yet the manager must also plan, organize, and control. Broadly speaking, leadership deals with the interpersonal aspects of a manager's job, whereas planning, organizing, and controlling deal with the administrative aspects. According to current thinking, leadership deals with change, inspiration, motivation, and influence. In contrast, management deals more with maintaining equilibrium and the status quo.

DuBrin, *Leadership,* p. 3.

4. Why does a new product fail? Mainly because the product and its marketing program are not planned and tested as completely as they should be. For example, to save on development costs, a firm may market-test its product but not its entire marketing mix. Or a firm may market a new product before all the "bugs" have been worked out. Or, when problems show up in the testing state, a firm may try to recover its product development costs by pushing ahead with full-scale marketing anyway. Finally, some firms try to market new products with inadequate financing.

Pride/Hughes/Kapoor, *Business,* p. 401.

5. The human brain in late adulthood, however, is smaller and slower in its functioning than the brain in early adulthood. This reduction is thought to be caused by the death of neurons, which do not regenerate. Neurons die at an increasing rate after age 60. The proportion of neurons that die varies across different parts of the brain. In the visual area, the death rate is about 50 percent. In the motor areas, the death rate varies from 20 to 50 percent. In the memory and reasoning areas, the death rate is less than 20 percent. The production of certain neurotransmitters also declines with age.

Payne/Wenger, *Cognitive Psychology,* p. 359.

6. America's political and intellectual leaders worked hard to inculcate virtue in their fellow countrymen and countrywomen. After 1776, American literature, theater, art, architecture, and education all pursued explicitly moral goals. The education of women was considered particularly important, for as the mothers of the republic's children, they were primarily responsible for ensuring the nation's future. On such matters Americans could agree, but they disagreed on many other critical issues. Almost all white men concurred that women, Indians, and African-Americans should be excluded from formal participation in politics, but they found it difficult to reach a consensus on how many of their own number should be included, how often elections should be held, or how their new governments should be structured.

Norton, *A People and a Nation,* p. 173.

7. Identities help determine whom people consider to be friends or foes. People have loyalties to numerous groups and identify with them—government, gender, employer, church, ethnicity, and so on. A person in France might identify with a feminist group seeking gender equality, a farm association trying to hold on to agricultural subsidies, a consumer who would like to reduce such subsidies and so lower food prices, the Catholic Church seeking state funds for parochial schools, or even a right-wing political party seeking to expel France's immigrant population. In complex societies, multiple identities are common.

Mansbach, *The Global Puzzle,* p. 163.

8. Many outdoor trainers and participants believe strongly that they derived substantial personal benefits from outdoor training. Among the most important are developing greater self-confidence, appreciating hidden strengths, and learning to work better with people. Strong proponents of outdoor training believe that those who do not appreciate the training simply do not understand it. Many training directors also have positive attitudes toward training. They believe that a work team that experiences outdoor training will work more cooperatively back at the office.

DuBrin, *Leadership,* p. 237.

9. Man probably used his own voice to produce the earliest music, and music through the ages has developed with reference to the voice. It seems likely that primitive human beings, discovering that their voices were capable of certain timbres and pitches, would have had a natural interest in similar sounds encountered by accident; a plucked bow string, wind blowing across the reeds in a brook. This natural tendency to relate new sounds to the human voice makes the voice the most fundamental of musical sounds.

Wink/Williams.

10. The word *civilization* is derived from the Latin adjective *civilis,* which means "political" or "civic." No matter how else we define civilization, an organized civic entity, known as a state, stands at the center of every society we call civilized. A state is a sovereign public power that binds large numbers of people together at a level that transcends the ties of family, clan, tribe, and local community and organizes them for projects far beyond the capabilities of single families or even villages and towns.

Andrea/Overfield, *The Human Record,* p. 5.

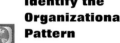

Identify the Organizational Pattern

Comprehension involves more than identifying the main ideas of paragraphs. Unlocking the meaning of text also involves understanding the relationships among the details within paragraphs. For writing to be coherent and make sense, the supporting details within a paragraph need to be organized logically. The ideas within the paragraph need to flow with a natural progression. Five **organizational patterns** for organizing details within a paragraph frequently appear in college textbooks. If you have taken any college composition classes, these organizational patterns are the same that you have learned to use in your own writing.

The five common patterns are shown below. Following each pattern is an example of a visual form that you could use to show the relationships between two or more items in the paragraph. While there are many ways to pictorially show the information, the examples given are excellent starting points.

Chronological Pattern If you look carefully at the details, you may notice that they are presented in a logical time sequence called *chronological order.* Chronological order is often used when a story is being told (a narrative) or when a procedure or process is being explained. The **chronological pattern** indicates that the details happen in a specific, fixed order to get to a conclusion or a result.

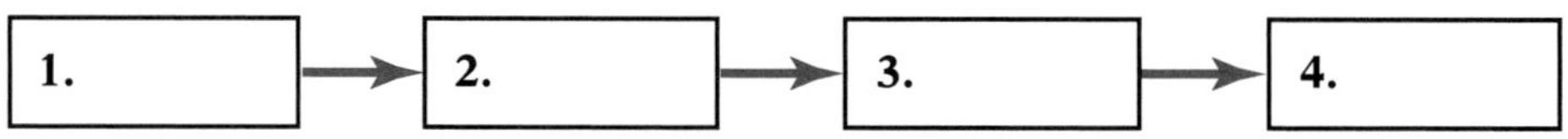

Clue words used in this pattern: *when, then, before, next, after, first, second,* and *finally.*

Comparison or Contrast Pattern When two or more objects or events are being discussed, a **comparison pattern** is being used. This pattern can include both likenesses and differences. However, if only differences between two or more objects are being discussed, a **contrast pattern** is used. After you are able to identify the comparison or the contrast pattern, you will more easily understand what is being said about each subject.

Features	A	B

Clue words used to signal likenesses: *also, similarly,* and *likewise.* Clue words used to signal differences: *but, in contrast, on the other hand, however, although,* and *while.*

Definition Pattern Many textbook paragraphs simply explain the meanings of terms. If the term being used is vital to comprehending more complex information, an entire paragraph may be devoted to helping you grasp the meaning of the term through the use of explanations, negations, analogies, or examples. A **definition pattern** often has the term to be defined in bold letters in the first sentence of the paragraph.

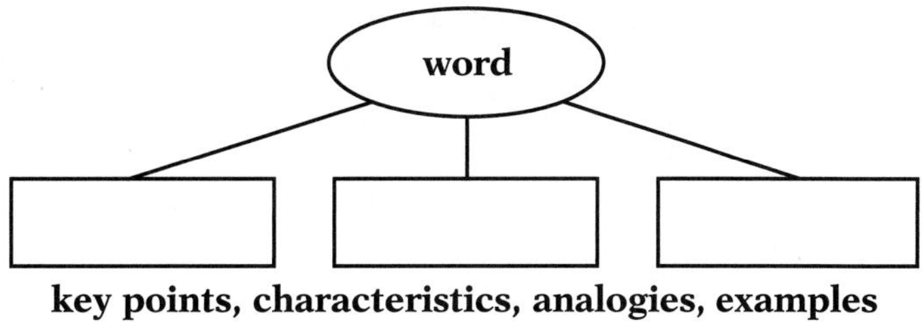

Clue words used in this pattern: *means, is, can be considered,* and *is defined as.*

Examples Pattern In the **examples pattern**, once an important idea, term, or theory is presented, the author expands your understanding by giving you clear examples of the theory before moving on to new information.

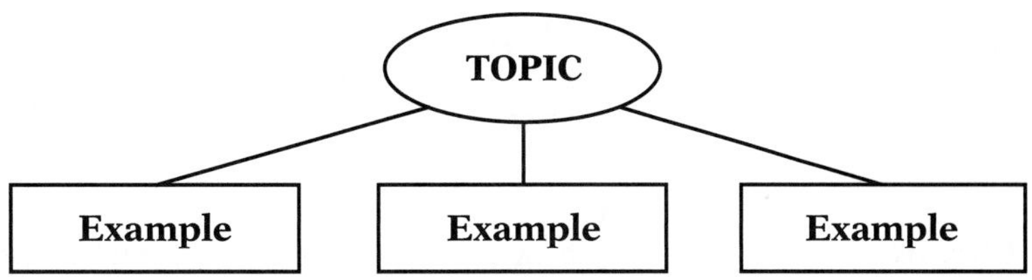

Clue words used in this pattern: *for example, another example,* and *an illustration of this.*

Cause/Effect Pattern Often the relationship between two items shows that one item caused the other to happen. Sometimes one cause can have more than one outcome or effect. In other cases, several causes can produce a given effect or outcome. Whenever there is a relationship that shows that one item caused the other to happen, a **cause/effect pattern** is being used.

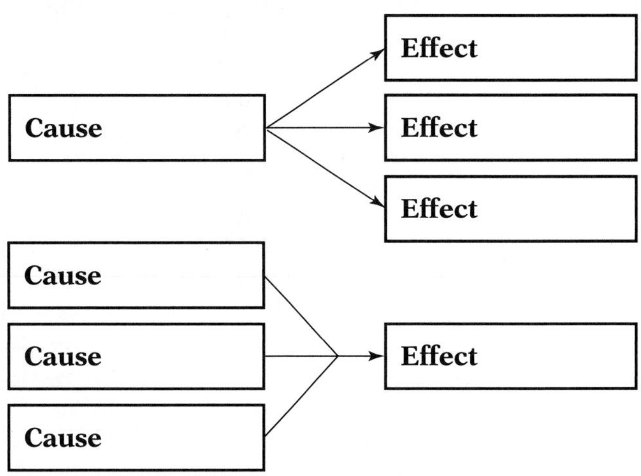

Clue words for this pattern: *because, since, so, therefore, caused by,* and *result in.*

Summary Chart for Organizational Patterns

Pattern	Purpose Is to Show:	Clue Words
Chronological	logical time sequence	when, then, before, next, after, first, second, finally, while, since, until
Comparison	likenesses or differences	also, and, similarly, likewise, but, in contrast, on the other hand, however, although, while
Contrast	differences	but, in contrast, on the other hand, however, although, while, yet, whereas, nevertheless
Definition	the meaning of course-specific words (terminology)	mean, is, can be considered, is defined as
Examples	examples that clarify an idea, term, or theory	for example, another example, an illustration of this, similarly
Cause/Effect	relationship between two items that have a cause and an outcome/effect	because, since, so, so that, therefore, caused by, result in, consequently, as a result

Draw a Picture of the Paragraph

Converting printed information in paragraphs into pictures promotes careful reading, critical thinking, and comprehension. As you work your way through the paragraph by drawing a picture to show the significant details, the information in the paragraph becomes clearer. (Note that you may also draw a picture for information from multiple paragraphs that appear under the same heading or in the same chapter.) The process of drawing also helps you create a visual image of the information and use thinking processes that do not occur when you read printed materials. By labeling parts of your pictures with words, you also create a strong association between words and symbols. Both the words and the symbols serve as links to recall information later. Remember from Chapter 6 that pictures are also one form of mnemonics that serves as a memory trigger to help you later pull up information from long-term memory.

Greenhouse Effect:

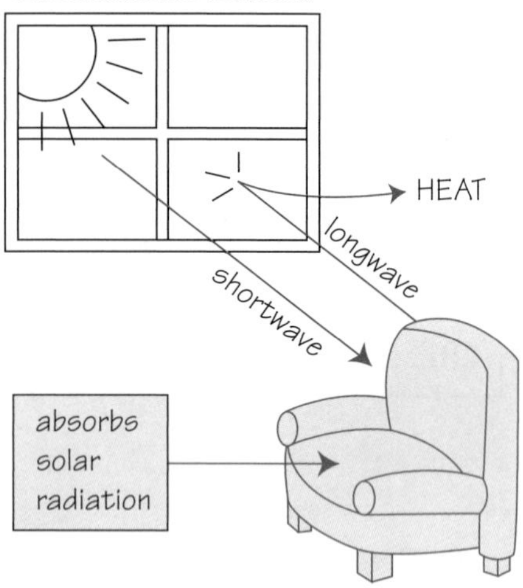

Place your hand over the picture at left; read the paragraph carefully. Visualize the information as you read. Then examine the drawing to see how the information has been converted to a picture.

A window pane transmits sunlight. It is nearly transparent, and much of the shortwave energy passes through. Only a little energy is absorbed to heat up the glass. However, the walls and furniture inside a room absorb a large part of the solar radiation coming through the window. The energy radiated from the furniture, unlike the original solar energy, is all long-wave radiation. Much of it is unable to pass out through the window pane. This is why the car seats get so hot on a hot, sunny day when all the windows are closed. Try putting a piece of glass in front of a hot object to see how the heat waves are cut off. A greenhouse traps energy in this way when the sun shines and so does the atmosphere.

Investigating the Earth, American Geological Institute

Exercise 8.5 Converting Words to Visual Forms

With a partner or on your own, convert the information in the following paragraphs to a visual form. You may use a visual form that shows the paragraph's organizational pattern, or you may use a picture that shows the significant details and their relationship. Complete your drawings on a separate piece of paper; number your drawings to correspond to the numbers given below.

1. The human costs of the Civil War were enormous. The total number of military casualties on both sides exceeded 1 million—a frightful toll for a nation of 31 million people. Approximately 360,000 Union soldiers died, 110,000 of them from wounds suffered in battle. Another 275,175 Union soldiers were wounded but survived. On the Confederate side, an estimated 260,000 lost their lives, and almost as many suffered wounds. More men died in the Civil War than in all other American wars combined until Vietnam. Fundamental disagreements that would continue to trouble the Reconstruction era had caused unprecedented loss of life.

Norton, *A People and a Nation,* p. 437.

2. The earth system contains a number of interconnected subsystems, often described as "environmental spheres." The four major subsystems are the *atmosphere,* or the ocean of air that overlies the entire earth's surface; the *hydrosphere,* or the water of the surface and near-surface regions of the earth; the *lithosphere,* or the massive accumulation of rock and metal that forms the solid body of the planet itself; and the *biosphere,* or the layer of living organisms of which we are a part. All four respond in various ways to the flow of energy and materials through the earth system.

Holt Atkinson, *Reading Enhancement and Development,* pp. 218–219.

3. The Celsius scale is *the temperature scale for general use in much of the world and for scientific use worldwide.* On this scale, the freezing point of water is 0°C, and the boiling point of water at normal barometric pressure is 100°C. On the Fahrenheit scale, *the scale in common usage in the United States,* the freezing point of water is 32°F, and the boiling point of water at normal barometric pressure is 212°F. Negative temperatures are possible with both of these scales. For example, liquid nitrogen boils at −321°F and −196°C. Another well-known temperature is discussed in the Chemical Perspective at the end of this section.

Ebbing, Wentworth, *Introductory Chemistry,* pp. 33–34.

4. Railroads altered conceptions of time and space. First, by overcoming physical barriers to travel, railroads transformed space into time. Instead of expressing the distance between places in miles, people began to refer to the amount of time it took to travel from one place to another. Second, railroad scheduling required the nationwide standardization of time. Before railroads, local church bells and clocks struck noon when the sun was directly overhead, and people set their clocks and watches accordingly. But because the sun was not overhead at exactly the same moment everywhere, time varied from place to place. Clocks in Boston, for instance, differed from those in New York by almost twelve minutes. To impose some regularity, railroads created their own time zones. By 1880 there were nearly fifty different standards, but in 1883 the railroads finally agreed—without consulting anyone in government—to establish four standard time zones for the whole country. Most communities adjusted their clocks accordingly, and railroad time became national time.

Norton, *A People and a Nation,* p. 437.

Exercise 8.6 Case Studies

Each of the following case studies describes a student situation. Read each case study carefully; highlight key ideas or student issues. Answer the question that ends each case study. In your response, address the key points that you highlighted and that directly relate to the question. Answer in complete sentences. These case studies are also available online; you can email your response to your instructor or print a copy of your work online.

1. Cecilia is taking a class in medical terminology. She is required to learn approximately fifty different medical terms each week. She has been trying to memorize each word and its definition. The words are grouped according to "word families." For example, one week she had to learn words such as *dermis, epidermis, dermatology,* and *dermatitis*. She is confused and is having difficulty learning all the words each week. What strategies would you recommend that would be more effective than memorizing each individual word?

2. Lisa has difficulty with reading comprehension. She encounters so many words that are unfamiliar to her; she is not able to understand many of the paragraphs she reads. She feels it will take too much time to use a dictionary to look up all the words. For now she is just getting by but is fearful of what will happen on the first test. What strategies would you recommend Lisa use to begin to deal with her problems?

3. Mayumi has a hard time learning the information in textbooks. Some of her difficulties may stem from her reading habits. She reads through several paragraphs at a time at a steady rate. She then returns to each paragraph to look for the main idea; however, all the sentences seem equally important to her. She realizes that she needs to learn how to identify the main ideas in paragraphs. What strategies would you suggest to Mayumi?

Exercise 8.7 LINKS

Work in a small group or with a partner to discuss one or more of the following questions. (Your instructor may assign your group or you and your partner a specific discussion question.) Compose an answer or explanation to present to the rest of the class.

1. In Chapter 7, you learned how to create flash cards or index cards to study terminology and lists of information. In this chapter, you learned about using word clues, word structure clues, and context clues to unlock the meanings of unfamiliar words. What principles of memory do you actively use when striving to improve your vocabulary with the above strategies?
2. When you read a paragraph carefully and then return to the paragraph to identify the main idea, which principles of memory are you most actively using?
3. Identify specific reading comprehension strategies that are well-suited to auditory learners. Explain how these strategies capitalize on auditory learners' strengths.
4. Identify specific reading comprehension strategies that are well-suited for visual learners. Explain how these strategies capitalize on the visual learners' strengths.
5. Explain which principles of memory are actively used when identifying and drawing the organizational patterns used in a paragraph to develop the supporting details.

Reflection Writing 2 — CHAPTER 8

On a separate piece of paper or in a journal, discuss the comprehension strategies in this chapter that address some of the difficulties you have encountered with reading comprehension in some of your courses. If you completed the Collaborative Learning Activity on page 198, refer to some of the problems you brainstormed with the members of your group. In your reflective writing, name specific strategies and how they will help you in specific courses.

Annotating Your Textbooks

An effective reader of textbooks must know how to identify and mark the information that he or she needs to learn. **Annotating** is the active learning process of marking textbooks to show the main ideas and supporting details, plus the sequence and relationships of ideas that appear in paragraphs. The primary goals of annotating are to interact with the printed text, analyze the contents of each paragraph, simplify the structure of the paragraph by selectively identifying the key elements of each paragraph, and create comprehensive understanding of the contents. Annotating reduces the amount of information that you need to study. When it is time to review textbook information for an upcoming test, your study time should be spent on focusing on the information that you marked, not on rereading entire chapters. In the long run, annotating saves you time, promotes critical thinking about what you are reading, and improves comprehension. Annotating a textbook involves the following active learning strategies.

Annotating a Textbook

1. Highlight the complete topic sentence, which states the main idea.
2. Selectively highlight key words or phrases that support the topic sentence.
3. Circle terminology that you need to be able to define.
4. Enumerate steps or lists of information.
5. Make marginal notes to emphasize important ideas and integrate information.
6. Use your annotations as guides for studying and reviewing.

Highlight the Topic Sentence

Highlighting involves the use of light-colored highlighter pens to mark the important information to learn. Selectivity is essential. Overmarking a paragraph defeats the purpose of highlighting. Strive to highlight 30–40 percent of the paragraph. Some students prefer to underline important information with a pencil or a pen; however, highlighting is recommended because the colors clearly separate the important information from the less important.

After you have read a paragraph, find the **topic sentence**—the main idea—and underline it completely. When you study, a clearly marked topic sentence helps you keep your focus on the author's main point. This is the *only* sentence in a paragraph that you should completely underline or highlight. Remember that the main idea or topic sentence must serve as an "umbrella sentence." It must be broad enough that all the other information in the paragraph "fits" under this sentence. Notice how the main ideas underlined in the following passage capture the main point of each paragraph.

> *Networking* In the job-getting process, networking refers to developing a group of acquaintances who might provide job leads and career guidance. The term has been used so much recently that it has perhaps become a buzzword, but it is still an important job-getting tool. Everyone—from the most recent college graduate to the president of a Fortune 500 firm—has a network on which to draw in searching for a job.
>
> Your initial network might include friends, family, professors, former employers, social acquaintances, college alumni, your dentist, family doctor, insurance agent, local business people, your minister or rabbi—in

short, everyone you know who might be able to help. Ideally, your network will combine both personal and professional connections. That's one benefit of belonging to professional associations, and college isn't too early to start. Most professional organizations either have student chapters of their associations or provide reduced-rate student memberships in the parent organization.

Ober, Scot. Contemporary Business Communication, 3e, p. 557.

Highlight Key Words or Phrases

By finding the topic sentence, you know the main idea or main point of the paragraph. Now you need to identify the important details that support this topic sentence. If you were asked to explain the topic sentence or "prove" the point made in it, which key words, phrases, definitions, facts, statistics, or examples would you use in your explanation? Locate these **supporting details** or key words and mark them. **The following suggestions will refine your marking:**

How does the use of different colors in studying affect memory? How could it hinder memory?

1. You can skip over words such as *to, and, with, also,* and *in addition* because they are not key words.
2. If a key word is used several times, you only need to mark it once.
3. As you are looking for key words, take note of lists, **bullets** (dashes or dots), and marginal notes. All these may indicate important supporting details.

Once you identify specific supporting details, ask yourself whether the details are important. Some details, such as extended explanations of examples, help you understand a concept but are not details you are expected to know. Selectivity is essential so that you do not highlight too much unnecessary information. Because you are selecting details that will serve as triggers or associations for *your memory,* you may select key words or phrases that other students may not feel are necessary. As long as you are targeting the essential details, do not be concerned if your highlighting is not exactly the same as another student's highlighting.

Notice which supporting details are underlined in the following example. Are these the same details you would choose to underline?

> Global politics, then, has many kinds of issues. Some, such as U.S.–Russian arms negotiations or Syrian–Israeli peace negotiations, involve the quest for security. Others, such as negotiations on trade barriers, focus on economic questions. Still others, such as controversies about acid rain, are about threats to the environment. In other words, the enormous range of issues in global politics covers diverse topics. Increasingly, the global agenda is attracting nontraditional issues that either produce cooperation or necessitate collaboration if disaster is to be avoided.
>
> Mansbach, *The Global Puzzle,* p. 19.

Most paragraphs that you read will have a topic sentence and supporting details. However, on occasion you may encounter a paragraph that does not seem to have any new information. This may be a **transition paragraph**; the information in it does not need to be marked. Transition paragraphs

- are designed to help ideas from one paragraph flow smoothly into the next paragraph.
- are usually short.
- do not contain strong main ideas or new details.

If the paragraph you are reading is more than a few sentences long and contains new terminology or new ideas, it is not a transition paragraph. Do not skip over it; read more carefully to find the important information to highlight.

Circle Terminology

More than 60 percent of most test questions are based directly on knowing and understanding specialized terminology (vocabulary words). For this reason, it is important to identify and mark the terms you need to define. Words that are underlined or printed in bold, italic, or colored print are usually terms to know. *Circle key terms to make them stand out.* Then mark the main points of the term's definitions. Use word clues, punctuation clues, and context clues to identify the definitions of course-specific terminology.

In the following example, notice how the main idea is completely underlined, terminology is circled, and only key words or phrases in the definitions are underlined. (The examples will show underlining; however, in your work you may prefer to highlight this information rather than underline.) As an optional way to highlight terminology and definitions, consider using a different color to highlight terminology and definitions; color coding in this manner helps separate terminology and definitions from the other kinds of supporting details. If you later create flash cards or index cards as study tools for the vocabulary terms to know, you can quickly identify key terms and key words in the definitions to transfer to your index cards.

> **Decisional Roles** As you might suspect, a **decisional role** is one that involves various aspects of management decision making. The decisional role can be subdivided into the following four specific managerial roles. In the role of *entrepreneur* the manager is the voluntary initiator of change. For example, a manager for Coca-Cola who develops a new strategy or expands the sales force into a new market is playing the entrepreneur's role. A second role is that of *disturbance handler.* A manager who settles a strike is handling a disturbance. Third, the manager also occasionally plays the role of *resource allocator.* In this role, the manager might have to decide which departmental budgets to cut and which expenditure requests to approve. The fourth role is that of *negotiator.* Being a negotiator might involve settling a dispute between a manager and a worker assigned to the manager's work group.
>
> Pride, *Business,* p. 196.

Enumerate Steps or Lists of Information

A paragraph that has a topic sentence that uses words such as *kinds of, reasons, advantages, causes, effects, ways,* or *steps* often has a list of supporting details. **Ordinals**, or "number words," such as *first, second,* or *third,* may point you in the direction of individual details. Use a pen to write the numerals (1, 2, 3) on top of the ordinals. Also watch for words such as *next, another* and *finally,* which are **place holder words** used to replace ordinals. Read carefully and write a new numeral on these words as well.

Sometimes ordinals are not used. A clue may be given, however, as to the number of details you should find. For example, saying that there are "five reasons" for something lets you know that you should find five details. You can then number these details clearly. With a pen, write *1* where the first item in the list is discussed, write *2* where the second item is discussed, and so on, until each supporting detail is numbered. Your final number of details should match the original clue (in this case, five reasons).

In the following example, notice how the main ideas (topic sentences) are *completely underlined,* key words of supporting details are underlined, and numbers are added to show lists of items. Brief notes in the margins summarize the information.

Consumerism

1. envir. protection
2. product performance
3. info disclosure

Consumerism consists of all activities undertaken to protect the rights of consumers. The fundamental issues pursued by the consumer movement fall into three categories: ① environmental protection, ② product performance and safety, and ③ information disclosure. Although consumerism has been with us to some extent since the early nineteenth century, the consumer movement became stronger in the 1960s. It was then that President John F. Kennedy declared that the consumer was entitled to a new "bill of rights."

The Six Basic Rights of Consumers

Consumer rights =
1. Safety
2. Informed
3. Choice
4. Be heard
5. Consumer educ.
6. Courteous service

President Kennedy's consumer bill of rights asserted that consumers have a right ① to safety, ② to be informed, ③ to choose, and ④ to be heard. Two additional rights added in the last decade are the right to ⑤ consumer education and to ⑥ courteous service. These six rights are the basis of much of the consumer-oriented legislation that has been passed during the last forty years. These rights also provide an effective outline of the objectives and accomplishments of the consumer movement.

Pride/Hughes/Kapoor, *Business,* p. 50.

Summary Chart: Signals Used to Guide Numbering in Notes

Topic Sentence Words:	kinds of, reasons, advantages, causes, effects, ways, steps . . .
Ordinals:	first, second, third . . .
Place Holders:	next, also, another, finally . . .
Number Word Clues:	five reasons, four ways, six steps . . .

Enumerating serves as a memory device, for it is easier to remember a fixed quantity of items than it is an unknown quantity of items. (For example, you are more likely to recall *Five* Theories of Forgetting than *theories of forgetting.*)

Make Marginal Notes

In Chapter 7, page 184, you learned that marginal notes can include the following information: lists of key points, key words or terminology, short definitions, personal comments, questions to ask in class, study questions, and diagrams or pictures. To work effectively, **marginal notes** must be brief to avoid cluttering the margins with difficult-to-read notes.

Use the following marking guidelines to create effective marginal notes.

1. When you encounter several sentences or a complete paragraph that is densely written with significant supporting details, rather than overmark the text or clutter the margins with too many details, you can use *brackets* next to the paragraph to draw your attention to that section of information. In the margins, use an abbreviation to indicate the content of the information you placed in brackets. You can create your own system of abbreviations, or you can use the following common abbreviations to label the content of brackets:

EX.	*example or examples*	DEF.	lengthy definition
IMP.	*important to reread*	REL.	relationship between two items
RE.	*reasons why . . .*	?	information you do not understand
DIFF.	*differences*	SUM.	summary

The following example demonstrates the use of brackets and abbreviations.

Feminism

Around 1910 some of those concerned with women's place in society began using a new term, *feminism,* to refer to their ideas. Whereas members of the woman movement spoke generally of duty and moral purity,

DIFF. feminists—more explicitly conscious of their identity as women—emphasized rights and self-development. Feminism, however, contained an inherent contradiction. ① On the one hand feminists argued that all women should unite in the struggle for rights because of their shared disadvantages as women. ② On the other, they insisted that sex-typing—treating women differently than men—must end because it resulted in

IMP. discrimination. Thus feminists advocated the contradictory position that women should unite as a gender group for the purpose of abolishing all gender-based distinctions.

Feminism focused primarily on economic and sexual independence. Charlotte Perkins Gilman articulated feminist goals in *Women and Economics* (1898), declaring that domesticity and female innocence were obsolete and attacking the male monopoly on economic opportunity.

SUM. Gilman argued that modern women must take jobs in industry and the professions and that paid employees should handle domestic chores such as cooking, cleaning, and childcare.

Norton, *A People and a Nation,* p. 616.

2. Use the margins to define or draw your attention to unfamiliar terms that are not course-specific terminology. Strive to increase your vocabulary each time you encounter an unfamiliar word. Take the time and make the effort to learn more about the words and add them to your working vocabulary. Recall from earlier in the chapter that you can use *word clues, word structure clues, context clues,* and dictionaries to unlock the meanings of unfamiliar words. You can substitute familiar words for the unfamiliar words to increase your comprehension. As with course-specific terminology, you can circle and define unfamiliar words in the margins. At some later time, on a test or in another context, you may encounter the new words once again, but the words will then no longer be unfamiliar.

greedy

fast & bright

> The voracious appetite of English mills caused a meteoric rise in cotton production. . . . From 1800 until the Civil War, British demand for cotton multiplied rapidly, and southern planters rushed to increase their acreage. Despite occasional periods of low prices, the demand for cotton surged ahead every decade. Southerners with capital bought more land and more slaves and planted ever more cotton. Cotton growers boosted production so successfully that by 1825 the South was the world's dominant supplier of cotton; by the 1850s the South was the source of over 70 percent of all the cotton that Britain imported.

def: antebellum

> Thus the antebellum South—the Old South before the Civil War—became primarily a cotton South. Large amounts of tobacco and hemp continued to be grown in the Upper South, and rice and sugar were important crops in certain coastal areas, especially in South Carolina, Georgia, and Louisiana. Thousands of southerners grew only food crops, but cotton was the largest and most widespread cash crop, and the wealth it generated shaped the society and fueled the South's hunger for new territory.
>
> Norton, *A People and a Nation,* p. 288.

3. Creating marginal notes is one of many options for notetaking. As you have seen, marginal notes may be used in addition to highlighting and enumerating. For textbooks that are not complex and do not contain extensive supporting details, you may use marginal notetaking as your primary method to record important information.

Use Your Annotations to Study and Review

The process of annotating your textbook is only the beginning step in learning. You must now *use* these markings, highlighted topic sentences and key words, circled terminology, numbered steps or lists, and marginal notes, to help you learn important information. Studying from your annotations may be done as a warm-up activity at the beginning of a study block, or as an immediate or ongoing review activity.

How to Use Annotations

1. Reread only the marked information.
2. String together the marked information to make sentences.
3. Recite using your own words.

Reread

Read what you have highlighted; include any numbering that you added. Do *not* let yourself reread the information that is not marked. Review these notes slowly to allow time for your mind to absorb, connect, and associate the information. You may want to read out loud to help your concentration and increase your comprehension. During this step, your reading will sound broken or fragmented. However, you will be reading all the main ideas and the key words of selected details.

String Ideas Together

Look at the marked information again. Instead of just reading, string the words, phrases, and sentences together by using some of your own words to connect the ideas in full sentences. As you begin **stringing ideas** together, include the main idea and the important supporting details. Include any marginal notes. This is an ideal time to turn on a tape recorder if you would benefit from having a review tape to use for studying. In addition to verbalizing the ideas, you can practice picturing or visualizing the information in the paragraph. Practice stringing the ideas together in your own words helps you *personalize* what you are reading. You are, in fact, converting textbook language into your own, more common form of language. In doing so, you practice expressing information in a more familiar form of language—your own.

Recite

After you have practiced stringing ideas together, you are ready to try **reciting** the same information out loud in full sentences and without looking. You will be **paraphrasing**, putting the information in your own words. If you were to recite word for word exactly as it was printed in the book, you would be emphasizing rote memory, a type of memory that is not as effective as thorough learning. After you have recited from memory, look back at your book to check your accuracy. Use your marginal notes and other markings as feedback to accuracy. If you made some mistakes, practice saying the information correctly.

Reciting reinforces the information you are learning and imprints the information more firmly in your long-term memory. As you remember, reciting is a principle of memory. It is powerful and it works! If you are an auditory learner, turn on a tape recorder while you are reciting. By recording yourself paraphrasing what you have read, you will create an excellent study tape that you can listen to for reviewing.

EXERCISE 8.8 Practicing Annotating Your Textbook

Your instructor may ask you to return to one or more of the following exercises to practice your annotation skills. If your instructor does not assign this exercise, return to the following excerpts for independent practice. Use the annotation suggestions in the box on page 216 to mark these excerpts. Remember that annotating a textbook is an individualized approach to comprehension, so your annotations will not be identical to those of another student. Also, remember to be selective.

Exercise 7.5, page 185, *Surveying, Questioning, Reading, and Recording*

Exercise 8.1, page 203, *Rereading, Verbalizing, and Visualizing*

Exercise 8.2, page 204, *Defining Words*

Exercise 8.3, page 205, *Substituting Common or Familiar Words*

Exercise 8.4, pages 208–209, *Identifying Main Ideas and Topic Sentences*

Exercise 8.5, page 213, *Converting Words to Visual Forms*

Writing Summaries

This chapter has shown you an array of reading comprehension and critical thinking skills that will help you learn from your textbooks more effectively. It is important to understand that improving your comprehension and critical thinking skills requires ongoing practice with a variety of textbooks. Writing *summaries* is a final study skills strategy for increasing your understanding and memory of important textbook information.

Summaries are paragraphs that present only the highlights of the information you read. A summary will definitely include the main ideas. A summary should briefly mention (summarize) the most important supporting details. Not all details will be expanded in depth. Minor details, such as examples that were used to develop a point, do not need to be included in the summary. Too many minor details will not result in a concise summary. Too few details will not provide you with much information when you later want to use your summary to review the information or prepare for a test.

Summary writing is valuable for several reasons:

1. Many students learn and remember information more readily if they have the opportunity to write it or type it on a computer.
2. Individuals with strong visual print memories can more readily recall the information when they see it in a shortened or condensed form.
3. Students who have difficulty expressing ideas on paper, especially during essay tests, have the opportunity to practice organizing and expressing ideas on paper *before the test.*
4. Summary writing has many of the same values as reciting. If you can express the information in your own words in a logical, clear manner, you know it.
5. Summaries with the main ideas and most important supporting details are excellent study tools to use for ongoing review of previously discussed chapters and for test preparation.

There are many methods that you may find helpful for structuring your summaries. Three common methods shown below are excellent choices to begin the practice of writing summaries.

Methods for Writing Summaries

1. Record on paper the same information that you speak when you "string ideas together."
2. Develop a chapter mapping. Use the mapping to guide your summary writing.
3. Use chapter outlines to guide the structure of your summary.

Write Summaries from Stringing Ideas

When you string together highlighted information, you are basically creating a verbal summary. This same information, when written on paper, becomes a written summary. This summary should state the main ideas and connect the important supporting details by using some of your own words. Following is a written summary for the "Decisional Roles" passage (page 218).

A decisional role is one that involves various aspects of management decision making. There are four specific managerial roles that are part of the decisional role. The first is the role of the entrepreneur where the manager becomes the voluntary initiator of change. The second decisional role is that of a disturbance handler in which the manager deals with specific kinds of disturbances. The third role is the resource allocator. The manager in this role makes decisions regarding budget expenditures to approve. The fourth role is that of negotiator; the manager assumes the role of settling disputes.

Write Summaries from Chapter Mappings

Chapter mappings are visual pictures of the topic of the chapter, its main points (headings), and important subpoints (subheadings). After a chapter mapping has been developed, write your summary by discussing each of the branches that stem from the center of the mapping. Your mapping will only show key words, so you will need to use your own words to string the words together into meaningful, organized sentences. In most cases, each heading can be written as a paragraph. Your summary of a chapter will consist of several paragraphs.

Write Summaries from Chapter Outlines

Some textbooks include chapter summaries that can become the "skeleton" or the structure for summary writing. If the chapter summary is written as a list of important points, expand the list with additional details. Look for meaningful ways to combine the chapter summary points into full paragraphs.

You can also use the table of contents or any chapter outlines presented in the introductory materials of a chapter. If the textbook does not give a chapter outline, you can create your own outline by listing the main headings on paper. Then list the subheadings under each main heading. You may add one or more additional levels of information to include some of the key supporting details of the chapter. (See Chapter 11 for more information about outlines.) Use this outline to guide your summary writing. Include each point in the order in which it is presented. Add your own words so the information flows together smoothly. For this chapter, the outline would look like this:

Chapter 8: Strengthening Comprehension and Critical Thinking Skills

I. Active Reading and Thinking
   A. Active Readers
   B. Active Thinkers
II. Understanding What You Read
   A. Reread, Verbalize, and Visualize
   B. Use Clues in Words and Sentences to Understand Unfamiliar Words
   C. Substitute Familiar Words for Unfamiliar Words
   D. Use the Natural Flow or Progression of Information
   E. Identify Main Ideas
   F. Identify Organizational Patterns
   G. Draw a Picture of the Paragraph
III. Annotating Your Textbook
   A. Highlight the Topic Sentence
   B. Highlight Key Words or Phrases
   C. Circle Terminology
   D. Enumerate Steps or Lists of Information
   E. Make Marginal Notes
   F. Use Your Annotations to Study and Review
IV. Writing Summaries
   A. Write Summaries from Stringing Ideas
   B. Write Summaries from Chapter Mappings
   C. Write Summaries from Chapter Outlines

Reflection Writing 3 — CHAPTER 8

On a separate piece of paper or in a journal, do the following:

Compare the way you previously read a textbook chapter to the way you plan to read a textbook chapter now that you have learned new textbook-reading strategies. You may write your response in paragraph form or in the form of a comparison chart.

SUMMARY

- Active learning requires active reading and active thinking skills. Active reading moves you beyond simply reading the words printed on the page. Active thinking, also known as critical thinking, promotes comprehension and lays a foundation for future learning.
- You can unlock the meaning of text by using seven different reading strategies:
  1. Reread, verbalize, and visualize.
  2. Use punctuation clues, word clues, word structure clues (prefixes, suffixes, word bases, and roots), and context clues (synonyms, antonyms, contrast, and comparisons/analogies) to learn meanings of unfamiliar words.
  3. Substitute familiar words for unfamiliar words.
  4. Use the natural flow or progression of information.
  5. Identify main ideas, which appear in topic sentences. These "umbrella sentences" may be found anywhere in paragraphs, although they are commonly the first sentence. Main ideas that are not stated are called implied main ideas.
  6. Identify the organizational pattern or patterns used for the supporting details. Five common organizational patterns appear in many college textbooks: chronological, comparison or contrast, definition, examples, and cause/effect.
  7. Draw a picture of the paragraph.
- Annotating textbooks is an active learning process that involves marking significant information that needs to be learned. Annotating reduces the amount of information to study and learn.
- Six active learning strategies can be used to annotate a textbook:
  1. Highlight the complete topic sentence that states the main idea.
  2. Selectively highlight key words or phrases that support the topic sentence.
  3. Circle terminology that you need to know how to define.
  4. Enumerate steps or lists of information by using ordinals, place holders, and number word clues.
  5. Make marginal notes to emphasize important ideas and integrate information.
  6. Use your annotations as guides for studying and reviewing. Reread the markings, string together the marked information, and then recite the information in your own words to personalize and internalize the information.
- Summaries are paragraphs that present the main ideas and a selective number of key supporting details. The structure of a summary can be based on the verbal information that you say when you string ideas together, chapter mappings, or chapter outlines.

ACE Practice Tests, which are scored online, supplementary exercises, enrichment activities, and related web site links are available online for *Essential Study Skills*, 4e. Use the following directions to access this web site:

Type: **http://college.hmco.com/collegesurvival/students**

Click on *List of Sites by Author.* Use the arrow to scroll down to Wong *Essential Study Skills*, 4e. Click on the title. If you are working on your own computer, bookmark this web site.

LEARNING OPTIONS

The following learning options provide you with opportunities to demonstrate your understanding of the topics in Chapter 8. Your instructor may assign one or more specific options or may ask you to select one or more options that interest you the most.

1. Expand the Chapter 8 mapping on page 195. Copy this structure on a blank piece of paper. Reread the information under each heading in your textbook. Extend branches on the mapping to show important key words or phrases for each heading. (See Chapter 11 for additional information.) You can add pictures and colors to your mapping to accentuate the points.
2. Copy any five pages from a textbook for another class. Use annotations on the pages to show effective use of underlining, circling, and marginal notes.
3. Use the Internet to locate informative web sites for the topic of *reading comprehension, textbook reading skills,* or *critical thinking skills.* Prepare a short presentation or a written summary of the most significant information. Include a list of the web site addresses and a short description of each web site content; this may be copied for the class.
4. Annotate Chapter 8. Use your annotations to create a study tape for Chapter 8.
5. Form a study group with three or more students to meet outside class to review the content of this chapter. Work together to complete any of the exercises that were not assigned in class. Write a summary paper that discusses the highlights of your study group.
6. Write a set of goals for yourself that identifies the active reading and active thinking strategies you will strive to incorporate in your study routine each time you begin reading a new chapter in one of your textbooks.
7. Use the chapter outline or the chapter visual mapping to write a summary for this chapter. Use paragraph form in your summary. Then, use a highlighter to mark those skills mentioned in your summary that are especially significant for you to master to increase your textbook reading and studying success.

Chapter 8 REVIEW QUESTIONS

Multiple Choice

Choose the best answer *for each of the following questions. Write the letter of the best answer on the line.*

_______ **1.** Which of the following is *not* true about writing summaries?
a. Summaries reflect the information that you highlighted in a paragraph.
b. Summaries must be presented in the form of short lists or categories.
c. Summaries include some textbook wording and some of your own wording.
d. Summaries show topic sentences and the supporting details of a paragraph.

_______ **2.** Which of the following is *not* true about annotating in a textbook?
a. It should be done only for textbooks that are difficult to read.
b. It uses selectivity to reduce the amount of information that a student needs to study.
c. It reduces overall reading time so more time can be devoted to the process of learning.
d. It can include highlighting, underlining, or making marginal notes.

_______ **3.** When you identify important supporting details in a paragraph, you
a. need to completely underline or highlight the sentence they are in.
b. select key words or phrases to highlight.
c. list each of the details in alphabetical order in the margins.
d. make a mental note to yourself that they support the main idea.

_______ **4.** Supporting details
a. can be words, phrases, definitions, or facts that support the topic sentence.
b. can sometimes be marked in the text with the use of bullets.
c. that are words you will need to define should be circled.
d. All of the above

_______ **5.** When careful highlighting and marking are used in a textbook,
a. every single paragraph will have important information marked.
b. approximately 80 percent of the paragraphs should be underlined or highlighted.
c. transitional paragraphs are the only paragraphs that will not be marked.
d. all important supporting details will be circled.

_______ **6.** If a topic sentence states, "Six strategies can be used to strengthen your vocabulary," the reader
a. should add numbers to his or her marking to indicate each strategy.
b. should watch for ordinals and use the ordinals to number each strategy.
c. needs to be aware of the use of "place holders" that replace ordinals.
d. All of the above

_______ **7.** After the important information in a chapter has been highlighted, the
a. student then needs to practice rereading the highlighted information out loud.
b. student has learned the information and can begin the next chapter.
c. highlighted information needs to be reread, strung together, and recited.
d. highlighted information needs to be copied in an outline form.

_______ **8.** When highlighted information is "strung together," the student
a. connects the marked words by adding his or her own words or sentences.
b. rereads aloud all of the information that was highlighted.
c. writes the information in phrases on paper in the same order they were found in the book.
d. connects all of the topic sentences together so they appear one right after another.

_________ 9. Paraphrasing
- **a.** is a process that students should use to promote rote memory.
- **b.** involves restating information in your own words.
- **c.** involves repeating information in the exact words that were given in the textbook.
- **d.** All of the above

_________ 10. Since many students find that writing reinforces the learning of information,
- **a.** short notes and lists of information can be written in the margins of the book.
- **b.** the highlighted or underlined information can be transferred to notes on notebook paper.
- **c.** ideas can be strung together verbally and then written in the form of a summary.
- **d.** All of the above

Annotating a Textbook Passage

Annotate the following passage by highlighting main ideas and important supporting details. Mark the text in whatever other ways seem appropriate. Create meaningful marginal notes.

Role of Concentration Undoubtedly one of the most difficult tasks we have to perform as listeners is concentration. Motivation plays an important role in activating this skill. For example, if you really want to listen to a speaker, this desire will put you in a better frame of mind for concentrating than will anticipating that the speaker will be boring.

Two other factors that affect listening concentration are interest level and difficulty of the message. Some messages may be boring, but if you need to get the information, careful concentration is imperative. You also may find the information so difficult that you tune out. Again, if it is imperative for you to understand the ideas, then you have to force yourself to figure out what you do not understand and find a way of grasping the meaning.

We can think three to four times faster than the normal conversation rate of 125 to 150 words per minute. And because we can receive messages much more quickly than the other person can talk, we tend to tune in and tune out throughout a message. The brain operates much like a computer: it turns off, recycles itself, and turns back on to avoid information overload. It is no wonder, then, that our attention fluctuates even when we are actively involved as listeners. A slight gap in your listening at times is a natural part of the listening process. When you tune out, the major danger is that you may daydream rather than quickly turn back to the message. But by taking notes or forcing yourself to paraphrase, you can avoid this difficulty.

Concentration also requires the listener to control for distractions. Rather than attempting to dismiss a whole list of things that you have to attend, control your concentration by mentally setting these other issues aside for the moment to give the speaker your full attention. It takes mental and physical energy to do this, but concentration is the key to successful listening.

Adapted from Berko, *Communicating,* pp. 89–90.

Chapter

9

Making Cornell Notes for Textbooks

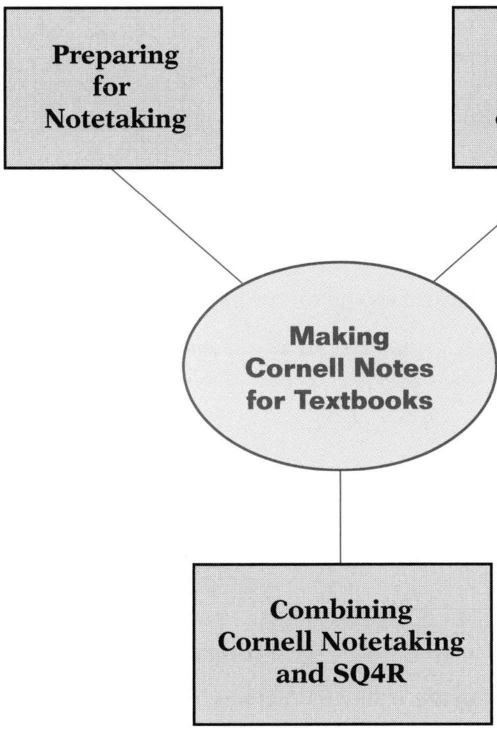

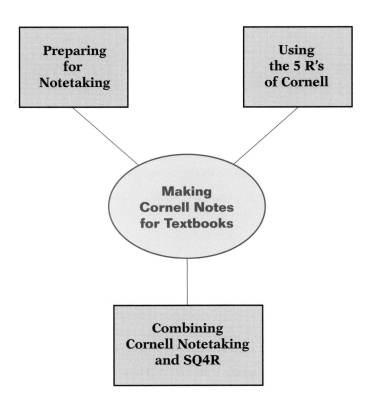

Effective notetaking is an essential skill for college students. By using the five-step Cornell notetaking system (record, reduce, recite, reflect, and review), you can take effective notes for textbook and lecture information. You can integrate the Cornell system into the SQ4R reading system; the result is a powerful textbook reading and notetaking system you can use for greater academic success.

Terms to Know

five *R*'s of the Cornell system
record
reduce
recall column
recite
feedback
reflect
immediate review
ongoing review
Maslow's Hierarchy of Needs
- physiological needs
- safety needs
- social needs
- esteem needs
- self-realization needs

encoding
acoustic codes
visual codes
semantic codes
storage
retrieval

CHAPTER 9 Cornell Notes Profile

DO, SCORE, and **RECORD** your profile before you read this chapter. If you need to review the process, refer to the complete directions given in the Profile for Chapter 1 on page 2.

ONLINE: You can complete the profile and get your score online at this textbook's web site.

	YES	NO
1. I take notes only on the front side of my notebook paper.	______	______
2. I spend little time studying from my notes.	______	______
3. I am selective when I take notes; I write down only the important ideas and details.	______	______
4. I take time to study and interpret graphs and charts.	______	______
5. I leave a double space in my notes before I begin a new heading.	______	______
6. After I take notes on a paragraph, I recite what I wrote before moving on.	______	______
7. My notes summarize important charts, graphs, or pictures in the textbook.	______	______
8. I practice reciting new information by using a special column with study questions or terminology to define.	______	______
9. I take time to think about and reflect on the information in the chapter.	______	______
10. I plan time each week to review information that I learned in previous weeks.	______	______

Reflection Writing 1 — CHAPTER 9

On a separate piece of paper or in a journal, do the following:

1. Discuss your profile score for this chapter. What was your score? What does it mean to you?
2. Discuss the effectiveness of your current notetaking system. Do you understand your notes when you study from them later? Do you have sufficient details in your notes? Are they organized neatly and logically?

Preparing for Notetaking

This chapter introduces the powerful five-step Cornell notetaking system, which you can use for taking notes from both textbooks and lectures. The strength of the system is in its steps; if you choose to eliminate any one step, you weaken the system. This notetaking system was designed by Dr. Walter Pauk at Cornell University more than forty-five years ago when he recognized students' need to learn how to take more effective notes. Many college and university teachers consider this the most effective notetaking system for college students.

Effective notetaking is important for several reasons:

1. You become an active learner when you seek out important information and write it down.
2. You focus on organizing the information logically.
3. You select the important information and reduce it to a form that is easy to study and review.
4. You have reduced notes to use for continual review throughout the term.

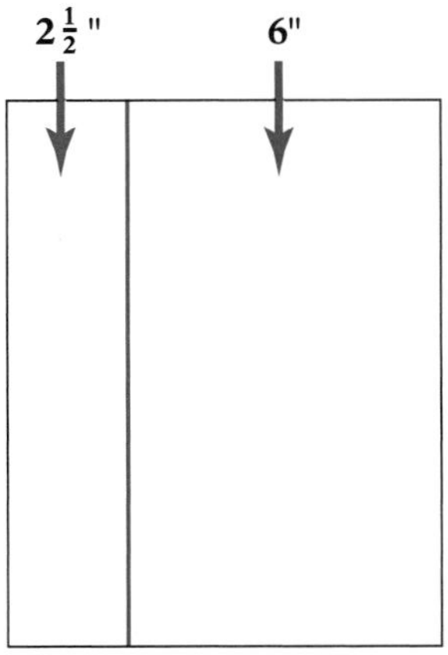

Setting up your paper

To begin, you need notebook paper with a *two-and-one-half-inch margin down the left side.* Many bookstores now carry Cornell notebook paper with this larger margin or a spiral "law notebook" with perforated Cornell-style pages. If you are not able to find the Cornell notebook paper for your three-ring notebook, draw a margin on the front side of regular notebook paper. All your notetaking is done on the front side only; the back of the paper is used for other purposes.

At the top of the first page, write the course name, chapter number, and date. For all the following pages, just write the chapter number and the page number of your notes. Later you may want to remove your notes from your notebook; having the pages numbered prevents disorganization.

EXERCISE 9.1 Creating a Sample Set of Notes

On your own paper, use your usual form of notetaking to take a set of notes on the information in the following excerpt. Save these notes for use later in the chapter.

Chronemics: Time as Communication

You communicate to yourself and others by the way you use time. The way people handle and structure their time is known as *chronemics.* "Each of us is born into and raised in a particular time world—an environment with its own rhythm to which we entrain ourselves." Time, as a communication tool, is sometimes greatly misunderstood. Only within certain societies, for example, is precise time of great significance. Some cultures relate to time as a *circular phenomenon* in which there is no pressure or anxiety about the future. Existence follows the cycle of the seasons of planting and harvesting, the daily rising and setting of the sun, birth and death. In *circular time,* there is no pressing need to achieve or create newness, or to produce more than is needed to survive. Nor is there fear of death. Such societies have successfully integrated the past and future into a peaceful sense of the present. Many Native Americans have been raised with this cultural attitude toward time.

Other societies operate on *linear time,* centered primarily on the future. These societies focus on the factual and technical information needed to fulfill impending demands. In most of Western Europe, North America, and Japan, punctuality is considered good manners. . . .

Time has become a critical factor in the U.S. workplace. Throughout a person's career, punctuality is often used as a measure of effectiveness. A person who arrives late for a job interview probably will have difficulty overcoming such a negative first impression, and employees who arrive late or leave early may be reprimanded and even dismissed.

Time is culture based. European Americans, Euro-Canadians, and Western Europeans, in general, are clock bound; African, Latin American, and some Asian Pacific cultures are not clock bound. Time is based on personal systems. European Americans traveling abroad often are irritated by the seeming lack of concern for time commitments among residents of some countries. In Mexico and Central America, tours may be late; guides may fail to indicate the correct arrival and departure times. Yet in other places, such as Switzerland, travelers can set their watch by the promptness of the trains. Businesspeople may get confused over what "on time" means as they meet those from other cultures. "In Britain and North America one may be 5 minutes late for a business appointment, but not 15 minutes and certainly not 30 minutes late, which is perfectly normal in Arab countries." In Latin America one is expected to arrive late to an appointment. This same tardiness for Germans or European Americans would be perceived as rudeness. . . .

In cultures that value promptness, one of the questions raised about time centers on the person who is constantly late. What does habitual tardiness reveal about the person? Chronic lateness, in a formal time culture, may be deeply rooted in a person's psyche. Compulsive tardiness is rewarding on some level. A key emotional conflict for the chronically late person involves his or her need to feel special. Such a person may not gain enough recognition in other ways; people must be special in some way, so the person is special by being late. Other reasons include needs for punishment, power, or as an expression of hostility. Tardiness can be a sign that a person wants to avoid something or that the activity or person to be met is not important enough to warrant the effort to be on time. Procrastinators are often not valued in a linear time-focused culture.

Adapted from: Berko, Wolvin, Wolvin, *Communicating,* pp. 61–62.

Using the Five *R*'s of Cornell

The goal of notetaking is to take notes that are so accurate and so detailed that you *do not need to go back to the book to study.* Your studying, your learning, can take place by working with your notes as you use the **five *R*'s of the Cornell system**: record, reduce, recite, reflect, and review.

The Five *R*'s of Cornell

1. *Record* your notes in the right column.
2. *Reduce* your notes into the recall column on the left.
3. *Recite* out loud from the recall column.
4. *Reflect* on the information that you are studying.
5. *Review* your notes immediately and regularly.

Step One: Record

The wider right column is for your notes. In this first step—**record**—read each paragraph carefully, decide what information is important, and then record that information on your paper. Your notes should be a *reduced version* of the textbook. Be selective, or you will wind up wasting your notetaking time and your studying time.

Headings and subheadings provide organization or structure in textbooks. They can also help you organize and structure your notes. Use these headings and the following suggestions for the first *R* of Cornell.

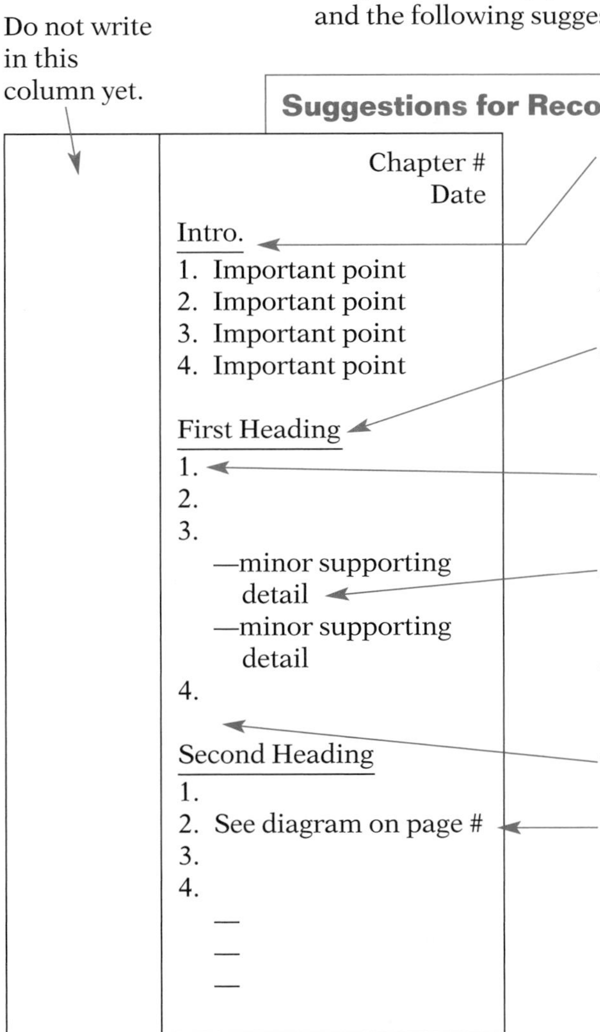

Do not write in this column yet.
Chapter #
Date
Intro.
1. Important point
2. Important point
3. Important point
4. Important point
First Heading
1.
2.
3.
—minor supporting detail
—minor supporting detail
4.
Second Heading
1.
2. See diagram on page #
3.
4.
—
—
—

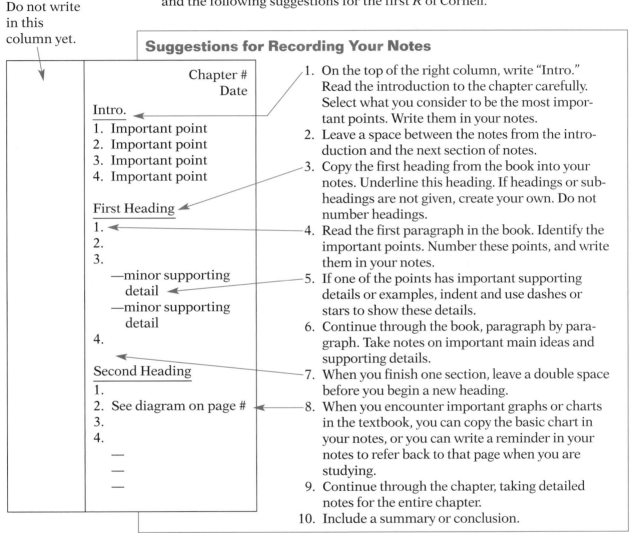

Suggestions for Recording Your Notes

1. On the top of the right column, write "Intro." Read the introduction to the chapter carefully. Select what you consider to be the most important points. Write them in your notes.
2. Leave a space between the notes from the introduction and the next section of notes.
3. Copy the first heading from the book into your notes. Underline this heading. If headings or subheadings are not given, create your own. Do not number headings.
4. Read the first paragraph in the book. Identify the important points. Number these points, and write them in your notes.
5. If one of the points has important supporting details or examples, indent and use dashes or stars to show these details.
6. Continue through the book, paragraph by paragraph. Take notes on important main ideas and supporting details.
7. When you finish one section, leave a double space before you begin a new heading.
8. When you encounter important graphs or charts in the textbook, you can copy the basic chart in your notes, or you can write a reminder in your notes to refer back to that page when you are studying.
9. Continue through the chapter, taking detailed notes for the entire chapter.
10. Include a summary or conclusion.

Take Notes on the Introduction The introduction often provides a brief overview of the content of the chapter. By listing the key ideas in your notes, you will be able to see later whether you understood and captured all the key points.

Leave Spaces Between Sections Notes that are crowded or cluttered are difficult to study. By leaving a double space between each new heading or section of your notes, you are visually grouping the information that belongs together. You are also *chunking* the information into smaller units, which will help your memory.

Use the Headings The headings are the *skeleton*, or outline, of the chapter. Take advantage of this structure by always starting a new section of notes with the heading. Underline the heading so that it stands out from the rest of your notes. If the textbook does not have headings or subheadings, look for categories of information and make your own headings. If the information will be clearer to you, create your own headings and group related information under each heading. (See the example on Theories of Forgetting, p. 237.)

Record Important Points Because you will use your notes for studying, you want to see the big picture and the small pictures (details). *Record enough information to be meaningful later:*

- Avoid using only individual words or short phrases that will lose their meaning when you return to them later.
- Use short sentences when necessary to avoid meaningless phrases.
- Do not copy down information word for word. Shorten the information by rewording or summarizing it.
- If you find some sentences or short sections that are so clearly stated that you want to copy them, omit any of the words that are not essential for your understanding.
- If you have already highlighted the information, move the same information into your notes.
- Number the ideas as you include them in your notes. Numbering helps you remember how many important points are under each heading and breaks the information into smaller, more manageable units.
- For math problems or formulas, copy examples or problems and clearly show each step needed to solve the problem or use the formula. Include words next to unfamiliar symbols.

Record Important Minor Details You will frequently encounter minor details that belong under an idea that you already numbered. Indicate these details by *indenting* and then using *dashes* or *stars* before writing the details.

Include Graphs and Charts Visual materials such as graphs, charts, and pictures contain valuable information. Usually you are not expected to know every fact or statistic depicted by the graph, chart, or other forms of visual materials. You are, however, expected to identify important patterns, relationships, or trends shown by the visual materials. Do not overlook these graphic materials; you can *copy* the graphic material into your notes or *summarize* the conclusions you make by studying the graphic materials. By taking the time necessary to study graphic materials, you will be able to:

1. Study large amounts of information in a condensed form.
2. Identify patterns, relationships, or trends more easily.
3. Imprint information in a visual form in your long-term memory.
4. Create a visual memory cue to recall information at a later time.

Include a Summary or Conclusion Summaries or conclusions pull the main ideas together to help you see the "big picture." If the book has a summary, include the summary as the last heading in your notes. If there is no summary, write your own conclusion to pull the main ideas together.

Highlight the Text First if Necessary If you have difficulty developing detailed notes, you may find that highlighting and annotating the text helps you identify the most important ideas of the paragraph. Use your annotations as guides; transfer the annotated information into your Cornell Notes.

Exercise 9.2 Creating Cornell Notes for *Chronemics*

Following is an incomplete set of Cornell notes for Chronemics *(Exercise 9.1). Complete the notes by adding details under each numbered point. Use dashes rather than numbers or letters to indicate significant details. Do not write in the left column (the recall column) at this time.*

Chronemics: Time as Communication

	1. *Chronemics*—the way people handle and structure time
	2. Circular time
	3. Linear time
	4. Time in the workplace
	5. Time: culture based
	6. People who are constantly late

Step Two: Reduce

After you have finished taking notes for the chapter, you are ready to close the book and **reduce**. Now, for the first time, you will be writing in the left column, the **recall column**. Remember, in step one you reduced the textbook information to the most important points and details. In step two, you are going to reduce your notes one step further. These reduced notes will provide you with a feedback system so you will know what information you have learned well and what information needs more effort. You will also refer to this column frequently for review.

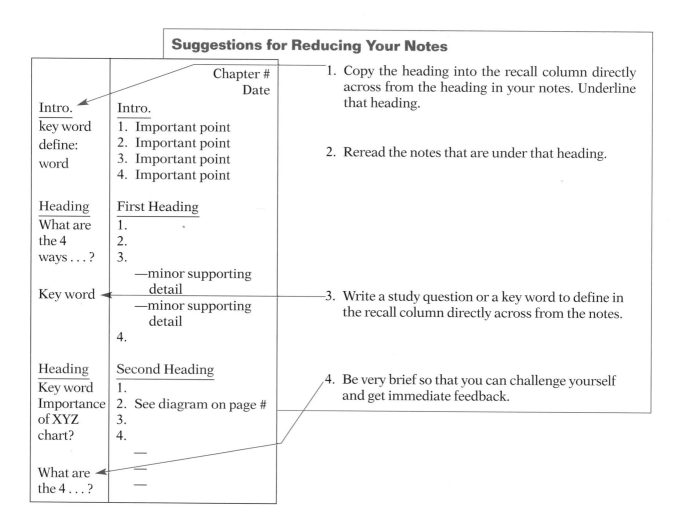

Suggestions for Reducing Your Notes

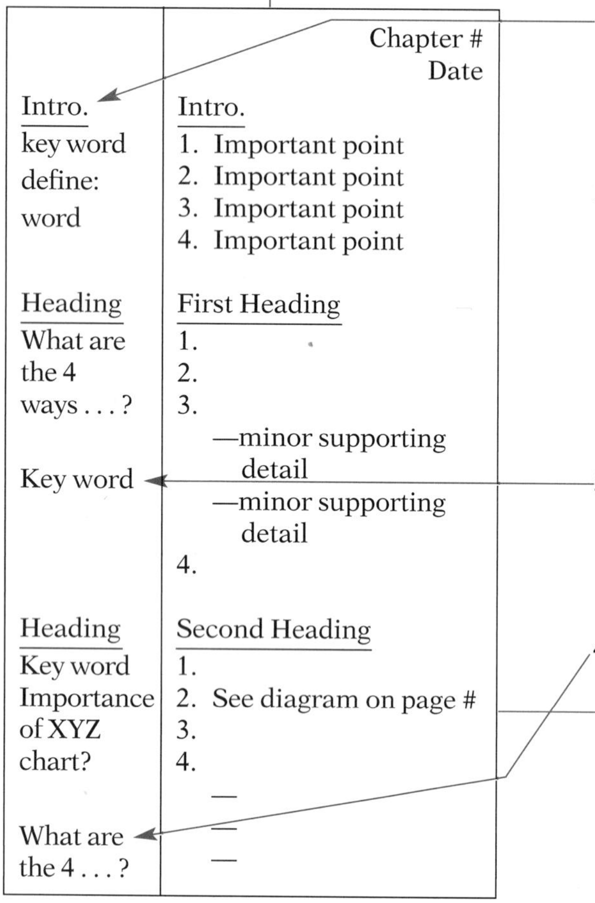

Chapter #
Date
Intro.
key word
define:
word
Intro.
1. Important point
2. Important point
3. Important point
4. Important point
Heading
What are
the 4
ways . . . ?
First Heading
1.
2.
3.
—minor supporting
detail
—minor supporting
detail
4.
Key word
Heading
Key word
Importance
of XYZ
chart?
Second Heading
1.
2. See diagram on page #
3.
4.
—
—
—
What are
the 4 . . . ?

1. Copy the heading into the recall column directly across from the heading in your notes. Underline that heading.
2. Reread the notes that are under that heading.
3. Write a study question or a key word to define in the recall column directly across from the notes.
4. Be very brief so that you can challenge yourself and get immediate feedback.

Copy the Heading In your notes, the heading provided organization. The same is true in the recall column. To avoid having rambling, unorganized reduced notes, *place the heading directly across from the heading in your notes.* Make it stand out by underlining it.

Reread the Notes Learning the information continues as you reread your notes. If your notes seem vague, incomplete, or nonsensical, go back to the book and add any necessary details.

Write Study Questions and Key Words to Define Directly across from each important detail, write a *brief study question.* You do not need to use complete sentences; abbreviated forms, such as the following, work: *Why? How many kinds of . . . ? Name the 6 . . . . Related to* X *how?* Another option is to simply write *key words* that you will need to define or relate to other ideas.

Be Brief You will be using this recall column for the next step of studying. It is important that the column not be cluttered with too much information. If you give yourself all the answers, you will end up reading the information and not challenging your memory. *Remember to be selective by focusing only on key words or study questions.* Do not give all the answers!

The following Cornell notes come from the Five Theories of Forgetting in Chapter 6 (pages 139–140). After you read the notes, notice the brief questions and key words that the notetaker used in the recall column.

	5 Forgetting Theories
Intro principles—forgetting	Intro 1. Even when use principles of memory, info can be forgotten.
Decay Theory Where in Info Proc. Model? What happens?	Decay Theory 1. Occurs in STM 2. Stimuli is too weak so info fades before it is processed
Displacement Theory Which memory? What happens with info? Why?	Displacement Theory 1. Occurs in STM 2. Too much info comes in too quickly, so some info is shoved aside 3. Not enough time given to process
Interference Theory I. LTM—What happens?	Interference Theory 1. In LTM 2. New and old info interfere with each other 3. Happens when new and old info are similar
Incomplete Encoding Happens where? Describe what happens Imprinted?	Incomplete Encoding Theory 1. Happens when info is not rehearsed 2. Info is only partially learned or learned inaccurately 3. Info cannot be recalled because it was never imprinted in LTM
Retrieval Failure Which memory? Why can't info be found? Schemas	Retrieval Failure Theory 1. Info learned but can't be found in long-term memory bank —weak organizational or filing system used in memory —lack of use—no ongoing review —not associated to schemas
Summary model—strategies—eliminate	Summary Info can be forgotten during several different stages of the Info Processing Model. Effective strategies can reduce/eliminate effects of forgetting theories.
Name the 5 theories of forgetting (D-D-I-I-R)	5 theories: decay, displacement, interference, incomplete encoding and retrieval failure

Step Three: Recite

The third step is to **recite** from the recall column. *Reciting involves speaking out loud and expressing ideas in your own words.* Reciting is a powerful tool for learning information and strengthening memory. If you are able to recite information accurately, you are learning. If you are not able to recite information accurately, you immediately know that more time and attention are needed. This immediate **feedback** is the strong benefit of this third step of Cornell.

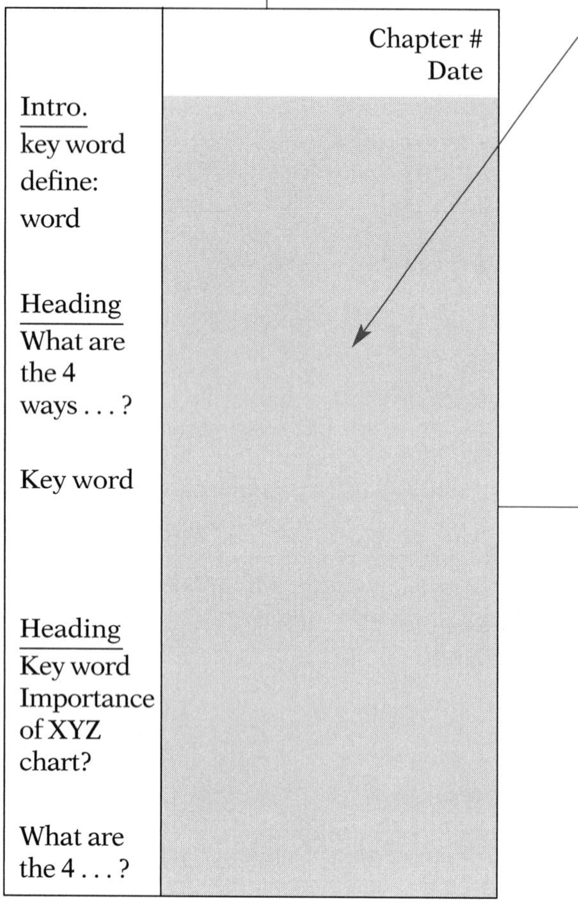

Suggestions for Reciting

1. Cover up the notes on the right.
2. Start at the top of the recall column. Read the heading and the first key word or question.
3. Talk out loud in complete sentences. Explain the information.
4. If you do not remember the information, uncover the right column. Reread the information. Cover it up and try reciting it again.
5. Move through your notes in this manner.
6. Adjust the recall column as needed.

Cover the Notes Use a blank piece of paper to cover the notes on the right side. Since you see only the recall column, you can now understand the importance of putting the headings in the recall column to help you remember the overall organization.

Read and Then Recite Read the headings and the key words or questions. Without looking at your notes, answer the questions and tell what you remember about the key words. Pretend you are explaining the information to a friend. *Talk out loud in complete sentences.*

- If you can verbalize the information accurately, you probably understand it.
- If you "go blank," that is valuable feedback that you are not yet ready to move on. Simply pull the paper down, read the information, cover it up, and try again. Reciting after you reread enables your memory to begin processing the correct information.

- If you are not sure whether you recited the correct information, also pull the paper down to check your accuracy. The positive feedback you receive for correct answers will strengthen your memory and provide motivation.

Continue Reciting Move through your entire set of notes by reciting, checking accuracy, and reciting again. Remember to take full advantage of this system by using the feedback to look at your notes and recite again.

Adjust the Recall Column Sometimes it is difficult to know how much and what kind of information to put in the recall column.

- If you found that you did not give yourself enough cues to recite important points, add more key words or study questions to the recall column.
- If you found that you wrote all the important information in the recall column and you ended up reading what was there, you had nothing left to recite from memory. Cross out (or white out) some of the details before you recite again.
- Star the information you did not recall the first time. Pay extra attention to these areas the next time you recite.

EXERCISE 9.3 Reciting with a Partner

Review the Five Theories of Forgetting *in Chapter 6 (pages 139–140). Then review the notes for the forgetting theories (page 237). Cover up the notes so you only see the recall column. Either you or your partner recite out loud, in complete sentences, information in the first four headings in the recall column. If the person reciting is not able to recall the information, he or she may pull the paper down, review briefly, cover up the notes, and try reciting again. Then reverse roles so the other person can recite information for the remainder of the notes.*

Step Four: Reflect

To **reflect** means to "think or consider seriously." The reflect step can be individualized and can include a wide variety of activities and study tools. Several reflect activities are listed here.

Suggestions for Reflecting

1. Take time to think about the information in your notes.
2. Line up your recall columns to see the overall structure of the chapter.
3. Write your own summary at the bottom of your notes.
4. Use the back side of your notepaper to make lists of information or questions.
5. Make your own study tools such as index cards, visual mappings, or pictures for later reviews.
6. For math, make a three-column reflect page for key words, steps for problem solving, or formulas.

Take Time to Think Reflecting lets the information register and settle in your brain. It also allows you to look at the information from your own perspective and experiences, look for connections or relationships between ideas, and think of ways to extend the information beyond its original context. The process of reflecting involves a wide variety of critical thinking skills.

Line Up the Recall Columns To gain an overview of the entire chapter, remove your notepaper from your notebook. Arrange your notes on a table so that you can see all the recall columns lined up in sequence from left to right. By looking at the headings and the details, you will see the entire outline for the chapter. If you enjoy studying from outlines, you could convert this information into outline form to use for review. (See Chapter 11 for outline form.)

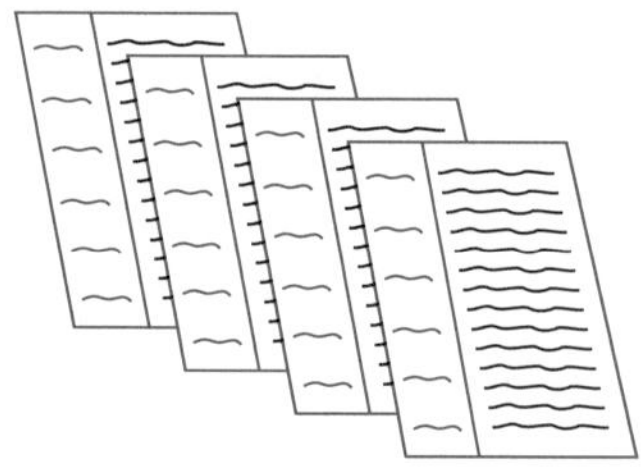

Write a Summary Look only at the information in the recall columns. Write a summary that explains the important points. Include the main ideas and brief statements of major supporting details. Your summary should be written in full sentences and paragraphs. Save this summary because it is a good review tool to use before tests. (See Chapter 8, pages 223–224, for more information about writing summaries.)

Write on the Back Side of Your Notepaper The back of your notepaper is now available for you to make additional lists of information or reminders. You can also include diagrams or charts to show how different ideas are related. If you have questions that you would like to ask the instructor, jot them down on the back as well. The backs are convenient and available, so use them as needed.

How would you apply Cornell notetaking to learning a foreign language?

Make Your Own Study Tools for Later Review The reflect step is a creative and highly individualized step. No two students will do the exact same activities in the reflect step. This is the time for you to decide *what will work best for you.* Consider the many different kinds of study tools you know how to make (or will be learning how to make). Select one or more that would help you learn the information more thoroughly, as well as provide you with study tools to use as you review throughout the term. Here are just a few options:

- Make index cards of all the key vocabulary terms, lists of information, or study questions.
- For math, make a list of symbols and their equivalent English words, or make a list of mathematical equations and their equivalent English sentences.
- Make a visual mapping, hierarchy, or outline of the chapter or parts of the chapter. As an option, write a summary of your work.
- Practice drawing or copying diagrams from the chapter.
- Add pictures, cartoons, or stick figures that can serve as memory triggers for parts of your notes later.
- Make study tapes that review the recall column or list the important points you want to remember.
- Use any of the study strategies described for each of the three learning styles (visual, auditory, kinesthetic).

How does taking notes in a math class differ from taking notes in a literature class?

For Math, Make a Three-Column Reflect Page Using a three-column notetaking system as a reflect activity for math textbooks promotes critical thinking and understanding of math terminology, problems, and formulas. This notetaking technique, presented by Paul D. Nolting in *Math Study Skills Workbook* as an alternative to the Cornell two-column system, shows key words, example problems, and explanations and rules for solving math problems or applying formulas. To use this technique and to create a reflect study tool, divide your notetaking paper into three columns, and then do the following:

1. Record each problem step in the *Examples* column.
2. Record the reasons for each step in the *Explanations/Rules* column.
3. Record key words and concepts in the *Key Words* column.
4. Cover up the *Examples* and the *Explanations/Rules* columns. Recite out loud the meanings of the key words or concepts.

The following examples shows this three-column system for one section of a math chapter.

Key Words	Examples	Explanations/Rules
$-n$	$-n$ If $n = s$, Then $-n = -s$ $-(-10) = 10$ $-(-15)(-15) = -15$ Opposite of $-x$ is x	Opposite of any number Count the number of signs; even means +, odd means −
Rational	Rational numbers are fractions ($^1/_4$, $^1/_2$, $^3/_4$).	A/B, $B/0$ is rational Division by 0 undefined
Numerator Denominator	numerator/denominator N/D	Numerator on top Denominator on bottom (D = Down)

Adapted from Nolting, *Math Study Skills Workbook*, pp. 50–51.

Step Five: Review

This last step of the Cornell system keeps the information active in your memory. Review provides the repetition you need to retrieve information quickly and accurately from your long-term memory.

Suggestions for Reviewing

1. Plan time for immediate review.
2. Plan time weekly for ongoing review.

Do an Immediate Review Reviewing actually begins when you are working at the fourth step. In the reflect step, you take time to think about the information you have covered, and you take time to create additional study tools. However, **immediate review** goes one step further. Before you close your book and quit studying, take a few additional minutes to review your recall columns. This provides one final opportunity to strengthen your memory for the organization and content of the material.

Ongoing Review **Ongoing review** means reviewing previous work so that you are continually practicing learned information. Ongoing review is necessary because you will be storing more and more information in your long-term memory as the term progresses, so you must make sure that you practice "old" information. In addition, by including ongoing reviews in your weekly study schedule, you save time in the long run. When tests, midterm exams, or final exams approach, you won't need to cram, for you will have kept the information active.

Several activities can take place during ongoing review:

- Review the recall columns of your notes. The more frequently you review these, the faster you can move through the columns. Also, as the term progresses, you will find that information placed in your notes early in the term is now clear and easy to understand.
- Review any reflect or review materials that you created earlier.
- If you have a list of questions from the second step of SQ4R or your own written summary, review these.
- Review chapter introductions, summaries, and lists of vocabulary terms for the chapter.

Now that the five *R*'s of the Cornell system have been discussed, take time to learn to use each of the steps. Remember, omitting any one step will weaken the system. The following pictures may help you learn and remember the steps more quickly.

1. Record

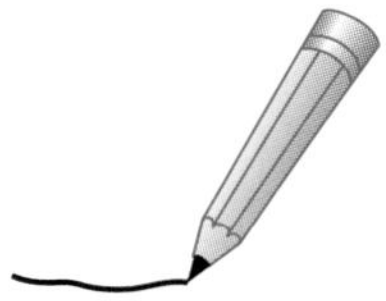

2. Reduce

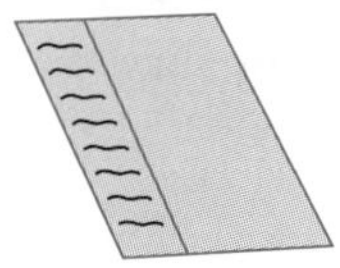

3. Recite

4. Reflect

5. Review

EXERCISE 9.4 Making Cornell Notes for Maslow's Hierarchy of Needs

Read the excerpt on ***Maslow's Hierarchy of Needs*** *on page 244. If you wish, highlight the important information in each paragraph.*

1. **Prepare:** Draw a two-and-one-half-inch margin down the left side of your notebook paper.
2. **Record:** Use the strategies presented in this chapter for taking notes in the right column. (See the Self-Assessment Form on page 245.)
3. **Reduce:** Reduce the notes in the left column. Write the heading and the key words or very brief study questions. Do not write too much information.
4. **Recite:** Cover up the right side of your notes. Practice reciting your notes out loud and in complete sentences. Check your accuracy.
5. **Reflect:** Do *one* of the following reflect activities:
   - **a.** THINK about the information and the following questions. Then summarize your ideas in a short paper.

     Do I believe that people are "wanting beings" who seek to fulfill needs?

     Do I believe this is really how needs we want to fulfill are arranged?

     Could emphasis on the various needs occur in a different order?

     Do my needs fall into this sequence? How?
   - **b.** The article suggests ways the business world can meet the different levels of needs of their employees. Brainstorm how colleges and universities strive to meet the different levels of needs of students. Summarize your ideas in paragraph form.
   - **c.** If you were in marketing or sales, how could you advertise in different ways to meet different levels of need? What would advertisements look like for each of the five kinds of needs?
   - **d.** Make vocabulary cards or a visual mapping of the information.
6. **Review:** Review your work so that you will be prepared to discuss this excerpt in class.

Special Note: Make multiple copies of the Self-Assessment Form on page 245 so you will have forms available for various notetaking assignments.

EXERCISE 9.4 continued

Maslow's Hierarchy of Needs

The concept of a hierarchy of needs was advanced by Abraham Maslow, a psychologist. A **need** is a personal requirement. Maslow assumed that humans are "wanting" beings who seek to fulfill a variety of needs. He assumed that these needs can be arranged according to their importance in a sequence known as **Maslow's hierarchy of needs**.

At the most basic level are **physiological needs**, the things we require to survive. These needs include food and water, clothing, shelter, and sleep. In the employment context, these needs are usually satisfied through adequate wages.

At the next level are **safety needs**, the things we require for physical and emotional security. Safety needs may be satisfied through job security, health insurance, pension plans, and safe working conditions.

Next are the **social needs**, the human requirements for love and affection and a sense of belonging. To an extent, these needs can be satisfied through the work environment and the informal organization. But social relationships beyond the workplace—with family and friends, for example—are usually needed, too.

At the level of **esteem needs**, we require respect and recognition (the esteem of others), as well as a sense of our own accomplishment and worth (self-esteem). These needs may be satisfied through personal accomplishment, promotion to more responsible jobs, various honors and awards, and other forms of recognition.

At the uppermost level are **self-realization needs**, the needs to grow and develop as people and to become all that we are capable of being. These are the most difficult needs to satisfy, and the means of satisfying them tend to vary with the individual. For some people, learning a new skill, starting a new career after retirement, or becoming the "best there is" at some endeavor may be the way to satisfy the self-realization needs.

Maslow suggested that people work to satisfy their physiological needs first, then their safety needs, and so on up the "needs ladder." In general, they are motivated by the needs at the lowest (most important) level that remain unsatisfied. However, needs at one level do not have to be completely satisfied before needs at the next-higher level come into play. If the majority of a person's physiological and safety needs are satisfied, that person will be motivated primarily by social needs. But any physiological and safety needs that remain unsatisfied will also be important.

Maslow's hierarchy of needs provides a useful way of viewing employee motivation, as well as a guide for management. By and large, American business has been able to satisfy workers' basic needs, but the higher-order needs present more of a problem. They are not satisfied in a simple manner, and the means of satisfaction vary from one employee to another.

Pride, *Business*, pp. 270–271.

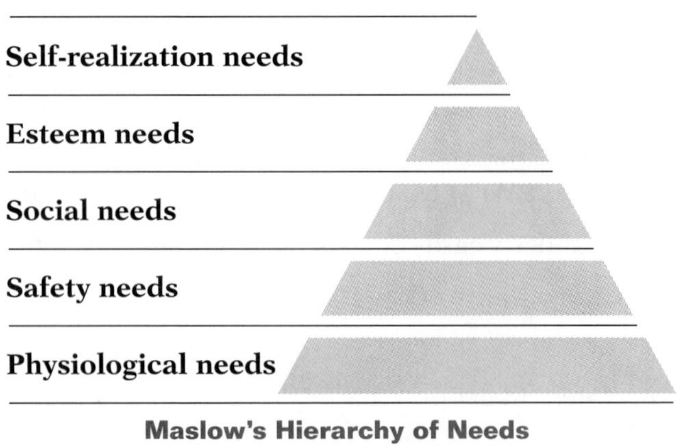

Maslow's Hierarchy of Needs

Maslow believed that people seek to fulfill five categories of needs.

Cornell Notetaking Self-Assessment Form 1

Name ______________________ Date ______________

Topic of Notes ______________________ Assignment ______________

Record Step

	YES	NO
1. Did you clearly show headings in your notes so you can see the main topics?	____	____
2. Did you underline the headings and avoid putting numbers or letters in front of the headings?	____	____
3. Did you leave a space between headings or larger groups of information so your notes are not cluttered or crowded?	____	____
4. Did you include sufficient details so that you do not need to return to the textbook to study this information?	____	____
5. Did you use numbering between the different details under the headings?	____	____
6. Did you indent and uses dashes or other symbols to show supporting details?	____	____
7. Did you use meaningful phrases or shortened or complete sentences so that the information will be clear at a later time?	____	____
8. Did you paraphrase or shorten the information so your notes are not too lengthy?	____	____
9. Did your notes refer to important charts, diagrams, or visual materials in the chapter, or did you make reference to the textbook pages in your notes?	____	____
10. Did you write on only one side of the paper, leaving the back side blank?	____	____
11. Did you write a heading on the first page of your notes and page numbers on the other pages?	____	____
12. Did you write your notes so that they are neat and easy to read?	____	____

Recall Column (Reduce Step)

	YES	NO
1. Did you move each heading into the recall column and underline it?	____	____
2. Did you use a two-and-one-half-inch margin on the left for the recall column?	____	____
3. Did you include study questions in the recall column for the key points in your notes?	____	____
4. Did you include enough information in the recall column to guide you when you recite your notes?	____	____
5. Did you include in the recall column some key words that you need to define or explain?	____	____
6. Did you write the questions and the key words directly across from the corresponding information in your notes column?	____	____
7. Did you avoid writing too much information or giving yourself all of the information in the recall column, thus leaving you with little to recite from memory?	____	____
8. Did you try using the recall column?	____	____
9. Did you add or delete information in the recall column after you tried using that column for reciting?	____	____

Cornell Notetaking Self-Assessment Form 2

Name ______________________________ Date ______________

Topic of Notes ______________________________ Assignment ______________

Record Step

	YES	NO
1. Did you clearly show headings in your notes so you can see the main topics?	____	____
2. Did you underline the headings and avoid putting numbers or letters in front of the headings?	____	____
3. Did you leave a space between headings or larger groups of information so your notes are not cluttered or crowded?	____	____
4. Did you include sufficient details so that you do not need to return to the textbook to study this information?	____	____
5. Did you use numbering between the different details under the headings?	____	____
6. Did you indent and uses dashes or other symbols to show supporting details?	____	____
7. Did you use meaningful phrases or shortened or complete sentences so that the information will be clear at a later time?	____	____
8. Did you paraphrase or shorten the information so your notes are not too lengthy?	____	____
9. Did your notes refer to important charts, diagrams, or visual materials in the chapter, or did you make reference to the textbook pages in your notes?	____	____
10. Did you write on only one side of the paper, leaving the back side blank?	____	____
11. Did you write a heading on the first page of your notes and page numbers on the other pages?	____	____
12. Did you write your notes so that they are neat and easy to read?	____	____

Recall Column (Reduce Step)

1. Did you move each heading into the recall column and underline it?	____	____
2. Did you use a two-and-one-half-inch margin on the left for the recall column?	____	____
3. Did you include study questions in the recall column for the key points in your notes?	____	____
4. Did you include enough information in the recall column to guide you when you recite your notes?	____	____
5. Did you include in the recall column some key words that you need to define or explain?	____	____
6. Did you write the questions and the key words directly across from the corresponding information in your notes column?	____	____
7. Did you avoid writing too much information or giving yourself all of the information in the recall column, thus leaving you with little to recite from memory?	____	____
8. Did you try using the recall column?	____	____
9. Did you add or delete information in the recall column after you tried using that column for reciting?	____	____

EXERCISE 9.5 Cornell Notes for Math

Read the following excerpt from a math textbook. Take a complete set of Cornell notes. After you complete your notes, your instructor may provide you with a sample set of notes to use for a comparison or he or she may discuss sample notes in class. Following the excerpt, you will find a beginning set of notes to use as a model.

A. Well-Defined Sets and Notation

We study sets in this book not only because much of elementary mathematics can be stated and developed by using this concept but also because many mathematical ideas can be stated most simply in the language of sets.

Definition 1.1

A **set** is a well-defined collection of objects, called **elements** or **members** of the set.

The main property of a set in mathematics is that it is **well defined**. This means that given any object, it must be clear whether that object is a member of the set. Thus, if we consider the set of even whole numbers, we know that every even whole number, such as 0, 2, 4, 6, and so on, is an element of this set but nothing else is. Thus, the set of even whole numbers is well defined. On the other hand, the set of funny comic strips in the daily newspaper is *not* well defined, because what one person thinks is funny may not be the same as what another person thinks is funny.

Example 1

Which of the following descriptions define sets?

(a) Interesting numbers (b) Multiples of 2

(c) Good writers (d) Current directors of General Motors

(e) Numbers that can be substituted for x so that $x + 4 = 5$

Solution Descriptions (b), (d), and (e) are well defined and therefore define sets. Descriptions (a) and (c) are *not* well defined, because people do not agree on what is "interesting" or what is "good." Descriptions (a) and (c) therefore do not define sets.

We use capital letters, such as A, B, C, X, Y, and Z, to denote sets, and lowercase letters, such as a, b, c, x, y, and z, to denote elements of sets. It is customary, when practical, to list the elements of a set in braces and to separate these elements by commas. Thus, $A = \{1, 2, 3, 4\}$ means that "A is the set consisting of the elements 1, 2, 3, and 4." To indicate the fact that "4 is an element of the set A," or "4 is in A, " we write $4 \in A$. To indicate that 6 is not an element of A, we write $6 \notin A$.

Example 2

Let $X = \{\text{Eva, Mida, Jack, Janice}\}$. Which of the following are correct statements?

(a) Mida $\in X$ (b) Jack $\notin X$

(c) Janice $\in$ {Eva, Mida, Jack, Janice}

(d) $E \in X$ (e) $X \in X$

Solution Statements (a) and (c) are the only correct ones.

B. Describing Sets

Sets can be defined in three ways.

1. By giving a verbal description of the set
2. By listing the elements of the set (roster method)
3. By using set-builder notation

Following are some sets defined in words and by lists.

Description	*List*
The set of counting numbers less than 5	{1, 2, 3, 4}
The set of natural Earth satellites	{Moon}
The set of counting numbers	[1, 2, 3, . . .} The three dots, called an *ellipsis,* mean that the list goes on in the same pattern without end.
The set of odd counting numbers less than 15	{1, 3, 5, . . . , 13} The three dots mean the odd numbers after 5 and before 13 are in the set but not listed.
The set of whole numbers less than or equal to 3	{0, 1, 2, 3}

In set-builder notation, we use a defining property to describe the set. A vertical bar (|) is used to mean "such that." Thus, the preceding sets can be written as follows:

Set-Builder Notation	*Read*
{*x* | *x* is a counting number less than 5}	The set of all elements *x*, such that *x* is a counting number less than 5
[*x* | *x* is a natural Earth satellite}	The set of all elements *x*, such that *x* is a natural Earth satellite
{*x* | *x* is a counting number}	The set of all elements *x*, such that *x* is a counting number
{*x* | *x* is an odd counting number less than 15}	The set of all elements *x*, such that *x* is an odd counting number less than 15
{*x* | *x* is a whole number less than or equal to 3}	The set of all elements *x*, such that *x* is a whole number less than or equal to 3

Example 3

Write verbal descriptions for the following sets:

(a) {a, b, c, . . . , z} (b) {1, 3, 5, . . . } (c) {3, 6, 9, . . . , 27}

Solution

(a) The set of letters in the English alphabet

(b) The set of odd counting numbers

(c) The set of counting numbers that are multiples of 3 and less than or equal to 27

Example 4

(Omitted for this exercise. Continue with Definition 1.2.)

Definition 1.2

The symbol { } or ∅ represents the *empty*, or *null*, set.

Example 5

Write the following sets using the listing (roster) method:

(a) $\{x \mid x$ is a counting number less than 10 and x is divisible by 4$\}$

(b) $\{x \mid x$ is a counting number between 8 and 13 and x is divisible by 7$\}$

Solution

(a) The counting numbers less than 10 that are divisible by 4 are 4 and 8. Hence, the required set is {4, 8}.

(b) None of the numbers between 8 and 13 are divisible by 7. Thus, the required set is empty and the answer can be written as { } or ∅.

Note: It would *not* be correct to write {∅} for the answer to part (b), because the set {∅} is not empty; it contains the element ∅.

C. Equality of Sets

Clearly, the order in which the elements of a set are listed does not affect membership in the set. Thus, if we are asked to write the set of digits in the year in which Columbus discovered America, we may write the set as {1, 4, 9, 2}. Someone else may write the set as {1, 2, 4, 9}. Both are correct! Thus, we see that {1, 4, 9, 2} = {1, 2, 4, 9}. Similarly, {*a, b, c, d, e*} = {*e, d, c, b, a*}.

Definition 1.3

In general, two sets A and B are *equal*, denoted by $A = B$, if they have the same members (not necessarily listed in the same order).

For example, {1, 3, 2} = {1, 2,3} and $\{20, \frac{1}{2}\} = \{\frac{1}{2}, 20\}$.

Notice also that repeated listings do not affect membership. For example, the set of digits in the year in which the Declaration of Independence was signed is {1, 7, 7, 6}. This set can also be written as {1, 6, 7}. Therefore, the set {1, 7, 7, 6} = {1, 6, 7}. In the same way, {*a, a, b, b, c, c*} = {*a, b, c*}, because the two sets have the same elements. By convention, we do not list an element more than once.

Bello, Britton. *Topics in Contemporary Mathematics*, pp. 13–17.

Sample Notes:

Math Pages 13–17	
<u>Well-Defined Sets/Notation</u>	<u>Well-Defined Sets and Notation</u>
Define: —set —elements/members of a set	1. Definition 1.1 set = well-defined collection of objects (*elements/members* of the set) —Can clearly tell if object is a member of the set —Explanation: set of even whole numbers. 0, 2, 4, 6 and all even whole numbers are elements/members of the set
Which are well-defined sets? Why? a. interesting numbers b. multiples of 2 c. good writers d. current directors of General Motors e. numbers can substitute for x so $x + 4 = 5$	2. Example 1 Which are definite sets? a. interesting numbers — No. Members of set unclear. b. multiples of 2 — YES. Clear members of set. c. good writers — No. Members of set unclear. d. current directors of General Motors — YES. Clear members of set. e. numbers can substitute for x so $x + 4 = 5$ — YES. Clear members of set.
These mean what? *A, B, C* . . . capital letters *a, b, c* . . . lowercase letters { } $\in$ $\notin$ Read: $4 \in A$	3. Important letters and symbols for sets —Capital letters to denote sets *A, B, C, X, Y, Z,* etc. —Lowercase letters for elements of sets *a, b, c, x, y, z* —List elements of a set in braces and use commas to separate elements $A = \{1, 2, 3, 4\}$ —$\in$ means element belongs to set: $4 \in A$ —$\notin$ means element not a part of set: $6 \notin A$ 4. Example 2: $X = \{$Eva, Mida, Jack, Janice$\}$

Group Processing: A Collaborative Learning Activity

Form groups of three students. Complete the following directions.

1. Use six index cards or pieces of paper. Write the following on the cards:
   1. Record 2. Reduce 3. Recite 4. Reflect 5. Review 6. 5 *R*'s of Cornell
2. Shuffle the cards and place them face down. Each student draws two cards.
3. The person with card 1 begins by telling everything he or she knows about *Record* (in the Cornell system). Continue with students reciting the cards according to the order above. After a student recites what he or she remembers about the category on the card, other group members may add additional information.

Reflection Writing 2

CHAPTER 9

On a separate piece of paper or in a journal, do the following:

1. In Exercise 9.1, you used your usual form of notetaking to take notes on *Chronemics*. In Exercise 9.2, you completed the notes for *Chronemics* by adding details to a set of notes with the key ideas numbered. Discuss the differences between your original notes in Exercise 9.1 and your notes in Exercise 9.2. Which notes are more organized, clearer, and easier to use? Explain.
2. What do you see as the greatest benefits of learning to use the 5 *R*'s of Cornell?

Combining Cornell Notetaking and SQ4R

You have now learned two very powerful study methods for mastering learning. SQ4R (Chapter 7) is a six-step system for reading a textbook; Cornell is a notetaking system that can be used with textbooks. The following chart shows how you can effectively combine these two methods.

Combining SQ4R and Cornell

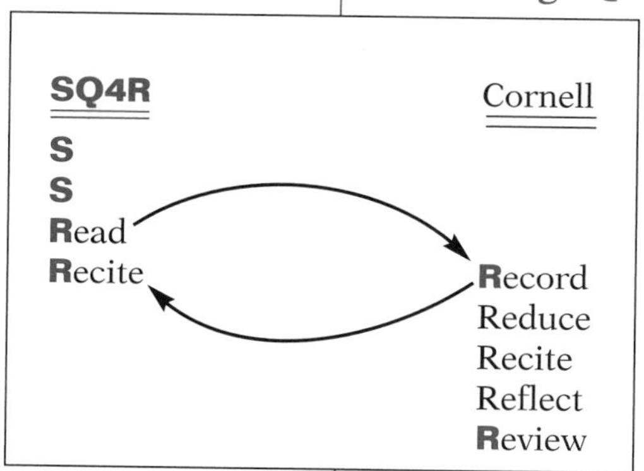

Begin the SQ4R Steps

1. **Survey:** Do an overview for the chapter.
2. **Question:** Write questions for each heading.
3. **Read:** Read one paragraph.
4. **Record:** Take Cornell notes on separate paper.
5. **Recite:** Recite the important information in the paragraph.
6. Continue to read-recite-record to the end of the chapter.

Continue the Cornell Steps

7. **Reduce:** Make your recall column.
8. **Recite:** Cover your notes and recite from your recall column.
9. **Reflect:** Do one or more reflect activities.
10. **Review:** Review your notes and complete the chapter and the questions you made in the second step of SQ4R.

Note that you begin with the first three steps of SQ4R: survey, question, and read. The Cornell system then merges with the reading system for the record step. (Record is step four of SQ4R and step one of Cornell.)

Once you have completed the reading and have taken the notes, put the book aside. Focus your attention on the Cornell notes you have taken and the remaining steps of Cornell: reduce, recite, reflect, and review. Join the review steps in SQ4R with the review step in Cornell. You have now successfully combined two powerful systems for learning.

EXERCISE 9.6 Case Studies

Each of the following case studies describes a student situation. Read each case study carefully; highlight key ideas or student issues. Answer the question that ends each case study. In your response, address the key points that you highlighted and that relate directly to the question. Answer in complete sentences on a separate piece of paper. These case studies are also available online; you can email your response to your instructor or print a copy of your work online.

1. Labrishun learns by writing information and studying from information that she has handwritten. Initially she thought the Cornell notetaking system would be perfect for her. However, after she had taken notes on two different chapters, she was ready to abandon the use of the Cornell system. When asked why, she responded that her notes were longer than the textbook chapters and that her hand was getting too tired copying everything from the textbook into her notes. What recording techniques does Labrishun need to learn to use more effectively and efficiently so her notes are not so lengthy and her hand does not tire from such extensive writing?
2. Joey has learned to condense information effectively into the right column. In his recall column, Joey makes lists of important information, writes definitions for key terms, and writes study questions with their answers. He reads all the information out loud. A tutor suggested to Joey that he practice reciting the information instead of simply reading the recall column. Joey realizes that he does not know the difference between reading out loud and reciting. How would you explain the differences to Joey?
3. In Damon's opinion, his "short-cut method" for taking textbook notes for his biology class results in neat and logically structured notes. He writes the headings and underlines them. He lists the subheadings that appear under each heading. In many ways, his notes look like a formal outline with only two levels of information: headings and subheadings. Damon's instructor announces that the majority of the upcoming midterm will focus on terminology and definitions. When Damon pulls out his notes to begin studying for the test, he realizes that the method of notetaking he has used all term is ineffective. Which of the 5 *R*'s of Cornell notetaking does Damon need to use in order to have more effective and useful notes?

Exercise 9.7 LINKS

Make a complete set of Cornell notes for one *of the following. (See the Self-Assessment Form on page 245 for the key elements that should appear in your notes.) After you complete the recall column, practice reciting the information in your notes. At the end of your notes, write a summary that highlights the most important information from the excerpt.*

Multiple Intelligences, Chapter 1, pages 19–22
Twelve Principles of Memory, Chapter 2, pages 42–48
Decreasing Procrastination, Chapter 5, pages 127–132
Exercise 7.5, Approaches to Psychology, pages 185–189
Chapter 8 Review Questions, Role of Concentration, page 228

EXERCISE 9.8 Working with Another Textbook

Select three or more pages from one of your textbooks for another class. Choose pages that have at least two headings and several paragraphs of text. Make a complete set of Cornell notes. (Review the Self-Assessment Form on page 245 for key elements to include in your notes.) Photocopy the pages and turn them in with your notes.

Exercise 9.9 Cornell Notes on Thinking Critically

Take a complete set of notes on the following section from a psychology textbook. Create a recall column and then write a short summary at the bottom of your notes.

Francine Shapiro, a clinical psychologist practicing in northern California, had an odd experience one day in 1987. She was walking in the woods, thinking about some distressing events, when she noticed that her emotional reaction to them was fading away (Shapiro, 1989a). Upon reflection, she realized that she had been unconsciously moving her eyes back and forth. Did the eye movements have anything to do with the change? When she made the eye movements deliberately, the emotion-reducing effect was even stronger. Curious, she examined the effect in others, first among friends and colleagues, then with clients who had suffered traumatic experiences such as childhood sexual abuse, military combat, or rape. She asked these people to think about their unpleasant experiences while following her finger with their eyes as she moved it back and forth in front of them. Like her, they said that their reactions to the memories faded. And her clients reported that emotional flashbacks, nightmares, fears, and other trauma-related problems dropped dramatically, often after only one session (Shapiro, 1989a).

Dr. Shapiro eventually called her new treatment *eye movement desensitization and reprocessing*, or *EMDR* (Shapiro, 1991). Today, Dr. Shapiro and other therapists are using EMDR to treat a wide range of anxiety-related problems, from simple phobias to disorders caused by the trauma of military combat (e.g., Manfield, 1998; Parnell, 1997; Shapiro, 1996). But the question remains: Can severe anxiety be permanently reduced by anything as simple as eye movements?

Psychologists still do not know what to make of EMDR. Is it a breakthrough in the treatment of anxiety disorders or a flash in the pan? When one is examining any aspect of behavior and mental processes, it is vital to determine, first, what specific questions to ask about the phenomenon of interest and, then, how to go about searching for the answer. Deciding on what questions to ask depends on an ability to think critically about the world; making progress toward answers depends on translating critical thinking into scientific research methods. As described in Chapter 1, psychologists use these methods to study a wide range of behavior and mental processes. In the pages that follow, we summarize some of the basic questions that emerge from thinking critically about psychology, describe the methods of science, show how some of these methods have been applied in evaluating the effectiveness of EMDR, and discuss the importance of ethics in scientific research. At the conclusion of the chapter, we present the first "Linkages" section, containing a discussion of how the contents of this chapter are related to another subfield of psychology. As we mentioned in the first chapter, discussions of this sort, and corresponding diagrams, appear throughout the book.

Thinking Critically About Psychology (Or Anything Else)

Often, people simply accept what they are told because it comes from a believable source or because "everyone knows" it is true. Indeed, some advertisers, politicians, TV evangelists, and social activists hope for this kind of easy acceptance when they seek your money, vote, or allegiance. They want you to believe their promises or claims without careful thought; they don't want you to think critically. Often, they get their wish. In 1997, for example, when a Canadian gold mining company called Bre-X claimed to have found the world's largest vein of gold in a remote area of Indonesia,

> thousands of people poured millions of dollars into its stock. Their uncritical belief in this claim eventually cost them every last penny because, after the stock skyrocketed—and the company's president and chief geologist made a fortune by selling out—the company was forced to admit that there was no gold (Spaeth, 1997). And this is just the tip of the iceberg. Millions of people waste billions of dollars every year on worthless psychic predictions, on bogus "cures" for cancer, heart disease, and arthritis, on phony degrees offered by nonexistent "universities" on the Internet, and on "miracle defrosting trays" and other consumer products that simply don't work (Beyerstein, 1997; Tuerkheimer & Vyse, 1997; Wolke, 1997).

Critical thinking is the process of assessing claims and making judgments on the basis of well-supported evidence (Wade, 1988). Consider Shapiro's EMDR treatment. Does it reduce anxiety-related problems, as reports by Shapiro and others suggest? One strategy for applying critical thinking to this or any other topic is to ask the following five questions:

1. *What am I being asked to believe or accept?* In this case, the assertion to be examined is that EMDR causes reduction or elimination of anxiety-related problems.

2. *What evidence is available to support the assertion?* Shapiro began her research on EMDR by gathering information about whether the reduction of her own emotional distress was related to her eye movements or simply a coincidence. When she found the same effect in others, coincidence became a less plausible explanation.

3. *Are there alternative ways of interpreting the evidence?* The dramatic effects experienced by Shapiro's friends and clients might be due not to EMDR but to factors such as their motivation to change or their desire to please her. Even the most remarkable evidence cannot be accepted as confirming an assertion until all equally plausible alternative assertions have been ruled out, which leads to the next step in critical thinking.

4. *What additional evidence would help to evaluate the alternatives?* The ideal method would be to identify three groups of people who are identical in every way except for the anxiety treatment they received. If a group receiving EMDR improved to a much greater extent than those given an equally motivating but inherently useless treatment, or no treatment at all, it would become less likely that EMDR effects could be explained on the basis of clients' motivation or the mere passage of time. The ways in which psychologists and other scientists collect evidence to test alternative explanations constitute the methods of scientific research, which we describe in detail later.

5. *What conclusions are most reasonable?* The evidence available thus far has not yet ruled out alternative explanations for the effects of EMDR (e.g., people's *beliefs* in EMDR rather than the treatment itself may be responsible for its positive effects), so the only reasonable conclusions to be drawn at this point are that (a) EMDR remains a controversial treatment, (b) it seems to have an impact on clients, and (c) further research is needed in order to understand it.

Does that sound wishy-washy? Critical thinking sometimes does seem indecisive because conclusions must be tempered by the evidence available. But critical thinking also opens the way to understanding.

Bernstein, *Psychology*, pp. 27–29.

Reflection Writing 3 — CHAPTER 9

On a separate piece of paper or in a journal, discuss the following:

1. What do you *like* about the Cornell notetaking system and what do you *dislike* about this system? Be specific.
2. Is it necessary to use the Cornell notetaking system for every one of your textbooks? Explain your answer.

SUMMARY

- The Cornell system provides you with a five-step method for recording and learning information accurately and thoroughly.
- You will become an active learner when you use all five *R*'s of Cornell:
  1. Select the important information and record it in the right column of your notepaper.
  2. Reduce the information to key terms or study questions; write this reduced information in the left column.
  3. Cover up the right side of your notes while you recite information in complete sentences; use the left column as a guide for reciting.
  4. Reflect on the material, finding relationships and creating study tools.
  5. Use immediate and ongoing review to rehearse information.
- The Cornell notetaking system can easily be incorporated into the SQ4R reading system; thus, two powerful study systems are combined to increase your learning potential.

ACE Practice Tests, which are scored online, supplementary exercises, enrichment activities, and related web site links are available online for *Essential Study Skills*, 4e. Use the following directions to access this web site:

Type: **http://college.hmco.com/collegesurvival/students**

Click on *List of Sites by Author.* Use the arrow to scroll down to Wong *Essential Study Skills*, 4e. Click on the title. If you are working on your own computer, bookmark this web site.

LEARNING OPTIONS

The following learning options provide you with opportunities to demonstrate your understanding of the topics in Chapter 9. Your instructor may assign one or more specific options or may ask you to select one or more options that interest you the most.

1. Expand the Chapter 9 mapping on page 229. Extend branches on the mapping to show important key words or phrases for each heading. (See Chapter 11 for additional information.) Add pictures and colors to your mapping to accentuate the points. (See the example in Chapter 1, page 25.) Write a summary in paragraph form of the chapter mapping.
2. Take a complete set of Cornell notes for any chapter in a mathematics textbook. Do a self-evaluation by using the Cornell Notetaking Self-Assessment Form printed on page 245. Design a *reflect* activity for this chapter and include it with your project. Photocopy the pages of the chapter or schedule a time to show your instructor the textbook, your notes, and your reflect activity.

3. Select an historical event, a geographic location, an inventor, or a geological or meteorological topic (volcanoes, earthquakes, hurricanes, comets). Use the Internet or your library resources to locate an informative article about your topic. The article must be two or more pages long. Print or photocopy the article. Make a complete set of Cornell notes on its content and create a reflect activity for your topic. Do a self-evaluation by using the Cornell Notetaking Self-Assessment Form printed on page 245.
4. Create a comparison chart for Maslow's Hierarchy of Needs. (For information about comparison charts, review pages 16 and 125.) Identify three or more categories of information for your chart so you have three or more columns of information. Refer to the reflect activities in Exercise 9.4 if you need ideas for your columns.
5. Create an informative brochure or one-page flyer that instructs other students how to use the Cornell notetaking system. Your brochure or flyer needs to show creativity, clarity, and accuracy; it may be reproduced by your instructor for distribution or display.
6. Work with a partner to select ten or more pages from a chapter in this textbook that your instructor has not yet assigned. Make a complete set of notes for these pages. You and your partner may make identical notes, or you may discuss the information together but then vary the way you develop your notes. Take turns covering your notes and reciting the recall column to your partner. Do a self-evaluation using the Cornell Notetaking Self-Assessment Form on page 245. When you turn in your notes, include the name of your partner and a short paragraph discussing the results of the reciting process you used together.
7. Conduct an Internet search for *notetaking, notetaking systems,* and *Cornell notetaking*. Print web site information that you deem valuable. Organize and compile the information into a *notetaking notebook* that you can use as a resource. Be sure that each entry in your notetaking notebook provides a web site address. Compile a list of all the useful web sites you located in your search. After each address, provide a brief summary of the web site; this page may be reproduced for other class members. You may be asked to give a presentation to the class on your project.

Name ______________________________ Date ______________

CHAPTER 9 REVIEW QUESTIONS

True-False

Carefully read the following sentences. Pay attention to key words. Write T *if the statement is true. Write* F *if the statement is false.*

_______ **1.** The majority of your review time should be spent working with your notes.

_______ **2.** Cornell notes are a reduced version of textbook information.

_______ **3.** It is best to read the whole chapter first and then go back to take notes.

_______ **4.** It is not necessary to take notes on graphs, charts, or pictures because they are always easy to remember.

_______ **5.** When you integrate the Cornell system and the SQ4R reading system, you begin taking notes during the second step of SQ4R.

_______ **6.** Too much information in the recall column causes you to read and not do much reciting.

_______ **7.** You can add more questions or key words to the recall column if there are too few cues to help you recite.

_______ **8.** If you are short on time, it is always best to skip the fourth step of Cornell.

_______ **9.** Ongoing review gets you in the habit of using repetition as a regular part of studying.

_______ **10.** If you highlight your textbook and take Cornell notes, essentially the same information will appear in both.

Short Answer

Complete the following chart by listing the five steps of the Cornell system in order and explaining the purpose of each step.

Steps of Cornell	The *purpose* of this step is to:
R	
R	
R	
R	
R	

Application

Take a complete set of Cornell notes on the following information from a psychology textbook. Organize your notes neatly and logically. Be sure to develop the recall column.

Basic Memory Processes

We know a psychologist who sometimes drives to work and sometimes walks. On one occasion, he drove, forgot that he had driven, and walked home. When he failed to find his car in its normal spot the next morning, he reported the car stolen. The police soon called to say that "some college kids" had probably stolen the car because it was found on campus (next to the psychology building!). What went wrong? There are several possibilities, because memory depends on three basic processes—encoding, storage, and retrieval. . . .

First, information must be put into memory, a step that requires **encoding**. Just as incoming sensory information must be coded so that it can be communicated to the brain, information to be remembered must be put in a form that the memory system can accept and use. In the memory system, sensory information is put into various *memory codes*, which are mental representations of physical stimuli. For example, **acoustic codes** represent information as sequences of sounds. **Visual codes** represent stimuli as pictures. **Semantic codes** represent an experience by its general meaning. Thus, if you see a billboard that reads "Huey's Going Out of Business Sale," you might encode the sound of the words as if they had been spoken (acoustic coding), the image of the letters as they were arranged on the sign (visual coding), or the fact that you saw an ad for Huey's (semantic coding). The type of coding used can influence what is remembered. For example, semantic coding might allow you to remember that a car was parked in your neighbors' driveway just before their house was robbed. If there was little or no other coding, however, you might not be able to remember the make, model, or color of the car.

The second basic memory process is **storage**, which refers to the maintenance of information over time, often over a very long time. When you find it possible to use a pogo stick or to recall a vacation from many years ago, you are depending on the storage capacity of your memory.

The third process, **retrieval**, occurs when you find information stored in memory and bring it into consciousness. Retrieving stored information such as your address or telephone number is usually so fast and effortless it seems automatic. Only when you try to retrieve other kinds of information—such as the answer to a quiz question that you know but cannot quite recall—do you become aware of the searching process. Retrieval processes include both recall and recognition. To *recall* information, as on an essay test, you have to retrieve it from memory without much help. *Recognition* is aided by clues, such as the alternatives given in a multiple-choice test item. Accordingly, recognition tends to be easier than recall.

Basic Memory Processes Remembering something requires, first, that the item be encoded—put in a form that can be placed in memory. It must then be stored and, finally, retrieved, or recovered. If any of these processes fails, forgetting will occur.

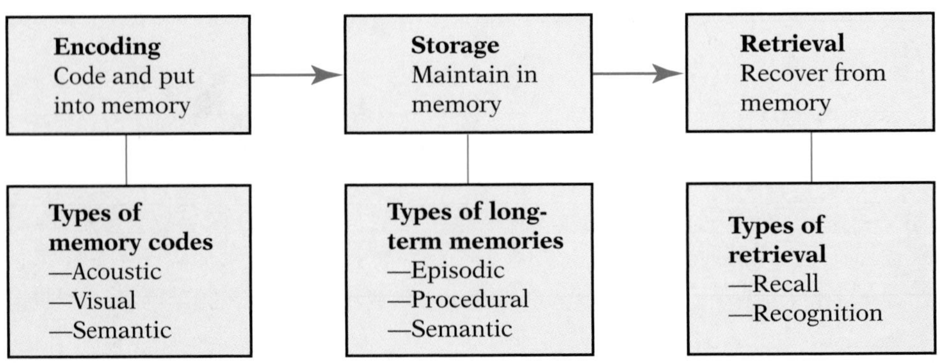

Bernstein, Douglas A., Thomas K. Srull, Christopher D. Wickens, and Edward J. Roy, PSYCHOLOGY, Fourth Edition. Copyright © 1997 by Houghton Mifflin Company. Used with permission.

CHAPTER 10

Listening and Taking Lecture Notes

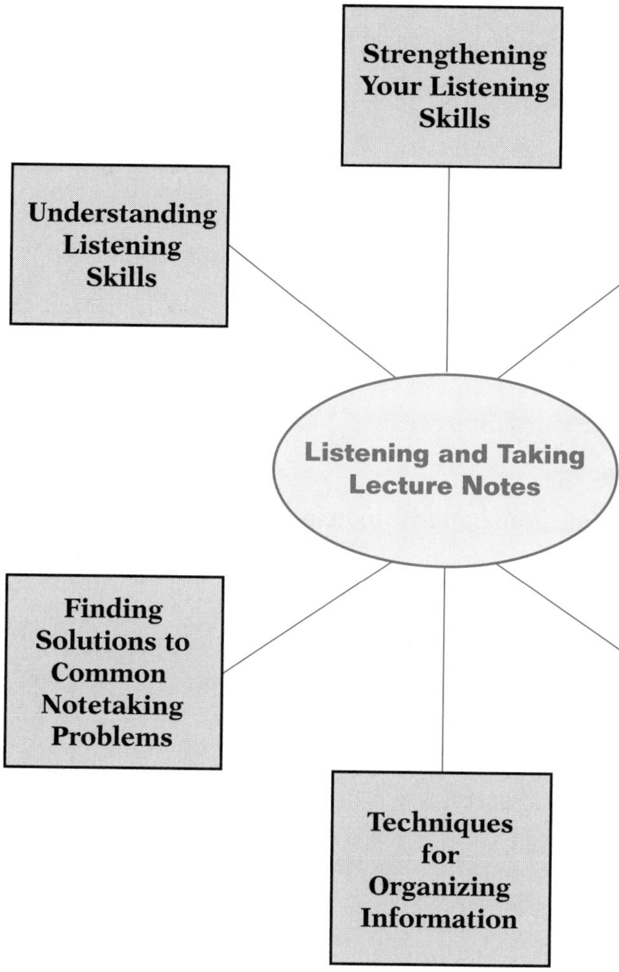

Terms to Know

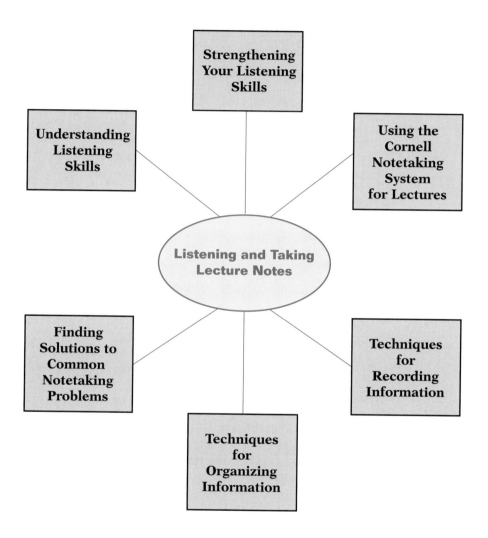

listening
reception
attention
perception
assignment of meaning
response
active listening
five *R*'s of Cornell
rate of speech
rate of writing
paraphrasing
ordinals
verbal clues
nonverbal clues
rate of thinking
sidetracks

Understanding factors that affect listening and the steps involved in active listening can help you learn to use effective listening strategies. This chapter presents twelve strategies for strengthening your listening skills; strong listening skills are essential for taking effective lecture notes. You can use the five *R*'s of Cornell notetaking during lectures. Specific techniques for recording and organizing lecture notes help you keep up with the lecturer's rate of speech, capture important main ideas and supporting details, and produce accurate notes that you can use for studying and ongoing review. This chapter also includes solutions for common notetaking problems that occur during lectures.

CHAPTER 10 Lecture Notes Profile

DO, SCORE, and **RECORD** your profile before you read this chapter. If you need to review the process, refer to the complete directions given in the profile for Chapter 1 on page 2.

ONLINE: You can complete the profile and get your score online at this textbook's web site.

	YES	NO
1. I have problems knowing what information to put into lecture notes.	______	______
2. I stop taking notes when the speaker sidetracks from the topic, I lose interest in the topic, or I cannot keep up with the pace.	______	______
3. I spend time going over my notes and filling in missing information as soon after the lecture as possible.	______	______
4. The main ideas and important details are easy to identify in my notes.	______	______
5. Internal and external distractors often interfere with my ability to concentrate during a lecture.	______	______
6. I can usually take notes that are adequate and easy to use for studying.	______	______
7. I frequently use symbols, abbreviations, and shortened sentences in my lecture notes.	______	______
8. I reword (paraphrase) what is said so I do not write word for word.	______	______
9. I practice reciting important information in my notes.	______	______
10. I use the instructor's verbal and nonverbal communication patterns to help me identify which information is important.	______	______

Reflection Writing 1 — CHAPTER 10

On a separate piece of paper or in a journal, do the following:

1. Discuss your profile score for this chapter. What was your score? What does it mean to you?
2. Discuss how comfortable and pleased you are with your ability to take effective notes in lecture-oriented classes.

Understanding Listening Skills

Of the four verbal communication skills (listening, speaking, reading, and writing), listening skills are often the weakest. You may think that as long as you have ears that work, you can listen. If your auditory channels are functioning, you can *hear,* but that does not necessarily mean that you are *listening.* Listening requires more than taking in sounds and being aware that words are being spoken.

Why is it important that reporters have good listening skills? Does a public relations person need to have good listening skills as well? Why or why not?

Listening involves understanding what you are hearing and having the ability to attach meaning to the words and to interpret what the speaker is saying. Frequently, people incorrectly perceive *speaking* as an active process and *listening* as a passive process. The truth is that *listening is an active process that engages the listener in a variety of mental processes*. The poor listening habits that many people have tend not to come from the training given in schools; instead, the poor listening habits often are learned because of the *lack* of training or instruction.

Influencing Factors

A person may begin listening to a speaker with the complete intention of "staying tuned in," listening attentively, following the ideas, and making every effort to understand the information. However, good listening is similar to concentration: It's here one second and then it's gone. All of the following factors can influence your ability to be a good listener.

- interest in the topic
- attitude toward the subject
- attitude toward the speaker
- tone of voice
- rate of speech
- speech patterns and mannerisms
- degree of organization of the lecture
- teaching/lecture style
- distractions from people nearby
- room temperature or lighting
- number of interruptions in the speech
- degree of insulation from outside sounds
- familiarity with words, terminology, or the topic
- length of time required to remain seated
- difficulty level of the course
- quantity of information presented
- sitting posture during the lecture
- seating location in relation to the speaker
- personal physical level (tired, sick)
- personal emotional level at the time
- personal background experiences
- learning style
- cultural background

Notice that the first few items are related to *attitude.* Positive attitudes toward the topic, the subject or the class, and the speaker lead to positive listening. A negative, disinterested, judgmental attitude will bring negative results by putting up barriers or shutting down your auditory channels, which are required for good listening. Some of the factors in the previous list are directly related to the speaker. Ideally, all speakers should automatically use an appropriate tone of voice, rate of speech, and pleasing speech patterns and mannerisms, and be well organized. However, this sometimes is not the case. You, the listener, need to find ways to overcome the barriers that are directly related to the speaker and his or her form of delivery of information. External distractors that were previously discussed in Chapter 5 that occur while you are studying also occur while you are listening. You can apply many of the same techniques for improving concentration to improving your listening skills. The factors listed at the top of the right column relate to your level of understanding of the course work. The time-management, goal-setting, and reading techniques learned in previous chapters will result in greater familiarity and understanding of the course work so these factors do not become barriers to good listening. The remaining factors are all related to *you* on a personal level.

Steps in the Listening Process

Listening is an active process that occurs in five distinct steps. These five steps, discussed in *Communicating,* a college textbook by Berko, Wolvin, and Wolvin (pp. 52–58), are summarized below. Notice the relationship of each step to the steps in the Information Processing Model (Chapter 2, pages 31–36).

1. *Reception:* **Reception** involves receiving auditory and visual stimuli, such as facial expressions, body language, and appearance. These stimuli enter your short-term memory and the process of listening begins.
2. *Attention:* **Attention** involves concentration, selectivity, motivation, and intent. In this step of listening, the stimuli enter the short-term memory system. You must actively focus your attention on the incoming stimuli, block out distractions and other insignificant stimuli, and concentrate on the message with the intent to comprehend what you hear. To avoid having the information drop out of your memory system, you must apply motivation and effort to give the stimuli your full attention.
3. *Perception:* **Perception** involves an initial attempt to evaluate the information received. During this process, you become aware of the information you understand and the information that does not make sense. Your educational background, your personal experiences, culture, attitude, values, and your mental and emotional states affect how you perceive the information.
4. *Assignment of meaning:* The **assignment of meaning** is the process of interpreting or attaching meaning to what you hear by categorizing the information into schemas, which are categories or clusters of information in long-term memory (see Chapter 2, page 35). As you interpret information and assign meaning to what you hear, you link the information to existing schemas and associate it to personal experiences. One of the greatest difficulties with this step occurs in the process of interpreting the message as the speaker intended, without distorting or altering the speaker's message by reacting emotionally, being judgmental, or confusing facts and opinions.
5. *Response:* After you assign meaning to the message, the process of listening continues with an intellectual or emotional **response** to the information. Your response may include a nonverbal form of feedback, such as a nod of your head to indicate understanding, or it may include verbal feedback, such as *paraphrasing* the speaker so you can check the accuracy of your perception and interpretation of the message. It may also include asking a question to seek clarification or gain more supporting information.

Another form of response may be to couple the information with a memory technique that can help you efficiently retrieve the information from your long-term memory at a later time.

Active listening is an essential skill required for taking effective classroom lecture notes. It is also a skill that will benefit you in classroom discussions and small group interactions, in your career field, and in your personal relationships. By understanding each step, you will be better equipped to analyze your listening patterns, which include your strengths and weaknesses, and to seek strategies to improve your active listening skills. The Listening Inventory in Exercise 10.1 will help you analyze your effectiveness in using each of the five steps of listening.

EXERCISE 10.1 Listening Inventory

Janusik/Wolvin Student Listening Inventory

Directions: The process of listening includes the five steps of Reception, Attention, Perception, Assignment of Meaning, and Response. As a process, listening can break down at any of the five steps. This inventory will help you to identify your strengths and weaknesses in terms of the steps within the context of the classroom. After reading each statement below, code the item with the most appropriate response within the context of the college classroom. Remember, "speaker" can mean the instructor or fellow students, so you may have to average your responses. **(1) almost never, (2) not often, (3) sometimes, (4) more often than not, and (5) almost always.**

______ **1.** I block out external and internal distractions, such as other conversations or what happened yesterday, when someone is speaking.

______ **2.** I feel comfortable asking questions when I don't understand something the speaker said.

______ **3.** When a speaker uses words that I'm not familiar with, I jot them down and look them up later.

______ **4.** I identify the speaker's credibility while listening.

______ **5.** I paraphrase the speaker's main ideas in my head as he or she speaks.

______ **6.** I concentrate on the main ideas instead of the specific details.

______ **7.** I am able to understand those who are direct as easily as I can understand those who are indirect.

______ **8.** Before making a decision, I confirm my understanding of the other person's message with her or him.

______ **9.** I concentrate on the speaker's message even when what she or he is saying is complex.

______ **10.** I really want to understand what the other person has to say, so I focus solely on his or her message.

______ **11.** When I listen to someone from another culture, I understand that the speaker may use time and space differently, and I factor that into my understanding.

______ **12.** I make certain to watch a speaker's facial expressions and body language for further clues to what he or she means.

______ **13.** I encourage the speaker through my facial expressions and verbal utterances.

______ **14.** When others are speaking to me, I make sure to establish eye contact and quit doing other tasks.

______ **15.** When I hear something with which I disagree, I tune out the speaker.

______ **16.** When an emotional trigger is activated, I recognize it for what it is, set aside my feelings, and continue to concentrate on the speaker's message.

______ **17.** I try to be sure that my nonverbal response matches my verbal response.

______ **18.** When someone begins speaking, I focus my attention on her or his message.

______ **19.** I understand that my past experiences play a role in how I interpret a message, so I try to be aware of their influence when listening.

______ **20.** I attempt to eliminate outside interruptions and distractions.

______ **21.** I look the speaker in the eye to focus on her/his message.

______ **22.** I tune out messages that are too complicated to understand.

______ **23.** I try to understand the other person's point of view and why she/he feels that way even when it is different from what I believe.

______ **24.** I am nonjudgmental and noncritical when I listen.

______ **25.** As appropriate, I self-disclose a similar amount of personal information as the other person shares with me.

Scoring

Directions: Write your responses in the appropriate positions. For example, if you gave yourself a "3" for the first statement, transfer the 3 to the first slot under Reception. When you've transferred all of your scores, add up all five scores for each step. The step with the highest score is your strength. The step with the lowest score is the step that can use the most improvement.

	Reception	Attention	Perception	Assignment of Meaning	Response
	1. ______	5. ______	3. ______	4. ______	2. ______
	9. ______	10. ______	6. ______	7. ______	8. ______
	12. ______	14. ______	15. ______	11. ______	13. ______
	18. ______	20. ______	16. ______	19. ______	17. ______
	21. ______	22. ______	23. ______	24. ______	25. ______
Total	______	______	______	______	______

Now add up your scores for all five steps, and use the following as a general guideline:

125–112	You perceive yourself to be an outstanding listener in the classroom.
111–87	You perceive yourself to be a good listener in the classroom, but there are some steps that could use improvement.
86–63	You perceive yourself to be an adequate listener in the classroom, but attention to some steps could really improve your listening effectiveness.
62–0	You perceive yourself to be a poor listener in the classroom, and attention to all of the steps could really improve your listening effectiveness.

Berko, Wolvin, Wolvin, *Communicating,* pp. 109–111.

Short Answers

1. In which step or steps did you excel?

2. Which step or steps indicated the most need for improvement?

Reflection Writing 2 — CHAPTER 10

On a separate piece of paper or in a journal, do the following:

1. In Chapter 1, pages 15–16, you completed a Dominance Inventory that provided you with information about being a linear or a global thinker and listener. In Exercise 10.1, you completed a second inventory that provided you with information about the way you tend to perform in each of the five steps of listening. Use the information from both inventories to discuss what you have learned about yourself as a listener.
2. Do your listening skills vary in different settings or situations? Discuss your effectiveness as an active listener in each of these four situations: with a close friend or partner, in social settings, in a small-group class discussion, and in college lectures.

Strengthening Your Listening Skills

Now that you have a better understanding of the many factors involved in listening, the next step is to begin applying strategies that strengthen your listening skills and assist you in becoming a good (or better) listener. The following strategies promote **active listening**. Active listening is the process of concentrating intently on what is being communicated. You focus your attention on the information coming into your short-term memory. The intent is to receive the information, understand it, and begin the task of processing its meaning. Active listening requires effort and mental discipline. The following twelve strategies are keys to strengthening your listening skills and becoming a more effective listener.

Twelve Strategies for Strengthening Listening Skills

Strategy	Further Explanations
Eliminate distractors	Use the Chapter 5 techniques to eliminate internal and external distractors. *Take charge* by selecting a location away from external distractors (specific individuals, window, door, and so on).
Attend to levels of information	Capturing only the main ideas is not sufficient; capturing every detail is not possible or recommended. Strive to follow the speaker's ideas by seeing the relationships between the information presented. Identify the "big picture" and recognize the important details that develop the big picture or main idea. Think in terms of "levels" of information.
Stay tuned in	Resist the temptation to tune out when information is too technical, difficult, unclear, or boring. Force yourself to listen more intently to identify trends or the sequencing used with the information. Work hard to achieve the mental discipline required to stay tuned in with the speaker.
Monitor your emotional response	Emotions can interfere with listening, distort the information, and set up barriers to understanding. Push yourself to put your own emotions aside so you can give the speaker the opportunity to develop his or her ideas. Jot your emotional responses on a piece of paper; save the discussion of your point of view for an appropriate time after the presentation or lecture.
Create an interest	The attitude you bring with you will affect your ability to listen. Genuine interest occurs when you are familiar with the topic, have an existing interest or curiosity about the topic, or have an excellent motivational speaker. When these situations do not exist, the responsibility to create an interest is on your shoulders. Relate the topic to your overall goals, write questions that may generate your curiosity, or involve yourself in discussions with people who already have a genuine interest in the topic.
Ask relevant questions	Many teachers and students value questions that ask for clarification or additional information when the questions are asked at appropriate times and are related to the topic being presented. If the speaker prefers not to address questions until the end of the lecture, jot questions on the side of your paper so you can ask them at the appropriate time. Asking questions is a sign of interest and a desire to learn; do not hesitate to ask questions when the time is appropriate.
Be nonjudgmental	Paying too much attention to a speaker's clothing, mannerisms, speech patterns, or appearance can be a major distraction from hearing and understanding the content of the message. Strive to focus on the information, not the person. Avoid criticism or judgments about the person. If for some reason the physical presence of the person is too much of a distraction, focus your eyes on the chalkboard or on your notes.
Posture and position yourself for listening	Body postures and position affect the quality of your listening and your level of attentiveness. Slouching conveys an image of disinterest; sit straight in the chair or lean forward slightly with your pen in hand ready to take notes. The back of the room tends to have more distractors, and seeing the overhead transparencies or the chalkboard tends to be more difficult; position yourself closer to the front of the classroom where concentration, attention, and interest often increase.
Visualize the topic and the content	Connecting visualization to the listening process helps imprint information into your memory system and makes retrieval of information more efficient and accurate. Strive to "make a movie in your mind" of the information presented by the speaker.

(continued)

Strategy	Further Explanations
Paraphrase the speaker	For effective notetaking, understanding the information presented in a lecture and then quickly rephrasing it for your notes is essential. Rephrasing (paraphrasing) results in a shorter, more condensed form of an idea. Practice paraphrasing and condensing rather than attempting to write word for word what the speaker says.
Attend to nonverbal clues and body language	Listening also involves picking up nonverbal messages presented through a speaker's gestures, mannerisms, stance, facial expressions, and pauses in verbal presentation. Carefully watch the speaker for nonverbal clues or body language clues that signal important ideas, shifts in ideas, or important supporting details. Many people give nonverbal clues without being aware of this behavior; however, you as a listener should strive to detect the nonverbal patterns used.
Enroll in a listening class	Check to see if your school has a listening class. When listening courses are available, they often focus on critical listening skills, which increase a person's auditory memory and expand the ability to remember verbal information more accurately.

EXERCISE 10.2 Identifying Poor Listening Habits

Poor listening habits appear in many forms. Following are nine types of listeners rated poor, based on their primary behavior in listening situations. Read the descriptions carefully; then complete the directions on page 268.

1. **Mind reader.** You'll hear a little or nothing as you think, "What is this person really thinking or feeling?"
2. **Rehearser.** Your mental tryouts for "Here's what I'll say next" tune out the speaker.
3. **Filterer.** Some call this selective listening—hearing only what you want to hear.
4. **Dreamer.** Drifting off during a face-to-face conversation can lead to an embarrassing "What did you say?" or "Could you repeat that?"
5. **Identifier.** If you refer everything you hear to your own experience, you probably didn't really hear what was said.
6. **Comparer.** When you get sidetracked assessing the messenger, you're sure to miss the message.
7. **Derailer.** Changing the subject too quickly soon tells others you're not interested in anything they have to say.
8. **Sparrer.** You hear what's being said but quickly belittle it or discount it. That puts you in the same class as the derailer.
9. **Placater.** Agreeing with everything you hear just to be nice or to avoid conflict does not mean you're a good listener.

SOURCE: *Communication Briefings,* as adapted from *The Writing Lab,* Department of English, Purdue University, 1356 Heavilon Hall, West Lafayette, IN 47907; Berko, *Communicating,* p. 53

Directions: *Copy the following comparison chart on your own paper. (You may also prepare this assignment on a computer using tables.) Provide sufficient writing space in each cell or box for your answers. The left column gives you three listening situations. In the middle column, write one of the categories of poor listeners that represents a behavior you tend to exhibit in that specific listening situation. Briefly describe a specific situation in which you exhibited this behavior. In the right column, write suggestions you can use to improve your listening skills in each listening situation.*

Listening Situation	Type of Poor Listener	Suggestions to Improve
Discussing a personal issue with a family member		
Talking with a small group of friends at a social event		
Participating in a small group discussion in class		

Using the Cornell Notetaking System for Lectures

Many classes will require you to have strong listening skills in order to understand the lectures you will hear and to capture the information to place in your notes for future studying. Capturing the information from lectures is important for several reasons:

- Lectures help you understand the course content better.
- Lectures often clarify or expand textbook information.
- Lectures help identify and emphasize the important course information that you are expected to learn.
- Lectures provide additional information or points of view that are not included in the textbook.

The Cornell notetaking system presented in Chapter 8 is the same notetaking system you will use to take effective lecture notes. For many students, taking notes from a textbook is not too difficult because the information is printed and the pace for taking notes is controlled by you. During lectures, however, you do not have the advantage of controlling the pace, and you often do not have the advantage of knowing the overall organization that will be presented in the lectures. Some teachers do provide students with an outline for the lecture or begin the lecture by listing the main topics that will be covered. Even with an initial outline, you will need to learn new skills that will allow you to keep up with the lecture and select the appropriate information for your notes. You will also need several new techniques for organizing notes during a lecture. Begin by reviewing the **five *R*'s of Cornell** that you will be using for your lecture notetaking: *record, reduce, recite, reflect,* and *review*.

1. Record

2. Reduce

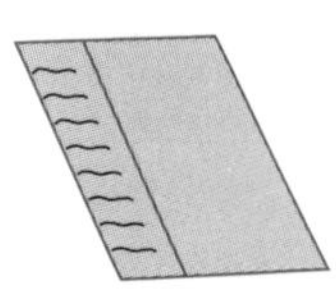

3. Recite

4. Reflect

5. Review

Group Processing: A Collaborative Learning Activity

Form groups of three or four students. Complete the following directions.

1. On a large chart, make two columns. In the left column, brainstorm problems that students encounter when they take lecture notes. List as many problems as you can think of in ten minutes.
2. In the right column, brainstorm possible solutions for each of the problems. Include solutions you know from personal experience and solutions you have read in this textbook. You may use information that appears later in this chapter as well.

Techniques for Recording Information

The following techniques are designed specifically for taking lecture notes. When you use them properly, you will have less difficulty "keeping up" and will be able to capture the most important information in your notes. These techniques are needed to deal with the discrepancy between rate of speech and rate of writing. The average **rate of speech** during a lecture is 100–125 words per minute. The **rate of writing** is about 30 words per minute. Noticing the discrepancy between the rate of speech and the rate of writing makes it apparent that you will not be able to write word for word. The following techniques will help you modify your writing so that you will be able to "keep up with the speaker."

Techniques for Recording Information

1. Familiarize yourself with the lecture topics before the lecture.
2. Paraphrase the speaker by shortening and rewording.
3. Use abbreviations to reduce the amount of writing.
4. Create a set of common symbols.
5. Use a modified form of printing/writing.
6. Practice often.

Familiarize Yourself with the Lecture Topics

Taking effective lecture notes can be difficult if the instructor presents unfamiliar terms and concepts. You can be better prepared for taking notes from lectures by familiarizing yourself with new terminology and concepts *before* the lecture. Refer to your course syllabus or previous class notes so you know the topic for the upcoming lecture. Survey (preview) the chapter if you do not have time to read the entire chapter before class. Becoming familiar with chapter terminology (and new symbols) before the lecture is especially important for math classes. Preparing a special list of new terminology, which includes new symbols, and keeping this list next to your notetaking paper can facilitate the process of taking lecture notes and can help you learn the new terminology more quickly. Becoming familiar with new terminology and concepts before the lecture increases your effectiveness. By knowing the contents of the chapter in advance, you gain a sense of confidence and know that you can return to the textbook for further explanations or clarifications, if needed, after the lecture.

Paraphrase

Paraphrasing means to put information into your own words. By paraphrasing, you will be able to shorten the information. Paraphrasing is a mental process that must be done quickly. As soon as you capture the speaker's words and interpret the message, write the information in a shortened form. Your sentences do not need to be grammatically correct. Words such as *the, an, and, there,* and *here* may be left out of your sentences, for they do not add to the overall meaning. Paraphrasing is perhaps one of the most difficult parts of notetaking, but with practice and familiarity with different teachers' lecture styles, your skills at paraphrasing will improve.

Use Abbreviations

Many words can be abbreviated to reduce the amount of writing. When you find content-related words that are frequently used, create your own abbreviations for the terms. Other common abbreviations, such as the following, can also be used.

BC. for *because*	**PRES.** for *president*
EX. for *example*	**SOC.** for *social* or *sociology*
IMP. for *important*	**SOL.** for *solutions*
POL. for *politics*	**W/OUT** for *without*

Create a Set of Symbols

Frequently used words can also be represented by symbols. The following symbols are often used in notes to reduce the amount of writing.

&	and	$\rightarrow$	leads to/causes
@	at	$<$	less than
$\downarrow$	decreases	$>$	more than
$\neq$	doesn't equal	#	number
$=$	equals	$+/-$	positive/negative
$\uparrow$	increases	$\therefore$	therefore

In lecture notes from a math class, you will need to use symbols frequently. Become familiar with the frequently used math symbols so you can use them when you take notes. You may want to create an ongoing list of symbols and their English words that you can refer to quickly when needed.

( )	quantity	$p \wedge q$	conjunction *and*
$>$	greater than	$p \vee q$	disjunction *or*
$<$	less than	$\sim p$	negation (not *p*)

Use Modified Printing

It is not uncommon to hear a person say that college ruined his or her handwriting. Lecture notetaking requires quickness; time is of the essence. As a result, many students move toward a style of handwriting that is functional without great emphasis on style, neatness, or consistency. One way to increase your writing speed is to use a modified form of writing that consists of a mixture of cursive writing and printing. Feel free to experiment with this mixture of cursive writing and printing to see if it increases your speed. Of course, when you are required to handwrite a personal letter or a job application, return to your neater, more consistent style of writing. Since your notes are usually only for you to see, relax your handwriting standards (but not to the degree that your writing is illegible).

Practice Often

Notetaking gets easier if you practice often. You can practice Cornell notes in every class and also at home. Practice taking notes as you watch educational television, attend meetings, listen to a sermon, or even talk on the phone! Many situational opportunities are available to practice your skills. Practice will increase your ability to paraphrase quickly and capture the speaker's main points.

Techniques for Organizing Information

Knowing how to structure notes is sometimes difficult because you do not have a clear sense of the overall organization of the content of the lecture. Most lectures are organized with headings (main ideas) and supporting details; the problem is that you don't usually have access to the instructor's notes that show this outline. Sometimes instructors provide students with an outline or may provide students with an outline if it is requested or suggested. If no outline is available, you will need to listen carefully for the main headings or shifts in ideas. In all situations, you will then need to listen and select the important details.

Selecting the important information and the right amount of information can be challenging. If your notes are too brief and lack sufficient details, they will not be very helpful when you need to study the information or prepare for tests. Notes that are too detailed can always be reduced during the reduce step of Cornell, so don't worry about having too many notes. More is better than not enough. Selectivity is the key. If you know some information is not essential, do not add unneeded information to your notes. If you are not sure if some information is going to be meaningful or essential, try to include it in your notes to be safe. The following techniques will help you organize your notes in meaningful ways:

Techniques for Organizing Your Notes

1. Listen for key words that signal headings and main points.
2. Listen for terminology and definitions.
3. Listen for important details (dates, names, facts, and statistics).
4. Listen for ordinals (number words).
5. Listen for examples.
6. Use verbal and nonverbal clues as signals.
7. For math lectures, copy every step of the problems and write explanations for each step.

Listen for Key Words

The words in the following list often signal a new heading or a new supporting detail. As soon as you hear these key words, ask yourself if the topic (heading) has shifted in the lecture, or if the instructor shifted to a new supporting detail.

advantages	effects	parts	stages
benefits	factors	principles	steps
causes	findings	purposes	techniques
characteristics	functions	reasons	types of
conclusions	kinds of	rules	uses
disadvantages	methods	solutions	ways

Listen for Terminology

In Chapter 8 you learned the importance of identifying and taking notes on terminology you encounter when you read. For the same reasons, getting terminology and definitions in your notes is important: understanding the terminology lays a strong foundation for learning course content. Word clues often signal definitions and signal you to get the information in your notes:

X *means . . .*	X *is defined as . . .*	*The definition of* X *is . . .*
X *is also called . . .*	X, *also referred to as . . .*	X, *also known as . . .*

When you hear these words, use the abbreviation *DEF,* to signal you are writing a definition. Or you may want to use the equal sign (=) as your own symbol to connect a word to a definition: *X* = definition. . . .

Listen for Details

As discussed in Chapter 8, supporting details are dates, names, facts, statistics, definitions, and examples that develop or "prove" the main idea. Notes with sufficient details for future use need to include the above kinds of information. If you find yourself only writing headings or just listing a few points and writing very little, chances are you need to start adding more supporting details to strengthen your notes.

Listen for Ordinals

When you hear "first," make that point number 1 in your notes. **Ordinals** (number words) help you organize the details in your notes and confirm that you are selecting the correct number of separate points for your notes. In addition to the ordinals that are number words, there are also *place holders,* or words that *represent* a number. The following words are examples of ordinals and place holders:

first	next	in addition
second	also	last
third	another	finally

Listen for Examples

Examples often serve as vivid triggers or reminders about a specific main idea or point that is being developed. Frequently, examples are informative and interesting; association between the example and what you are expected to learn is easier. For that reason, reference to the example should be in your notes. Sometimes, however, a considerable amount of time is spent on the example, especially if it is an anecdote of a personal experience. Your notes only need to show the basic idea of the example as a reminder of the placement of the example in the lecture; your notes do not need to "retell the whole story."

Use Verbal and Nonverbal Clues

Key words such as *kinds of, steps, advantages of,* and so forth, are verbal clues that signal the information is important. The following **verbal clues** are even stronger signals of information that should be included in your notes:

How does a newscaster's voice change during a story? What words receive more emphasis?

"This is important. You need to know and understand this."

"This will be on the next test."

"As I have already said . . ." (ideas are repeated).

"Be sure you copy this information (from the overhead or chalkboard)."

"If you haven't already done so, be sure you read carefully the information on pages . . . ."

"I can't emphasize enough the importance of . . . ."

A person's intonation (pitch of his or her voice), volume of voice, and rate of speech are also verbal clues. Listen to your instructor's patterns carefully. Does he or she speak louder, more enthusiastically, faster, slower, or at a different pitch when giving important information? Many speakers may not even be aware of the verbal patterns they use to emphasize important points, but focused listeners can identify the patterns and use the information to help select the important ideas for their notes.

Information that is written on the chalkboard or charts or graphs that are displayed on an overhead projector are actually visual clues that information is important. As the information is discussed, you have another verbal clue that the chart, graph, or information on the board is important. If it were not important, why would the instructor spend time displaying it? Information on the board or on overheads should appear in your notes on a regular basis.

Watch your instructor's **nonverbal clues** or patterns as well. Body stance, hand gestures, and facial expressions (forehead wrinkles, eyebrows rise) are nonverbal clues that communicate to observant listeners. If the instructor pauses to look at his or her notes or simply pauses to allow you time to write, the pauses are nonverbal clues. Writing information on the board, pointing to parts of it over and over, and circling words on the board are also nonverbal clues indicating that information is important.

Copy Every Step in Math Problems and Write Explanations for Each Step

The majority of lecture time in math classes involves the discussion and explanation of solving math problems. As the instructor writes math problems on the board, strive to copy the exact information in your notes. Next to each step of the problem-solving process, write brief explanations or paraphrase the instructor's explanation of the step. Include as much other information as possible, such as when to use a given theorem or sequence of problem-solving steps. If you miss some information, insert question marks; you can return to these questions marks after the instructor completes the problem, or you can refer to your textbook to fill in the missing information.

Finding Solutions to Common Notetaking Problems

Learning to take effective lecture notes occurs through experience with different teachers, lecture styles, and content. The following problems that you may encounter in taking lecture notes are common to many college students. Solutions for these problems follow.

- "Keeping up" even after using the techniques previously discussed
- A wandering mind because of a slow lecture style
- Sidetracking by the instructor
- Spelling problems
- Poor concentration and inattentiveness
- Disorganized notes
- Lectures that follow the book exactly and move too quickly
- Frustration and the tendency to stop writing

Solutions to Common Notetaking Problems

1. To help you "keep up," leave a gap and continue, or shift to paragraph form.
2. Use active listening techniques when the rate of speech is too slow.
3. Take notes on "sidetracking."
4. Spell as it sounds and check the spelling later.
5. Use active listening techniques to combat inattentiveness, boredom, or poor concentration.
6. Work with your notes immediately after the lecture.
7. Highlight and take notes in the book instead of on paper when the lecture follows the book.
8. Keep writing even though information is difficult, confusing, or unorganized.

Leave a Gap or Shift to Paragraphs

If you fall behind, do *not* stop writing and decide to just listen. Instead, leave a gap in your notes and start taking notes again for as long as you can keep up with the instructor. After class, ask another student or the instructor to help fill in the gaps. The more you practice and use the strategies in this chapter, the less frequent and the smaller will be the gaps in your notes.

You can also shift to paragraph form. Notes are definitely easier to work with when they are clearly organized. However, you will encounter times when you simply cannot keep up with the instructor and organize your notes at the same time. If you find yourself slowing down by trying to decide if a detail is a supporting detail or one that should be indented, shift to writing in paragraph form. Simply keep writing what you hear; paraphrase by restating the information in your own words or write abbreviated sentences. Later, when you have more time, you can reread the paragraph and organize it in a more meaningful way when you make the recall column.

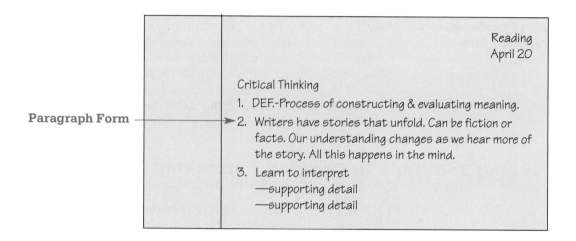

Reading
April 20

Critical Thinking
1. DEF.-Process of constructing & evaluating meaning.
2. Writers have stories that unfold. Can be fiction or facts. Our understanding changes as we hear more of the story. All this happens in the mind. ← **Paragraph Form**
3. Learn to interpret
   —supporting detail
   —supporting detail

Use Active Listening

There are times when you may find your mind wandering because the speaker is talking too slowly. Again, the problem is attributed to a discrepancy between rates. The *rate of speaking* may be one hundred words or less or an example may go on too long to be meaningful. The **rate of thinking** is about four hundred words per minute. Your mind is moving much more quickly than the words of the speaker. The result is often daydreaming, doodling, or losing focus. In addition to the listening techniques covered at the beginning of this chapter, the following techniques can help you become an active listener:

Keep Writing Even if the details do not seem vital to your notes, write them anyway. You can always eliminate them later by not including them in the recall column of your notes. By continuing to write, you remain actively involved with the lecture.

Mentally Summarize In your mind, run through the main ideas and the supporting details that have been discussed. Try to mentally review and summarize them.

Anticipate the Next Point With focused listening, you can often tune in to the speaker's outline. Keeping in mind the points that have already been discussed, anticipate or guess the next point. Then listen carefully to determine whether your prediction was correct.

Mentally Question the Information Ask yourself several basic questions. Do you agree with the information? Does it agree with the textbook? Does it go beyond the textbook? How does it relate to other areas previously presented?

Take Notes on Sidetracking

Some organizational problems occur because the instructor **sidetracks** by discussing something that does not seem to fit the outline of the lecture. When you know this has happened, continue to *take notes on any of the "sidetracked" information* that may be important. Try to organize this information under headings with main ideas and important supporting details. Where should you place this information in your notes? There are two options that work well:

- Since you are taking notes on only one side of the paper, use the back side of the previous page of notes. Record your sidetracked notes here.
- Continue to take notes in the Cornell column. When you finish taking the sidetracked notes, draw a box around this information to set it off from your regular set of notes.

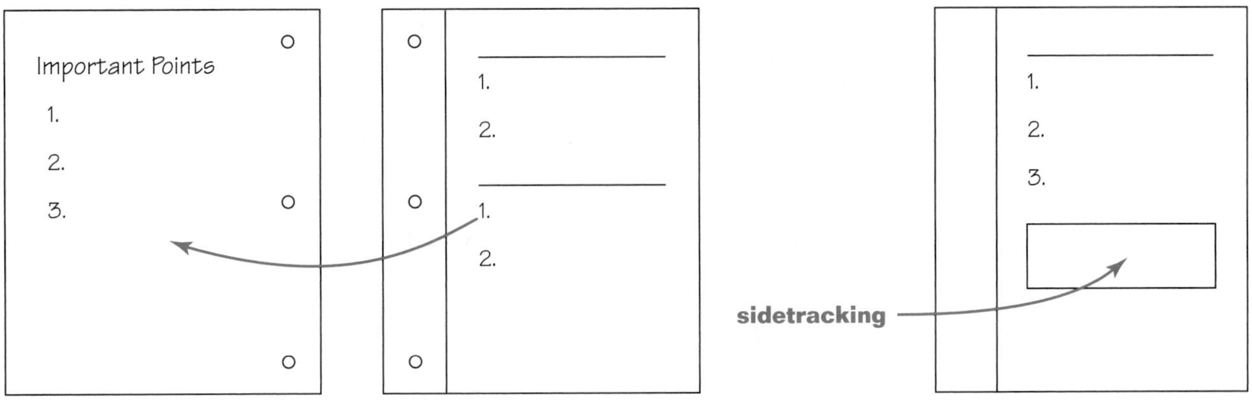

Spell What You Hear

Write what you hear, even if you know it is misspelled. As soon after class as possible when you develop the recall column, correct the spelling by any of the following methods:

- Use a portable spell checker or language master for quick correcting.
- Enter the word on a computer and run the spell checker command.
- Check the textbook chapter, index, or glossary.
- Use a reference book of common misspellings and correct spellings.
- Ask another student for the correct spelling.
- Use a dictionary. (This is the most lengthy process if your spelling is too far from the correct spelling.)

Many strategies are available to help you, an adult, learn to be a better speller and "sound words out" more accurately. You may shudder at the thought of a spelling class if you remember the problems you had in your younger years. Good news! Approaches in teaching spelling have changed drastically over the years, so explore the new strategies and take the initial steps to become a stronger speller.

Use Active Listening Strategies

Review the section on active listening, and then identify specific strategies you can use to strengthen your listening skills. You can also use the following techniques to increase your attentiveness, concentration, and listening comprehension:

1. Sit near the front of the room. You will encounter fewer distractions and be able to see the board or the overhead screen more easily.
2. Set goals for yourself that include specific strategies you wish to implement during lectures. This may include becoming comfortable with asking questions, using techniques to eliminate internal and external distractions, creating a stronger interest in the subject, or using mental discipline to follow your instructor's lecture outline.
3. Be prepared by having sufficient notebook paper, pencils or pens, and your textbook ready to use at the beginning of the lecture. Begin notetaking as soon as the lecture begins; continue taking notes through to the end of the class.

Work with Your Notes

A time-management technique discussed in Chapter 3 (page 70) recommends that you schedule a study block as soon after a lecture class as possible so you can work with your notes while the information is still fresh in your mind. During this study block, work with your notes in the following ways:

1. Add missing details or fill in gaps that you left in your notes. Confer with other students or your instructor, or refer to your textbook for missing information.
2. If your notes appear disorganized, you do not need to rewrite them simply for the sake of producing a neater set of notes. Instead, find ways to add more structure or organization to the existing notes. You might want to insert headings or number individual details. You might want to highlight the most important information or circle important terminology. Since you will be working mainly with your recall column, your time will be better spent creating an organized recall column than it would rewriting your notes.
3. On the back side of the opposing page, you can make lists of important information, a brief outline of the key points, or a list of questions you would like to ask in class.
4. Some students insist on rewriting their notes or typing them on a computer. Some teachers advise against this practice because of the time involved. For many students, this advice is good; time can be better spent on reciting, reflecting, and reviewing activities. However, students who are kinesthetic or highly visual may find value in rewriting or typing notes. The physical process of rewriting boosts memory and recall of the information. If this is the case, rewriting notes, reordering information, and adding more structure to the notes is a meaningful and effective use of time.
5. After you have spent some time rereading your notes, focus on creating an effective recall column. Begin by moving the headings from your notes into the recall column. Reread each section of your notes; create study questions in the recall column. Because the study questions function as a form of self-quizzing, do not include answers. Add individual words, such as terminology, in the recall column so you can practice reciting definitions. Remember that a well-organized recall column that will guide you through the reciting process is more important than organized notes in the right column.

Highlight and Take Notes in the Book

You will encounter a wide variety of lecturing styles in college. Lecturing straight from the book is not very common, but it does occur. If you try taking notes from a teacher who lectures from the book, the rate of speech is too rapid. When this occurs, save the Cornell notetaking for later. Instead, follow along in the book. Highlight the points as they are mentioned in class. Make marginal notes throughout the book. After class, if you want to have Cornell notes as one of your methods of studying for the class, use the highlighting, the marginal notes, and the organizational structure (headings and subheadings) to guide you in making Cornell notes.

Keep Writing

One of the most common mistakes students make when information is difficult, confusing, or unorganized is to stop writing and just listen. In actuality, this is the time that writing is more important than ever. If you can write down the information, even if you are not understanding what is being said and have difficulties paraphrasing, the information you write will provide you with material to look over later, to ask other students or the teacher about, and to compare to the information in the textbook. So, when the task gets difficult, *keep writing.* You can sort it out later.

Exercise 10.3 Lecture Notes on Vocabulary

If your instructor elects to use this exercise in class, he or she will present a lecture on vocabulary skills. *As you listen to this lecture, take a complete set of Cornell notes. Your instructor may then provide you with a sample set of notes for comparison. Though your notes will not be identical to the sample notes, your notes should contain the same main ideas and similar supporting details. The Assessment Form on page 279 may be used to evaluate your notes.*

Exercise 10.4 Taking Lecture Notes

Select any one of your classes. Use the Cornell system to take notes from one of the lectures. On your own paper, identify the class, the topic, and the instructor's name. Answer the following questions. Turn your answers in with your lecture notes. (Your lecture notes may be evaluated by the Assessment Form on page 279.)

1. What problems did you have taking notes from this lecture?
2. What are possible solutions for the problems you had?
3. How soon after the lecture did you work on the recall column? Did this seem effective? Why or why not?
4. Did the recall column work for you? Did it give you enough or too much information to help you with reciting? Explain.

EXERCISE 10.5 Case Studies

Each of the following case studies describes a student situation. Read each case study carefully; highlight key ideas or student issues. On separate paper, answer the question that ends each case study. In your response, address the key points that you highlighted and that directly relate to the question. Use complete sentences in your answers. These case studies are also available online; you can email your response to your instructor or print a copy of your work online.

1. Calib has learned the five *R*'s of Cornell. His notes are well organized; his recall columns give complete lists or complete sentences to summarize his notes. To study and review his notes, he rereads the recall column. Calib usually does well on all the test questions that cover the textbook information, but he frequently misses questions that come from lectures. He does not understand why, since it seems to him his notes are thorough and he spent time reading the recall columns. How does he need to modify his approach?
2. Kimberly is very uncomfortable sitting in a classroom. She often feels like other students are watching her so she sits in the back corner. She has a lot of problems taking notes. Her notes are too brief and ineffective for studying. Sometimes she has problems with her notes because she cannot clearly see what is written on the board. Other times she simply loses her concentration by watching other students. When she does try taking notes, she cannot write fast enough to get all of the teacher's words on her paper. What would you recommend?
3. Alex has an outgoing personality. He enjoys discussions and contributing his ideas in class. However, he frequently annoys his classmates and instructors during lectures. He seems to verbalize every thought that enters his head. Thinking he is participating in class, he often interrupts the instructor with irrelevant questions, or he asks the instructor to repeat information or slow down so he can write the information in his notes. What techniques does Alex need to learn in order to be a more effective listener and positive contributor to the class environment?

Exercise 10.6 LINKS

Work in groups of three or four students. On legal-sized paper or chart paper, draw and label the Information Processing Model. Use your understanding of the listening process and the five R*'s of the Cornell notetaking system to show what occurs in each step of the Information Processing Model when you take and study lecture notes. You and the members of your group may be asked to explain your work to the rest of the class.*

Reflection Writing 3 — CHAPTER 10

On a separate piece of paper or in a journal, do the following:

1. **Discuss specific difficulties you have taking lecture notes for two or more of your classes.**
2. **For each class, discuss techniques you can use to overcome these difficulties to create more effective lecture notes.**

Cornell Notetaking Assessment Form 1

Name ________________ Date ________ Notes for ________________

Strengths of Your Notes

Your Notes Column

_____ You clearly showed and underlined the headings.
_____ Your notes will be easier to study because you left a space between new headings or sections of information.
_____ Your notes show accurate and sufficient details.
_____ You used meaningful phrases or shortened sentences effectively so the information is clear and understandable.
_____ You paraphrased and shortened information effectively and captured the important ideas.
_____ Your notes are well organized. You effectively used numbering and indentations for supporting details.
_____ You included important visual information that appeared on the board or the overhead.
_____ Your notes are neat and easy to read.
_____ You used notetaking standards effectively: you wrote on one side of the paper, you included a heading, and you numbered pages.
_____ You completed your notes by filling in any gaps, correcting spelling, or adding details after class.

Your Recall Column

_____ You used a 2½-inch column.
_____ You placed your headings, questions, and key words directly across from the information in your notes.
_____ Your questions and key words are effective.
_____ Use the recall column to check its effectiveness. Add more self-quizzing questions, visual cues, or hints to guide reciting if necessary.

Areas for Improvement in Your Notes

_____ Strive to identify and underline headings.
_____ Leave a space before you begin a new heading or section of information so your notes will be less crowded or cluttered.
_____ Include more information in your notes. Your notes lack some important details.
_____ Short phrases or isolated words lose meaning over time. Use more sentences or more detailed phrases to capture important ideas.
_____ Use paraphrasing or shortened sentences to capture the important ideas. Your notes are unnecessarily lengthy.
_____ Strive for clearer organization. Number and indent supporting details.
_____ Include information that appears on the board or the overhead.
_____ Strive for neater penmanship and readability.
_____ Write on one side of the paper. Include a heading on the first page. Number all the pages of your notes.
_____ Complete your notes by filling in any gaps, correcting spelling, or adding details after class.

_____ Use a 2½-inch column on the left.
_____ Place the headings, questions, and key words directly across from the information in your notes.
_____ You need more meaningful questions and key words in the recall column.
_____ You are giving yourself too much information in the recall column; use questions without answers so you will have more to recite.
_____ Use the recall column to check its effectiveness. Add more self-quizzing questions, visual cues, or hints to guide reciting if necessary.

Other Comments:

Photocopy this form before you use it.

Cornell Notetaking Assessment Form 2

Name ______________________ Date ________ Notes for ______________________

Strengths of Your Notes

Your Notes Column

______ You clearly showed and underlined the headings.
______ Your notes will be easier to study because you left a space between new headings or sections of information.
______ Your notes show accurate and sufficient details.
______ You used meaningful phrases or shortened sentences effectively so the information is clear and understandable.
______ You paraphrased and shortened information effectively and captured the important ideas.
______ Your notes are well organized. You effectively used numbering and indentations for supporting details.
______ You included important visual information that appeared on the board or the overhead.
______ Your notes are neat and easy to read.
______ You used notetaking standards effectively: you wrote on one side of the paper, you included a heading, and you numbered pages.
______ You completed your notes by filling in any gaps, correcting spelling, or adding details after class.

Your Recall Column

______ You used a 2½-inch column.
______ You placed your headings, questions, and key words directly across from the information in your notes.
______ Your questions and key words are effective.
______ Use the recall column to check its effectiveness. Add more self-quizzing questions, visual cues, or hints to guide reciting if necessary.

Areas for Improvement in Your Notes

Your Notes Column

______ Strive to identify and underline headings.
______ Leave a space before you begin a new heading or section of information so your notes will be less crowded or cluttered.
______ Include more information in your notes. Your notes lack some important details.
______ Short phrases or isolated words lose meaning over time. Use more sentences or more detailed phrases to capture important ideas.
______ Use paraphrasing or shortened sentences to capture the important ideas. Your notes are unnecessarily lengthy.
______ Strive for clearer organization. Number and indent supporting details.
______ Include information that appears on the board or the overhead.
______ Strive for neater penmanship and readability.
______ Write on one side of the paper. Include a heading on the first page. Number all the pages of your notes.
______ Complete your notes by filling in any gaps, correcting spelling, or adding details after class.

Your Recall Column

______ Use a 2½-inch column on the left.
______ Place the headings, questions, and key words directly across from the information in your notes.
______ You need more meaningful questions and key words in the recall column.
______ You are giving yourself too much information in the recall column; use questions without answers so you will have more to recite.
______ Use the recall column to check its effectiveness. Add more self-quizzing questions, visual cues, or hints to guide reciting if necessary.

Other Comments:

Photocopy this form before you use it.

SUMMARY

- Listening is an active process that involves understanding and attaching meaning to what you hear.
- A wide variety of factors influence a person's ability to be a good listener. They include attitude, interests, environment, experiences, learning styles, and personal background.
- The process of listening occurs in five steps: reception, attention, perception, assignment of meaning, and response. Each of these steps corresponds to steps in the Information Processing Model.
- Twelve different strategies can be used to strengthen your active listening skills:

  1. Eliminate distractors.
  2. Pay attention to levels of information.
  3. Stay tuned in.
  4. Monitor your emotional response.
  5. Create an interest.
  6. Ask relevant questions.
  7. Be nonjudgmental.
  8. Posture and position yourself for listening.
  9. Visualize the topic and content.
  10. Paraphrase the speaker.
  11. Pay attention to nonverbal clues.
  12. Enroll in a listening class.

- The same five steps for the Cornell notetaking system for textbook notes are used for lecture notes: record, reduce, recite, reflect, and review.
- Discrepancies between the rate of speech (100–125 words per minutes) and the rate of writing (30 words per minute) can create notetaking problems. You can overcome the effects created by these discrepancies by familiarizing yourself with the topic, paraphrasing, using abbreviations and symbols in your notes, using modified printing, and frequently practicing your notetaking skills.
- Techniques for organizing information involve listening for key words, terminology, important details, ordinals, and examples.
- Verbal and nonverbal clues often signal important information to include in your notes. For math classes, your notes should include nonverbal or visual clues (problems written on the board and solved in class) and verbal clues (explanations for each step of the math problem).
- Learning to take effective lecture notes requires that students adjust to a variety of teachers, lecture styles, and content. Additional notetaking strategies exist to deal with specific notetaking problems. These include:

  1. Leaving gaps or shifting to paragraph form
  2. Using active listening techniques to combat slow rates of speech
  3. Taking notes on sidetracking information
  4. Spelling unfamiliar words by the way they sound
  5. Using active listening techniques to combat inattentiveness and poor concentration
  6. Organizing notes by working with them immediately after a lecture
  7. Highlighting and taking notes in the textbook for lectures that follow the textbook
  8. Continuing to write even though information is difficult, confusing, or unorganized

ACE Practice Tests, which are scored online, supplementary exercises, enrichment activities, and related web site links are available online for *Essential Study Skills*, 4e. Use the following directions to access this web site:

Type: **http://college.hmco.com/collegesurvival/students**

Click on *List of Sites by Author*. Use the arrow to scroll down to Wong *Essential Study Skills*, 4e. Click on the title. If you are working on your own computer, bookmark this web site.

LEARNING OPTIONS

The following learning options provide you with opportunities to demonstrate your understanding of the topics in Chapter 10. Your instructor may assign one or more specific options or may ask you to select one or more options that interest you the most.

1. Expand the Chapter 10 mapping on page 259. Reread the information under each heading in your textbook. Extend branches on the mapping to show important key words or phrases for each heading. You can add pictures and colors to your mapping to accentuate the points. (See the example in Chapter 1, page 25.)
2. Create a listening log for one week. Record the various situations you encounter in which you need to assume the role of a listener. Record the situation and your listening behavior. Discuss any specific listening strategies you were aware of using. Evaluate your effectiveness in each situation; include suggestions for ways you could have handled the listening situation even more effectively.
3. Use the Internet or your library system to locate an informative web site or periodical for the topic *listening* or *listening skills.* Print or copy the information. Prepare a short presentation or a written summary of the most significant information. In your presentation or summary, explain how the contents of the web site or the periodical relate to the content of Chapter 10.
4. Conduct an Internet search for the topic *lecture notes.* Print the web sites that are informative and provide new information on lecture notetaking. Prepare a handout that gives the web site addresses and a brief summary of each web site. This handout may be distributed to other class members, so give due attention to its accuracy and visual format.
5. Create a poster, a collage, or a brochure that depicts one of the following: the steps in the listening process, techniques for active listening, or notetaking skills for lectures. You may use magazine pictures, photographs, your own drawings, or computer graphics. Organize the information in a logical, appealing manner. Provide written explanations as needed to convey significant points about your project.
6. Form a group with three or more students to meet outside class for notetaking practice. Each student needs to prepare a five-minute lecture-style presentation that provides information about a topic from one of his or her classes. The other students in the group practice taking notes on the presentation. Each presenter should then discuss his or her main points and details so the group members can evaluate the completeness of their notes. Complete sets of notes for each presentation need to be turned in after the group work is finished.
7. Compile a set of three or more lecture notes that show the content of three lectures from any of your classes. You may substitute lecture notes with notes from videotapes if you prefer. (Check your school library for available videotapes for topics that interest you.) When you turn in your notes, be sure to complete the recall column and include the source of your information.

CHAPTER 10 REVIEW QUESTIONS

True-False

Carefully read the following sentences. Pay attention to key words. Write T *if the statement is true. Write* F *if the statement is false.*

______ **1.** Active listening involves attaching meaning to verbal and nonverbal communication.

______ **2.** A person's levels of concentration, motivation, stress, and intent affect his or her listening effectiveness.

______ **3.** In the listening process, a person provides a verbal or a nonverbal response after he or she has received, attended to, perceived, and assigned meaning to the content of a spoken message.

______ **4.** Creating an interest in a subject and visualizing the information presented by the speaker are two strategies that help to strengthen a person's listening skills.

______ **5.** When you fall behind and miss information in a lecture, you should stop writing and rely on your auditory memory skills.

______ **6.** During a lecture, you should develop the recall column whenever the rate of speech of the lecturer slows down or the lecturer spends excessive time expanding an example.

______ **7.** Listening for key words that signal headings, writing and underlining headings, numbering major points under headings, and leaving two inches of space between each new heading are effective strategies for creating well-organized notes.

______ **8.** You can increase your speed of writing lecture notes by paraphrasing, using abbreviations and symbols, writing shortened sentences, and using a form of modified printing.

______ **9.** When you begin to lose your concentration because the speaker is talking too slowly, you can maintain your level of concentration by summarizing the lecture information, anticipating the next point, or creating mental questions about the content of the lecture.

______ **10.** Some listening problems stem from the differences that occur in the average rate of speech (100–125 words per minute), the average rate of writing (30 words per minute), and the average rate of thinking (400 words per minute).

Listing

List the 5 R's of Cornell notetaking. After each step, briefly explain what you do during that step.

Short Answer and Critical Thinking

1. Briefly discuss two *external factors* and two *internal factors* that may affect a person's ability to be an active listener.

2. Label the five steps of the listening process. Below each step, briefly define or explain what happens during that step.

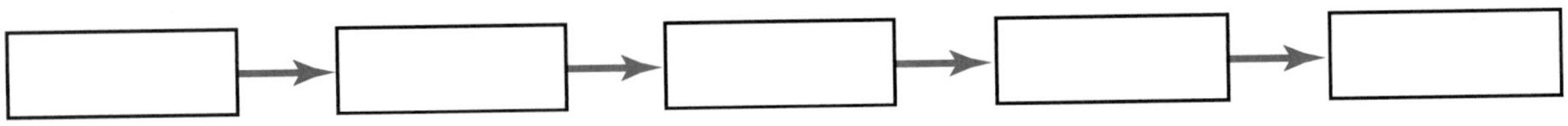

3. Marshall becomes easily frustrated when he needs to take lecture notes in his math class. He doesn't understand the terminology his instructor uses, so he quickly loses his focus on the lecture. He struggles to see the problems on the board and to get the problems written in his notes. What notetaking strategies do you recommend Marshall learn to use to produce a higher-quality set of lecture notes?

CHAPTER 11

Using a Variety of Notetaking Systems

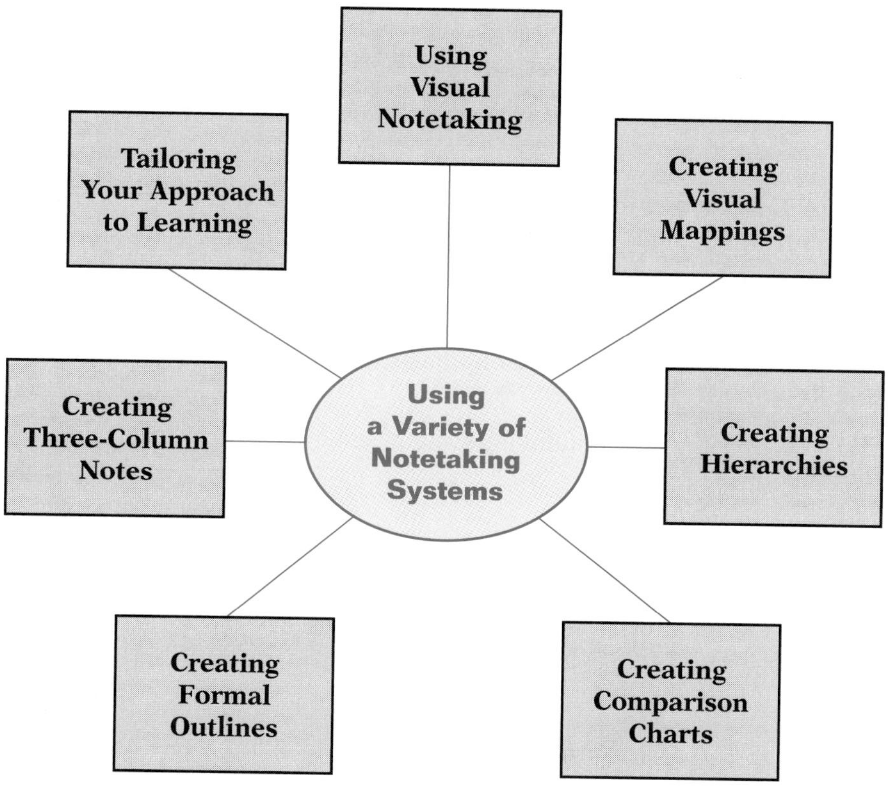

Terms to Know

visual notetaking
visual mappings
level one information
level two information
level three information
hierarchies
comparison charts
formal outlines
Roman numerals
three-column notes

Tailoring your approach to learning involves becoming familiar with an array of strategies, learning to use the strategies, and then selecting those strategies that work most effectively for you and the content or course you are studying. Visual notetaking provides you with an avenue to use your visual skills and creativity to capture important information in the form of visual mappings, hierarchies, or comparison charts. Structured formal outlines are another option that provides you with a study tool for reciting and explaining information. The last notetaking option in this chapter, the three-column notes, provides you with an alternative format that can serve multiple functions. By learning to use all of these notetaking options, you will be better equipped to individualize the process of learning to achieve greater success.

CHAPTER 11 Using a Variety of Notetaking Systems Profile

DO, SCORE, and **RECORD** your profile before you read this chapter. If you need to review the process, refer to the complete directions given in the profile for Chapter 1 on page 2.

ONLINE: You can complete the profile and get your score online at this textbook's web site.

	YES	NO
1. I am comfortable reorganizing or rearranging information instead of studying it in the same order it was presented.	______	______
2. I use reciting frequently when I study.	______	______
3. I draw various kinds of pictures to help me remember what I have read.	______	______
4. I understand the concept of different levels of information and know how to show these levels in my notes.	______	______
5. I learn main ideas well but I often overlook important details.	______	______
6. I use these two principles of memory frequently when I study: recite and review.	______	______
7. I close my eyes or look up into the air to visualize or picture charts.	______	______
8. When I recite, reflect, and review, I stop to get feedback so that I know whether I am remembering information correctly.	______	______
9. I know how to make mappings, hierarchies, comparison charts, formal outlines, and three-column notes.	______	______
10. I am familiar and comfortable with one specific notetaking system, so I use that system in all notetaking situations.	______	______

Reflection Writing 1

CHAPTER 11

On a separate piece of paper or in a journal, do the following:

1. Discuss your profile score for this chapter. What was your score? What does it mean to you?
2. Do you currently have one specific type of notetaking system that you use consistently, or do you use a variety of notetaking methods? Briefly describe your current approach to taking notes.
3. Discuss the benefits you will gain by knowing how to use a variety of notetaking formats.

Tailoring Your Approach to Learning

Learning effective college study strategies involves becoming familiar with an array of strategies, learning to use the strategies, and then tailoring your individual approach to learning by selecting the strategies that work most effectively for you and the courses you are studying. In the following list, notice the extent of study skills options you have already learned to use from previous chapters. Needless to say, using *all* of these strategies is not feasible; instead, after experimenting with the strategies, you should select specific ones to incorporate in your personal approach to learning.

1. Strategies that capitalize on visual, auditory, or kinesthetic learning styles (Chapter 1)
2. Strategies for rehearsing and retrieving information along the paths of the Information Processing Model (Chapter 2)
3. Techniques for creating four kinds of time-management schedules that meet your individual needs and lifestyle (Chapter 3)
4. Techniques to keep your momentum to achieve goals (Chapter 4)
5. Strategies to increase concentration, decrease stress, and decrease procrastination (Chapter 5)
6. Mnemonics and other strategies to boost your memory and help you prepare for tests (Chapter 6)
7. Notetaking options to use for the *record* step and study options for the *review* step of SQ4R (Chapter 7)
8. Reading strategies to strengthen comprehension and critical thinking skills (Chapter 8)
9. *Reflect* and *review* options for the Cornell notetaking system (Chapters 9 and 10)

The first seven notetaking options in the following list have been introduced in previous chapters. In this chapter you will learn more about visual mappings, hierarchies, comparison charts, formal outlines, and the eighth option, three-column notes. You may use all of these options for taking notes from textbooks and, with practice, you can also use these options, with the exception of marginal notes, for taking notes from lectures.

What kind of information is presented in an art history course? Which notetaking system do you think would be most helpful in a course such as this?

1. Notes on index cards (see Exercise 4.6, page 106, and Chapter 7, page 183)
2. Marginal notes (see Chapter 7, pages 184–185)
3. Underlining or highlighting (see Chapter 8, pages 219–221)
4. Cornell notes on paper (see Chapters 9 and 10)
5. Visual mappings or hierarchies
6. Comparison charts
7. Formal outlines
8. Three-column notes

The goal of any notetaking system is to capture important information in notes so you have a condensed version of lecture or textbook material that you can use to study and review. You will need to determine in each notetaking situation which of the eight notetaking options seems the most appropriate for the material. Frequently, after you take notes on a lecture or a textbook chapter, you may find that you want to create a second set of notes to *reflect* or *review* the information. Using a different notetaking format for a second set of notes is one kind of *elaborative rehearsal* and application of the Memory Principle of Organization. Though you will want to create your own notetaking options, the following demonstrate several possibilities.

1. Take notes using the Cornell notetaking system. Then use the information in your notes to create a set of index cards. The index cards show key words, short definitions, categories with lists of important information, and study questions with answers.
2. Highlight the textbook. Then make a formal outline of the chapter or a set of Cornell notes to use to recite the main ideas and significant supporting details.
3. Make a set of Cornell notes. Then convert the notes into a visual mapping, a hierarchy, or a comparison chart.
4. Create marginal notes in the textbook. Then convert specific sections of material into a comparison chart or make a set of index cards.

When you are enrolled in a course that is difficult or challenging, you may feel that you need "all the help you can get." You may find using *three* notetaking options is beneficial and provides you with the opportunity to work with the information in a variety of ways. For both lecture and textbook information, experiment with the various notetaking systems and combinations until you find the most suitable approach for the situation and the one that produces the best result.

Using Visual Notetaking

In Chapter 1 you explored your learning styles or learning preferences. If you have strong visual skills, **visual notetaking** such as visual mappings, hierarchies, and comparison charts may become your preferred methods for learning new information.

What are the benefits of converting textbook information into visual notes? How does the use of pictures and color strengthen visual memory?

Although visual notetaking is generally used to create reflect activities, some students become so proficient with visual notetaking that it can replace the Cornell notetaking system. The goal of this book is to help you find the methods that work best for you. Use visual notetaking as your main system of notetaking if it helps you learn and remember new information more easily.

Visual notetaking offers you an opportunity to organize, rearrange, and record information in *creative* ways. It incorporates the use of colors, pictures, symbols, and graphic formats that utilize visual memory skills. Because it draws on your originality, there is more than one way to correctly present information. You do not need to be artistically talented to use visual notes; stick figures or basic sketches are sufficient as long as you understand the pictures you create. Color-coding for levels of information or visual components in your notes accentuates information and strengthens the visual appeal and visual memory. Because visual methods involve a relatively new form of notes, you may at first feel uncomfortable with these methods. Give yourself time and practice to learn these tools; they just may be your key to a stronger memory and system for recalling information quickly.

Students with weak visual skills may want to adapt some of the steps used to study from visual notes. If picturing or visualizing information is a struggle, the following suggestions are recommended; they help transfer the visual aspects of the study tools in this chapter to an auditory approach:

1. Complete the visual notes as discussed in this chapter.
2. Turn on a tape recorder. Look at the visual notes you created.
3. Follow the recommended steps for studying the information. Instead of visualizing, verbalize. Discuss the information out loud and speak in complete sentences.

Creating Visual Mappings

You have already had some experience with **visual mappings** in this textbook. (Note that visual mappings in other textbooks and web sites are also referred to as *cognitive maps, mind maps,* or *clusters.*) You learned the basic techniques for creating visual mappings in the Chapter 1 Learning Options (page 25). You also learned about visual mappings in the Chapter 2 Links exercise (page 52).

Mappings can be used in a variety of ways. You can make a visual mapping of

- A paragraph or a group of paragraphs under one heading.
- A topic or a subject presented in several chapters and lectures.
- Your lecture notes (in addition to Cornell or an alternative notetaking method).
- Information to review for a test.
- Each chapter you have covered.
- Ideas brainstormed for a paper or a speech.

How to Create Visual Mappings

Four basic steps are involved in creating visual mappings. Your choice of borders, shapes, pictures, and colors in each step gives you the opportunity to be creative.

How to Create Visual Mappings

1. Write the topic in the center of your paper (level one information).
2. Write the main ideas or the main headings; use lines to connect them to the topic (level two information).
3. Add major details to support the main ideas (level three information).
4. Add any necessary minor details.

Write the Topic In the center of your paper, write **level one information**—the topic. The topic can be the title of a chapter, the name of a lecture, or the subject you wish to map. For example, SQ4R is a subject, not the name of a chapter or a lecture.

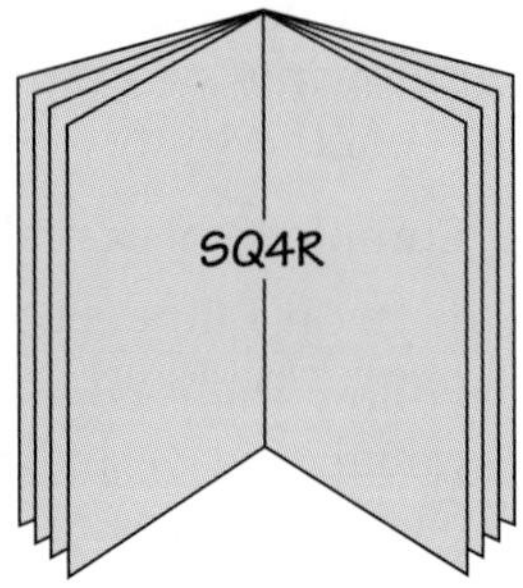

Border The border can be a box, a circle, or even a picture. If you are making a mapping of types of real estate investments, you may want the center picture to be a house or a building. If you are making a mapping on memory, you may want the center picture to be a person's head.

Paper size If you know that your mapping will include many details, you may want to work on legal-size paper (eight-and-a-half by fourteen inches) or drawing paper that is even larger. If your mapping is on a smaller topic, notebook-size paper is sufficient.

Write Main Ideas Next add the **level two information**, the main ideas of the topic. For a visual mapping of a chapter, use the main headings found in the chapter. For a visual mapping of a subject, show the main categories of information related to the subject. (See sample mapping on p. 291.)

Borders, Shapes, or Pictures To make the main ideas or categories stand out, place a border or shape around each item on level two. You may want to use a different shape than you used for the topic. Pictures can be used instead of geometric shapes or pictures can be placed inside shapes.

Colors Some people's memories are strengthened with the use of color. Experiment with colors by shading in the main ideas. Use different colors for each level of information.

Spacing Visually appealing and uncluttered mappings are easier to visualize or memorize. Before you begin adding the level two information, count the number of main ideas to decide how to space them evenly around the page. Place them relatively close to the topic so you'll have room to add details later.

Organization The most common organization for this level-two information is clockwise, beginning at the eleven o'clock position. If there is a definite sequence to the information, such as steps that must be learned in order, you may want to add numbers to the lines that extend from the topic or inside the borders.

Connections Draw a line from each main idea to the topic. This gives a visual representation of their relationship. Each main idea is thus represented as a subtopic of the topic in the center of the paper.

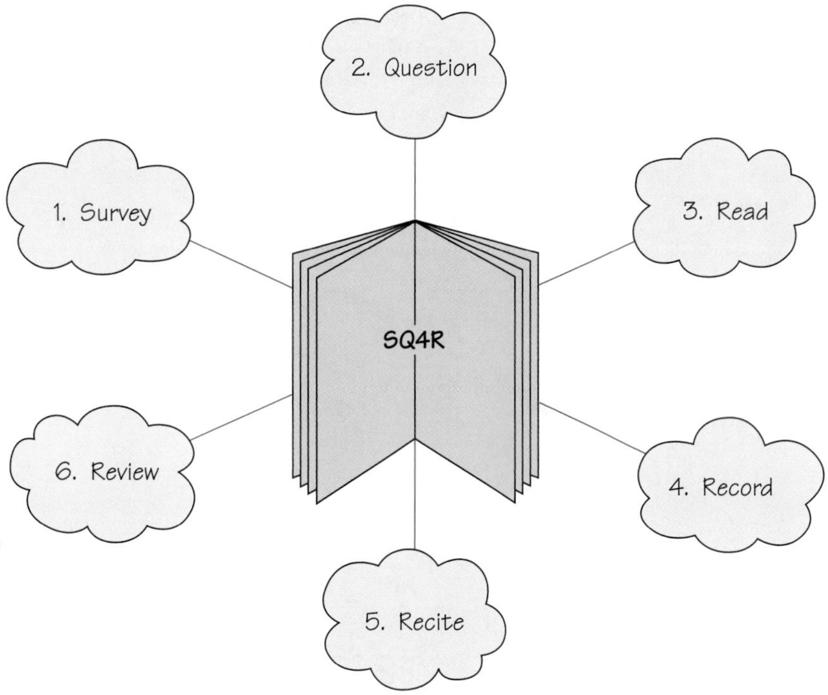

Add Major Details Now add the major supporting details for each main idea. This is the **level three information**. Write only key words that serve as "triggers" for you to recite in full sentences. Avoid the tendency to write long phrases or full sentences; your mapping will become too cluttered. Draw lines from these key words to the main ideas they support. Level three information does not need to be in clockwise order or to start at the eleven o'clock position. (See sample mapping on page 292.)

Quantity of Details Be selective. Include only as many major details as you need to help you remember the important information. You do not need to have the same number of details for each main idea. It is up to you to determine how many details will help your memory.

Horizontal Writing To make your mapping easy to read, keep all your writing horizontal. Avoid writing at a slant or sideways, or turning the paper as you write, resulting in words written upside down.

Borders If the mapping details stand out clearly without borders (as shown in the SQ4R mapping), do not include any. If you are color coding levels of information, you may also want to enclose these major details within a border.

Personalize with Pictures Pictures help imprint the information in your visual memory. Many times it is easier to recall pictures than it is words, so include pictures when appropriate.

Add Minor Details If you need some minor details, use the same guidelines as for major details. (Note the minor details for the record step in the following example.) If you find that you need one or more levels of information beyond the minor details, such as may be the case with a long chapter, consider reorganizing the information into several different topics and creating several mappings. You may find that narrowing or limiting the topic of a mapping will be

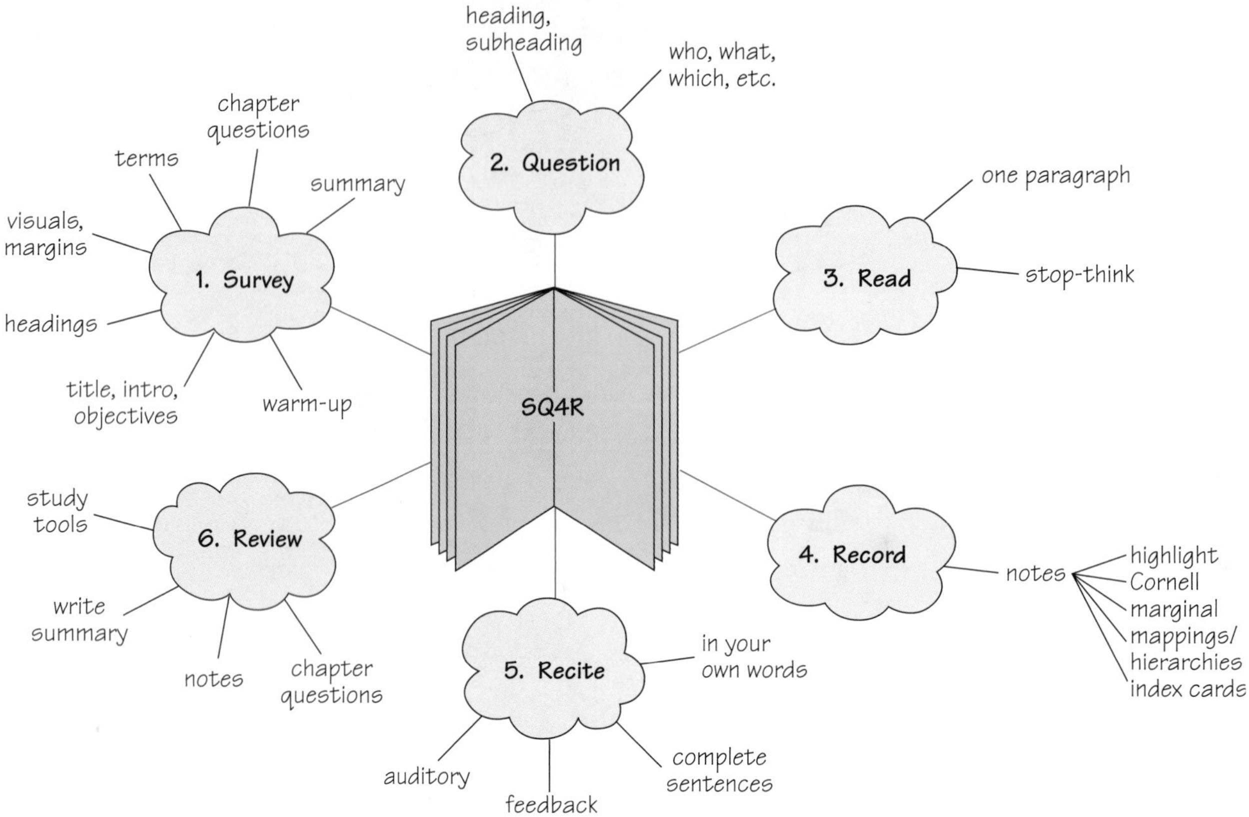

more beneficial for visualizing and studying. By reorganizing, you chunk information into more meaningful groups. Your big picture is not so big that it is difficult to memorize, visualize, or comprehend.

The following mapping on a lecture about vocabulary skills is an example of converting your notes into a mapping. Assume the instructor first discussed two kinds of vocabulary (receptive and expressive) and then discussed six strategies for finding definitions, providing details and examples for each of the strategies. Your visual mapping of the lecture would look something like this:

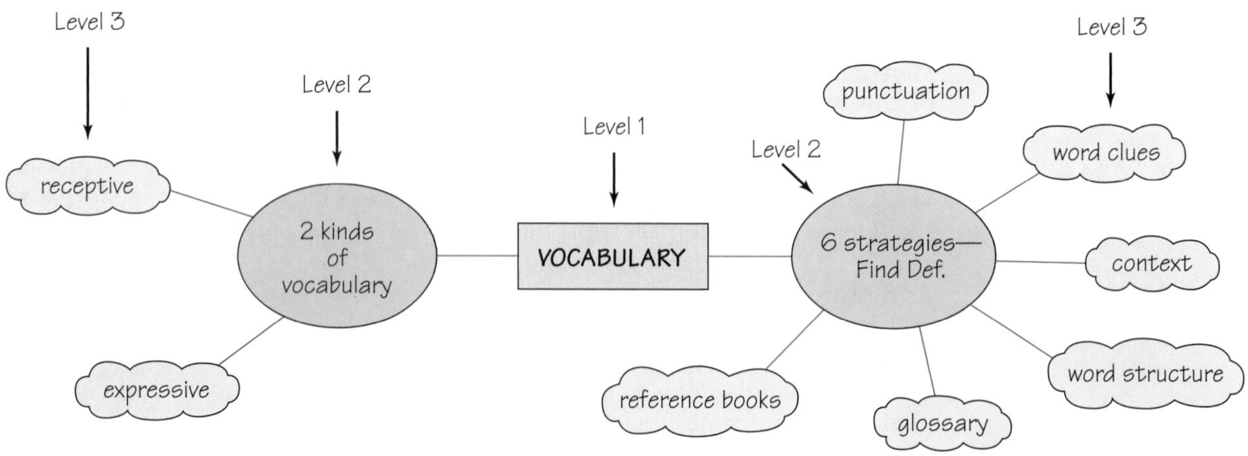

How to Study from Visual Mappings

Visual mappings are powerful and work effectively because they are based on memory principles that boost your ability to learn new information. The information in mappings is organized logically, shows relationships, and helps you associate one idea with another. Concentration and interest increase as you work to present information creatively. As you recite, review, receive feedback, and visualize, the process of learning is enhanced.

How to Study from Mappings

1. Look intently (stare) at your visual mapping until you think you have a mental picture of level one and level two information in your memory.
2. Close your eyes or look away. Visualize and recite the topic (level one information) and each main idea (level two information). Check your accuracy.
3. Visualize one main idea at a time. Recite the details. Check your accuracy.
4. Use reflect activities.
5. Use ongoing review.

Look Intently at Your Mapping Stare at the visual mapping you created. Pay attention to the words, shapes, and colors; try to engrain in your memory the level one topic and the locations and topics of the level two information. Your goal is to carve a mental image of *the level one and level two information,* the skeleton of your visual mapping. You do *not* need to attempt to visually remember the level three information. Move to the next step when you feel you have the mental image learned.

Visualize and Recite the Topic and Main Headings Close your eyes, look away, or look "up and to the left" toward the ceiling. Try to picture the topic and the main ideas of your mapping. Practice seeing the words, the shapes, and the colors (if any were used). Now recite by naming the topic and each of the main ideas. Your reciting may *sound* like this: "In SQ4R, there are six main ideas branching off the topic SQ4R. They are survey, question, read, record, recite, and review."

Check your accuracy Refer back to your mapping to verify that you recited correctly. If you were correct, move on to the next step. If you were not correct, study the skeleton with the topic and the main ideas. Look away to visualize and recite again. Get more feedback.

Visualize and Recite Main Ideas and Details Now that you can clearly picture the skeleton, return to the first main idea. Without looking, try to tell all that you remember about this main idea. Your goal is to include all the key words (major and minor details) that appear on your mapping. When you recite, talk to yourself in complete sentences. It is not necessary to visualize all major and minor details written on your paper. It is important, however, that you include these details in your reciting.

Check your accuracy Refer to your mapping to see whether you included all the major and minor details for the main idea you just recited. Did you forget to include some information? If yes, try reciting and including the information as you look at your mapping. The major and minor details can be visual clues for you. Then look away and recite. Get feedback again to be sure that this time you incorporated the details in your reciting.

Continue this process for each of the main ideas. Do not rush the process; work through each category in a careful, thoughtful way. When you are finished with the entire mapping, move on to a reflect activity.

Use Reflect Activities *You can reflect several ways:*

1. Copy the skeleton of your visual mapping on paper. Then, without referring to the mapping, fill in the words for the topic and the main ideas.
2. Try to redraw the visual mapping with as many major and minor details as possible without looking and without first giving yourself the skeleton.
3. Repeat the process of visualizing and reciting the entire visual mapping. Turn on a tape recorder as you recite. The tape can become auditory notes for review.
4. Convert the visual information back into print form by summarizing. Use the main headings of the visual mapping as your guide and the structure for your summary. Write one paragraph (or more) for each heading. Summarize the details related to that heading. Writing summaries from visual mappings begins to prepare you for essay writing and short-answer questions that may appear on future tests.

Use Ongoing Review Because visualizing does not require you to have materials such as notebooks, paper, or pencil available, you can review any time you have a few available minutes. As you wait in between classes, ride a bus, take a shower, or wash dishes, try to reconstruct the mapping in your mind.

You may want to make a smaller version of your mapping to place on index cards for review. These cards can also be placed around your house where they are easily seen and reviewed.

As you remember, the final step of the Information Processing Model is retrieval. To access this mapping from your long-term memory, practicing retrieval is essential. With more practice, you will see the picture more sharply and more readily.

EXERCISE 11.1 Creating a Visual Mapping

Read the following excerpt from a psychology textbook. Convert the information into a visual mapping. In the center of your visual mapping and for level one information, write Coping Strategies—Cognitive Restructuring. *To add visual appeal and make the information easier to recall later, use colors and/or pictures in your visual mapping.*

Developing Coping Strategies Like stress responses, strategies for coping with stress can be cognitive, emotional, behavioral, or physical. *Cognitive coping strategies* change how people interpret stimuli and events. They help people to think more calmly, more rationally, and constructively in the face of stress and may generate a more hopeful emotional state. For example, students with heavy course loads may experience anxiety, confusion, discouragement, lack of motivation, and the desire to run away from it all. Frightening, catastrophic thoughts about their tasks (for example, "What if I fail?") can amplify stress responses. Cognitive coping strategies replace catastrophic thinking with thoughts in which stressors are viewed as challenges rather than threats (Ellis & Bernard, 1985). This substitution process is often called **cognitive restructuring** (Lazarus, 1971; Meichenbaum, 1977; see Chapter 16). It can be done by practicing constructive thoughts such as "All I can do is the best I can." Cognitive coping does not eliminate stressors, but it can help people perceive them as less threatening and thus make them less disruptive.

Seeking and obtaining social support from others are effective *emotional coping strategies.* The perception that one has emotional support, and is cared for and valued by others, tends to be an effective buffer against the ill effects of many stressors (Taylor, 1995). With emotional support comes feedback from others, along with advice on how to approach stressors. Having enhanced emotional resources is associated with increased survival time in cancer patients (Anderson, 1992), improved immune function (Kiecolt-Glaser & Glaser, 1992), and more rapid recovery from illness (Taylor, 1995).

Behavioral coping strategies involve changing behavior in ways that minimize the impact of stressors. Time management is one example. You might keep track of your time for a week and start a time-management plan. The first step is to set out a schedule that shows how your time is now typically spent; then decide how to allocate your time in the future. A time-management plan can help control catastrophizing thoughts by providing reassurance that there is enough time for everything and a plan for handling it all.

Behavioral, emotional, and cognitive skills often interact closely. Discussing stressors and seeking feedback from others help you think more rationally and calmly, and make it easier to develop and use sensible plans for behavioral coping. When behavioral coping eliminates or minimizes stressors, people find it easier to think and feel better about themselves.

Physical coping strategies are aimed at directly altering one's physical responses before, during, or after stressors occur. The most common physical coping strategy is some form of drug use. Prescription medications are sometimes an appropriate coping aid, especially when stressors are severe and acute, such as the sudden death of one's child. But if people depend on prescriptions or other drugs, including alcohol, to help them face stressors, they often attribute any success to the drug, not to their own skill. Furthermore, the drug effects that blunt stress responses may also interfere with the ability to apply coping strategies. If the drug is abused, it can become a stressor itself. The resulting loss of perceived control over stressors may make those stressors even more threatening and disruptive.

Nonchemical methods of reducing physical stress reactions include progressive relaxation training, physical exercise, biofeedback training, and meditation, among others (Carrington, 1984; Dubbert, 1992; Tarler-Benlolo, 1978).

Bernstein, *Psychology,* p. 478.

Creating Hierarchies

Hierarchies are a form of visual mapping that arrange information in levels of importance from the top down. If visualizing mappings with lines extending in all directions is difficult for you, you may prefer the more organized structure of hierarchies. Three different hierarchies for SQ4R follow:

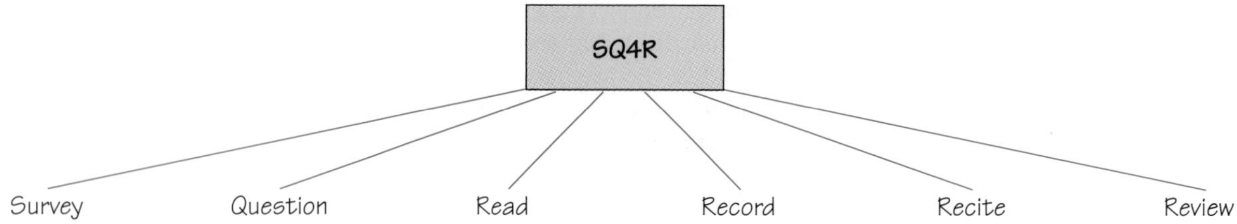

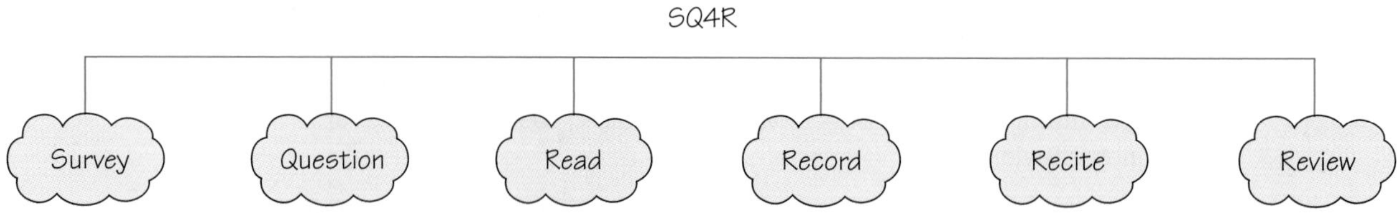

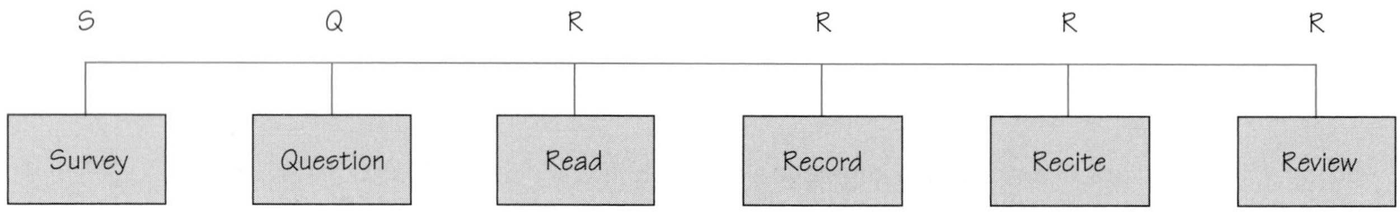

How to Create Hierarchies

The steps for creating hierarchies are similar to the steps for creating visual mappings. The same levels of information are used: topic, main idea, major details, and minor details.

How to Create Hierarchies

1. Write level one information (the topic) on the top line of the hierarchy.
2. Draw lines downward from the topic to show level two information (the main ideas).
3. Under each main idea, branch downward again for level three information (major details).
4. Add level four information (minor details) under the major details if needed.

Write Level One Information Place the topic or the subject on the top line. You do not need to put a box or border around the topic, but you can if you wish.

Show Level Two Information When hierarchies are created for textbook chapters, the headings in the book become level two information. When you create a hierarchy for a general topic such as SQ4R, level two information represents general categories.

Determine the number of main ideas to be placed under the topic. Branch *downward* to level two to write the main ideas. Consider using legal-size paper for more extensive hierarchies. Space the main ideas evenly on the paper to avoid a cluttered or crowded look. Always write horizontally. Try adding color coding and various shapes or pictures to strengthen the visual image.

Many textbooks provide informative introductions; these can be included in your hierarchies under a category labeled "Intro." Key words, concepts, or objectives can now be added to the hierarchy. Another category can also be included, if needed, to show graphs, visual aids, lists of terminology, or any other information you want to remember.

Add Level Three Information Because level three often has numerous supporting details, you need to consider how you will place the details on the paper. To avoid a cluttered or crowded look, the details can be staggered or arranged in a variety of layouts, as shown in the following illustrations.

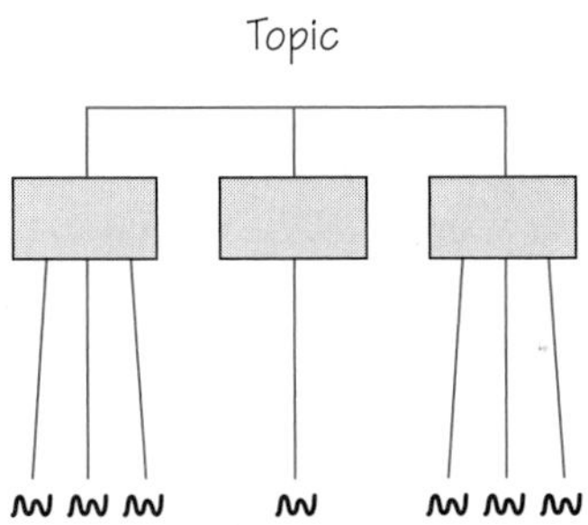

Equal-length lines—on the same plane

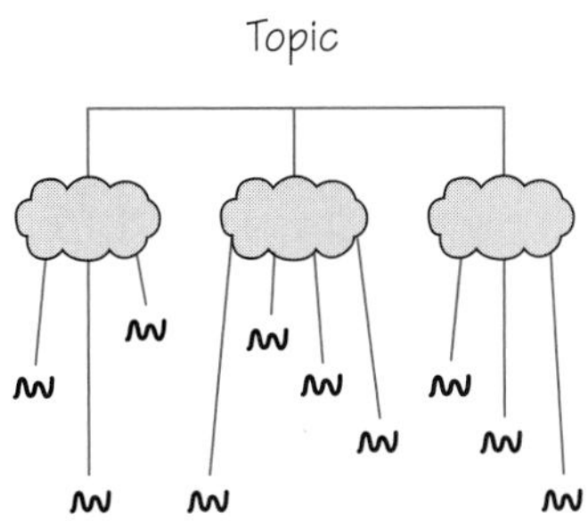

Unequal-length lines—staggered

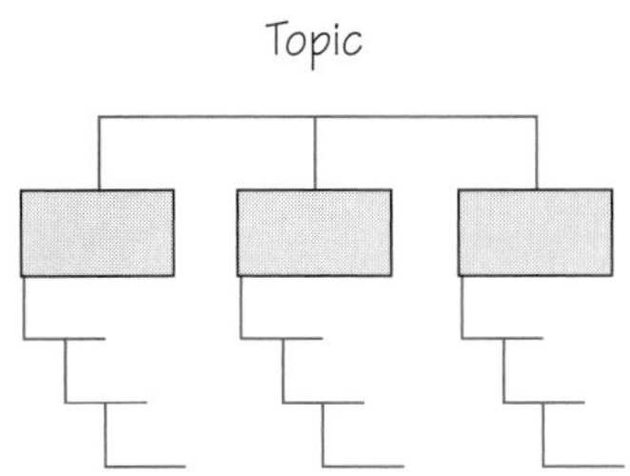

Steps

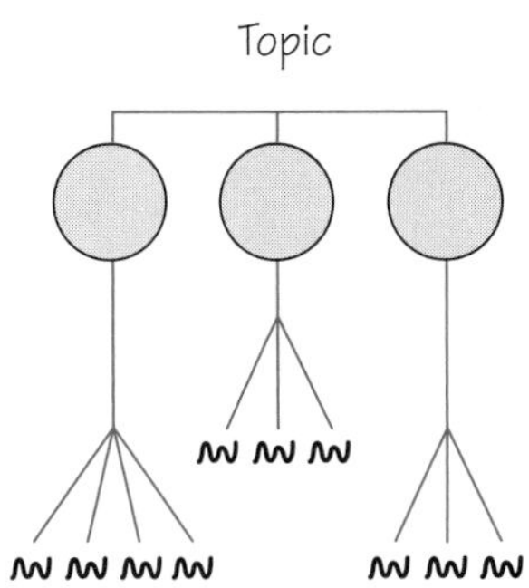

One main line—spread-out lines

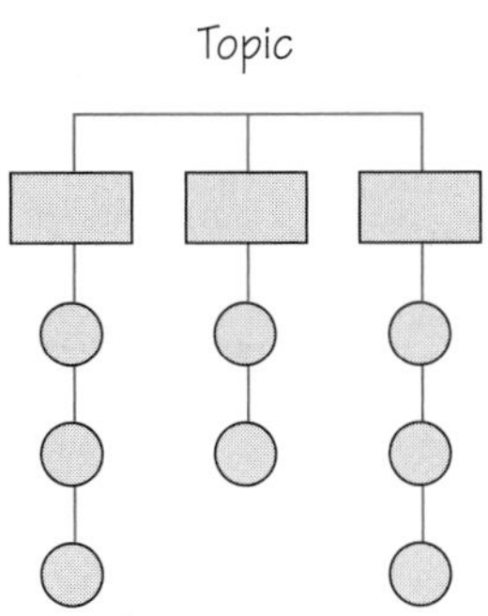

Chain

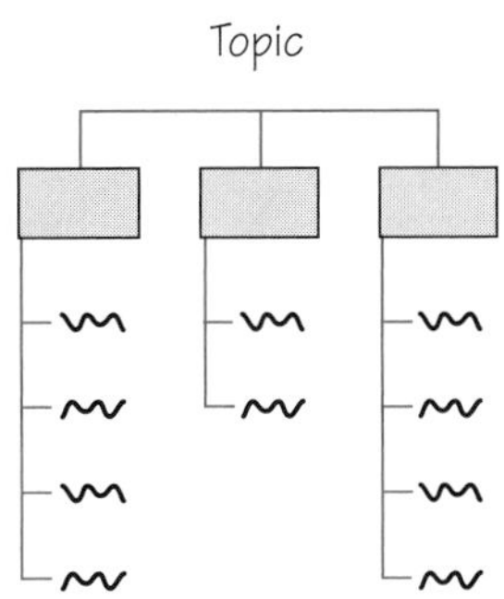

Half ladder

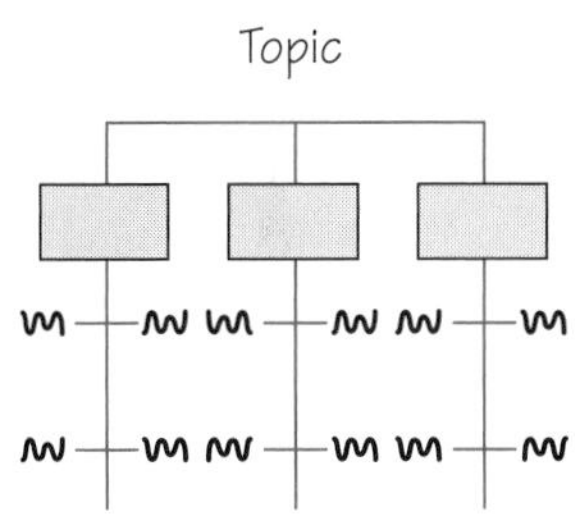

Full ladder

Provide Level Four Information Minor details can be added by branching *downward* from level three. Be selective. Include only essential key words that you feel you need to help you remember the information. Again, select a layout that will organize the details clearly. Borders, pictures, and color coding can also be used.

How to Study from Hierarchies

As with mappings, hierarchies need to be visualized, recited, and reviewed to work as effective study tools. Because the study techniques are the same as those used with visual mappings, they are summarized, rather than detailed, below.

How to Study from Hierarchies

1. Look intently (stare) at your hierarchy until you think you have a mental picture of level one and level two information in your memory.
2. Close your eyes or look away. Visualize and recite the skeleton.
3. Visualize one main idea at a time. Recite the details. Check your accuracy.
4. Use reflect activities.
5. Use ongoing review.

Reciting, reflecting, and reviewing are essential. In Chapter 2 you learned that short-term memory can handle only a limited amount of information at one time. If your hierarchy has more than seven main ideas on level two, you are wise to divide your reciting, reflecting, and reviewing into smaller sections.

For example, if you are studying a mapping or a hierarchy for the Twelve Principles of Memory, find ways to divide the information into smaller parts. Visualize and recite the first section; then continue to work with additional sections. Your reciting may sound like this: "There are Twelve Principles of Memory. The first four are selectivity, association, visualization, effort; they spell the word *SAVE.* The second four spell the word *CRIB:* concentration, recitation, interest, and big picture–little pictures. The last four (*FOTO*) are feedback, organization, time on task, and ongoing review. Selectivity means . . . ."

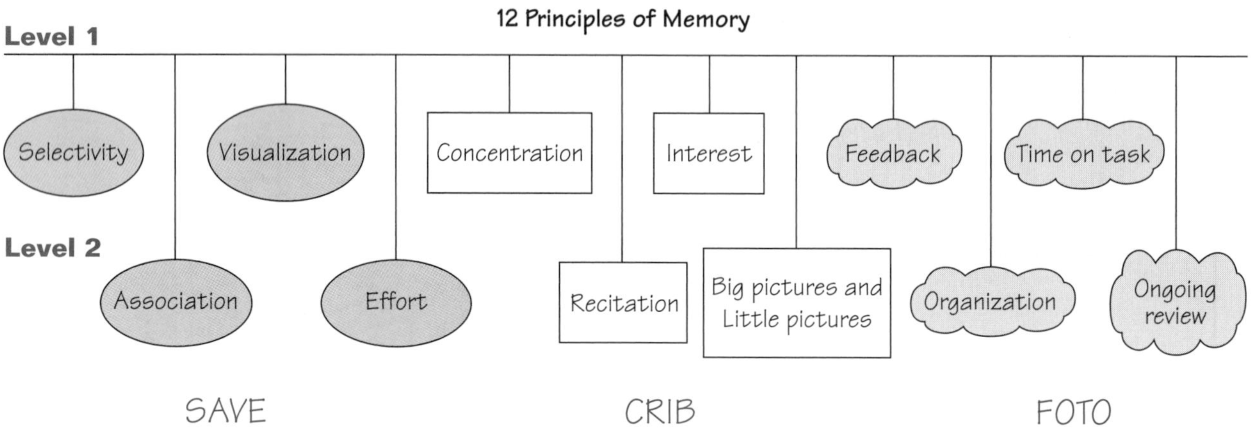

EXERCISE 11.2 Creating a Hierarchy

Read the following information from a chemistry book. Convert the information to a hierarchy. On the top line and for level one information, write The Scientific Method. *Include at least three levels of information on your hierarchy. Note: the last paragraph may help you organize the skeleton of your hierarchy.*

1.3 The Scientific Method

Objectives

- Differentiate among the terms *experiment, law, hypothesis,* and *theory.*
- Describe the scientific method.

The intertwined relationship of experiment and explanation . . . can be found in any modern science. The general scheme for carrying out a scientific investigation is called the *scientific method.* Before we describe this procedure in detail, you should know the precise definitions of several terms, some of which we have already used, such as *experiment* and *theory.* . . .

[A]n important requirement of scientific research is the careful design of experiments. An **experiment** is *the observation of some natural phenomenon under controlled circumstances.* Lavoisier, for example, showed that a component of air combined with mercury when both substances were heated in a closed apparatus. Merely heating mercury(II) oxide in the open would not have allowed him to show that a portion of the air had disappeared. Use of a closed vessel was part of the controlled circumstances of the experiment.

After performing many experiments, a scientist may note some pattern in the results. Scientists express such patterns in the form of a **law,** *a simple generalization from experiment.* We discuss a number of laws in this book, including the law of conservation of mass. That particular law comes from Lavoisier. He saw a pattern in his experiments: There is no change in mass during a chemical reaction.

Experiment and the statement of experimental results as laws are only one aspect of science; another is explanation. Explanation helps us organize knowledge and predict future events. A **hypothesis** is *a tentative explanation of a law, or regularity of nature.* Dalton explained the law of conservation of mass with his atomic hypothesis (later to become the atomic theory). He said that atoms are not created or destroyed during a chemical reaction—they are merely rearranged. Because the atoms have definite masses, the total mass after the reaction is the same as it was before the reaction.

A hypothesis is the starting point for devising new experiments. Having developed a hypothesis for the combustion of mercury in air, Lavoisier set up quantitative experiments to test this hypothesis. A very important part of any scientific investigation is to devise experiments to test whether or not the hypothesis agrees with [the] experiment. If the hypothesis does not agree with [the] experiment, it must be modified or discarded.

Once a hypothesis successfully passes many experimental tests and can explain a large body of experimental facts, it becomes known as a theory. A **theory** is *a tested explanation of some body of natural phenomena.* For example, the atomic theory explains a chemical reaction as the rearrangement of the atoms of the reacting substances to form new atomic arrangements, the products of the reaction. This theory has been tested by many chemical experiments and in each case has agreed with experimental results. Of course, even if an explanation becomes a theory, it may someday need to be modified if subsequent experiments make this necessary. Although Dalton believed that atoms were indivisible, it is now known that under the right circumstances one atom may break apart to form two different atoms.

The **scientific method** is *the general process involving experimentation (controlled observation) and explanation (hypothesis and theory) whereby scientific knowledge grows* (Figure 1.12). The scientist devises a series of experiments to test a hypothesis. As a result of these experiments, the scientist may amplify or modify the hypothesis. This scientist or others may then set up additional experiements to test this new hypothesis, which might result in a modified hypothesis, and so forth. In this way, the hypothesis is refined or is replaced by a better one. Eventually, a hypothesis that appears to agree with many experiments will be called a *theory.*

Adapted from Ebbing, Wentworth, *Introductory Chemistry*, pp.10–11.

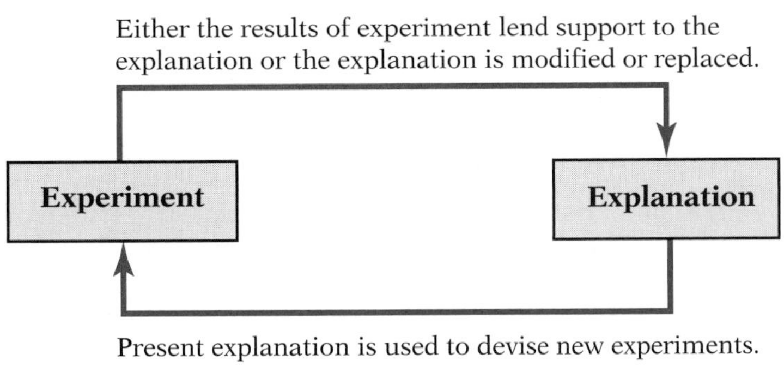
Either the results of experiment lend support to the explanation or the explanation is modified or replaced.
Experiment
Explanation
Present explanation is used to devise new experiments.

Figure 1.12 The scientific method. This diagram shows the interplay between experiment and explanation in science.

Group Processing: A Collaborative Learning Activity

For this collaborative activity, you will need large poster or chart paper and colored pens. Divide the class into eight groups. Complete the following directions.

1. Each group assumes responsibility for developing one of the following:
   a. a **visual mapping** for Exercise 7.5, *Approaches to Psychology,* page 185.
   b. a **hierarchy** for Exercise 7.5, *Approaches to Psychology,* page 185.
   c. a **visual mapping** for *Reasons for Procrastinating,* Chapter 5, pages 128–129.
   d. a **hierarchy** for *Reasons for Procrastinating,* Chapter 5, pages 128–129.
   e. a **visual mapping** for *Basic Memory Processes,* Chapter 9, page 258.
   f. a **hierarchy** for *Basic Memory Processes,* Chapter 9, page 258.
   g. a **visual mapping** of *Maslow's Hierarchy of Needs* (Chapter 9, page 244)
   h. a **hierarchy** of *Maslow's Hierarchy of Needs* (Chapter 9, page 244)
2. Work as a group to convert the information from the textbook into either a visual mapping or a hierarchy according to your assigned directions. Be creative! Be accurate! Be organized!
3. Plan to share your final product with the class.

Creating Comparison Charts

Comparison charts (also known as matrixes, grids, or tables) are designed to organize a large amount of information into a format that is visual and easy to use to compare and contrast information. Comparison charts are organized with columns and rows. The category or characteristics that are being compared or contrasted are placed at the top of each column. The subjects that are being compared or contrasted are placed at the beginning of each row. Whenever you are working with several related subjects that each have specific characteristics, this form of visual notetaking is useful. (For examples of comparison charts, see Chapter 1, Exercise 1.4, or Chapter 5, Exercise 5.2.)

Categories → **Subjects ↓**	**Column 1**	**Column 2**	**Column 3**
Subject A			
Subject B			
Subject C			

How to Create Comparison Charts

In a comparison chart, *columns* run up and down, and *rows* run across the page. Important information about each subject is written inside the boxes (cells). The number of columns and rows is determined by the amount of information being covered. The following steps show how to organize information for matrixes. If you use a computer, matrixes can be made through "table" commands.

How to Create Comparison Charts

1. Identify the number of subjects to be compared or contrasted. Write one subject on each row.
2. Identify the categories of information to be discussed. Write one category at the top of each column.
3. Complete the comparison chart by writing key words in each box where columns and rows intersect.

Identify Subjects and Label Rows Comparison charts are designed to compare or contrast information for two or more subjects, so begin by identifying the number of subjects. Many times the number of subjects (topics) is given in the printed text information. Once you have identified the number of subjects, you can begin to make the rows for your comparison chart. If you have two subjects, your chart will have only two rows. Write the names of the subjects on the rows.

As you become more familiar with visual materials and recognize different kinds of visual materials from your textbooks, you will note that some tables or informational charts in textbooks place the subjects at the tops of the columns instead of at the beginnings of the rows.

Identify Categories and Label Columns Identifying categories requires you to think carefully about the information you have read. What categories of information were discussed for all or most of the subjects? You can almost always use a general category titled "Characteristics," but more specific categories are more useful. The number of categories you select determines the number of columns in your comparison chart. Label the top of each column.

If you have difficulties finding appropriate labels for the columns, try using this approach to help you organize important information for the chart:

1. List each of the subjects across the top of a piece of paper.
2. Under each subject, list important details associated with that subject.
3. Look at your list of details. Can you group the details into larger categories?
4. If you see a logical category of information under one subject, is that same kind of information also given for other subjects? If so, you have discovered an appropriate title for a category.

Complete the Comparison Chart Complete one *column* at a time by providing essential details for each subject that is listed down the side of the chart, or complete all the boxes in one row at a time. With this method, all the essential details about one subject are given before you work with the details of the other subjects.

How to Study from Comparison Charts

When you are the creator of comparison charts, you need to ask yourself, "What information am I expected to know?" For some comparison charts, the most valuable information to know will be patterns or trends. For other comparison charts, you will be expected to know the details within each cell of the chart. Once you are able to identify the information that you are expected to know, you will be able to select the most appropriate methods to study the information.

Reciting and visualizing from comparison charts can be more demanding than reciting and visualizing from mappings or hierarchies because you are telling about more than one subject or main idea. You are also comparing or contrasting it to other subjects or main ideas. If you are expected to know the specific details inside the cells, use the following steps to recite and learn the information.

How to Study from Comparison Charts

1. Name and visualize the topic, the subjects in the rows, and the categories across the top of the comparison chart.
2. Recite information by moving across the rows or down the columns. Check your accuracy.
3. Use reflect activities.
4. Use ongoing review.

Name and Visualize the Rows and Columns The skeleton of the chart includes the title, the subjects written down the side (labels of the rows), and the categories written across the top of the chart (labels of the columns). Take time to create a strong visual image of this chart before reciting information inside the boxes. Explain the chart to yourself as you try to restructure it visually without looking.

Recite and Check Your Accuracy Recite in a logical order. Decide if you want to recite row by row, telling everything about one subject at a time, or column by column, telling how one specific category is used for each of the subjects. After you recite either a row or a column, refer back to the chart to check your accuracy. Immediate feedback is important; recite again if you found that you made mistakes. Continue until you can recite the entire chart.

Use Reflect Activities If adding pictures to visual notetaking helps you remember information, add pictures inside each box. If color helps you remember visual information more easily, add color. You can use colored pencils to shade each subject (each row) in a different color or to complete the boxes of the chart so that the key words appear in different colors.

There are three basic reflect activities that are effective for comparison charts. The first two can be done by looking at the chart.

- Read through the chart row by row. Turn the key words in the boxes into complete sentences. Speak so that the information is clear and organized. Use a tape recorder to record your presentation. Listen to the recorder several times for review. Visualize each part as you hear it on the recorder. Use the same process, reading and speaking in full sentences, as you explain each column.
- With the chart in front of you, write a summary that includes all the key points. First write a summary that explains all the categories one row at a time. Then write a summary that explains one category at a time as it relates to each subject. This activity is basically the same as the first activity above, except that it is a written, rather than a verbal, exercise.
- Try to redraw the entire chart without looking at your original. Label first your rows and then your columns. Go back to each box and fill in the key words.

Use Ongoing Review As with any form of notetaking, comparison charts need to be reviewed often so that they stay fresh and accessible in your mind. Because a comparison chart contains so much information, practice retrieving it frequently.

Exercise 11.3 Case Studies

Each of the following case studies describes a student situation. Read each case study carefully; highlight key ideas or student issues. On separate paper, answer the question that ends each case study. In your response, address the key points that you highlighted and that directly relate to the question. Use complete sentences in your answers. These case studies are also available online; you can email your response to your instructor or print a copy of your work online.

1. Monica, who would like to study graphic arts, is intrigued by the use of visual mappings as a form of notetaking. After some practice, she feels this notetaking approach suits her learning style. The following is her first attempt at creating a visual mapping; she used the information from Chapter 9 on *Chronemics*.

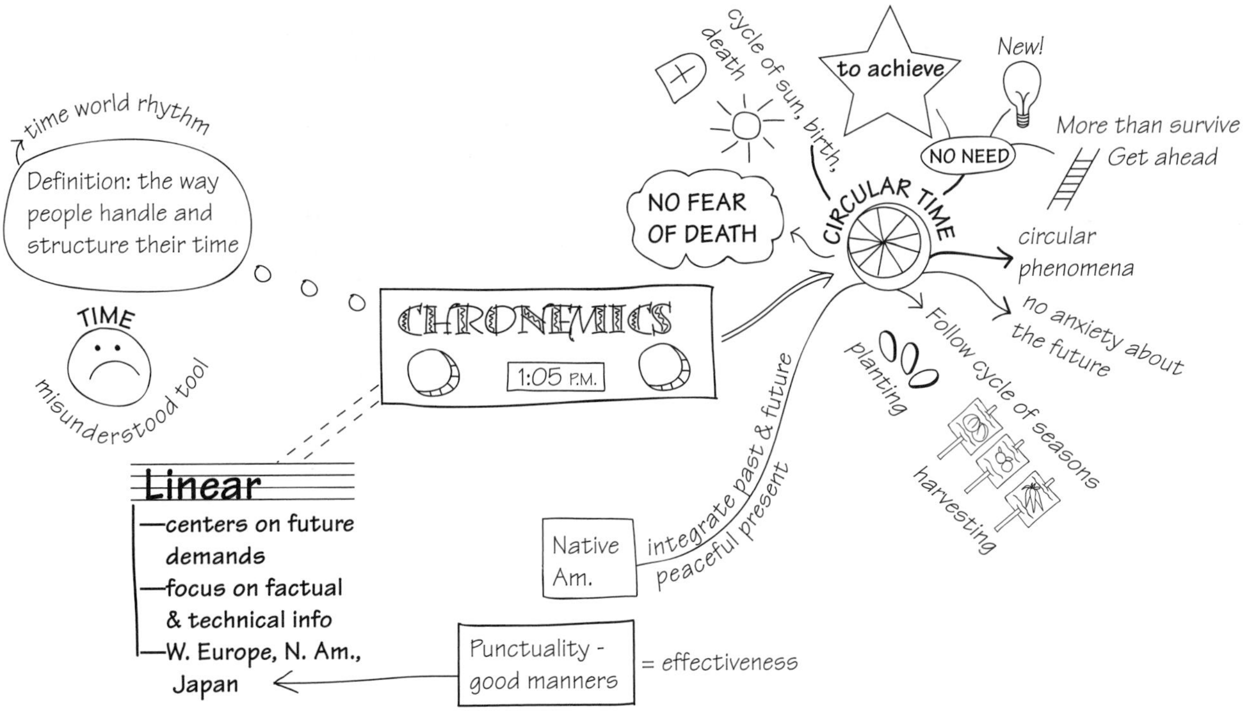

Several students in Monica's study group admired her visual mapping, but Monica was disappointed with the results. She found studying from her mapping difficult because it seemed to her "too busy" and "too disorganized." What techniques could Monica try that might result in a visual mapping that might be easier to read and better suited to her?

2. Darrel prefers organizing information into comparison charts whenever possible. He finds that comparison charts are logically organized and a perfect way to condense large amounts of information. However, he often struggles with the process of identifying the number of columns he needs and then labeling the columns. What suggestions might help Darrel identify and label effective columns for a comparison chart about three Southwest Indian tribes he is studying in his Native American Studies class?

3. Mickey creates many visual mappings and hierarchies as a second form of notetaking after she has taken Cornell notes for a textbook or a lecture. She finds that the process of reorganizing and writing information in her own handwriting helps her remember better. She would like to know how to use her visual mappings and hierarchies to study for tests. What suggestions can you give her?

EXERCISE 11.4 Creating a Comparison Chart

By yourself or with a partner, read the following information about diabetes *carefully. Convert the information into a comparison chart.* Type 1 *and* Type 2 *are your two subjects. You will need to decide on the number of columns, the titles for the columns, and the information to write in each cell.*

Though both Type I diabetes and Type II diabetes are metabolic disorders that affect the way the body uses food, they are more dissimilar than similar. Type I diabetes, the insulin-dependent diabetes, affects 5% to 10% of the 16 million Americans who have diabetes. Type I diabetes surfaces during childhood or young adulthood; for that reason, it is called *juvenile onset diabetes.* With Type I diabetes, the immune system attacks the pancreas and destroys its ability to make insulin. As a result, diabetics need to track the food they eat, their activity levels, and their blood sugar levels several times during the day. They must inject themselves with insulin to keep the body's sugar levels in balance. Type II diabetes has different characteristics. Type II diabetes, the non–insulin-dependent diabetes, affects 90% to 95% of Americans who are diagnosed with diabetes. Type II diabetes usually surfaces after the age of forty. It is called *adult onset diabetes.* With this form of diabetes, the pancreas produces insulin, but the body and its tissues, especially its muscles, do not use the insulin effectively. Type II diabetes is linked to inactivity, weight gain, and obesity. Eighty percent of the people with Type II diabetes are overweight. Type II diabetics can reduce or eliminate the health threats related to diabetes by lifestyle changes, more exercise, better nutritional habits, and possibly medication. Even though Type I and Type II diabetes differ considerably in their time of onset, effects on the body, and forms of treatment, both are autoimmune disorders that must be diagnosed and treated in order to avoid serious, life-threatening health problems.

Modified from Wong, *Paragraph Essentials,* p. 259.

Reflection Writing 2 — CHAPTER 11

1. On a separate piece of paper or in a journal, discuss your reaction to visual notetaking systems such as visual mappings or hierarchies. Are these systems new to you?
2. What do you like and dislike about them? What are the advantages of visual notetaking?
3. Are you familiar enough with these systems that you will use them at times for taking notes or creating review study tools?

Creating Formal Outlines

You may already be familiar with formal outlines because many composition courses require you to include formal outlines with your essays or papers. Recall from Chapters 9 and 10 that in the Cornell notetaking system, formal outlining is not recommended, especially for lecture notes, because too often students spend too much time and concern on the numbering and lettering systems used in formal outlines. However, **formal outlines** created from textbook chapters can be used effectively as study tools to recite and review textbook chapters. If you become comfortable with formal outlines and do not have difficulty organizing information, you can use formal outlines for lecture notes as well.

Using a Formal Structure for Your Outline

In formal outlines you arrange the information in the order in which it is presented. By using Roman numerals, capital letters, numerals, lowercase letters, and numerals inside parentheses, you can show the relationship of the larger concepts to the smaller details. Different levels of information appear in the following standard format.

Title:

I. Main headings or topics appear with Roman numerals.
  A. Subtopics appear with capital letters.
  B. Subtopic
    1. Arabic numerals show important supporting points or details.
    2. Supporting detail
      a. Lowercase letters show minor details.
      b. Minor detail
        (1) Arabic numerals inside parentheses show subideas of minor details.
        (2) Subideas of minor details
  C. Subtopic

The following points are important to use when you create a formal outline using the standard format:

1. When you indent to show a subtopic of a larger category, place the new letter or the new number directly under the first word that appears above in the larger category.
2. Each level of the formal outline must have *at least two subtopics* under each category. If you do not have two items [A, B; 1, 2; a, b; or (1), (2)], try renaming the larger category so you do not end up with only one item under that category. For example, notice how the incorrect form on the left is reworded on the right.

Incorrect	*Correct*
1. Tax benefits a. Individuals	1. Tax benefits for individuals

3. Use **Roman numerals** for main topics. Roman numerals from one to fifteen are written as follows: I, II, III, IV, V, VI, VII, VIII, IX, X, XI, XII, XIII, XIV, and XV.
4. Most outlines consist of key words and short phrases; full sentences are seldom used.

How to Create Outlines for Textbook Chapters

1. Write the chapter number and title on the top of your paper.
2. Locate the first main heading in your textbook. Label it with a Roman numeral.
3. Locate all the subheadings for your main heading. Label them with capital letters.
4. Use numerals and lowercase letters for supporting details under each subheading.
5. Use numerals inside parentheses for smaller details if needed.

Most textbooks provide you with the main headings and the subheadings, so items for the Roman numerals and capital letters are easy to identify and incorporate into a formal outline. At times, however, you may need to create your own subheadings to reflect the important information in the chapter. (For example, compare II. Strengthening Your Listening Skills to the textbook, page 265. Notice how subheadings did not appear in the textbook, so the person creating the formal outline read the information carefully and assigned two important topics to the outline as main topics with capital letters.) More careful thought must be given to the supporting details, the information in your outline that appears with lowercase letters and numerals inside parentheses. By using the main headings and the subheadings in Chapter 10, the beginning of a formal outline for the chapter would show the following:

Chapter 10: Listening and Taking Lecture Notes

I. Understanding Listening Skills
  A. Influencing Factors
    1. Listener's attitude
    2. Speaker's form of delivery
    3. Listener's level of familiarity and understanding
  B. Steps in the Listening Process
    1. Reception
    2. Attention
    3. Perception
    4. Assignment of Meaning
    5. Response
II. Strengthening Your Listening Skills
  A. Active Listening
  B. Twelve Strategies

EXERCISE 11.5 Completing an Outline

Use the beginning outline for Chapter 10. Complete the outline by referring to the headings and subheadings of your book. Add as many key words or phrases as you feel are valuable to have in your notes. Write your formal outline on your own paper.

How to Study from Formal Outlines

Outlines provide an excellent study tool to practice reciting, which involves explaining information *out loud* and *in complete sentences.* Reciting from outlines provides you with immediate feedback about your level of understanding and recall of textbook information. As a study tool, you may break away from the formal structure by adding clue words, specific facts, or other kinds of information that you need to learn or failed to include initially in your reciting.

How to Study from Formal Outlines

1. Read one line or item at a time; explain the line or item by reciting.
2. Check your accuracy or completeness.
3. Add clue words to the right of the lines or items.
4. Repeat the process of reciting from the outline.

Read and Explain Begin with the first Roman numeral on your outline. Read the information on that line of the outline. Then begin the process of reciting. Tell what you know about the topic. Speak in complete sentences; imagine you are explaining the information to someone who is unfamiliar with the topic. This form of reciting promotes integration of information that you have learned; you do not have to limit what you recite to the structure of the outline. Instead, make a concerted effort to link ideas together and explain relationships clearly.

Check Your Accuracy or Completeness As you recite, you will quickly become aware of your level of comfort and familiarity with the topic. Listen to what you say when you recite. If some information does not sound accurate or complete, use this feedback wisely. Refer to your textbook to check your accuracy or see what kinds of information you did not include in your reciting.

Add Clue Words You can break away from the formal structure of the outline at this point by jotting down key words or details that you did not initially include in your reciting. These clue words can guide you through the reciting process the next time you use your outline to review the contents of the chapter. You may want to write your clue words in a different color so they stand out more readily. The following example shows clue words that a student added for several sections of part B of the Chapter 10 outline. He added the clue words because of feedback he received during the initial attempt to recite from his outline.

B. Steps in the Listening Process
   1. Reception *auditory and visual stimuli*
   2. Attention
   3. Perception *evaluate what makes sense/understand*
   4. Assignment of Meaning
   5. Response *verbal or nonverbal feedback; intellectual or emotional*

Creating Three-Column Notes

In Chapter 9 (page 242), you learned about making three-column reflect pages for math textbooks. Key words or key components in a math problem appeared in the left column. The center column stated the math problem or formula.

Explanations or rules used to solve the math problem appeared in the right column. Thus, each column had a distinct purpose.

You can use **three-column notes** in many creative ways and for many purposes; the following illustrations provide you with a few of the possibilities. You are encouraged to explore other uses for this system, which helps you compile information from more than one source or break information into separate aspects so the individual parts are easier to learn and remember.

Example 1:
Select key topics or concepts. Write the term in the left column. Compile your textbook notes in the middle column. Refer to lecture notes on the same concept. Add additional information that your instructor provided to reinforce the textbook information.

Topic/Concept	**Textbook**	**Instructor**
product life cycle	1. Introduction 2. Growth 3. Maturity 4. Decline	Class example: 3M (Post-it Notes) Sony digital cameras

Example 2:
Write the key term, concept, or formula in the left column. Write the definition, explanation, or steps in the middle column. In the right column, list or discuss applications.

Topic/Concept	**Definition or explanation**	**Applications—when, where, how to use**
infomercial	A form of television advertisement that appears as a 15–30-minute program	Often used with exercise equipment and videos (ex. Tae-Bo), weight loss programs, cosmetics, and "get rich quick" programs.

Example 3:
Write the original math problem in the left column. You may want to use this format throughout the week to write random math problems discussed in class, or you may want to write only the problems that you initially worked incorrectly. Leave the middle column blank until you are ready to rework the problem. Write the original solution on the right. When you rework the problem, *fold the right column back* so you cannot see the solution. Unfold the column to check the accuracy of the problem you reworked.

Original math problem	**Space to rework the problem**	**Original solution from textbook or class**
Leave the answer in exponential form: $4^5 \times 4^7$		$4^5 \times 4^7 = 4^{5+7} = 4^{12}$

Exercise 11.6 LINKS

Work in a small group, with a partner, or on your own to create a comparison chart for the different kinds of notetaking systems you can use. Identify the characteristics or elements you would like to discuss for each of the notetaking systems below; use this information to label the columns in your comparison chart. You may use as many columns as you wish; however, you must include at least two *columns. You may be asked to share your work with the class.*

	?	?	?
Cornell notes			
Visual mappings			
Hierarchies			
Index cards			
Outlines			

Reflection Writing 3 — CHAPTER 11

On a separate piece of paper or in a journal, do the following:

1. **Discuss any changes you have made in your attitude toward notetaking. Be specific.**
2. **Which forms of notetaking do you prefer? Does your preference vary by class? Which forms of notetaking are easier for you to use when you study and review? Explain.**
3. **What do you see at this time as your biggest notetaking challenge or difficulty? What ideas or plans do you have for overcoming this challenge?**

SUMMARY

- Tailoring your approach to learning involves understanding and knowing how to use a variety of strategies and then selecting the strategies that work most effectively for you and the courses you are studying.
- Visual notetaking, which includes visual mappings, hierarchies, and comparison charts, provides you with creative ways to organize and record important information that you need to learn.
- You can use visual mappings to record information from individual paragraphs, chapter headings, complete chapters, lectures, or for specific topics to review for tests or to use in papers or speeches. Visual mappings include multiple levels of information. Level one information is the topic. Level two information shows the main ideas. Level three information consists of supporting details.
- A hierarchy is a form of visual mapping that arranges information in levels of importance from the top down. As with visual mappings, the use of colors and pictures enhances the effectiveness and recall of visual information.
- To study from visual mappings and hierarchies, begin by visually memorizing the skeleton of your drawing. The skeleton consists of the topic and the main ideas. Recite the details for each main idea; check your accuracy by referring to level three information in your drawing.
- Comparison charts organize large amounts of information into columns and rows. List the subjects in the left column. Identify categories

of information; label each column with these categories. Use key words or short phrases in the cells of the comparison chart to show similarities and differences among the subjects.

- Formal outlines use a standard structure consisting of Roman numerals, capital letters, Arabic numerals, and lowercase letters to show levels of information and their relationships to each other. After you create a formal outline, you can use it to recite the information and receive feedback. You may add clue words to your formal outline to guide you in the process of reciting.
- Three-column notes provide you with a notetaking system that compiles information from more than one source or separates information into three distinct categories. This form of notetaking is ideal for review work and test preparation.

ACE Practice Tests, which are scored online, supplementary exercises, enrichment activities, and related web site links are available online for *Essential Study Skills*, 4e. Use the following directions to access this web site:

Type: **http://college.hmco.com/collegesurvival/students**

Click on *List of Sites by Author.* Use the arrow to scroll down to Wong *Essential Study Skills*, 4e. Click on the title. If you are working on your own computer, bookmark this web site.

LEARNING OPTIONS

The following learning options provide you with opportunities to demonstrate your understanding of the topics in Chapter 11. Your instructor may assign one or more specific options or may ask you to select one or more options that interest you the most.

1. Expand the Chapter 11 mapping on page 285. Copy this structure on a blank piece of paper. Reread the information under each heading in your textbook. Extend branches on the mapping to show important key words or phrases for each heading. You can add pictures and colors to your mapping to accentuate the points.
2. Convert the chapter mapping on page 285 to a hierarchy. Include at least three levels of information. You can add pictures and colors to your hierarchy to accentuate the points.
3. Use the Internet to locate informative web sites for one topic: *visual mapping, visual notetaking, mind mapping,* or *clustering.* Print the information. Make a list of the web sites with their URLs (web site addresses); include a brief summary of the contents of each web site. Organize your information neatly and accurately, as your list may be copied for the class.
4. Apply one of the forms of notetaking from Chapter 11 to one of your textbooks from a different class. Take notes on the entire chapter. If the chapter is more than fifteen pages long, take notes on just the first fifteen pages. Schedule a time to meet with your instructor so he or she can compare your notes to the textbook pages.
5. Work with a partner to create a formal outline for Chapter 11. Recite from your outline; ask your partner to listen to your reciting and give feedback about the completeness and accuracy of your explanations. Then listen to your partner recite from his or her outline.
6. Use your library to locate a magazine article about a topic that interests you. Photocopy the article. Create a visual mapping, hierarchy, classification chart, or formal outline for the information in the article. Turn in the article with your final work.
7. Create a three-column set of notes to review ten or more problems from your math textbook or math lectures. Fold the right column back before you rework the problems. After you rework the problems and check your accuracy, write a one-paragraph summary of the effectiveness of this system.

Chapter 11 REVIEW QUESTIONS

Multiple-Choice

Choose the best answer *for each of the following questions. Write the letter of the best answer on the line.*

______ **1.** Visual mapping can be used to
a. take lecture notes.
b. take textbook notes.
c. make reflect activities.
d. All of the above

______ **2.** Hierarchies
a. use rows and columns.
b. show only the main ideas of what you read or heard.
c. contain the same information found on visual mappings.
d. always arrange information chronologically.

______ **3.** Visual notetaking requires the use of
a. visualization.
b. creativity.
c. recitation.
d. All of the above

______ **4.** If you have large amounts of information for a visual mapping,
a. use complete sentences.
b. use larger paper.
c. omit some ideas.
d. All of the above

______ **5.** It is acceptable to
a. write full sentences in each cell of a comparison chart.
b. write sideways if needed.
c. add information to a visual form of notetaking after you begin reciting.
d. None of the above

______ **6.** When you first visualize your notes, you should
a. try to see the skeleton first.
b. be creative and make changes as you go.
c. stare at the paper for five minutes.
d. add new information that you forgot to put in the original mapping.

______ **7.** Feedback
a. is nonessential when you work with visual notetaking.
b. lets you know how well you are learning.
c. comes only in auditory form.
d. requires that you work with a partner.

______ **8.** Reflect activities may include
a. making tapes as you recite in full sentences.
b. reproducing the visual notes from memory.
c. summarizing the information in new ways.
d. All of the above

______ **9.** To avoid having cluttered hierarchies,
a. stagger the information on lower levels.
b. write more complete sentences.
c. eliminate some main ideas.
d. eliminate some key words.

_______ **10.** When reciting is done with visual notetaking, it should
a. begin from the bottom up.
b. move counterclockwise.
c. go from details, to main ideas, to topic.
d. go from topic, to main ideas, to details.

_______ **11.** The columns on comparison charts
a. show the percentages to use.
b. show the categories, characteristics, or traits to be compared and contrasted.
c. cannot contain more than five cells.
d. label the rows to be studied.

_______ **12.** In the structure of a formal outline for textbook information,
a. capital letters reflect the primary headings in the chapter.
b. Roman numerals reflect the main headings in the chapter.
c. lowercase letters appear immediately under information that is labeled with capital letters.
d. it is acceptable to have only one item under a larger category.

_______ **13.** When you study from a formal outline, you should
a. read the outline out loud at least three times.
b. re-create the outline from memory and then check your accuracy.
c. include only two levels of information.
d. add clue words if you need additional guidance for the reciting process.

_______ **14.** The three-column notetaking system can be used to
a. compile lecture notes and textbook notes for a specific topic.
b. summarize two different parts or aspects of a specific term or concept.
c. rework math problems that initially caused you some problems.
d. All of the above

_______ **15.** When you need to take notes from a lecture or a textbook, you should
a. select a notetaking format that seems best suited for the material.
b. begin with one notetaking format and then consider creating a second type of notes to reflect on or review the information.
c. include elaborative rehearsal strategies as part of your learning process.
d. All of the above

Short Answer—Application

Create a hierarchy *to show eight different notetaking options available to you when you need to take notes from a textbook. You only need to include two levels of information on your hierarchy.*

CHAPTER 12

Developing Strategies for Objective Tests

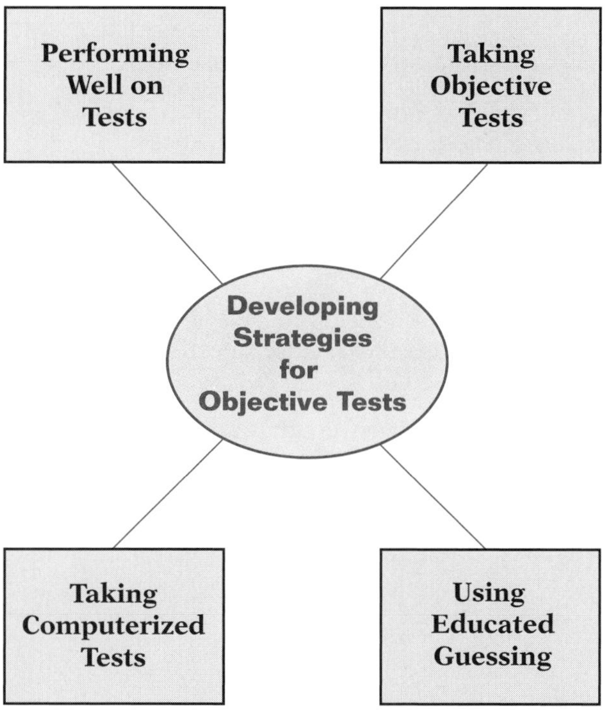

You can increase your performance on tests by using strategies to calm your mind, create quick test plans, increase your concentration, manage your time well, and take advantage of four levels of response for answering questions. This chapter focuses on answering objective questions, which include true-false, multiple-choice, and matching questions. You can use educated guessing strategies for these types of test questions, but educated guessing should only be used as a last resort and after you have tried immediate, delayed, and assisted responses. Many of the strategies in this chapter apply to computerized tests as well as to handwritten tests. Using the skills in this chapter will help you improve your test performance.

Terms to Know

four levels of response
immediate response
delayed response
assisted response
educated guessing
objective tests
memory search
negatives
modifiers
100 percent modifiers
in-between modifiers
definition clues
relationship clues
stem
options
distractors
paired associations
word or grammar clues
wild-shot guess

CHAPTER 12 Developing Strategies for Objective Tests Profile

DO, SCORE, and **RECORD** your profile before you read this chapter. If you need to review the process, refer to the complete directions given in the profile for Chapter 1 on page 2.

ONLINE: You can complete the profile and get your score online at this textbook's web site.

	YES	NO
1. I am able to answer true-false questions without making many mistakes.	______	______
2. True-false questions confuse me because I do not understand what they are asking.	______	______
3. I read both columns of items on a matching test before I even begin answering.	______	______
4. I have a system for answering matching questions so that I do not use an answer twice.	______	______
5. I watch for modifiers such as *no, never, some, few, always,* and *often* because they can affect the meanings of questions.	______	______
6. I can tell when a question is testing a definition or a cause/effect relationship.	______	______
7. I make too many careless mistakes on tests.	______	______
8. I turn each part of a multiple-choice question into a true-false question before I select a final answer.	______	______
9. The first time I work through a test, I leave blank the answers that I do not know and then return to them when I have time.	______	______
10. I use other parts of the test to help me find answers I don't immediately know.	______	______

Reflection Writing 1 — CHAPTER 12

On a separate piece of paper or in a journal, do the following:

1. Discuss your profile score for this chapter. What was your score? What does it mean to you?
2. Describe your general performance level and confidence level for taking tests that involve true-false, multiple-choice, and matching questions.

Performing Well on Tests

In Chapter 6, you learned strategies to prepare for tests and to reduce test anxiety. You are now ready to focus your attention on strategies to use *during* tests to increase your performance and your grades.

Begin with a Calm Mind

Feeling slightly nervous or apprehensive when you first enter the classroom or when the instructor distributes the test is a normal reaction to testing situations. Strive to focus your mind on the test and prepare yourself mentally for the challenge as quickly as possible. The following tips can help you get off to a positive start.

1. *Use a familiar relaxation or visualization strategy that you learned in Chapters 5 and 6.* This will not take long but will help you calm your nerves and set the stage for concentration.
2. *Jot down important information that you may want to refer to during the test.* As soon as you receive your test, jot down any formulas, mnemonics, lists, or facts that you want to be sure to remember accurately during the test. You can jot this information on the back of the test, in the margins, or on a blank piece of paper if your instructor allows you to use paper to organize ideas.
3. *Listen carefully to the directions.* Your instructor may announce corrections on the test, suggestions for completing the test, the amount of time available for the test, or other important instructions. You may save yourself stress or confusion by listening to your instructor's initial directions.

Create a Quick Plan

1. *Survey the test.* Glance through the test to become familiar with the types of questions used, the point value of different sections of the test, and the overall length of the test. Be sure to check if questions appear on the backs of the test pages.
2. *Budget your time.* Take a minute or two to estimate the amount of time you will spend on each section of the test. This is especially important if you have essay questions because essay answers require adequate time to organize, develop, and proofread. If you wish, jot down estimated times to begin each section of the test.
3. *Decide on a starting point.* Many students prefer to work through the pages of a test in the order in which the questions are presented. Recognize, however, that you do not have to do the test pages in order. Decide which section of the test you would like to do first; you may feel more comfortable with one kind of question format, or you may feel more confident about the content of a specific section of the test. Quickly decide which section of the test will be your starting point.

Maintain a Focus on the Test

1. *Read all the directions carefully.* For multiple-choice questions, note whether more than one answer per question can be used. For matching questions, note whether items can be used more than once. If the directions are long or confusing, take time to circle the key words in the directions to help you understand them accurately. Ask for clarification if the directions still are not clear.
2. *Recognize and deal with signs of test anxiety.* As soon as you start feeling panicky or frustrated, your attention shifts away from the test. You may begin negative chatter or negative self-talk, or your eyes may start jumping

from one line to another or skipping over words in the questions. Try these methods to get yourself back on task:

- Become more active and interactive with the test. Circle direction words so they stand out more clearly. Underline key words in directions and in questions.
- Mouth or whisper the directions or questions to yourself. This activates your auditory channel so you call on more than one sense to help you.
- Use your arm or a blank piece of paper to block off the rest of the test. Restricting your vision to the question you are contemplating helps you focus and helps calm your mind.
- Use positive self-talk. Remind yourself that you have prepared for this test, that you are capable of figuring out the answer, and that you can work to do your best.

3. *Ignore other students.* Do not watch other students or compare your progress with theirs. Work at your own pace rather than the pace set by one or more other students. Avoid wasting valuable test time by worrying about others or watching how they are handling the test. Ignore students who finish early and leave; an early departure does not necessarily mean those students knew the material better than you or that they performed better than you. The students who are the last to finish the test are some of the best test takers, for they use all the available time to complete and check their answers.

Manage Your Time Well

1. *Use your test time wisely.* If you have time available after you have answered all the questions, proofread for mistakes and strengthen any answers. Students often wonder whether they should change answers when they proofread. Do *not* change answers if you are panicking or feel time running out. *Do* change answers if you can justify the change; perhaps other questions on the test gave you clues or helped you recall information that would lead to a different answer.
2. *Do not leave answers blank if you start to run out of time.* You will automatically lose points if you do not write *some* kind of answer. When you feel you are running out of time, pick up your pace, which means you may not be able to reason or ponder questions as carefully. At times you may even need to guess at answers or jot down partial answers to avoid leaving blank spaces instead of answers.

Use Four Levels of Response

Some students who have not learned effective test-taking strategies move through a test methodically. They read a question, answer it the best way possible, and move to the next question; this process continues until they reach the end of the test. Performing well on tests is often the result of moving through tests by completing some answers, leaving some questions blank and returning to them later, and changing some answers if proofreading time is available. Performing well also improves when students understand that taking objective tests involves **four levels of response**, which are explained in the following chart.

Levels of Response	Description
Immediate response	As soon as you read the question, you immediately know the answer. The question automatically triggers an association to information in your long-term memory. This is the payoff for effective studying.
Delayed response	When you cannot immediately respond, read the question a second time. Do a quick memory search; try to recall the information by linking or associating key words in the question to information in your long-term memory. Try *visualizing* the information as it appeared in your notes, in your study tools, in the textbook, or in the lecture. If no answer surfaces, *place a small checkmark next to the question and move on to other questions.* Return to the question after you have answered as many questions on the test as possible.
Assisted response	Return to the unanswered questions. Use other parts of the test to help you find possible answers. Skim through the test and look for key words that appear in the question. Information used in other questions may assist you in finding the information you need or may trigger an association that will lead you to the answer.
Educated guessing	Use educated guessing strategies only when all else fails. These strategies are not guaranteed to work all the time, but they may improve your odds in selecting the correct answer. Educated guessing strategies are *never* more effective than arriving at the answer through other means.

Group Processing: A Collaborative Learning Activity

Form groups of three or four students. Complete the following directions.

1. As a group, brainstorm to list the kinds of problems you encounter when you take objective tests. List as many problems as possible in random order.
2. On large chart paper or an overhead transparency, organize your information by creating logical categories for the different kinds of test-taking problems you encounter. Rewrite your list of problems by putting problems under the categories you create. Be prepared to share your work with the class.

Taking Objective Tests

Objective tests involve true-false, multiple-choice, and matching questions. Objective test questions, also called *recognition questions*, are often considered the easiest form of test questions to answer because you are basically required to *recognize* the correct answer or *recognize* whether or not a statement is accurate. This process of recognition often requires you to do a **memory search**, which involves locating information in your long-term memory, associating or linking the test question to information in a long-term memory schema, or applying information you already know in order to select the correct answer. Before we consider more specific strategies for taking objective tests, the following test-taking strategies apply to the three kinds of objective tests:

1. Prepare for the test by reciting and reviewing terminology, categories or lists of information, and important supporting details, such as names, dates, events, theories, rules, or principles.
2. Create a five-day study plan for major tests (Chapter 4, pages 100–102).
3. Prepare *summary notes* for the chapters that will be covered on the test (Chapter 4, pages 100–101).

Many professional degree programs require entry-level exams that consist mainly of objective test questions. In what other situations will you frequently encounter objective test questions?

Tips for Answering Objective Questions

1. When answering *true-false questions,* pay close attention to key elements in the true-false statements.
2. When answering *multiple-choice questions,* use a two-step approach to identify the correct answer.
3. When answering *matching questions,* use the four steps for matching two columns of information.

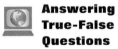

Answering True-False Questions

True-false questions are one of the most basic forms of objective questions, for they take less time to read and can easily be scored by hand, by machines (the tests in which you fill in the numbered bubbles to indicate your answer), or by computer. Students sometimes feel that some true-false questions are "trick questions" mainly because they do not know how to read and interpret the questions correctly.

The following guidelines can help you improve your performance on true-false tests:

1. *Read the statement carefully.* If you tend to misread questions, point to each word as you read the statement. *Circle key words used in the question.*
2. *Be objective when you answer.* Do not personalize the question by interpreting it according to what you do or how you feel. Instead, answer according to the information presented by the textbook author or your instructor in class.

3. *Mark a statement as True only when the statement is completely true.* If any one part of the statement is inaccurate or false, you must mark the entire statement *False*.
4. *Check items in a series of items very carefully.* Every item must be true for you to mark *T*.
5. *Do not take the time to add your reasoning or argument to the side of the question.* Frequently, the only information that will be looked at is the *T* or *F* answer, so other notes, comments, or clarifications will be ignored during grading.
6. *If you are taking a true-false test using paper and pencil, make a strong distinction between the way you write a* T *and the way you write an* F. Trying to camouflage your answer so it can be interpreted as a *T* or an *F* will backfire. Answers that cannot be clearly understood are marked as incorrect.

In addition to the above guidelines, it is important that you pay close attention to four key elements of true-false questions. Learning to identify these key elements will result in more careful reading of true-false questions and more accuracy in your choice of answers.

Key Elements in True-False Questions

1. Negatives in the form of words or prefixes
2. Modifiers in the form of 100 percent modifiers and in-between modifiers
3. Definition clues signaling the definition of a term is being tested
4. Relationship clues signaling the relationship between two items is being tested

Watch for Negatives As you read true-false questions, pay close attention to any negatives. **Negatives** are words or prefixes in words that carry the meaning of "no" or "not." *Negatives do not mean that the sentence is going to be false.* Instead, negatives affect the meaning of the sentence and require you to read and think carefully. Watch for the following negatives in questions.

Negative Words	Negative Prefixes
no	dis (disorganized)
not	im (imbalanced)
but	non (nonproductive)
except	il (illogical)
	in (incomplete)
	ir (irresponsible)
	un (unimportant)

Sentences with negatives can be confusing and can leave you wondering what is really being asked. One method of working with statements that have a negative word or a negative prefix is to *cover up the negative* and read the sentence without it. If you are able to answer *true* or *false* to the statement without the negative, the correct answer for the statement with the negative will be the *opposite* answer.

Watch for Modifiers **Modifiers** are words that tell to what degree or frequency something occurs. There is a huge difference between saying that something *always* happens and saying that something *sometimes* or *often* happens. You must learn to pay close attention to these words to determine how often or how frequently something actually occurs. As you notice in the following list, there are other kinds of modifiers. Words such as *best* or *worst* show the extremes and indicate that there is *nothing* that is greater or better.

Modifiers can be shown on a scale. The **100 percent modifiers** are on the extreme ends of the scale. They are the absolutes with nothing beyond them. The **in-between modifiers** are in the middle of the scale. They allow for more flexibility or variety because they indicate that a middle ground exists where situations or conditions do not occur as absolutes (100 percent of the time).

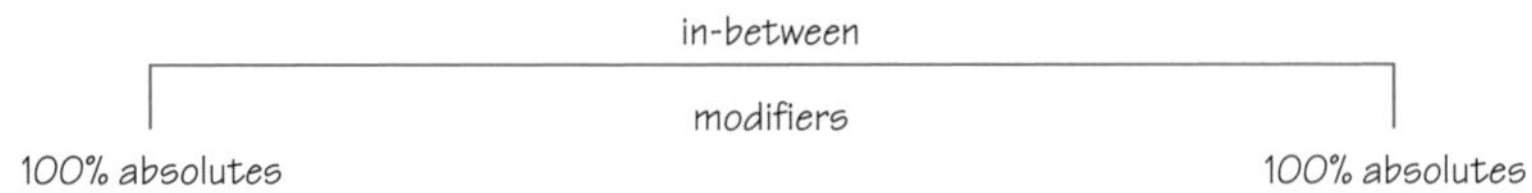

Modifiers

100 Percent	In-Between	100 Percent
all, every, only	some, most, a few	none
always, absolutely	sometimes, often, usually, may, seldom, frequently	never
everyone	some/few/most people	no one
everybody		nobody
best	average, better	worst
any adjective that ends in *est*, which means "the most," such as largest, smallest . . .	any adjective that ends in *er*, which means "more," such as larger, smaller . . .	least fewest

Watch for Definition Clues A test writer must find ways to create false statements for true-false tests; one common way to develop false statements is by testing your understanding of the definition of a specific term. The following words, called **definition clues**, often signal that a question is evaluating your understanding of a definition.

Definition Clues

Clues That Signal Definitions		Sentence Pattern Used
defined as are/is states that referred to as is/are called	also known as means which means which is/are involves	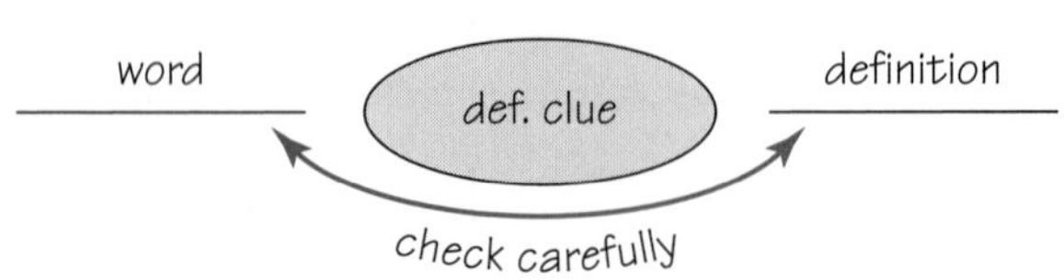

For definition questions, circle the clue words that signal definitions. Underline the key term that is being defined. Then ask yourself, "What is the definition I learned for this word?" Once you can recall the definition you learned, compare it to the definition that is given. If your definition and the test question definition are the same, the statement is *true*. If there is a discrepancy, analyze the test question definition carefully because it may be saying the same thing but simply using different words. If the definitions are not the same, the answer will be *false*.

Watch for Relationship Clues Some true-false questions test whether a certain relationship exists. Relationships often show cause/effect—one item causes another item to occur. Become familiar with the following words for relationships. When you see these **relationship clues** in true-false sentences, think carefully about the relationship being discussed before you decide whether the statement is true or false.

Relationship Clues

Clues That Signal Relationships		Sentence Pattern Used
increases	result	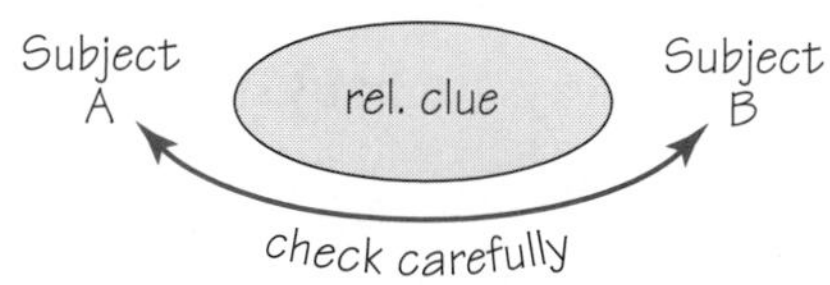
produces	since	
reason	so, so that	
affects	creates	
because	decreases	
causes	effects	

In relationship questions, circle the relationship clues. Underline the key terms that are involved in the relationship. Then ask yourself, "What do I know about how these two terms are related or associated to each other?" Once you have a relationship idea in your mind and before you mark *true* or *false*, compare your idea with the one presented in the question.

✎ EXERCISE 12.1 Answering True-False Questions

Read the following true-false questions, which test information learned in previous chapters. Pay close attention to items in a series; when you find negatives, definition and relationship clues, or modifiers, circle them. Write T *for true and* F *for false.*

_______ **1.** The three areas of life that need to be balanced are school, leisure, and studying.

_______ **2.** You can increase your speed in notetaking by paraphrasing, using abbreviations, and writing sentences that are not grammatically correct.

_______ **3.** The recall column in the Cornell system should have headings, key words, study questions, and all the answers.

_______ **4.** When you create a goal organizer, you identify benefits you will gain, obstacles you may encounter, and resources you could use.

_______ **5.** Ongoing review is essential in the Cornell system but is optional in the SQ4R system.

_______ **6.** Index cards should be used only when you need to learn terminology.

_______ **7.** Reciting is important because it utilizes the auditory channel and provides feedback for understanding.

_______ **8.** Spaced practice is preferred so that the student can usually avoid rote memory and cramming techniques.

_______ **9.** Too much information in the recall column of Cornell causes you to read instead of recite.

_______ **10.** The amount of time you spend on social or leisure activities should always be more than the total hours spent on work.

_______ **11.** Concentration is defined as the ability to focus on two or more things at one time without being distracted.

_______ **12.** In a formal outline, Roman numerals are never used to label supporting details under a subheading.

_______ **13.** *Schema* is another term for the feedback loop.

_______ **14.** Everyone should always try to divide her or his "life's pie" into three equal parts.

_______ **15.** It is always best and most productive to study late at night when there is no one around to bother you.

_______ **16.** Always begin by studying your favorite subject first so that you can get motivated.

_______ **17.** Reading and speaking are active processes, but listening is an inactive process.

_______ **18.** Most people are a combination of global and linear learners and thinkers.

_______ **19.** Procrastination is defined as a self-defeating behavior that always occurs when a person has a fear of failure.

_______ **20.** All cultures place a high premium on the same good listening behaviors.

_______ **21.** A disorganized desk is not an external distractor.

_______ **22.** The process of selectivity is not used during the fourth step of SQ4R.

_______ **23.** Students should use every concentration technique during a study block.

_______ **24.** Cramming can frequently be avoided if ongoing review is used each week.

_______ **25.** Test anxiety may stem from being underprepared or lacking test-taking skills.

_______ **26.** Semantic encoding is defined as the process of coding words for long-term memory.

_______ **27.** The Interference Theory of Forgetting states that information in short-term memory is confused because too much information enters the system too quickly.

_______ **28.** Increasing the amount of information in a schema often makes learning information on that subject easier to do.

_______ **29.** Spaced practice is preferred for studying because it encourages students to avoid marathon studying.

_______ **30.** Because test anxiety is a learned behavior, it can be unlearned through the use of strategies, practice, and willingness to change.

Answering Multiple-Choice Questions

Careful reading is also essential for answering multiple-choice questions correctly. For multiple-choice questions, there are two parts to the question: the stem and the options. The **stem** is the beginning part of the statement. The **options** are the choices for the correct answer. Usually there are four options, and only one of the options is the correct answer. Your goal is to eliminate the options that are incorrect. These incorrect options are referred to as **distractors**.

The following guidelines will help you improve your performance on multiple-choice questions:

1. *Read the directions carefully.* Usually the directions say to choose *one answer.* However, variations of this do exist; you may find directions that say you may use *more than one* answer. If no mention is made about the number of answers to choose, always select only one.
2. *Choose the best answer.* One or more of the answers may be correct, but the answer that is the most inclusive (includes the most or the broadest information) is the best answer.
3. *Read all of the options before you select your answer.* Some students stop as soon as they find a good answer. It is important to read all the options so you are sure you are finding the best option.
4. *Write your letter answer on the line.* Some students make careless mistakes writing the correct answer on the line. If this is a tendency of yours, first *circle* the letter answer and then write the letter on the line. Using this method, you are able to quickly check that you wrote what you circled and what you believe is the correct answer.

The following steps will guide you through the process of answering multiple-choice questions. Use each step before you write your final answer.

Steps for Answering Multiple-Choice Questions

1. Read the stem, finish the statement in your mind, and check to see if the answer is one of the options.
2. Read the stem with each option as a true-false statement. Eliminate the distractors and select from the remaining options.

Finish the Stem The first step with a multiple-choice question is to read the stem and finish the stem in your mind. This helps you "get into the correct memory schema" and relate the rest of the question to something you already know. The answer that you get may or may not be one of the answers given as an option, but you will be thinking along the same channels. For practice, how would you complete each of the following stems in your mind?

_______ **1.** The principle of Big Picture–Little Pictures _______________

____

_______ **2.** Visual encoding refers to _______________________

____

_______ **3.** Howard Gardner's eighth intelligence is called _______________

____

Read as Four T-F Statements When you read the stem of a multiple-choice question with just one of the options, the result is a one-sentence statement that can be treated as a true-false statement. This process can continue until each of the options has been analyzed as a true-false statement. The strategies you learned previously for true-false statements will be used in exactly the same way for multiple-choice questions. Here is the process:

1. Read the stem with the first option.
2. If the statement is false, *cross off the letter of that option.* This is a distractor and will not be the correct answer.
3. If the statement is true, *it may be the correct answer.* You won't know for sure until all the options have been read with the stem. If you would like, you may write a *T* at the end of all the options that make a true answer when they are added to the stem.

The following example demonstrates the use of this strategy:

b **1.** In the listening process, *assignment of meaning*

a. occurs before the attention and response steps. F

b. requires the listener to categorize information into schemas and interpret the message without distorting it. T

c. requires the listener to check the accuracy of his or her perception by asking a question or providing nonverbal feedback. F

d. requires the listener to interpret a message. T

Exercise 12.2 Answering Multiple-Choice Questions

For each of the following questions, read the stem and answer the question in your own words. Look to see if your answer matches one of the options. Then make a true-false statement by reading the stem with each of the options. Write T *or* F *at the end of each option. Cross off the false statements. Select the best answer from the remaining options.*

______ **1.** Maslow's hierarchy of needs is a theory that explains
a. people's needs.
b. how people are motivated by their needs.
c. why needs are sustained over time.
d. universal behaviors that exist in all cultures.

______ **2.** You can use visual mappings to
a. take lecture notes.
b. take textbook notes.
c. make review study tools.
d. All of the above

______ **3.** It is acceptable to
a. put many key words in each cell of a comparison chart.
b. write sideways on visual mappings if needed.
c. write a single item under a subheading in a formal outline.
d. None of the above

______ **4.** When you visualize a mapping, you should
a. try to see the skeleton first.
b. always be creative and make changes as you go.
c. never stare at the paper for as long as five minutes.
d. add new information that you forgot to put in the original mapping.

_______ **5.** When making a hierarchy of information from a chapter, level two information
a. should reflect only the chapter headings.
b. should show all important terminology.
c. should always include pictures.
d. may include your own categories and chapter headings.

_______ **6.** Cramming
a. is one of the most effective short-term memory processing strategies available.
b. uses all the memory principles.
c. processes large amounts of information efficiently.
d. is not a technique used by prepared students.

_______ **7.** Anxiety refers to
a. controlled stress.
b. uncontrolled stress.
c. a natural form of stress.
d. motivational stress used to be productive.

_______ **8.** Test anxiety can be reduced by focusing on
a. test-taking tasks, such as circling key words or mouthing the question.
b. outward thoughts and ignoring others.
c. your strengths and accomplishments.
d. All of the above

_______ **9.** The principle of Big Picture–Little Pictures
a. encourages you to memorize individual facts and details.
b. is based completely on rote memory.
c. recommends that you process information only in clusters.
d. recommends that you try to "see the trees" *and* "see the forest" when you study.

_______ **10.** The memory principle of organization is often used
a. in the third step of the SQ4R reading system.
b. each time a student reads a textbook chapter.
c. in more than one step of SQ4R and the Cornell notetaking system.
d. when a student organizes his or her work space and notebook.

Answering on Matching Tests

Matching questions are based on paired associations. **Paired associations** are items that were linked together when you learned the information. For example, a word is linked or paired to its definition. When you think of the word, you associate it with the definition. When you think of the definition, you pair it with the word. Paired associations for matching may include:

- Words and their definitions
- People and what they did
- Dates and events
- Terms and their function or purpose
- Problems and their solutions

When you are faced with matching questions on tests, you will see a list of words on the left and their paired association on the right. The key to answering matching questions is to work through them in a systematic way. The following steps will help you avoid confusion and perform better on tests that have matching questions.

Four Steps for Working Through Matching Questions

1. Read the directions carefully.
2. Count the number of items in each list to see if the lists are equal.
3. Begin by reading the column that has the shorter entries.
4. Use the four levels of response to match the columns.

Read the Directions Begin by reading the directions carefully. Usually each item on the right can be used only once; if an item can be used more than once, the directions should say so.

Count the Items Count the number of items in the left column and then the number of items in the right column. If the lists contain an equal number of items, each item will be used once. Sometimes the list on the right is longer, indicating that some of the items will not be used. Extra items make matching questions a little more difficult because you cannot automatically match up whatever is left over.

Read the Shortest List Usually the column on the left will have the shortest entries. These may be words (terminology), names, dates, or events. Read these so that you are aware of the choices that are available. Also notice what types of pairing will be used. Are these people, events, dates, or vocabulary terms? Below, the list on the left has shorter entries; read this list first.

________	**1.** intrinsic rewards	**a.** a technique used to switch the time blocks of specific activities
________	**2.** trading time	**b.** material items or activities used when goals are met
________	**3.** motivation	**c.** a feeling, emotion, or desire that moves a person to take action
________	**4.** extrinsic rewards	**d.** feeling proud, relieved, or satisfied

Use the Levels of Response Now that you are familiar with the items on the left, begin reading the first item on the right. Read the item carefully, and quickly search your memory for an association to that item. Look on the left to see whether the associated word is on the list. For example, if the item on the right is a definition, search your memory for the vocabulary term. Then use the **four levels of response**:

Immediate Response Immediate response can be used when you immediately know the answer. Once you see a definite match, write the letter on the line and *cross off the letter you used so you do not reuse it*. If you do not immediately know the answer, move to delayed response. Do not guess or write any answer that you are not absolutely certain is correct.

Delayed Response Use delayed response when you do not immediately know the answer. In addition to the techniques discussed on page 317, use **word clues** and **grammar clues**. For example, if you see *system, technique,* or *rule,* you would narrow your focus by looking for choices in the shorter list that deal specifically with a system, a technique, or a rule. When you read and connect the item on the left with the item on the right, a meaningful "thought unit" or sentence should emerge. To find this meaningful connection, *mentally chatter your way* to the answer.

If none of these techniques works, do *not* guess. If you are not able to identify the correct answer after trying one or more of the above techniques, *leave the answer space blank*. Use some type of symbol, like a checkmark, in the left margin as a reminder that you need to return to this question later. Move on to the next item. Always work your way from the top down to the bottom of the list.

Assisted Response Scan through the test to look for any of the key words used on either side of your matching list. Other parts of the test may have information that helps you recall associations or jogs your memory about the information in the matching questions. If you cannot find any clues in other parts of the test, move on to educated guessing.

Educated Guessing If you have exhausted the above techniques and still have not come up with the correct answer, use educated guessing. If you put nothing on the line, it will be wrong; you might as well take the remaining items that you could not match and fill in any empty lines with any of those remaining letters. Be sure to make a mental note of those items so you can check your book and notes right after class.

Matching

① Directions say to use each answer once.

② Two answers are extra and won't be used.

Match the items on the left to the items on the right. Write the letter of each answer on the line. Each item on the right may be used only one time.

③ Read the shorter list. ④ Start with "a." Do only the ones you know.

h 1. circadian rhythms	a. creating a border for visualization
___ 2. motivation	b. associating items together
a 3. framing	c. short-term memory and feedback loop
j 4. affirmations	d. feeling, emotion, or desire that elicits an action
f 5. chunking	e. feedback
___ 6. sensory stimuli	f. breaking tasks into more manageable units
b 7. linking	g. procedural memory
i 8. memory storage centers	h. body's natural patterns and rhythms
___ 9. active memory paths	i. long-term and short-term memory
___ 10. result of self-quizzing	j. positive statements written in present tense
	k. rehearsal and retrieval
	l. words, sounds, pictures, tactile sensations

⑤ Use delayed response. Use helper words to try to connect the items that you do not know well.

⑥ Use assisted response. Use the rest of the test for assistance in finding more answers.

⑦ Use educated guessing. Fill in any remaining blanks with letters you did not already use.

EXERCISE 12.3 Matching Problems and Solutions

Read each problem on the left. Find the solution on the right. Write the letter of the solution on the line. You may use each answer only once.

_______ **1.** I highlight too much.

_______ **2.** I don't know how to study from underlining.

_______ **3.** When I read, I need to find a way to make important terminology stand out more clearly

_______ **4.** I have trouble finding the topic sentence.

_______ **5.** I have problems finding definitions for key words in the book.

_______ **6.** I don't feel like I really understand how to use the textbook features very well.

_______ **7.** I need a fast way to look up page numbers to find information in my book.

_______ **8.** The teacher said to check our work with the answer keys in the book, but I can't find any answer keys in my chapters.

_______ **9.** I have trouble getting started when I have a reading assignment. I'm just not motivated to "dig right in" and do the serious reading.

_______ **10.** I go into "automatic pilot" every time I try to read pages in my textbook.

_______ **11.** I can't write fast enough to write down everything the teacher says in a lecture.

_______ **12.** When the teacher talks too slowly, my mind wanders to other things.

_______ **13.** My notes are a jumbled mess. The information all runs together.

a. Circle the words that you need to be able to define.

b. Survey the book at the beginning of the term.

c. Use punctuation, word clues, word structure clues, and context clues.

d. Try to organize with headings and numbered details. Leave spaces between headings.

e. Only mark the main idea and the key words for details.

f. Read one paragraph at a time. Stop. Take time to comprehend what you read.

g. Use your own words to string together the ideas you marked.

h. Use the index.

i. Survey the chapter first as a "warm-up" activity.

j. Paraphrase with shortened sentences. Abbreviate. Use symbols.

k. Check the first and the last sentences to see if one has the main idea that controls the paragraph.

l. Keep writing, anticipate new points, question ideas, or mentally summarize.

m. Check the book's appendix.

Exercise 12.4 Case Studies

Each of the following case studies describes a student situation. Read each case study carefully; highlight key ideas or student issues. On separate paper, answer the question that ends each case study. In your response, address the key points that you highlighted and that relate directly to the question. Use complete sentences in your answers. These case studies are also available online; you can email your response to your instructor or print a copy of your work online.

1. Alonzo usually does well on essay tests but has problems on tests with multiple-choice questions. He knows the information; therefore, he believes his errors are simply careless mistakes. Alonzo realizes that he tends to select answers too quickly and that he needs to learn to use a systematic approach to identify the correct answers. What systematic approach would you recommend?
2. Shaina learned long ago that either you know the answer or you don't. Consequently, she works through the test questions in the order in which they are presented. She reads each question once and answers the questions to which she knows the answers. She gets annoyed with herself for not knowing the other answers, so she leaves the remaining questions blank. Which of the four levels of response does Shaina need to learn to use in order to improve her performance on tests?
3. Courtney frequently experiences test anxiety. She often wastes the first five minutes of a test trying to get herself calmed down enough to read the questions. Her anxiety only increases each time she is not able to answer a question. Her eyes dart across the test and she loses her focus. In her state of panic, she misreads questions, skips over important words, and then randomly selects an answer. Later, when she rereads her test without the time pressure, her comprehension and selection of correct answers improve. What strategies can Courtney use to improve her test performance?

Exercise 12.5 LINKS

Assume that your instructor announces an objective test in this class for the last three chapters you discussed. To prepare for the test, you develop sample test questions. Follow the directions below to create a practice test.

Use information from the last three chapters you studied to write five ***true-false*** *questions.*

_______ 1. ______________________________

_______ 2. ______________________________

_______ 3. ______________________________

_______ 4. ______________________________

_______ 5. ______________________________

Use information from the last three chapters to write three ***multiple-choice*** *questions.*

_______ **1.** ______________________________

a. ______________________________

b. ______________________________

c. ______________________________

d. ______________________________

_______ **2.** ______________________________

a. ______________________________

b. ______________________________

c. ______________________________

d. ______________________________

_______ **3.** ______________________________

a. ______________________________

b. ______________________________

c. ______________________________

d. ______________________________

Use the terminology at the beginning of the last three chapters you studied to create matching questions. *Write any ten terms in the left column and short definitions for each term in the right column. Remember to scramble the order of the definitions.*

_______ **1.**	**a.**
_______ **2.**	**b.**
_______ **3.**	**c.**
_______ **4.**	**d.**
_______ **5.**	**e.**
_______ **6.**	**f.**
_______ **7.**	**g.**
_______ **8.**	**h.**
_______ **9.**	**i.**
_______ **10.**	**j.**

Reflection Writing 2 — CHAPTER 12

On a separate piece of paper or in a journal, do the following:

1. Examine two or more previous objective tests you completed for any of your classes. Look for the use of *modifiers, negatives, definition clues,* and *relationship clues* in the questions. Analyze any questions you answered incorrectly. Discuss what you discovered by examining your previous tests.
2. How do the objective test-taking strategies in this chapter relate to your test questions? How would the knowledge you acquired in Chapter 12 have helped you achieve a better grade on those tests? What do you notice now about those tests that you were not aware of at the time you took the tests? Be specific in your answers.

Using Educated Guessing

Educated guessing is the fourth level of response for answering objective test questions. Educated guessing involves using specific strategies to improve your odds for supplying the correct answers on objective test questions. On page 327 you learned about educated guessing for matching questions. You can also use educated guessing for true-false and multiple-choice questions.

Precautionary Notes

Understanding educated guessing strategies often improves critical reading skills, for you learn to notice the significance of individual words and details in questions. Even though educated guessing strategies may help you gain a few additional points on a test, you need to be aware of the following precautionary notes about using educated guessing:

1. The phrase *educated guessing* is used instead of simply *guessing* because you use some background information, logic, and common sense to approach questions that you cannot answer through immediate, delayed, or assisted response.
2. Educated guessing is not foolproof. These strategies only increase the odds that you will reach the final answer.
3. Do not become overly confident about taking tests simply because you know how to use educated guessing. Educated guessing strategies do not guarantee a correct answer.
4. Limit the use of educated guessing strategies to situations in which nothing else has produced an answer. Educated guessing is a last resort!

Ten Educated Guessing Stategies

The following ten educated guessing strategies apply to true-false and multiple-choice questions. Remember that multiple-choice questions may be seen as a series of true-false questions, so the same strategies used for true-false questions will apply to multiple-choice questions.

Ten Educated Guessing Strategies

1. Guess *false* if there is a 100 percent modifier.
2. Guess *true* if there is an in-between modifier.
3. Guess *false* if there is a relationship clue.
4. Guess *false* if the statement is ridiculous, foolish, insulting, or has unfamiliar terms.
5. Guess *true*, the wild-shot guess, if there are no other clues in a true-false question.
6. If there are numbers as options, eliminate the highest and the lowest; guess one of the options that remain.
7. If there are multiple-choice options that are almost identical (look alike), choose one of those two options.
8. If one multiple-choice option is longer in length or more inclusive in content, choose it.
9. If the last option is "all of the above" and this option is not used throughout the test, choose it.
10. Guess *c*, the wild-shot guess, if there are no other clues in a multiple-choice question.

100 Percent Modifiers (False)

The *100 percent modifiers* are the *absolutes*, meaning that they are the extremes, no exceptions are allowed. Few things happen or exist without exceptions, so the odds are in your favor that questions with 100 percent modifiers will be false. Guess *false*. (See page 320 to review the modifiers.)

Notice how the 100 percent modifiers make the following statements false:

___F___ **1.** Attendance in college is required in every class.

___F___ **2.** Always begin by studying your favorite subject first.

___F___ **3.** Never use a tape recorder in class.

When a multiple-choice option with a 100 percent modifier is added to the stem, a true-false question is created. The true-false guessing strategy for 100 percent modifiers is to guess *false*. Notice how this same strategy works in the following example:

______ **1.** The prefix *intra-*
- a. is never used in English words.
- b. always means "between."
- c. means "within" or "inside of."
- d. None of the above

___F___ a. The prefix *intra-* is never used in English words.

___F___ b. The prefix *intra-* always means "between."

___T___ c. The prefix *intra-* means "within" or "inside of."

In-Between Modifiers (True)

The *in-between modifiers* make room for exceptions or for the statement to sometimes apply and sometimes not apply. If you are using educated guessing and you see an in-between modifier, guess *true*. Odds will be in your favor. Notice how the in-between modifiers make these statements true:

__T__ **1.** Reviewing notes from a previous paragraph can sometimes be used to help understand a difficult paragraph.

__T__ **2.** In a sole proprietorship, the person who owns the business is usually the one who operates it.

The same is true for multiple-choice questions because each option can be converted to a true-false statement when it is added to the stem. If more than one option is true, remember to then select the answer you believe is the *best* answer.

______ **1.** Intrapersonal intelligence is an intelligence that
a. always shows leadership and group charisma.
b. often involves a special interest in personal growth and insights.
c. seldom is combined with linguistic or interpersonal intelligence.
d. is never taught in schools.

Notice how option *a* and option *d* have 100 percent modifiers. If guessing strategies are used, these would be marked *false*. Both option *b* and option *c* have in-between modifiers. For a guessing strategy, guess one of these two options. However, before you purely guess, think it through more carefully. Option *c* is not accurate information; option *b* makes sense and is the correct answer. If you didn't know this, by reducing the choices to two options, you have a fifty-fifty chance of guessing correctly. (Needless to say, *knowing* the correct answer is always preferred!)

Relationship Clues (False)

True-false questions often test your knowledge of facts; on a higher level, true-false questions can test your understanding of relationships. Two common kinds of relationships questioned on tests are cause/effect and explanation through reason. When you see one of the common relationship clues (*because, since, so, cause, effect,* or *reason*), first try immediate, delayed, and assisted responses. If you cannot figure out the answer, guess *false*. Why? These higher-level thinking skills questions can easily be written to show false relationships. Notice how the two parts of the following questions do not show a true relationship.

__F__ **1.** Lack of motivation is the reason unsuccessful students avoid using time management.

__F__ **2.** Cramming is not recommended because it uses only eight of the twelve principles of memory.

This same strategy can be used for multiple-choice questions. After each option below, you will see the true or false answer that would be used for that option.

______ **1.** Systematic desensitization
~~a~~. causes a person to react more mildly to criticism. (F)
~~b~~. works because the immune system is strengthened. (F)
~~c~~. should never be used to avoid undesirable situations. (F)
d. helps a person change his or her negative reaction to specific events. (T)

Ridiculous, Foolish, Insulting, or Unfamiliar Terms (False)

If you see statements that are meant to be humorous, ridiculous, or unreasonable, mark them false for true-false questions, and mark them as distractors in multiple-choice questions. If you have attended class regularly and have done all the reading assignments and you encounter unfamiliar terms on a test, odds are in your favor that the statement is false or it is a distractor in a multiple-choice question. Notice how this works in the following examples.

___F___ **1.** Howard Gardner's multiple intelligences theory applies only to people with IQs over 175. *(ridiculous)*

___F___ **2.** Howard Gardner's multiple intelligences theory added an eighth intelligence called psychic/intuitive. *(unfamiliar terms)*

___F___ **3.** Interpersonal intelligence is shown by those who party instead of study. *(ridiculous)*

___d___ **4.** When you don't know the answer to a test question, you should
a. try using the rest of the test to trigger your memory. (T)
~~b~~. try looking at another student's answers. *(ridiculous)* (F)
~~c~~. cry. *(ridiculous)* (F)
d. use delayed or assisted response before educated guessing. (T)

___a___ **5.** Interpersonal intelligence is
a. seen in people with social and leadership skills. (T)
~~b~~. associated with immaturity. *(ridiculous)* (F)
~~c~~. not a useful quality in school beyond the first grade. *(silly)* (F)
~~d~~. a form of type B behavior. *(unfamiliar term)* (F)

Wild-Shot Guess (True)

If there are no modifiers to use and there is no relationship shown, you will need to take a **wild-shot guess**. If you run out of time on a test and simply must guess, *guess true*. There is a logical reason for this. When teachers write tests, they usually prefer to leave the correct, accurate information in your mind. They know that you are likely to remember what you read. Therefore, they tend to write more true statements than false statements.

Eliminate the Highest and Lowest Numbers

When the options are numbers, chances are better that the correct answer is one of the numbers in the middle range. Therefore, treat the highest and the lowest numbers as distractors. That leaves you with two options. Try to reason through to make the better choice. If any one of the other guessing strategies applies (such as choose *c*), incorporate that strategy as well to choose your answer.

______ **1.** An average rate of thinking speed is
~~a~~. 800 words per minute. (Eliminate the highest.)
b. 600 words per minute. } Choose between these
c. 400 words per minute. } two options.
~~d~~. 200 words per minute. (Eliminate the lowest.)

Choose One of the Look-Alike Options

Some questions have two options that look almost the same. Perhaps only one or two words are different. Chances are good that the correct answer is one of these two. Eliminate the other options and focus on these two look-alikes. Carefully think through and associate the information with what you have learned. If you can't decide, choose either one.

_________ **1.** Compared to the left hemisphere of the brain, the right hemisphere of the brain
a. understands spoken language better.
b. has better logical abilities.
c. perceives words better.
d. perceives emotions better.

Focus on *c* and *d* because they are look-alikes. Now try to reason your way through this. You have already eliminated *a,* which deals with language. Because *c* also relates to language, it, too, must be incorrect. This leaves you with *d* as the correct answer, which it is. (Notice in this case how the guessing strategy to use *c* does not work—there are no guarantees!)

Choose the Longest or Most Inclusive Option

This guessing strategy is based on two premises. First, sometimes more words are needed to give complete information to make a correct answer. Second, an answer that covers a wider range of possibilities is more likely correct.

You can begin by looking at the *length* of the answer. If one option is much longer than the others, choose it. Also look at the content of the answers. Sometimes two or three answers may be correct to some degree, but one answer contains more information or a broader idea. This answer is the most inclusive. Notice how the *most inclusive answer* in the following is the best answer.

_________ **1.** Test anxiety can be reduced by focusing on
a. yourself and ignoring others.
b. outward thoughts and actions.
c. your strengths and accomplishments.
d. the four strategies to reduce test anxiety.

All of the answers are correct to some degree. However, *d* is the longest and includes a wider range of information. The answers *a, b,* and *c* fit under the information given in *d*.

Choose "All of the Above"

If you know for sure that two options are correct, but you are not sure about the third option and the fourth option is "all of the above," choose it. This is a safe guess since you can choose only one answer and you know that two are correct. If you do not know for certain that two are correct and you have tried each option in a true-false form and don't know the answer, go ahead and choose "all of the above." This strategy is not very reliable, especially if "all of the above" is used throughout the test. Be sure to check out all other possibilities before you decide to use this strategy.

_________ **1.** Cramming is
a. the result of being underprepared. T
b. a frantic attempt to learn a lot of information in a short amount of time. T
c. a method that does not use very many memory principles. ?
d. All of the above

Your first reaction might be to choose *b* because it is the longest answer. However, if you know that at least two of the choices are correct, your only choice then is to choose *d,* which is correct.

Choose C as a Wild-Shot Guess

Many teachers favor the *c* answer for the correct answer. If you try writing some of your own multiple-choice questions, you may find that you, too, tend to put more correct answers in the *c* position than in any other position. Here are a few explanations for why *c* is the most common answer:

- *A* is not used as often because many students would stop reading the questions and stop thinking about the answer if the correct answer were given first.
- *B* is not used as often for the same reason that *A* is not.
- *C* seems to hide the answer best and force the reader to read through more of the options.
- *D* seems to be too visible because it is on the last line.

EXERCISE 12.6 Using Educated Guessing on True-False Questions

This exercise has test questions on topics that may not be familiar to you. However, if you apply the educated guessing strategies to answer these questions, you will be correct. Work with a partner and discuss your answers.

________ **1.** In 1913, President Woodrow Wilson believed that concentrated economic power threatened individual liberty and the monopolies had to be broken up to open up the marketplace.

________ **2.** All matter exists in only one of three physical forms: solid, liquid, or gas.

________ **3.** The liquid form of a given material is always less dense than the solid form.

________ **4.** Prolonged overuse of alcohol can result in life-threatening liver damage, vitamin deficiencies that can lead to irreversible brain disorder, and a host of other ailments.

________ **5.** Rome's early wars often gave plebeians the power to demand that their rights be recognized, but their demands were seldom met.

________ **6.** Because monasteries believed in isolation, they never conducted schools for local people.

________ **7.** In 1013, the Danish ruler Swen Forkbeard invaded England.

________ **8.** The only objective of medieval agriculture was to produce more cattle for meat and dairy products.

________ **9.** Historians have determined for certain that the bubonic plague originated in southern Russia and was carried to Europe by traveling soldiers.

________ **10.** Economic growth was rapid during the Italian Renaissance.

________ **11.** The first movies, which began in the late 1880s, were slot-machine peep shows in penny arcades.

________ **12.** The Warren Court in 1962 declared that schools would always have the right to require prayers in public schools, but students had the right to refrain from praying.

________ **13.** The world's population has more than doubled since 1950.

________ **14.** The behavioral theory suggests that people learn to use alcohol because they want to become more sensitive to others.

________ **15.** Alcoholic parents, hyperactivity, and antisocial behavior in childhood are reasonably good predictors of alcoholism in adults.

________ **16.** The Dow Jones Industrial Average, established in 1897, is a stock index still in use today.

________ **17.** The Standard & Poor's 500 Stock Index and the New York Stock Exchange Index never include more stocks than the Dow Jones averages.

________ **18.** The Securities and Exchange Commission (SEC) was created in 1934 because stock-brokers wanted access to a compiled list of all trading.

________ **19.** The abolitionist newspapers frequently attacked the Fugitive Slave Act as a violation of fundamental American rights.

________ **20.** In the 1970s, unemployment was high due mainly to the oil embargo.

EXERCISE 12.7 Using Educated Guessing on Multiple-Choice Questions

Use the educated guessing strategies for the following multiple-choice questions. Remember to convert each option into a true-false question before you select the best answer.

_______ **1.** A response pattern known as *cynical hostility*
a. is linked to coronary heart disease and heart attacks.
b. develops in childhood years.
c. is characterized by resentment, frequent anger, and distrust.
d. All of the above

_______ **2.** Signs of post-traumatic stress disorder are
a. never being able to sleep.
b. shown in a frequency histogram.
c. poor concentration, anxiety, and nervousness.
d. apparent at the time of the trauma.

_______ **3.** The domestication of plants and animals began around
a. 7000 B.C.
b. 4000 B.C.
c. A.D. 1200.
d. 9000 B.C.

_______ **4.** The mental shortcuts called *heuristics* are
a. informal reasoning based on which events or hypotheses are likely.
b. informal reasoning based solely on using a given algorithm.
c. formal reasoning based on the use of an algorithm and logic.
d. required in at least one stage of every scientific model.

_______ **5.** With a *balloon automobile loan,* the
a. buyer feels stupid when the balloon payment is due.
b. buyer must sell the car back to the lender at the end of the loan.
c. first six monthly payments are large but later payments are reduced.
d. monthly payments are lower but the final payment is much greater.

_______ **6.** Reinforcement theory is
a. based on giving rewards for behavior you want repeated.
b. based on forcing issues.
c. never to be used by effective managers.
d. the very best training to use for infants.

_______ **7.** In business, the agency shop
a. never charges dues.
b. charges annual fees of $10 or less.
c. requires employees to pay dues even if they do not join.
d. requires employees to always be union members.

_______ **8.** Volcanic mountains are formed from
a. cinder piles and ash.
b. cinder piles, lava rock, ash, and shields of magma.
c. erosion.
d. sandstone and shale.

_______ **9.** Consumer spending reports have shown that _______ percent of Americans' disposable income in 1994 was spent on food.
a. 5
b. 9
c. 15
d. 28

Taking Computerized Tests

Computerized tests usually consist of multiple-choice questions. These tests may be written by the instructor, but more often they consist of a test bank generated by the textbook publisher. Some of the test banks randomly assign test questions of varying levels of difficulty; other test banks allow the instructor to tag the questions to be used on the test. The following chart shows some advantages and disadvantages of computerized testing.

Advantages	Disadvantages
1. You get immediate feedback and a score on your test. 2. Positive feedback that an answer is correct increases your confidence level. 3. The time limits to complete the tests are less rigid than when you take a test in class. 4. You may feel less stress because you can control your pace for answering questions.	1. Immediate feedback that indicates your answer is incorrect may cause stress and frustration. 2. Most computerized tests do not allow you to go back to previous questions so you cannot use the test-taking strategies of assisted response. 3. You cannot go back to previous questions to review or change your answers. 4. You usually do not get a printed copy of the test to review or use to study when you prepare for a final exam.

What are some of the difficulties with taking computerized tests? How can you effectively deal with these difficulties?

Computerized testing speeds up the grading process for instructors and provides a record sheet of student grades. When classes are large and instructor workloads are high, instructors may prefer computerized testing over hand-graded testing formats. If you have not already experienced computerized testing, chances are good that you will some time during your college career. When you are faced with taking a test on a computer, allow yourself ample time to complete the test. For many students, taking a computerized test requires more time than tests in the classroom. Therefore, you will want to avoid going into the lab when you are rushed. Select a time of day when you feel mentally sharp and best able to concentrate. The following strategies can also help you perform more effectively when you are sitting at a computer in a test-taking situation.

Strategies for Taking Computerized Tests

1. Read the directions carefully so you understand the program and how to respond.
2. Use the multiple-choice test-taking strategies previously discussed in this chapter.
3. If you give an incorrect answer, study the question before you move on.
4. Use strategies to stay relaxed, positive, and focused.
5. Explore options that may be available to you in the computer lab.

Read the Directions

Computerized programs vary, so it is important to read the directions carefully. Learn the basic options or commands that are available for the program you will be using. Frequently asked questions are: How do I log on? Is there a time limit? How do I delete an answer before entering my choice? Can more than one answer be correct? May I have a blank paper with me to work out problems or jot down ideas as I think? Is there a way to see all the questions before I start answering? Is a screen reader program with voice (and earphones) available for this program? Is there a practice test I can do first? May I take the test a second time?

Use the Multiple-Choice Strategies

Use the same multiple-choice strategies that were presented earlier in this chapter. Read the stem and try to complete the stem with your own words. See if one of the options matches your words. Then read the stem with each option and convert each option into a true-false question. Eliminate any of the options that would be false. Remember that you are doing this *with your eyes.* Pay close attention to key words, modifiers, negatives, and relationship and definition clues. Once you have decided on an option, reread the question with your option one more time. This is important because you do not usually have the opportunity to go back and change your answer.

Study the Question After an Incorrect Answer

If you answer incorrectly and the screen tells you that you have made a mistake, avoid the tendency to get away from that question and move quickly to the next question. If the test questions are given randomly, it is possible that a future question on the same material may be given. Take time to reread the question and understand your error. If the question gives the correct answer, learn the information with that answer. The information may also help you later with another closely related question. Taking the time to learn from the question helps to keep your mind focused on the material and reduces the tendency to move to the next question too hastily and with a negative attitude.

Use Stress-Reducing and Concentration Strategies

If you find yourself tensing up, feeling discouraged, impatient, angry, or irritated, stop for a few short minutes to do a relaxation technique. Breathe by threes, use the relaxation mask, or give yourself some positive self-talk. Stretch your arms, roll your head around, shake out your hands, roll your shoulders around, or even stand up for a minute to reduce the building stress. If you are finding yourself losing concentration, try to identify the distractors. Use any of the concentration strategies to get your mind on track and back to the task at hand. If the location of your computer station is a distractor, remember the next time to select a computer that is removed from the steady flow of traffic. Your goal is to work as much as possible with the relaxed "ahhhhh" state of mind.

Explore Options

If you are uncomfortable taking computerized tests or find computerized tests a difficult format to use to perform well, communicate your concerns with your instructor. Perhaps he or she will be able to provide you with additional suggestions for effectively taking computerized tests. The following are other options you may want to explore. After all, it never hurts to ask.

1. Ask the lab assistant if a *hard copy* (printed copy) of the test questions can be made available while you take the test. Explain that sometimes you find it helpful to be able to write on the test, circle words, and see all the questions as you work.
2. Ask your instructor if tests can be taken a second time. If yes, ask if you may take notes during the first test.
3. Ask your instructor or the lab assistant if you may have a hard copy of the test questions and your answers so you can study and learn from the errors.
4. Try to remember questions that puzzled you or that you did not think were discussed much in class. Talk to your instructor about those questions.
5. Ask if there are options available other than the computerized tests. Could essays or short answers on paper be done instead? Could a project or portfolio assignment be used in lieu of a computerized test?

Computerized tests will likely become more interactive and more sophisticated as technology advances. Learning to be comfortable working on a computer and taking computerized tests is essential if the trend to assess student performance continues in the direction of computerized testing. Be an active learner by asking lab assistants, instructors, and other students for additional strategies that can help you with computerized tests for specific classes. You may end up being a member of the group of students who prefer computerized testing!

Reflection Writing 3 — CHAPTER 12

Refer to the Group Processing: A Collaborative Learning Activity on page 317. On a separate piece of paper or in a journal, discuss solutions to the problems your group listed. If you did not do the group activity in class, list the kinds of problems you most frequently encounter with objective questions; then discuss solutions for each of the problems.

SUMMARY

- Performing well on tests involves beginning with a calm mind, creating a plan, maintaining a focus, managing time well, and using the four levels of response.
- Objective questions utilize the steps of immediate response, delayed response, assisted response, and educated guessing.
- Recognition questions, also called objective questions, include true-false, multiple choice, and matching.
- Words used in objective questions must be read more carefully:
  1. Definition clues
  2. Negatives
  3. 100 percent and in-between modifiers
  4. Relationship clues
- Both the stem and all the options in a multiple-choice question should be read as true-false statements before they are answered.

- A two-step strategy can enable you to answer multiple-choice questions.
- A four-step approach is recommended when you answer matching questions.
- Some strategies can be used to increase your odds at guessing on true-false and multiple-choice questions.
- Do not become falsely confident because you know educated guessing strategies; the best approach is to be prepared and learn as much information as possible so that you do not need to use educated guessing on a regular basis.
- Special strategies can be used to increase your performance on computerized tests.

ACE Practice Tests, which are scored online, supplementary exercises, enrichment activities, and related web site links are available online for *Essential Study Skills*, 4e. Use the following directions to access this web site:

Type: **http://college.hmco.com/collegesurvival/students**

Click on *List of Sites by Author*. Use the arrow to scroll down to Wong *Essential Study Skills*, 4e. Click on the title. If you are working on your own computer, bookmark this web site.

LEARNING OPTIONS

The following learning options provide you with opportunities to demonstrate your understanding of the topics in Chapter 12. Your instructor may assign one or more specific options or may ask you to select one or more options that interest you the most.

1. Expand the Chapter 12 mapping on page 313. Extend branches on the mapping to show important key words or phrases for each heading. (See Chapter 11 for additional information.) You can add pictures and colors to your mapping to accentuate the points. In paragraph form, summarize the key points in your mapping.
2. Create a visual mapping or a hierarchy that shows effective test-taking strategies to use *before a test, during a test*, and *after a test*. Use information from this chapter, as well as from previous chapters, to create this mapping.
3. Use the Internet to locate informative web sites for *one* of the following topics: *objective tests, test anxiety, or test-taking strategies.* Print the web pages. Prepare a short presentation or a written summary of the most significant information. In your presentation or summary, explain how the contents of the web site relate to the content of Chapter 12.
4. Create a chart or diagram for one of your classes this term, the test grades you have received, and the types of tests that were given. Then analyze the last test from each class to see the kinds of questions you missed or errors you made. Include your findings on your chart or diagram.
5. Take notes on Chapter 12 using the Cornell notetaking format, index cards, or a formal outline. Include significant lists of information and definitions for key terms.
6. Arrange an interview with three instructors on your campus to gain insight into their approaches to tests. Create a standard set of questions to use with each instructor. The following questions are provided only as suggestions, but you may use them if you wish:

   What types of questions do you prefer to use on your tests? Why?

   What test-taking suggestions or tips do you give your students?

   What are two test preparation strategies that work well in studying for your course?

   Do you assign computerized tests? Why or why not?
7. Create a study tape for yourself for Chapter 12. On your tape, summarize or explain the most important points of the chapter that you need to learn. This tape will serve as an excellent review tape later in the term.

Chapter 12 REVIEW QUESTIONS

True-False

Carefully read the following sentences. Pay attention to key words. Write T *if the statement is true. Write* F *if the statement is false.*

_______ **1.** Jotting down reminders on your test can help you keep a calm mind before you begin a test.

_______ **2.** The words *reason, because,* and *since* are often relationship clues.

_______ **3.** All items listed in a series must be false before you can use a false answer.

_______ **4.** True-false statements that use negatives are always false.

_______ **5.** The most inclusive option in a multiple-choice question is often the best answer.

_______ **6.** You should always work systematically through a test by completing questions in the order in which they appear.

_______ **7.** If a multiple-choice question has four options, the question should be read as four true-false statements.

_______ **8.** If you cannot give an immediate response, you should use educated guessing.

_______ **9.** In matching questions, an item from each column can be formed into a sentence by using helper words during the delayed response step.

_______ **10.** If you give an incorrect answer on a computerized test, you should quickly move to the next question to keep your confidence level high.

Multiple-Choice

Write the letter of the best answer *on the line.*

_______ **1.** If you start to feel anxiety during a test, you can
a. become more active with the test by circling directions and underlining key words.
b. activate your auditory channel by rereading questions with a whispering voice.
c. help keep your eyes focused on the question by blocking off the rest of the test with your arm or a piece of paper.
d. All of the above

_______ **2.** The _________ of a multiple-choice question should be used with each option.
a. distractors
b. directions
c. stem
d. All of the above

_______ **3.** Educated guessing should be used after
a. the recall step of response.
b. the immediate response step.
c. all other options have been tried.
d. the delayed response step.

_______ **4.** When you first read the stem of a multiple-choice question, you should
a. decide you really don't like the question.
b. turn it into a true-false question.
c. finish the stem with your own words and then see whether an option matches your words.
d. identify the distractors immediately, using educated guessing strategies.

_______ **5.** When you are told your answer is incorrect on a computerized test, you should
a. take a deep breath, relax, and try not to get irritated.
b. try to remember the test question so you can discuss it later.
c. take time to learn the information with the correct answer.
d. All of the above

Matching

Match the items on the left to the items on the right, writing the letter answer on the line. You may use each answer only once.

_______ **1.** Paired associations
_______ **2.** 100 percent modifiers
_______ **3.** In-between modifiers
_______ **4.** Relationship clues
_______ **5.** Prefixes with negative meanings
_______ **6.** Recognition questions
_______ **7.** Delayed response
_______ **8.** Assisted response
_______ **9.** Stem
_______ **10.** Distractors

a. words such as *sometimes, often, some, perhaps*
b. units of meaning at the beginning of words that mean "no" or "not"
c. guessing true or the letter *c*
d. the linking of two ideas together
e. the beginning part of a multiple-choice question
f. answers that you immediately know
g. options that are incorrect answers
h. involves rereading, looking for clues, and doing memory searches
i. words that are absolutes
j. objective questions
k. a response you give after you skim the test for clues
l. words that often show cause/effect

Short Answer and Critical Thinking

Answer the following questions on your own paper. Use paragraph form for your answers.

1. Zach frequently has problems managing his time on tests. For math tests, he starts with the most difficult problems because they represent the most points, but then he does not have enough time to work the rest of the problems. In history class, he usually does well on objective questions but runs out of time for answering the essay questions. Discuss two test-taking strategies Zach could use to manage his time on tests more effectively.
2. Discuss the difference between *delayed response* and *assisted response* that can be used for objective test questions.

Developing Strategies for Recall, Math, and Essay Tests

CHAPTER 13

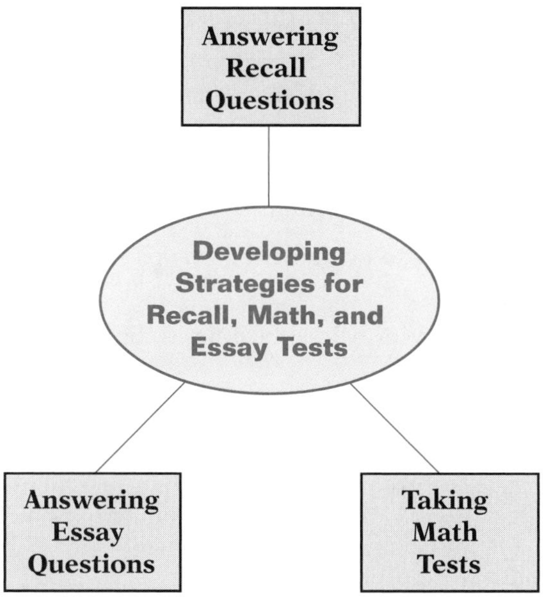

During your college career, you will likely encounter recall, math, and essay tests. In this chapter you will learn effective strategies to answer recall questions, which include fill-in-the blanks, listing, definition, and short-answer questions. You will also learn strategies to avoid common errors on math tests and strategies for increasing your performance on math tests. Essay tests—the most challenging type of test for many students—require you to know the information thoroughly, organize your thoughts logically, and express your ideas in well-written sentences and paragraphs. The strategies given here for answering essay questions will strengthen your performance on essay tests.

Terms to Know

- recall questions
- fill-in-the-blank questions
- immediate response
- delayed response
- memory search
- assisted response
- synonym
- listing questions
- closed questions
- open-ended questions
- definition questions
- short-answer questions
- direction word
- RSTUV Problem-Solving Method
- summary notes
- thesis sentence
- organizational plan for an essay
- five-paragraph essay format
- body of the essay
- concluding paragraph

CHAPTER 13 Recall, Math, and Essay Tests Profile

DO, SCORE, and **RECORD** your profile before you read this chapter. If you need to review the process, refer to the complete directions given in the profile for Chapter 1 on page 2.

ONLINE: You can complete the profile and get your score online at this textbook's web site.

	YES	NO
1. My answers on questions that require lists of information or short answers are often incomplete or inaccurate.	______	______
2. I often have difficulty recalling a specific word to complete a fill-in-the-blank question.	______	______
3. Open-ended questions that have many possible answers are difficult for me to answer.	______	______
4. I write a one-sentence answer for most questions that ask me to define a term.	______	______
5. I understand the different answers required for questions that use the direction words *define, explain, compare, summarize,* or *evaluate.*	______	______
6. I know how to analyze my answers on math tests so I can identify my pattern of errors.	______	______
7. When I can, I take time to proofread all my answers before turning in the test and leaving the classroom.	______	______
8. I use my course syllabus, the table of contents of my textbook, and my class notes to predict themes or topics that might appear in essay questions.	______	______
9. I prepare summary notes before major tests, such as midterms or final exams.	______	______
10. I use a specific strategy for answering math word problem questions.	______	______

Reflection Writing 1 — CHAPTER 13

On a separate piece of paper or in a journal, do the following:

1. Discuss your profile score for this chapter. What was your score? What does it mean to you?
2. Discuss your general attitude toward tests. How do you react when your instructor announces a test? How do you rate your overall test-taking skills?

Answering Recall Questions

The four most common types of **recall questions** are fill-in-the-blank questions, listing questions, definitions, and short answers. Elaborative rehearsal, thorough learning, and efficient long-term memory retrieval techniques are essential for answering such questions. No educated guessing strategies are available for these questions. The following chart summarizes the kind of information to study and forms of practice to include when you prepare for recall questions.

Recall Questions

Study This Kind of Information:	Practice May Include:
• Information presented in lists • Definition cards —say and spell words on the fronts for fill-in-the blank tests —three-part definitions on the backs of cards for definition and short-answer tests • Category cards • Cornell recall columns • Questions created in the *Q* step of SQ4R • Summaries at the ends of chapters • Details on visual notetaking systems	• Reciting information in full sentences and in your own words • Writing short summaries to practice expressing ideas on paper • Writing answers to the questions created in the *Q* step of SQ4R • Writing your own questions for fill-in-the-blank, listing, definition, and short answer questions • Working with a study partner to exchange practice questions

Fill-in-the-Blank Questions

A **fill-in-the-blank question** is a sentence with one or more words missing. You must read the sentence carefully and decide which key words will complete the sentence correctly. If you know a test will have fill-in-the-blank questions, you can predict that the majority of answers will relate to terminology. The following strategies provide you with methods for studying and completing this kind of recall question.

Strategies for Fill-in-the-Blank Questions

1. Study from the backs of your index cards.
2. Use immediate response.
3. Use delayed response; search your memory for the category and ask questions.
4. Use assisted response by skimming the rest of the test.
5. Substitute a related synonym or phrase.

Study from the Backs of Your Index Cards Many fill-in-the-blank questions are based on key vocabulary terms. Spend extra time studying from the *backs* of your index cards so that you can readily recall the terms on the fronts. If you are studying from vocabulary sheets (similar to the Cornell notetaking format) with the terminology on the left and the definitions on the right, cover up the left column. Read the definitions and practice reciting and spelling the terms in the left column. Your index cards or vocabulary sheets should include all the key terms in the chapter and other terms given in lectures.

Use Immediate Response If you created, recited, and reviewed vocabulary cards or vocabulary sheets using the method just described, you can often get an **immediate response**. The following points are important to remember when you fill in the blanks:

- Unless the directions say otherwise, write only one word on each blank line.
- The length of the line is not an automatic clue to the length of the word that will fit on the line.
- The completed sentence should make sense and be grammatically correct.
- Blanks that are separated by commas indicate a series of items.
- Several blank lines without commas between them indicate that you will be completing a phrase with a specific number of words.

Use Delayed Response To use **delayed response**, search your memory for the general category or topic related to the information in the sentence. Once you identify the category, search your memory for the details. Try to recall a specific chapter, a specific visual mapping, a study tool, or a mnemonic you rehearsed for the category. Then ask yourself questions, such as *What is . . . What do we call . . . Where is . . . When . . . Who . . . ?* "Talk" your way to the answer.

This **memory search**, or process of thinking back and connecting to information learned, needs to be done quickly. If you have difficulty identifying the category, recalling the study tool used, or answering the questions you formulate, delay your response. Do not spend too much time on one question. If you need to leave the question blank, put a checkmark next to the question so you remember to come back to it later. Move on to the next question.

Use Assisted Response After you have answered all the questions you can on the test, return to the unanswered ones and apply **assisted response**. Because fill-in-the-blank questions are usually key vocabulary terms, use the rest of the test to look for the terms or their categories. For example, if you know the term belongs to the category "test anxiety," skim through the test looking for other questions about test anxiety. Sometimes you will find the word or an item on the test that will trigger an association to the missing word.

Substitute a Related Synonym or Phrase You may be able to pick up partial points by writing something in the blank even though you know it is not the correct term. Try one of the following possibilities:

- Use a **synonym** (a word with a similar meaning) or a substitute word. You may not get full points for your answer, but you may be given partial credit.
- If necessary, write a short phrase. Some teachers (though not all) will recognize your effort.

Filling in the blank using synonyms, substitutions, or phrases does show an effort on your part. Be aware, however, that you may put effort into using this approach but your answer will be marked wrong because the *exact* answer was needed. Make a mental note to find the correct answers after the test.

EXERCISE 13.1 Filling in the Blanks

Work with a partner. Read the following questions carefully. They are all review questions based on key terms from previous chapters. First try an immediate response; then try a delayed response by doing a memory search and posing a question.

1. The ______________ ______________ technique is a concentration technique for letting other people know that you do not want to be disturbed.

2. The beginning part of a multiple-choice question is called the ______________.

3. ______________ time consists of a few hours each week added to your time-management schedule to allow for any extra study time beyond your regular study blocks.

4. Howard Gardner's ______________ intelligence refers to a person's ability to work cooperatively, understand people, and demonstrate leadership skills.

5. The second step of the Cornell system uses the memory principle of selectivity when information is selected to put in the ______________ column.

6. The memory principle of ______________ is used when two items are linked together in memory so one can trigger the recall of the other.

7. Maslow's highest level of needs in his hierarchy is called ______________-______________.

8. ______________ are clusters of related information that are imprinted in long-term memory.

9. Excessive stress is called ______________.

10. ______________ are number words such as *first, second,* and *third.*

11. A(n) ______________ is a "memory trick strategy" that involves making up a word by using the first letters of each of the key words that you need to remember.

12. A(n) ______________ learner describes a person who is a "right-brain dominant person" and tends to be intuitive, creative, and visual.

13. ______________ ______________ such as I, II, III, IV, and V are used to show main topics in a formal outline.

14. ______________ memory occurs when emphasis is on memorizing the exact wording of information instead of using elaborative rehearsal for more thorough understanding.

15. ______________ is the process of skimming through information before beginning the process of careful reading.

Listing Questions

Listing questions require you to recall a specific number of ideas, steps, or vocabulary words. The answers are usually key words; full sentences are not generally required. Listing questions often begin with the direction word *list* or *name*. Using the following strategies will improve your performance on listing questions.

Strategies for Listing Questions

1. Predict listing questions when you study.
2. Underline key words and determine whether the question is closed or open ended.
3. Use immediate response.
4. Use delayed response; do a memory search and ask questions.
5. Use assisted response.
6. Substitute a related synonym or phrase.

Predict Listing Questions When You Study You can predict listing questions as you read, take notes, and create study tools by recognizing or anticipating possible items for listing questions. Lists to study can be found

- on vocabulary category cards.
- in questions created for headings in the SQ4R system.
- in Cornell recall columns.
- in chapter objectives and introductions.
- in level one and level two information in mappings or hierarchies.
- in paragraphs that use ordinals (number words).
- in marginal notes written in your textbooks.

Underline Key Words In Closed and Open Ended Questions By underlining the key words in the question, you will be able to focus specifically on the information being asked. Notice how the underlining in the following question helps you focus:

1. Lining up the Cornell columns is one reflect activity you can do during the fourth step of the Cornell notetaking system. List five other study tools that you can make during the reflect step to reinforce the learning process.

Now decide whether the question has specific answers or a variety of possible answers. **Closed questions** require very specific answers, often in a specific order. **Open-ended questions** can have many possible answers. You can pull related ideas and information from throughout the term to develop your answer for an open-ended question. The above question about study tools during the reflect step of Cornell is an open-ended question. Any five of the following answers would be correct: visual mappings, cartoon/pictures, acronyms, outlines, study tapes, written summaries, predicted test questions, vocabulary flash cards, or hierarchies.

This is a *closed question:* List the five *R*'s of the Cornell notetaking system in the order in which they occur.

This is an *open-ended question:* List six concentration strategies to reduce attention to external distractors.

Use Immediate Response After you have underlined the key words in the directions, you may be ready with the answer. Being able to give an *immediate response* indicates that you organized and rehearsed information effectively, which enabled you to quickly retrieve what was needed from long-term memory.

Use Delayed Response If necessary, move to *delayed response*. Use association triggers to help you connect the key words in the directions to the information you want to find in your memory bank. Use the following techniques.

- Focus on the key words you underlined in the directions. These will help you identify the category.
- Search your memory for study tools that you created to rehearse the information. Try to picture the index cards, the Cornell recall column, the chapter headings, or the main topics in visual notes or outlines.
- Turn the information into a new *question*. In the preceding example, you might pose the question "What study tools help me reflect on information that I am learning?"

Because you probably have many other questions to deal with on the test, memory searching and questioning must be done relatively quickly. If you are able to retrieve an answer—or part of an answer—write it down. If you are not able to complete the listing, *place a checkmark next to the question*. You can come back to it later after you have completed as many questions as possible.

Use Assisted Response When you return to the unanswered or partially answered questions, skim through the rest of the test for possible clues. Many times important information appears in the test in more than one place but in a different questioning format. Focus on the key words that you underlined in the directions. When you find a possible answer, check it against the question that you posed earlier.

Substitute a Related Synonym or Phrase If you were not able to locate the exact terms for the listing, use synonyms or short phrases. These answers are not as accurate, yet they show your effort and general understanding. An empty space can bring only one result: no points. You may receive full points or partial points for using synonyms or short phrases.

EXERCISE 13.2 Practicing Closed and Open-Ended Questions

Work with a partner. Read the following questions carefully. In the margin, write C *if the question is a closed question and* O *if the question is an open-ended question. On separate paper, list answers for each question without referring to other pages in your textbook or your notes.*

_______ **1.** What are the steps, in order, for the SQ4R textbook reading system?

_______ **2.** List five strategies to reduce or eliminate procrastination.

_______ **3.** List five traits of active listeners.

_______ **4.** What are the eight intelligences in Howard Gardner's Theory of Multiple Intelligences?

_______ **5.** Name the four levels of response (in order) that you can use to answer test questions.

Definition Questions

Any questions that ask you to "define" a term are **definition questions**. This kind of question asks you to retrieve specific information from your memory and organize the information into sentences. *Paired association* is required and achieved if you have studied from vocabulary cards or vocabulary sheets. You can predict that these questions will come from the course-specific terminology that was defined in your textbook and in lectures. The following strategies will result in well-developed definition answers.

Strategies for Definition Questions

1. Read the question carefully. Underline the term to be defined.
2. Use the three steps for writing definitions.
3. Use delayed response and assisted response if necessary.

Underline the Term For a short definition question, the term is easy to identify. Underline the term to help you keep your focus on that one word. Sometimes definition questions begin by giving background information. Read all of the information carefully and then underline the term to be defined. The following examples are both definition questions.

1. Define the term *neurons*.
2. The human nervous system is comprised of two primary types of cells, the neurons and the glial cells. Glial cells provide physiological support to neurons. Define *neurons* in the central nervous system.

Use the Three Steps for Writing Definitions For powerful definition answers, include three levels of information. First, name the category associated with the term. Second, give the formal definition. Third, expand the definition with one more detail. The following examples show a weak answer and a strong answer.

Question: Define the term *distributed practice*.

Weak Answer: It means you practice at different times.

Strong Answer: Distributed practice is a time-management strategy that is also related to the memory principle of time on task. It means that study blocks are spread or distributed throughout the week. Distributed practice is the opposite of marathon studying.

Category → that is also related to the memory principle of time on task.
Definition → distributed throughout the week.
One more detail → is the opposite of marathon studying.

Expanding your definition is the open-ended part of a question that gives you the opportunity to show you know more about a word than just its most basic definition. The following chart shows seven methods, followed by an example, that are commonly used to expand a definition.

Method	Example
Add one more fact.	*Distributed practice often occurs when the 2:1 ratio is used.*
Give a synonym.	*Distributed practice is the same as spaced studying.*
Give an antonym, a contrast, or a negation.	*Distributed practice is the opposite of marathon studying or massed practice.*
Give a comparison or an analogy.	*Distributed practice is like working on a goal a little every day instead of trying to complete all the steps in one block of time.*
Define the structure of the word.	*The root of neuron is "neuro," which means nervous system.*
Give the etymology.	*The term locus comes from the Latin "loci," which means place, so locus of control refers to a place where there is the control.*
Give an application.	*Surveying can be used to become familiar with a new textbook, chapter, article, or test.*

Use Delayed and Assisted Response If you are not able to give an immediate response, the questions given for identifying the general category may help you with the delayed response. If your mind is blank and you cannot write the definition or expand the definition, *place a checkmark next to the question and move on.* After you have answered all the questions you can, skim through the rest of the test to search for additional clues or details to complete your answer. Remember that key terms are frequently used or referred to in other parts of the test in other questioning formats.

EXERCISE 13.3 Answering Definition Questions

Work with a partner. Write a three-part definition answer for the following definition questions.

1. Define the term *reciting*.

   category: ______________________________

   definition: ______________________________

   ____

   one more detail: ______________________________

   ____

2. You have learned many study strategies in this course. These strategies have one common characteristic: they all emphasize *elaborative rehearsal*. Define the term *elaborative rehearsal*.

   category: ______________________________

   definition: ______________________________

   ____

   one more detail: ______________________________

   ____

3. Learning involves intellectual and emotional growth. Self-talk has the power to enhance the learning process, but it can also hinder the learning process. In this course, the focus has been on the power of *positive self-talk*. Define what is meant by *positive self-talk*.

   category: ______________________________

   definition: ______________________________

   ____

   one more detail: ______________________________

   ____

4. Define *Memory Principle of Organization*.

category: ______________________________

definition: ______________________________

____

one more detail: ______________________________

____

Short-Answer Questions

Short-answer questions usually require a short paragraph of three to seven sentences for the answer. Sometimes they look like "mini-essays" and other times they look like expanded "listing questions" that use sentences to explain the items in a listing. With short answers, both the content of your answer and your writing skills are important. Some teachers will grade higher when you use correct grammar, punctuation, and spelling.

As with listing questions, short-answer questions may be *closed questions* in which very specific answers are expected. They may also be *open-ended questions* that require you to connect or relate ideas from different parts of the course, or they may require you to apply your knowledge to new situations. Both types of short-answer questions require sufficient details to show that you know the information. The following steps can help you write an effective answer.

Strategies for Answering Short-Answer Questions

1. Identify the direction word and underline the key words.
2. Make a mental plan or short list of key ideas to use in your answer.
3. Write a strong, focused opening sentence.
4. Add additional sentences with specific details.
5. Use delayed and assisted response if necessary.

Identify the Direction Word and Underline Key Words The first step is to pay attention to the **direction word** in each question. Each type of direction word requires a specific kind of answer. To get full points for your work, your answer must match the question. The following direction words are common for short-answer questions.

Direction Word	What Is Required
Discuss/Tell	Tell about a particular topic.
Identify/What are?	Identify specific points. (This is similar to a listing except that you are required to answer in full sentences.)
Describe	Give more specific details or descriptions than are required by "discuss."
Explain/Why?	Give reasons. Answers the question "Why?"
Explain how/How?	Describe a process or a set of steps. Give the steps in chronological (time sequence) order.
When?	Describe a time or a specific condition needed for something to happen, occur, or be used.

Circle the key direction word when you first read the question. Review in your mind what is required by this direction word. Because you want to respond quickly, become very familiar with the preceding descriptions of direction words. Then underline key words to use in your answer.

Each of the following test questions has the same subject: visual mappings. However, because of the different direction words, each answer will be slightly different.

Why is recitation important to use while studying a visual mapping?

Explain how to create a visual mapping.

How should you study from a visual mapping?

When should visual mappings be used?

Make a Mental Plan or a Short List of Key Ideas Look at the key words underlined in the step above. These words should be included in your answer. Pause and do a *memory search* for appropriate details for your answer. Either make a mental plan or jot down a short list of points that you will want to present in sentence form. Do only what is expected; do not pad the answer with unrelated information.

Write a Strong, Focused Opening Sentence Because you will not have much space to write a long answer, begin your answer with a sentence that is direct and to the point. Your first sentence should include the key words of the question and should show that you are heading in the direction required by the direction word. Do not beat around the bush or save your best information for last. The first sentence, when well written, lets the teacher know right away that you are familiar with the subject.

Notice the differences in quality in the following opening sentences. The first one does not get to the point. The second and third examples are direct and show confidence.

Question: Why is recitation important in the learning process?

Weak: Recitation is important because it helps a person learn better.

Strong: Recitation, one of the Twelve Principles of Memory, is important to use for studying for three reasons.

Strong: Recitation is important for studying because it involves the auditory channel, feedback, and practice expressing ideas.

Add Sentences with Specific Details After you write your opening sentence, expand your answer with more information. Give appropriate details to support your opening sentence; try to use course-related terminology in your answers.

Notice the difference between the weak answer and the strong answer in the following example.

Weak: Recitation is important because it helps a person learn. Everyone wants to do the very best possible and recitation helps make that happen. When you recite, you talk out loud. You practice information out loud before a test.

Strong: Recitation is important for studying because it involves the auditory channel, gives feedback, and provides practice expressing ideas. When a person states information out loud and in complete sentences, he/she activates the auditory channel, which results in a stronger imprint in long-term memory. Reciting also gives feedback so a person knows immediately whether or not the information is understood on the level that it can be explained to someone else. Taking time to recite also provides the opportunity to practice organizing ideas so they can be clearly expressed.

Use Delayed and Assisted Response if Necessary If you are unable to write a strong opening sentence for your short answer, do a memory search for the topic. Frequently students are able to write the opening sentence but have difficulty with the details necessary to expand the opening sentence. If the delayed response and the memory search do not result in sufficient information or details, place a checkmark next to the question and move on. After all other questions have been answered, skim through the test for related details that you can add to your short answer. Expand your answer with these details.

EXERCISE 13.4 Writing Answers to Short-Answer Questions

Select two *questions from the following list. Write your answers on a separate piece of paper, or use the computer to email your answers to your instructor. Be sure to include the numbers of the questions with your answers.*

1. Discuss the differences between *hearing* and *listening*.
2. Explain why *rote memory* is not a reliable method for studying in college.
3. Explain how *locus of control* affects a person's perception of his or her life.
4. Discuss any one strategy that you can use to comprehend a difficult paragraph.
5. Describe a *five-day study plan* for a major test.
6. Explain the process that stimuli go through to be imprinted in long-term memory.
7. When should you use educated guessing on tests?
8. Explain how the *Decay Theory of Forgetting* works.
9. Briefly discuss ways to keep your mind on the speaker when his or her rate of speech is very slow and your rate of thinking is very fast.
10. What occurs for a listener in the first step (reception) of the listening process?

Exercise 13.5 LINKS

Assume you are in a health class and are preparing for a test that includes the coping strategies presented in Exercise 11.1, page 294. Write the following kinds of practice questions on your own paper. Then present your questions to a partner to answer while you practice answering your partner's questions. Try answering these recall questions without looking back at the passage.

1. Write three fill-in-the-blank questions.
2. Write one listing question.
3. Write one definition question.
4. Write one short-answer question.

Group Processing: A Collaborative Learning Activity

Form groups of three or four students. Complete the following directions. You may be asked to share with the class the information your group generates.

1. Discuss strategies you use to prepare for a math test. After each member of your group discusses his or her strategies, compile a list of the strategies used by members of your group for math tests.
2. Brainstorm to make a second list that shows the kinds of errors you sometimes make on math tests.

Taking Math Tests

How can this student use a completed math test to improve her test-taking skills? What kinds of problem patterns should she look for on the test?

The test-preparation strategies and test-taking strategies discussed previously apply to test-taking situations for all math tests. Because most problems on math tests are patterned after math problems you worked on in the textbook and in class, reworking problems before a test is an excellent test-preparation technique. Reciting and reviewing steps of a specific process, formulas or theorems, and meanings of symbols, and translating algebraic symbols into English words should also be a part of your test-preparation strategy. Performing well on tests involves a variety of tasks:

1. You must read the directions and the problem carefully to identify the problem, the information that is provided, and the missing information that you will need to supply for the answer. Frequently, drawing a simple picture of the problem or expressing the problem in an algebraic formula will help you see the problem more clearly.
2. You must use the information to solve the problem. You can begin the process by first *estimating a reasonable answer*. After you work the steps to complete the problem, you can compare your final answer with your estimated answer. A discrepancy between the two answers provides you with feedback that you should examine the problem more carefully.
3. You must apply the appropriate problem-solving technique to reach the correct answer. Conduct a **memory search** for the problem-solving steps or formulas that you used in class for this type of math problem. Mentally compare the test problem to problems you practiced and reworked in class and in the textbook.
4. You must show your work all the way through to the last step of solving the problem. Showing all the steps of the process indicates that you understand how to use a set procedure to solve the problem; it can also show you or your instructor where errors occur if you do not solve the problem correctly. In addition, your instructor may award points for the work you show in the individual steps even if the final answer is incorrect.

Six Types of Test-Taking Errors

Recognizing six types of test-taking errors can help you strengthen your accuracy on math tests. Use the following information each time you do a math problem for homework, as well as on tests. After tests are returned to you, use the information to analyze your errors so you can adjust your strategies for future tests.

Six Types of Test-Taking Errors

1. Misread directions errors
2. Careless errors
3. Concept errors
4. Application errors
5. Test-taking errors
6. Study errors

Adapted from: Nolting, *Math Study Skills Workbook,* pp.92–95.

Misread directions errors occur when you skip directions or misunderstand directions, but you work the problems anyway. To avoid misread directions errors, read all the directions carefully and circle or underline key words. If you do not understand any of them, ask your instructor for clarification.

Careless errors are mistakes that you can catch automatically upon reviewing the test. Both good and poor math students make careless errors. Students who commit these errors know the math but simply make sloppy mistakes, such as calculation mistakes, or omission of a symbol or the steps used to solve the problem. If a student can point out the mistake upon examination of a problem at a later point, the error is one of carelessness. To reduce careless errors, use all available test time wisely to check your work.

Concept errors are mistakes made when you do not understand the properties or principles required to work the problem. Concept errors, if not corrected, will follow you from test to test, causing a loss of test points. After the test, go back to your textbook or notes and learn why you missed those types of problems. Rework several problems that use the concept that you need to learn more accurately. In your own words, write the concepts that you use to solve these kinds of problems.

Application errors occur when you know the concept but cannot apply it to the problem. Application errors usually are found in word problems, deducing formulas (such as the quadratic equation), and graphing. To reduce application errors, you must predict the types of application problems that will be on the test. You must then think through and practice solving those types of problems using the concepts. Application errors can be avoided with appropriate practice and insight.

Test-taking errors apply to the specific way you take tests. The following list includes test-taking errors that can cause you to lose many points on an exam:

1. *Missing more questions in the first third or the last third of a test:* Errors in the first third of a test (the easiest problems) can be due to carelessness. Errors in the last part of the test can be due to the fact that the last problems are more difficult or due to increasing your test speed to finish the test.
2. *Not completing a problem to its last step:* Take time to review the last step to be sure you show all your work right up to the end of the problem.
3. *Changing test answers from correct to incorrect:* Changing answers without a logical reason for doing so is a sign of panic or test anxiety. Keep your original answer unless you locate an error in your work when you review your work a final time.
4. *Getting stuck on one problem and spending too much time on it:* Set a time limit for each problem. Working too long on a problem without success will increase your test anxiety and waste valuable time that could be better used solving other problems or reviewing your test.
5. *Rushing through the easiest part of the test and making careless errors:* Work more slowly and carefully. Review the easiest problems first if you have time to go back over your work during the allotted test time.
6. *Miscopying an answer from your scratch work to the test:* Systematically compare your last problem step on scratch paper with the answer written on the test. Always hand in your scratch work with your test.
7. *Leaving answers blank:* If you cannot figure out how to solve a problem, rewrite the problem and try to do at least the first step.
8. *Solving only the first step of a two-step problem:* Write *two* in the margin of the test when you first read the problem. This reminds you that you need to show two steps or two answers to the problem.
9. *Not understanding all the functions of your calculator* can cause major testing problems. Take time to learn all the functions of your calculator *before* the test.
10. *Leaving the test early without checking your answers:* Use the entire allotted test time. Remain in the room and use the time to check each problem.

Study errors occur when you study the wrong type of material or do not spend enough time on pertinent material. Use your time management skills to allocate sufficient time to review problems and formulas that have been covered in class. Create study tools such as three-column notes and index cards to review frequently before the test.

Adapted from: Nolting, *Math Study Skills Workbook,* pages 92–95.

The RSTUV Problem-Solving Method

In *Topics in Contemporary Mathematics*, the **RSTUV Problem-Solving Method** serves as a model to solve *any* word problem.

RSTUV Problem-Solving Method

1. **R**ead the problem, not once or twice, but until you understand it.
2. **S**elect the unknown; that is, find out what the problem asks for.
3. **T**hink of a plan to solve the problem.
4. **U**se the techniques you are studying to carry out the plan.
5. **V**erify your answer.

1. **Read** the problem.

Mathematics is a language. As such, you have to learn how to read it. You may not understand or even get through reading the problem the first time. Read it again and, as you do, pay attention to key words or instructions such as *compute, draw, write, construct, make, show, identify, state, simplify, solve,* and *graph.*

2. **Select** the unknown.

How can you answer a question if you do not know what the question is? One good way to look for the unknown is to look for the question mark "?" and carefully read the material preceding it. Try to determine what information is given and what is missing.

3. **Think** of a plan.

Problem solving requires many skills and strategies. Some of them are *look for a pattern; examine a related problem; make tables, pictures, and diagrams; write an equation; work backward;* and *make a guess.*

4. **Use** the techniques you are studying to carry out the plan.

If you are studying a mathematical technique, it is almost certain that you will have to use it in solving the given problem. Look for procedures that can be used to solve specific problems. Then carry out the plan. Check each step.

5. **Verify** the answer.

Look back and check the results of the original problem. Is the answer reasonable? Can you find it some other way?

Source: Bello and Britton, *Topics in Contemporary Mathematics,* pp. 5–6.

Reflection Writing 2 — CHAPTER 13

On a separate piece of paper or in a journal, discuss the strategies that you believe will be the most helpful to you on future tests involving recall questions and math problems. Which strategies deal directly with test-taking problems you have previously encountered? How might these strategies improve your performance?

Name ______________________________ Date ______________

Exercise 13.6 Looking at Test-Taking Errors on Math Tests

*Complete the following comparison chart. In the middle column, briefly describe or define each of the problems listed on the left. In the right column, personalize your chart by noting whether you tend to exhibit that type of error in your math tests. (*Note: *If you are not currently enrolled in a math course, you may complete this chart for any one of your courses.)*

Type of Error	Brief Description	Personal Assessment
1. Misread directions		
2. Careless		
3. Concept		
4. Application		
5. Test-taking		
6. Study		

EXERCISE 13.7 Case Studies

Each of the following case studies describes a student situation. Read each case study carefully; highlight key ideas or student issues. Answer the question that ends each case study. In your response, address the key points that you highlighted and that directly relate to the question. Answer in complete sentences. These case studies are also available online; you can email your response to your instructor or print a copy of your work online.

1. Armand takes effective notes in his science class. He does well on multiple-choice tests but frequently has difficulty with fill-in-the-blank tests. He realizes that he needs to adjust his study methods to prepare more effectively for this test format. Which study methods would you recommend he use to be better prepared for fill-in-the-blank questions?

2. Jessica's sociology instructor writes test questions that require listings and short answers. Jessica decides to form a study group to help her prepare for an upcoming sociology test. She wants the group to be productive, but she needs suggestions on an approach the study group can use to prepare for the test. Which study techniques would you suggest the group implement?

3. As a way to strengthen his math test-taking skills, Dimitri decides to do an error-pattern analysis of his previous math tests. He quickly discovers that most of his incorrect answers were due to his misreading the directions or making careless errors. What test-taking strategies could Dimitri use to eliminate these types of errors?

Answering Essay Questions

Essays are demanding. They require that you know the information thoroughly, be able to pull the information from your memory, and write about relationships rather than isolated facts. The way you express the information and the relationships needs to follow a logical line of thinking. Essays also require a sound grasp of writing skills (grammar, syntax, and spelling), as well as a well-developed, expressive vocabulary. If essay writing is intimidating to you, be assured that you can strengthen your essay-writing skills by using the following strategies and, if you feel it necessary, by enrolling in writing or vocabulary courses.

Preparing for Essay Tests

Preparation for essay tests involves gathering information about "the big picture" concepts, trends, and relationships and then associating supporting details to be used within the essay. The strategies used to prepare for essays vary based on the type of essay test that will be used.

Strategies for Different Kinds of Essay Tests

1. Predict and organize for essay tests when the topics are unknown.
2. Organize and practice writing essays when the *topics* are announced in advance.
3. Organize and practice writing essays when the *questions* are announced in advance.
4. Organize materials when the essay is an *open-book* test.
5. Organize and develop essay answers for *take-home* tests.

Unknown Topics *Predict and organize for essay tests when the topics are unknown.* The most challenging type of essay test is the one in which the topics for the essay questions are not announced in advance. For this type of test, your study strategies throughout the term need to include *elaborative rehearsal* of both the textbook and the lecture material. Elaborative rehearsal occurs when you work with the information; rearrange it; look for relationships, patterns, and trends; and work to recognize key concepts, main ideas, and themes, as well as significant supporting details for the "big pictures." The following strategies will help you prepare for essay exams when the topics are not announced in advance.

- *Focus on identifying the major themes that your instructor developed throughout the term.* Begin by examining your course syllabus and course outline. Your course syllabus and outline state the course objectives and learning outcomes, which basically are the themes or the *big pictures* you should know upon completion of the course. Next, examine the textbook's table of contents. Oftentimes the headings of units or groups of chapters form a theme; the chapter titles may also form themes. For example, in the sample table of contents in Chapter 7 (page 174), the unit headings reveal several themes: Chemical Substances and Reactions, Atomic Structure and Chemical Reactions, Different States of Matter, and Chemical Reaction Concepts. Some chapter titles may also reveal themes that your instructor emphasized in the course: Chemical Composition, Electron Structure of Atoms, Chemical Bonding, or Acids and Bases. Review the information in the introductory section of your textbook, for it often states major themes the author develops in the textbook. Finally, examine your course notes and any visual materials such as visual mappings, hierarchies, and comparison charts that you created throughout the term to identify additional recurring topics or themes. The following chart summarizes ways to identify major themes that your instructor may use to write essay questions.

Identifying Themes

1. Course syllabus and course outline
2. Unit titles and chapter titles in the table of contents
3. Introductory material in the front of the textbook
4. Course notes and visual materials

- *Create* **summary notes** *that pull together information from your textbook, lectures, and homework for each theme.* Essay questions often require you to compare, contrast, summarize, describe, explain, discuss, or apply information about major themes to specific situations, so your goal with summary sheets is to facilitate the review process by compiling and grouping related information. Summary sheets in the form of lists, visual mappings, hierarchies, outlines, or comparison charts help you group and organize information into a *big picture* (see Chapter 4, page 101).
- *Use the list of possible themes and your summary notes to predict and write test questions.* Refer to previous tests from the same instructor to become familiar with the types of essay questions your instructor uses. You may also want to talk to students who have already completed the course to gain insight into the types of essay questions the instructor uses. Consider working with a study partner so each of you can create practice questions to prepare for an upcoming test. Use the direction words on page 366 to add variety to the questions you compose.
- *Practice writing answers for the essay questions you created.* Set a realistic time limit to compose answers to your practice questions. If you practice expressing your ideas on paper *before the test,* dealing with essay questions on the test is much less stressful and intimidating. Even if your predicted questions do not appear in some form on the test, you will have had practice working with a variety of topics in depth. Strategies for organizing your ideas and writing an essay appear on pages 368–371.

Topics Announced in Advance *Organize and practice writing essays when the topics are announced in advance.* Sometimes instructors will indicate the *topics* that will be used for essay questions, although they do not provide you with the actual *questions.* This advance notice offers you the opportunity to generate detailed notes on the topics so you can predict test questions and practice developing comprehensive answers. Use the following strategies to prepare for this type of essay test.

- *Use the index of your book to locate page references for information about the topic.* Reread each of the pages; prepare a set of **summary notes**. (See Chapter 4, page 101.) Expand your summary notes by adding information from your lecture notes and homework assignments.
- *Use the strategies discussed on pages 368–371 to identify possible themes related to the topic and to write practice test questions.* Remember that essay questions usually focus on the *big pictures* or concepts. They may ask you to compare, contrast, discuss, explain, or summarize information about the topic. Use a variety of direction words from the chart on page 366 when you write practice questions.

- *Practice organizing information and answering your predicted questions.* If you work with a study partner, each of you should prepare separate practice answers. Begin by organizing the information into an outline or some form of visual notetaking. After you finish your essays, take time to compare the structures of your essays and the kinds of information each of you chose to include in the answer.

Questions Announced in Advance *Organize and practice writing essays when the questions are announced in advance.* Some instructors announce the exact essay questions in advance, or they provide you with a list of essay questions from which the test questions will be selected. By announcing essay questions in advance, instructors expect well-developed and thorough answers that include specific, relevant details. This advance notice offers you the opportunity to gather pertinent information, organize the information into paragraphs, and compose a comprehensive answer. Use the following strategies to prepare for this type of essay test.

- *After carefully reading each question, identify the direction words and key words so your answers reflect the questions.* Be certain that you understand what kind of information the instructor expects in each of your answers.
- *Gather information to use in each answer.* Use the index of your textbook, your notes, and your homework assignments to locate information that you can use to answer each question.
- *Organize your answers.* Create outlines, visual mappings, or hierarchies to show the structure you plan to use in each answer. Clearly identify the main ideas that you will use to develop the separate paragraphs to answer each question. Memorize the outlines or the skeletons of your visual mappings or hierarchies so you can mentally recall them when you are in class composing the answer to the essay question.
- *Practice writing the answers to the questions several times.* Without referring to your outline or visual mapping, write a strong answer for each of the essay questions. Then critique your answer. Does it include the key ideas on your summary notes? Does it use course terminology? Do the ideas flow together smoothly? Set aside the questions for one day. The following day, write new answers for the essay questions. Compare the effectiveness of your answers. Continue practicing writing answers to the test questions until your ideas flow smoothly and effortlessly onto the paper.

Open-Book Test *Organize materials for an open-book test.* Students are often excited and relieved to learn that an essay test will be an open-book test. However, the previous strategies for preparing for tests by anticipating test questions, preparing summary sheets, and practicing writing answers should still be used. In addition, the following strategies should also be used so you are not wasting valuable test time searching for needed information:

- *Become familiar with the index of your book* so you can look up the topic quickly.
- *Use a special highlighter for important facts* (significant dates, names, events, statistics, or terminology) *and quotations* you predict may be needed on the essay.
- *Use tabs to mark significant pages* such as important summary charts, tables, lists or steps, or visual materials.

Take-Home Test *Organize and develop answers for a take-home test.* Expectations for a polished essay are higher when the essay questions are given as a take-home test. The major problem many students face with take-home tests is not allowing enough time to develop essay answers. Use the steps presented in Chapter 4 (pages 102–103) for a term-project goal.

Take-home essays, which are written in untimed situations, use basically the same steps as classroom tests with a few modifications in the first and last paragraphs. In an essay test, the first paragraph is very brief; it basically gives the thesis sentence. In an untimed essay, this first paragraph can be written to create a stronger interest for the reader. The paragraph may begin with a captivating introduction, called a *lead-in,* and end with your thesis sentence. Introductions or lead-ins may include:

- A short personal experience, an incident, an analogy, or an event from the text that is closely related to the thesis
- Factual information from your text or from library research
- Brief background information that prepares the reader for your thesis
- A fictitious situation that introduces the thesis

The last paragraph continues to serve as a summary or conclusion. The first part of the paragraph will still echo your thesis sentence. However, it can also include implications or applications of the topic of your essay. This closing paragraph can be written to leave the reader with some new angles or thoughts to consider.

If you decide to use these variations for your introductory and concluding paragraphs, remember to be concise. Lengthy variations shift the focus away from your thesis and body, and that is not your intention.

Understanding Direction Words

Some of the direction words used in short-answer questions also appear in essay questions. Understanding the direction words is essential for your essay to address the question that was posed. Study the following direction words so that you will know the kind of information that is expected in your answer.

Direction Word	What Is Required
Compare	Show the similarities and differences between two or more items.
Contrast	Present only the differences between two or more items.
Define	Give the definition and expand it with more examples and greater details.
Trace/Outline	Discuss the sequence of events in chronological order.
Summarize	Identify and discuss the main points or the highlights of a subject. Omit in-depth details.
Evaluate/Critique	Offer your opinion or judgment, and then back it up with specific facts, details, or reasons.
Analyze	Identify the different parts of something. Discuss each part individually.
Describe	Give a detailed description of different aspects, qualities, characteristics, parts, or points of view.
Discuss	Tell about the parts or the main points. Expand with specific details.
Explain/Explain why	Give reasons. Tell why. Show logical relationships or cause/effect.
Explain how	Give the process, steps, stages, or procedures involved. Explain each.
Illustrate	Give examples. Explain each example with details.

As an example of the importance of understanding the direction word, assume a question on your literature test stated, "Compare the writing style of Homer in *The Odyssey* and John Milton in *Paradise Lost*." In your essay, you would want to focus on the similarities and differences between the two authors' writing styles. To simply write one paragraph describing Homer and another paragraph describing Milton, and assume that the teacher could infer the differences by reading the two paragraphs would not clearly show the relationships involved. The direction word requires you to identify specific elements of writing styles and compare or contrast the use of each element by Homer and by Milton. Responding appropriately to direction words is an essential key to well-written answers.

EXERCISE 13.8 Analyzing Essay Questions

Work with a partner or in a small group. Read each question carefully. On the line, write C *if the question is a* closed question *and* O *if the question is an* open-ended question. *Then circle the direction word and underline key words that you would use in your answers.*

_______ **1.** Discuss this statement: Business competition encourages efficiency of production and leads to improved quality control.

_______ **2.** Is gross national product really a reliable indicator of a nation's standard of living? Explain.

_______ **3.** Why should business take on the task of training the hard-core unemployed?

_______ **4.** What are the major differences between the economic model of social responsibility and the socio-economic model?

_______ **5.** Define the goal of affirmative-action programs and tell how the goal is achieved.

_______ **6.** Explain the differences between general partners and limited partners.

_______ **7.** Trace the incorporation process and describe the basic corporate structure.

_______ **8.** Discuss the changes made in Washington in the post-Watergate years to place greater restrictions on the executive power of the president of the United States.

_______ **9.** Contrast the opinions and sentiments expressed by the people of Panama and the American people in 1977 in regard to the ownership and rights to the Panama Canal.

_______ **10.** President Clinton's 1998 visit to China brought the Tiananmen Square event back into the public's awareness. Trace the events in China that led up to and followed the massacre in Tiananmen Square.

_______ **11.** In the late 1990s, environmental issues remained high on the international list of global problems. Summarize the global environmental issues that may have the greatest impact on the welfare of the world's population.

_______ **12.** Which leadership style or styles most closely conform to supportive communication? Explain.

_______ **13.** Think of and then discuss three examples of positive ethnic stereotypes.

_______ **14.** Compare the thinking styles of vertical thinkers and lateral thinkers. Include the characteristics of each type of thinker and give examples to clearly show the differences in the way each would operate in day-to-day situations.

_______ **15.** What are Piaget's stages of human development? Summarize each stage of his theory.

_______ **16.** Trace the path of blood in the circulatory system of mammals.

Strategies for Answering Essay Questions

The following strategies for answering essay questions are similar to the strategies used for short-answer questions (page 354). The procedures have been expanded to meet the essay requirement that full paragraphs be used to communicate the information. Understanding the general structure of an essay and using the following strategies will result in better performance on essay tests.

Strategies for Answering Essay Questions

1. Identify the direction word and underline the key words.
2. Write a strong, focused opening sentence called a *thesis sentence* or *thesis statement.*
3. Plan your answer before you begin writing. Make a brief outline, visual mapping, hierarchy, or list of ideas to develop the body of your essay.
4. Develop the body of the essay. A common format is the five-paragraph essay.
5. Summarize your main ideas in a short concluding paragraph.
6. Proofread and revise.

Identify the Direction Word As discussed in the previous section, the beginning step in writing an essay is knowing what kind of answer is expected. The direction word indicates what is expected and should guide the direction of your answer.

Write a Strong Thesis Sentence A **thesis sentence** directly states the main point you want to make in the entire essay. The thesis sentence for an essay test should be the first sentence on your paper. This sentence should:

- clearly state the topic of the essay.
- include key words that are a part of the question.
- show that you understand the direction word.
- indicate a given number of main ideas you will discuss.

The thesis statement is important to you and to your teacher. For you, it serves as a guide for developing the rest of your essay. It provides the basic outline of main ideas to develop with important supporting details. For the teacher, it serves as an immediate indicator that you understand the question and know the answer. Because of the significance of the thesis statement, take time to create a strong, direct, confident opening sentence.

In the following chart, notice how the direction word is identified and circled, and key words are underlined. Thought is given to the type of answer that is expected, based on the direction word. Finally, a possible thesis statement, which would help guide the direction of the body of the essay, is given.

Question	Direction	Possible Thesis Statement
Discuss the characteristics of each of Howard Gardner's multiple intelligences.	Discuss = tell about What are the eight intelligences?	*Each of Howard Gardner's eight intelligences has clearly recognizable characteristics.*
Explain why elaborative rehearsal is more effective for college learning than rote memory strategies.	Explain why = give reasons What are the reasons? How many reasons?	*Elaborative rehearsal is more effective than rote memory because more of the memory principles are used and information in memory is in a more usable form.*

Plan Your Answer Before You Begin Writing For many students, organizing information is the most difficult part of writing essays. Many students wander off course or are at a loss for ideas to write in essays without first making a plan. Outlines, visual mappings, hierarchies, or basic lists that are not as detailed as outlines are four common plans used to organize information for an essay. Explore the different formats and then decide which works best for you. The following examples show the use of a plan in outline form, visual mapping form, and hierarchy form.

Outline

Thesis: ______________________

A. ______________________
   1. ______________________
   2. ______________________

B. ______________________
   1. ______________________
   2. ______________________

C. ______________________
   1. ______________________
   2. ______________________
   3. ______________________

MAPPING

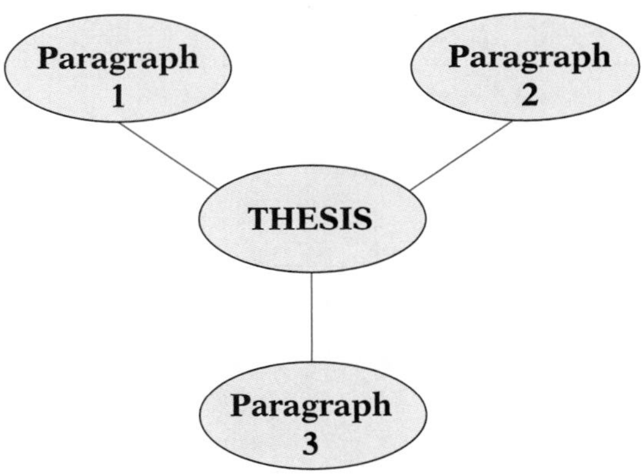

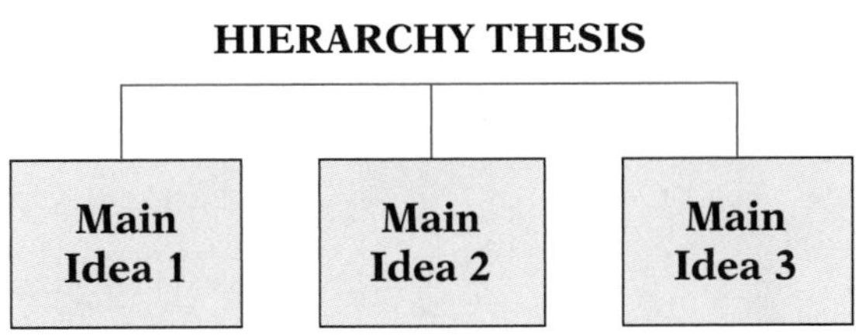

Develop the Body of Your Essay A strong thesis statement and a plan for the information you want to include in your essay lead naturally to the next step, the actual writing of the essay. *Each category or section* of information in your outline, visual mapping, or hierarchy can be expanded into sentences and developed into *one paragraph.* Each additional category or section would thus become another paragraph. Remember, however, that a person with strong writing skills is capable of combining ideas in a variety of ways, so devoting one paragraph to each section of your plan is one possible way to develop the body of the paragraph, but other options may also exist.

The following suggestions will help you develop a more effective essay answer:

- Limit each paragraph to one main idea. Shifting to a new main idea is the signal to move to the next line, indent (about five spaces), and begin a new paragraph.
- Complete sentences need to be used to express your ideas and present your information. Short phrases, charts, or lists of information are not appropriate for an essay.
- Supporting details are essential or your essay will be underdeveloped. Include facts such as names, dates, events, statistics; include definitions, examples, or appropriate applications of the information you are presenting. Do not make the mistake of assuming that information is obvious and your teacher knows what you are thinking or clearly sees the connection. Write as if your reader is *not knowledgeable* about the subject.
- Use course-specific terminology. You spent time studying all the vocabulary words, so strive to include them in your answers as much as possible. Use other words that you learned from class or the textbook and words you have added to your expressive vocabulary.
- Use the basic five-paragraph essay format or a variation of the format as discussed below.
- Use an **organizational plan for an essay**. The following organizational plan shows the five parts of this format for a sample essay question.

Q: Summarize strategies to use to strengthen a person's vocabulary, textbook reading, and test-taking skills.

Thesis: ______________________________

____

Thesis Statement

Body

P. 1: Vocabulary
- textbook clues to find definitions
- make flash cards
- study from fronts & backs
- recite often: linked associations

P. 2: Textbook reading
- use steps of SQ4R
- read carefully/thoroughly—not rush
- understand concepts/details
- substitute familiar words

P. 3: Test-taking
- reduce anxiety—be prepared
- use relaxation/self-talk
- use 4 stages of responses

Summary/conclusion

The **five-paragraph essay format** is a standard format that can be used effectively for most essay tests. It begins with the thesis statement, which is then followed by the **body of the essay**. The body often consists of three paragraphs developing three main ideas. Each paragraph includes specific supporting details that show your understanding and knowledge. (Additional paragraphs can be added for longer essays.) A short summary or **concluding paragraph** ends the essay.

Summarize Your Main Points Finish your essay with a short summary sentence or paragraph. Summarizing leaves a clear picture of your main points in the reader's mind and signals that you have finished with your thoughts. Your summary should reflect the same information you used in your thesis sentence. If your summary and thesis sentence do not focus on the same subject, check to see where you got sidetracked when you developed the body of your essay.

Proofread and Revise After you have completed your essay, take a few minutes to *proofread* for mechanical errors such as spelling, grammar, word usage, or sentence structure. Many teachers try to grade mainly on the content, but mechanical errors are distracting, and maintaining a focus on the ideas is therefore more difficult.

If your writing skills are still weak for college-level writing, consider enrolling in writing skill-building courses to improve your spelling, grammar, punctuation, and organizational skills. Also, ask your instructor if you can use a dictionary, thesaurus, spell checker, or laptop computer when you write essays.

Q: *This term, many study skills were discussed to help you become a successful college student. Select any four skills that you feel are most important for your personal success in college. Discuss the importance of those skills to you.*

Thesis: ____

____

Example of an organizational plan for a six-paragraph essay

Thesis Statement

Body:

P. 1: Importance of time management
- more productive
- less stress
- better balance in life

P. 2: Importance of concentration
- make best use of available time
- learn more thoroughly, less time going back
- develop mental discipline

P. 3: Importance of notetaking
- select info that needs to be learned
- puts info in own words
- steps help memory
- good ongoing study tool

P. 4: Importance of textbook reading
- read to understand
- efficient reading—don't need to go back over
- source of most class info

Summary/conclusion

EXERCISE 13.9 Strengthening a Weak Essay

Read the following essay question and one student's answer. Then work with a partner to discuss answers to the questions that follow the essay.

Question: *Discuss the parts of the Information Processing Model.*

There are six main parts to the Information Processing Model.

The first part of the model is the input. This is where we use our senses to get information. The information then starts into our memory system.

Short-term memory is the next part of the model. It really is short! It doesn't hold much here. Sometimes, in fact, information gets shoved out or forgotten here because it can't hold much.

If it makes it out of short-term memory, the information goes on the practice path. This is also called the rehearsal path. This is where a lot of practice takes place until ideas are learned. Rehearsal can include reading carefully, quizzing yourself, going over flash cards, or working on recall columns of notes. Any kind of activity that helps you work with the information and lets you know if you are learning works here.

Next, information goes into long-term memory. Well, not really all the time. If you rehearse and can't answer, you don't know it. It isn't in long-term memory. The information can go back up on this loop. Try again.

When you're successful in learning, the information goes into long-term memory. Somehow it finds its way around the brain and gets plunked in the right place. It is permanent. It's always in there. When you want to use it, you send yourself a message to get it out. The information you learned then goes out on the retrieval path. This is the path that leads to you being able to give an answer, show you know something or use the information in some way.

Those are all the parts of the Information Processing Model. The model takes you from the sensory input all the way through to the output. That's how we learn.

Questions:

1. Is the thesis statement strong, neutral, or weak? Explain your answer.
2. Is the body of the essay sufficiently developed? What details would you want to add?
3. Is the summary paragraph effective? Explain your answer.
4. Give examples of slang or language that is too informal for an essay.
5. Identify the places in this essay where the following writing tips could be used:
   - Avoid using the word *you*. Reword so *you* is not used.
   - Avoid vague pronouns such as *it* or *they*. Reword by using the noun word.
   - Avoid "weak sentence starters" such as *There is . . . There are . . . Here is . . . .* Reword.
6. Optional assignment: Go to this textbook's web site. Click on Chapter 13, Exercise 13.9. Revise the essay online; print a copy of your work or email it to your instructor.

Additional Essay Writing Tips

Writing strong essay answers becomes easier with practice. When you get your essay tests back, take time to read the comments and suggestions. You can learn to improve your essay-writing skills by analyzing your essays. Your analysis can also include looking for patterns to the kinds of questions your teacher tends to assign. Are the questions mainly from information in the textbook, in lectures, or both? Then look at other essay test-taking skills. Were you effective in predicting essay test questions? When you wrote your essays, did you answer the questions directly? Were your answers well organized? Did you provide sufficient details?

The following tips will also strengthen your essay-writing skills:

How can you use a computer to plan and develop essay answers?

- If you are given several choices of questions to answer, look at the choices carefully. The majority of students tend to choose the question that is the shortest and looks the easiest. However, these questions are usually more general and sometimes more difficult to answer. Questions that "look the most difficult" because they are longer may actually be more specific and easier to answer. Consider your choice of questions carefully.
- If you are required to do more than one essay question, begin with the one that is most familiar and easiest for you. Your confidence will be boosted and your mind will shift into the essay-writing mode.
- Strive to write as neatly as possible. Illegible handwriting will hurt your grade. If you need to delete some of the information, delete it by crossing it out with one neat line, or using liquid white-out.
- Consider writing on every other line so you have room to revise or add information if time permits before the test time ends.
- If you were not able to budget your time sufficiently, turn in your plan (outline, mapping, hierarchy, or list). You may earn some additional points for showing you knew the information and would have included it if you had not run out of time.
- If you have more than one essay to complete on a test, be sure to write something on each question. You will lose too many points by leaving out one question entirely. It is usually better to turn in *some* work on two essays versus only one essay completely developed.
- Weigh the value of different questions. If one question is worth more points, take more time to develop that answer or to return to that answer later and add more information to strengthen your answer.
- If your keyboarding skills are good and you have a laptop computer, ask if you can write your essay on the computer and turn in the disk. Work tends to appear neater and easier to read, and is less likely to include spelling errors.

Reflection Writing 3 — CHAPTER 13

On a separate piece of paper or in a journal, discuss important strategies you learned in this chapter for writing strong answers for essay test questions. Which strategies are new to you? Which strategies deal directly with difficulties you previously encountered on essay tests? Which strategies will strengthen your answers on essay tests?

EXERCISE 13.10 Writing Essay Answers

Select one of the following essay questions. Gather appropriate information. In the space at the bottom of this page create a visual mapping, hierarchy, outline, or an organizational plan for your answer. Then write your answer, including an introductory paragraph, paragraphs for the body, and a concluding paragraph. You may use this textbook's web site to write your essay; and then print it or email it to your instructor.

1. Define each of the *Five Theories of Forgetting* and discuss strategies that you can use to combat each form of forgetting.
2. Outline ways to use *recitation* in three or more strategies that strengthen the process of learning.
3. We have discussed many forms of notetaking. Some notetaking methods are more appropriate for global learners, whereas other forms are more appropriate for linear learners. Discuss the forms of notetaking that are geared toward global learners; then discuss those that are geared toward linear learners. Explain your reasoning.
4. Summarize ways the memory principle of *selectivity* is used in three or more study skills strategies.
5. Contrast major characteristics of active and passive learners.

Show your prewriting plan in the space below:

SUMMARY

- Recall questions include fill-in-the blank questions, listing questions, definition questions, and short-answer questions. Each requires a different type of answer:
  - **a.** Fill-in-the-blank questions often require specific vocabulary words as answers.
  - **b.** Listing questions require lists of information that do not need to be written as complete sentences.
  - **c.** Definition questions require a clear explanation of a vocabulary term; an effective answer consists of three levels of information: a category, a formal definition, and one more detail to expand the definition.
  - **d.** Short-answer questions require details, which can often be expressed in three to five sentences.
- The four levels of response can be used in recall questions; however, educated guessing is replaced by substituting words or synonyms when you cannot recall the exact answers.
- Recall questions and essay questions may be closed or open-ended questions.
- Math tests involve problem-solving strategies that begin by estimating a reasonable answer. They require application of specific skills and demonstration of the steps involved in solving each problem.
- Six common test-taking errors on math tests can be corrected through the use of effective studying and test-taking strategies.
- The RSTUV Problem-Solving Method can be used to solve any math word problem. The steps are *read, select, think, use,* and *verify.*
- To prepare for essay questions, you should spend time identifying possible themes for the question, predicting questions, writing your own questions, creating summary notes, creating an organizational plan for your answer, and practicing writing essay answers before test day.
- Direction words help you understand the type of answer expected for short-answer and essay questions.
- A basic essay structure includes a thesis statement, several paragraphs in the body of the essay, and a concluding paragraph.

ACE Practice Tests, which are scored online, supplementary exercises, enrichment activities, and related web site links are available online for *Essential Study Skills*, 4e. Use the following directions to access this web site:

Type: **http://college.hmco.com/collegesurvival/students**

Click on *List of Sites by Author.* Use the arrow to scroll down to Wong *Essential Study Skills*, 4e. Click on the title. If you are working on your own computer, bookmark this web site.

LEARNING OPTIONS

The following learning options provide you with opportunities to demonstrate your understanding of the topics in Chapter 13. Your instructor may assign one or more specific options or may ask you to select one or more options that interest you the most.

1. Expand the Chapter 13 mapping on page 345. Use large poster paper so you have adequate room for level three information. Add pictures and colors to your mapping to accentuate the main ideas and significant supporting details.
2. Create a visual mapping, hierarchy, or outline to show an organizational plan you could use to answer one of the following questions.
   - **a.** Summarize the relationship of the Twelve Principles of Memory to one of the following: SQ4R, Cornell notetaking, or visual notetaking.
   - **b.** Contrast the capabilities and the functions of short-term memory and long-term memory.
   - **c.** Discuss specific techniques to reduce or eliminate excessive stress.

3. Create summary notes for one of the following topics that might appear on the next test:
   a. recitation
   b. surveying
   c. test anxiety
4. Create three original case studies in which students have problems with any of the following: time management, concentration, weak vocabulary, or taking objective tests. End each case study with a question. Write a short answer for each of your case studies.
5. Write an essay that contrasts some aspect of your behavior as it occurred before you enrolled in this class and as it exists now. For example, your topic could be an earlier attitude toward learning, the physical environment where you study, your independent study strategies, or your ability to perform well on tests.
6. Create a set of Cornell notes for one of these sections of Chapter 13: Answering Recall Questions, Taking Math Tests, or Answering Essay Questions. Complete the recall column. Practice reciting from your recall column.
7. Conduct an Internet search for *writing essays* or *essay tests*. Print the web pages that provide meaningful information or additional essay test-taking strategies. Summarize each web site and include the web site addresses. Your summary may be copied for the class, so your information must be neat and accurate.

Chapter 13 REVIEW QUESTIONS

The following questions will provide you with practice using the test-taking techniques from Chapter 13 as well as provide you with the opportunity to review material from throughout the term.

Fill-in-the-Blank

Write one word on each line to correctly complete each sentence.

1. A ____________ is defined as a word that has the same or similar meaning as another.
2. ____________ questions on tests are questions that require very specific answers, often in a specific order.
3. A ____________ sentence states the writer's main point about an entire essay.
4. A ____________ sentence states the main idea for one specific paragraph.
5. ____________ are words used in objective tests that indicate how frequently or how completely something occurs. Examples are *sometimes, seldom, always,* and *never.*
6. When studying math, it is important to practice converting algebraic expressions into English ____________.
7. Students who have test anxiety due to ____________ often find the need for last-minute massed practice or cramming.
8. A ____________ ____________ is a type of visual graphic that organizes information to be compared by using columns, rows, and cells.
9. The ____________ step of the Cornell notetaking system is designed for the student to practice information by talking out loud and in complete sentences.
10. ____________ can be eliminated by using goal-setting and time-management techniques that encourage a person not to put things off for a later time.
11. The three basic cognitive learning modalities are ____________, ____________, and ____________.
12. When using the SQ4R textbook reading system, the first *R* of the Cornell system would begin during the ____________ step of SQ4R.

Definitions

Write a complete definition for each of the following terms.

1. Memory Principle of Organization

2. Distributed practice

3. Active learning

4. The *reflect* step in the Cornell notetaking system

Listing Questions

Use your own paper to write the answers to the following questions.

1. Name the eight intelligences as defined by Howard Gardner.
2. List the five steps in the listening process.
3. List the steps involved in effective goal setting.
4. Name any six concentration strategies to deal with internal or external distractors.
5. List the Twelve Principles of Memory.

Short-Answer Questions

Write the answers to the following questions on your own paper.

1. Explain how to study from the highlighting done in your textbook.
2. What are the three levels of information in a well-developed definition?
3. How do the discrepancies among the rate of speech, the rate of writing, and the rate of thinking affect a person's notetaking skills?
4. Tell how highlighting or a chapter visual mapping can be used to write summaries.

Essay Questions

Select one *of the following to develop into an essay. Write your answer on your own paper.*

1. Summarize the techniques that can be used to improve comprehension of a difficult paragraph.
2. Explain how to use the RSTUV Problem-Solving Method for math word problems.
3. Discuss the notetaking options that you can use in the fourth step of SQ4R.
4. Define *active learning* as it relates to a college student.
5. Illustrate ways that goal-setting strategies can be combined with time-management strategies.

Appendixes

APPENDIX A
Chapter Profile Materials

APPENDIX B
Useful Forms

Name ____________________ Date ________

APPENDIX A
Chapter Profile Materials

Master Profile Chart

	Learning Styles	Processing Memory	Managing Time	Setting Goals	Concentration, Stress, Procrastination	Boosting Memory; Preparing for Tests	Reading System	Comprehension; Critical Thinking	Cornell for Textbooks	Cornell for Lectures	Variety of Notetaking Systems	Objective Tests	Recall, Math, and Essay Tests
	1	2	3	4	5	6	7	8	9	10	11	12	13
100%	10	10	10	10	10	10	10	10	10	10	10	10	10
90%	9	9	9	9	9	9	9	9	9	9	9	9	9
80%	8	8	8	8	8	8	8	8	8	8	8	8	8
70%	7	7	7	7	7	7	7	7	7	7	7	7	7
60%	6	6	6	6	6	6	6	6	6	6	6	6	6
50%	5	5	5	5	5	5	5	5	5	5	5	5	5
40%	4	4	4	4	4	4	4	4	4	4	4	4	4
30%	3	3	3	3	3	3	3	3	3	3	3	3	3
20%	2	2	2	2	2	2	2	2	2	2	2	2	2
10%	1	1	1	1	1	1	1	1	1	1	1	1	1
0%	0	0	0	0	0	0	0	0	0	0	0	0	0

Beginning-of-the-Term Profile

1. As you begin a new chapter, complete the chapter profile chart. If you prefer, you can complete the profile online and then record your score above.
2. Score your profile. (See Chapter 1, page 2.) Find the chapter number above. Circle your score to show the number correct.
3. Connect the circles with lines to create a graph (your Master Profile Chart).

Profile Answer Keys

	1: Learning Styles	2: Processing/ Memory	3: Managing Time	4: Setting Goals
1.	Ⓨ N	Ⓨ N	Ⓨ N	Ⓨ N
2.	Ⓨ N	Y Ⓝ	Y Ⓝ	Y Ⓝ
3.	Ⓨ N	Y Ⓝ	Y Ⓝ	Y Ⓝ
4.	Y Ⓝ	Ⓨ N	Y Ⓝ	Ⓨ N
5.	Y Ⓝ	Y Ⓝ	Ⓨ N	Ⓨ N
6.	Ⓨ N	Ⓨ N	Ⓨ N	Y Ⓝ
7.	Y Ⓝ	Y Ⓝ	Ⓨ N	Y Ⓝ
8.	Ⓨ N	Y Ⓝ	Y Ⓝ	Ⓨ N
9.	Ⓨ N	Ⓨ N	Y Ⓝ	Y Ⓝ
10.	Ⓨ N	Ⓨ N	Ⓨ N	Ⓨ N

	5: Concentration, Stress, Procrastination	6: Boosting Memory; Preparing for Tests	7: Reading System	8: Comprehension; Critical Thinking
1.	Ⓨ N	Y Ⓝ	Ⓨ N	Ⓨ N
2.	Y Ⓝ	Ⓨ N	Y Ⓝ	Y Ⓝ
3.	Ⓨ N	Y Ⓝ	Y Ⓝ	Ⓨ N
4.	Y Ⓝ	Ⓨ N	Ⓨ N	Y Ⓝ
5.	Ⓨ N	Ⓨ N	Ⓨ N	Y Ⓝ
6.	Y Ⓝ	Y Ⓝ	Y Ⓝ	Ⓨ N
7.	Y Ⓝ	Ⓨ N	Y Ⓝ	Ⓨ N
8.	Ⓨ N	Ⓨ N	Ⓨ N	Y Ⓝ
9.	Y Ⓝ	Y Ⓝ	Y Ⓝ	Ⓨ N
10.	Y Ⓝ	Ⓨ N	Ⓨ N	Y Ⓝ

	9: Cornell for Textbooks	10: Listening and Lecture Notes	11: Variety of Notetaking	12: Objective Tests	13: Recall, Math, Essay Tests
1.	Ⓨ N	Y Ⓝ	Ⓨ N	Ⓨ N	Y Ⓝ
2.	Y Ⓝ	Y Ⓝ	Ⓨ N	Y Ⓝ	Y Ⓝ
3.	Ⓨ N	Ⓨ N	Ⓨ N	Ⓨ N	Y Ⓝ
4.	Ⓨ N	Ⓨ N	Ⓨ N	Ⓨ N	Y Ⓝ
5.	Ⓨ N	Y Ⓝ	Y Ⓝ	Ⓨ N	Ⓨ N
6.	Ⓨ N	Ⓨ N	Ⓨ N	Ⓨ N	Ⓨ N
7.	Ⓨ N	Ⓨ N	Ⓨ N	Y Ⓝ	Ⓨ N
8.	Ⓨ N	Ⓨ N	Ⓨ N	Ⓨ N	Ⓨ N
9.	Ⓨ N	Ⓨ N	Ⓨ N	Ⓨ N	Ⓨ N
10.	Ⓨ N	Ⓨ N	Y Ⓝ	Ⓨ N	Ⓨ N

End-of-Term Profile

1. Cut a two-inch-wide strip of paper to cover up the original answers on the profile questions at the beginning of each chapter (or complete the profiles on this textbook's web site). Redo all the profile questions so you can see changes that you have made this term. Write Y or N *next to the number of each profile question.*
2. Score your profile answers using the answer key above.
3. Chart your scores on the Master Profile Chart. Use different color ink so you can compare these scores to your original scores.

APPENDIX B
Useful Forms

Learning Options Assessment Form*

Name ______________________ Learning Option # ________ for Chapter ________

1. Write a short introduction that states your goals for this Learning Option.

2. Write a short self-assessment that states your view on the value and the quality of your work.

3. Your instructor will score the quality of your work based on the following criteria:

1	2	3	4	5	Sufficient details
1	2	3	4	5	Accurate information
1	2	3	4	5	Inclusion of required skills
1	2	3	4	5	Neatness, clarity of presentation
1	2	3	4	5	Originality, critical thinking
1	2	3	4	5	Other: ______________________

Total Points: __________

4. Instructor Evaluation Comments:

*Photocopy this form before you use it.

Class Schedule

Reg. #	Course Name	Time	Location	Instructor

Time	Mon.	Tues.	Wed.	Thurs.	Fri.	Sat.	Sun.
12–6 A.M.							
6–7:00							
7–8:00							
8–9:00							
9–10:00							
10–11:00							
11–12 NOON							
12–1:00							
1–2:00							
2–3:00							
3–4:00							
4–5:00							
5–6:00							
6–7:00							
7–8:00							
8–9:00							
9–10:00							
10–11:00							
11–12 A.M.							

Weekly Time-Management Schedule

For the week of ______________________

Time	Monday	Tuesday	Wednesday	Thursday	Friday	Saturday	Sunday
12–6 A.M.							
6–7:00							
7–8:00							
8–9:00							
9–10:00							
10–11:00							
11–12 NOON							
12–1:00							
1–2:00							
2–3:00							
3–4:00							
4–5:00							
5–6:00							
6–7:00							
7–8:00							
8–9:00							
9–10:00							
10–11:00							
11–12 A.M.							

Goal Organizer

1. What is your goal?	
2. What benefits will you gain by achieving this goal?	
3. What consequences will you experience by not achieving this goal?	
4. What obstacles might you encounter while working on this goal?	
5. How can you deal with the obstacles effectively if they occur?	
6. What people or resources could help you in achieving this goal?	

Identify Your Goal

Step 1: State your specific goal: ____________________

Step 2: State a specific target date and time to complete the goal:

____

Step 3: Identify the specific steps required to achieve your goal:

Step 4: State your intrinsic or extrinsic reward: ____________________

Name ______________________________ Date ______________

Personal Insights

1. Learning Style Inventory Score (Chapter 1, page 5)

   Visual ________ Auditory ________ Kinesthetic ________

2. Dominance Inventory—Left/Right, Linear/Global Dominance (Chapter 1, page 6)

   Left ______________________________________ Right

   1 2 3 4 5 6 7 8 9 10

3. Structured, Interactive, and Independent Learner (Chapter 1, page 17)

   Structured learner in these classes: ______________________________

   Interactive learner in these classes: ______________________________

   Independent learner in these classes: ______________________________

4. Multiple Intelligences (Chapter 1, page 19)

   Most developed intelligences: ______________________________

5. Circadian Rhythms (Chapter 3, page 67)

   Times during the day with highest concentration/alertness: ____________

   Times during the day with lowest concentration/alertness: ____________

6. Listening Inventory (Chapter 10, page 264)

   Reception Score: ________ Total Score: ________

   Attention Score: ________ You perceive yourself to be:

   Perception Score: ________ ______________________

   Assignment of Meaning Score: ________

   Response Score: ________

7. Preferred form of notetaking (you may check more than one)

   ________ Index cards ________ Hierarchies

   ________ Marginal notes ________ Comparison charts

   ________ Annotations ________ Formal outlines

   ________ Cornell notes ________ Three-column notes

   ________ Visual mappings

8. Most important concepts you learned about yourself this term:

Acknowledgments

The author is grateful to the following for granting permission to reprint excerpts from their works:

Andrea, Alfred J., and James Overfield, THE HUMAN RECORD, Third Edition. Copyright © 1998 by Houghton Mifflin Company. Used with permission.

Bello/Britton, TOPICS IN CONTEMPORARY MATHEMATICS, Sixth Edition. Copyright © 1997 Houghton Mifflin Company. Used with permission.

Berko, Roy M., Andrew D. Wolvin, and Darlyn R. Wolvin, COMMUNICATING, Seventh Edition. Copyright © 1998 by Houghton Mifflin Company. Used with permission.

Bloom, Benjamin S., TAXONOMY OF EDUCATIONAL OBJECTIVES: Book 1 Cognitive Domain. Copyright © 1984 by Allyn & Bacon. Adapted by permission.

DuBrin, Andrew, LEADERSHIP, Second Edition. Copyright © 1998 Houghton Mifflin Company. Used with permission.

Ebbing, Darryll D., and Rupert Wentworth, INTRODUCTORY CHEMISTRY, Second Edition. Copyright © 1998 Houghton Mifflin Company. Used with permission.

Ellis, Keith, THE MAGIC LAMP: Goal Setting for People Who Hate Setting Goals by Keith Ellis. Copyright © 1998. Published by Three Rivers Press. Reprinted by permission.

Garman, E. Thomas, PERSONAL FINANCE, Fifth Edition. Copyright © 1997 Houghton Mifflin Company. Used with permission.

Mansbach, Richard W., THE GLOBAL PUZZLE, Second Edition. Copyright © 1997 Houghton Mifflin Company. Used with permission.

Nolting, Paul, MATH STUDY SKILLS WORKBOOK. Copyright © 2000 Houghton Mifflin Company. Used with permission.

Norton, Mary Beth, David M. Katzman, Paul D. Escott, and Howard Chudacoff, A PEOPLE AND A NATION, Fifth Edition. Copyright © 1998 Houghton Mifflin Company. Used with permission.

Payne, David G., and Michael J. Wenger, COGNITIVE PSYCHOLOGY. Copyright © 1998 Houghton Mifflin Company. Used with permission.

Pride, William M., Robert J. Hughes, and Jagdish R. Kapoor, BUSINESS, Seventh Edition. Copyright © 2002 Houghton Mifflin Company. Used with permission.

Pride, William M., Robert J. Hughes, and Jagdish R. Kapoor, BUSINESS, Fifth Edition. Copyright © 1996 Houghton Mifflin Company. Used with permission.

Index